PETS AND PEOPLE

PETS AND PEOPLE

The Ethics of Our Relationships
with Companion Animals

Edited by

Christine Overall

OXFORD
UNIVERSITY PRESS

OXFORD
UNIVERSITY PRESS

Oxford University Press is a department of the University of Oxford. It furthers
the University's objective of excellence in research, scholarship, and education
by publishing worldwide. Oxford is a registered trade mark of Oxford University
Press in the UK and certain other countries.

Published in the United States of America by Oxford University Press
198 Madison Avenue, New York, NY 10016, United States of America.

CIP data is on file at the Library of Congress
ISBN 978–0–19–045608–5 (hbk.)
ISBN 978–0–19–045607–8 (pbk.)

9 8 7 6 5 4 3 2 1

Paperback printed by WebCom, Inc., Canada
Hardback printed by Bridgeport National Bindery, Inc., United States of America

To the memory of
Jean Harvey

CONTENTS

PART II: *Living with Companion Animals*

PREFACE

I originally became involved in this book because of the cats in my life.

In October 2013 my friend and colleague Dr. Jean Harvey, Professor of Philosophy at the University of Guelph in Ontario, Canada, contacted me to ask what she admitted might be a bizarre, out-of-the-blue question: "Do you have companion animals?" She added, "Nothing to do with trying to get anyone to adopt rescues, so don't worry about that."

I wrote back to tell her that my life-partner, Ted, and I had lived with many wonderful cats. After our Ozzie died (of acute kidney disease) in early 2011 at age sixteen, Ted and I were devastated. We waited until the summer of 2012 to adopt our current family member, Nekko (Japanese for "cat"), a grey tabby. But why was she asking?

Jean wrote again to tell me about an innovative project she was starting: a philosophical anthology on ethics and companion animals. The features of the anthology were, first, that it would focus on ethical issues relating to companion animals, primarily cats and dogs; second, that the chapters would be accessible not only to philosophers but also to people from other disciplines and to interested and educated people outside academia; and third, that each contributor would provide a distinct perspective on human relationships with companion animals. In particular, Jean wanted to encourage some potential contributors who had not previously written about animal ethics to think about how their published work on human-to-human ethics might apply to the ethics of human relationships with companion animals.

In my case, she suggested that I consider whether and to what extent some of my ideas in an earlier book, *Aging, Death, and Human Longevity: A Philosophical Inquiry* (2003), might apply to cats and dogs. I had not previously written much about animal ethics, but I was intrigued by Jean's suggestion and readily accepted her invitation to contribute. (The result is my chapter in this book, "Throw out the Dog? Death, Longevity, and Companion Animals.") I was happy to be included in what promised to be a groundbreaking collection.

But just over a month later Jean wrote again to say she had been hospitalized. In the course of treatment for appendicitis, it had been discovered that she had acute leukemia. As a result, she said, her schedule for the book (originally planned to be finished in 2014) would now be delayed. But, despite starting chemotherapy, she emphasized her commitment to completing the anthology.

Unfortunately, by February 2014, she was too ill to continue working on it. Her doctors had concluded that no further treatment was possible or likely to be effective, and she returned home from the hospital to spend time with the cats she called her "furry family." Jean was realistic about her own medical prospects. In an email message to me on February 3, 2014, she wrote,

> I now realize I will not be able to bring [the anthology] to completion, I wondered if there were another way to see it through. . . . I wondered if you would be willing to edit the collection? . . . I realize this is a bit of a cheek, asking about this, but I'm so passionate about the collection being published. In case you have any interest at all, I have attached the 'basic' information from each of the six committed contributors [they included her and me]. I'm so sorry this is so quick and business-like. Just really tired and rather anxious to see the email on its way. Every one of the pieces so far planned for is excellent, both in its focus (and therefore in the 'variety' in the collection) and in the qualities of the author.

I was deeply saddened by the revelation of the seriousness of Jean's illness. Although I could not yet accept that her illness was terminal, I agreed to help with the book. My thought was to work with her until she was sufficiently recovered to take it on again. My reasons for doing so were my respect for Jean's philosophical work and my belief in the value, importance, and timeliness of the book's theme.

Jean was delighted and relieved when I accepted her invitation, although she must surely have known that my main qualification as editor was not academic but personal: a simple determination to see the project through to its completion. Over the next months she and I discussed in more detail, via phone and email, the book's focus and goals. Jean also told me she had been warned that she had only about two more months of life. During that time she was working to finish her second single-author book, *Civilized Oppression and Moral Relations: Victims, Fallibility, and the Moral Community*,[1] which was edited by her colleague and friend Antonio Calcagno (who is also a contributor to this anthology) and subsequently published in 2015. Despite her own truly dire situation, Jean continued to be upbeat, appreciative, encouraging, and supportive of my work on the anthology.

Jean Harvey died on Sunday, April 20, 2014. Hers was a life well lived. I hope that *Pets and People: The Ethics of Our Relationships with Companion Animals* reflects her intentions, hopes, and scholarly values.

Note

1. This book is a follow-up to and development of her first, *Civilized Oppression* (1999).

References

Harvey, Jean. 2015. *Civilized Oppression and Moral Relations: Victims, Fallibility, and the Moral Community*. Edited by Antonio Calcagno. London: Palgrave Macmillan.
Overall, Christine. 2003. *Aging, Death, and Human Longevity: A Philosophical Inquiry*. Boston: MIT Press.

ACKNOWLEDGMENTS

This book was inspired and initiated by Jean Harvey, whose now-classic paper, "Companion and Assistance Animals: Benefits, Welfare Safeguards, and Relationships," was one of the earliest philosophical discussions of ethics and companion animals. Her paper is included here and is the only chapter that has been previously published. I am deeply grateful to Jean for starting this project, and to the *International Journal of Applied Philosophy* (22 [2], 2008: 161–76) for permission to reprint her paper.

I also thank all the contributors, whose enthusiasm, insight, and cooperation made creating this anthology such a pleasure. Special thanks to the original group of contributors who were with the book from the beginning: Maurice Hamington, Kathryn Norlock, Bernard Rollin, and Cynthia Townley.

I'm grateful to editor Peter Ohlin for believing in the value of the book. Thank you to Emily Sacharin and Andrew Ward, the editorial assistants who worked with me on this project, to Henry Southgate for his careful and professional work as copy editor, and to Shalini Balakrishnan, the project manager.

Many people supported my work on *Pets and People*. Thank you to my friends Tabitha Bernard, Kathy Silver, Ruth Dubin, Tom Russell, Carol Kavanagh, Stephen Leighton, Carlos Prado, Tam Mito, and Ahmed Kayssi for their kindness. My writers' group, "Writers Like Us"—Mary Cameron, Carla Douglas, Tara Kainer, and Kim Renders—has sustained and encouraged my writing, both academic and non-academic, over the past three years. I am especially grateful to Kim for the many opportunities she has given me to perform my words.

My friends from high school, Evan Alcock, Dave Beavan, Gisela Braune, and Nancy Chapple, connect me to our past and model hope for our future. My wonderful former students, especially Nikoo Najand, Christine Vidt, and Kassy Wayne, remind me of the value of philosophy and the importance of embedding it in our lives. Daily exercise at Kingston's Apex Indoor Cycling lowers both my blood pressure and my stress. Special thanks to Jeff Farmer and all the instructors for their encouragement.

My mother, Dorothy Overall, was my first model for living supportively with cat companions. She has always believed in me and my work. My life-partner Ted Worth lovingly plies me with excellent food and endures my scholarly ups and downs with grace and compassion. Our children, Devon Worth and Narnia Worth, and their spouses Julie Mayrand and Michael Ashton, connect me to warm family life outside work, and our grandchildren, Ewan, Nathan, Torin, and Darren, repeatedly reawaken my sense of wonder and joy.

Most of all, I acknowledge and thank the cats who have been and remain an irreplaceable part of my family and my life: Tiger, Nudnik, Ozzie, Nemo, and Nekko.

CONTRIBUTORS

David Benatar, Professor of Philosophy, University of Cape Town, South Africa

Antonio Calcagno, Professor of Philosophy, Department of Philosophy, King's University College, University of Western Ontario, London, Ontario, Canada

Michael Cholbi, Professor of Philosophy, California State Polytechnic University, Pomona, California, USA

Jessica du Toit, Teaching Assistant, Philosophy Department, University of Cape Town, South Africa; Former Fellow, Department of Bioethics, National Institutes of Health, Bethesda, Maryland, USA

Maurice Hamington, Executive Director of University Studies and Professor of Philosophy, Portland State University, Portland, Oregon, USA

Jean Harvey, Professor of Philosophy, University of Guelph, Guelph, Ontario, Canada (deceased)

Josh Milburn, Postdoctoral Fellow, Department of Philosophy, Queen's University, Kingston, Ontario, Canada

Tony Milligan, Teaching Fellow in Ethics and the Philosophy of Religion, Department of Theology & Religious Studies, King's College London, UK

Kathryn J. Norlock, Associate Professor and Kenneth Mark Drain Chair in Ethics, Department of Philosophy, Trent University, Peterborough, Ontario, Canada

Christine Overall, Professor Emerita of Philosophy and University Research Chair, Queen's University, Kingston, Ontario, Canada

Jennifer Parks, Professor of Philosophy and Director of the Undergraduate Bioethics Minor Program, Loyola University, Chicago, Illinois, USA

Bernard E. Rollin, University Distinguished Professor, Professor of Philosophy, Professor of Animal Sciences, Professor of Biomedical Sciences, University Bioethicist, Department of Philosophy, Colorado State University, Fort Collins, Colorado, USA

John Rossi, Assistant Professor and Co-Director, Program in Public Health Ethics & History, Department of Community Health and Prevention, Drexel University School of Public Health, Philadelphia, Pennsylvania, USA

Tina Rulli, Assistant Professor, Philosophy Department, University of California, Davis, California, USA

Chloë Taylor, Associate Professor, Department of Women's and Gender Studies and Department of Philosophy, University of Alberta, Edmonton, Alberta, Canada

Cynthia Townley, Research Associate, Macquarie University, Sydney, Australia

Gary Varner, Professor, Department of Philosophy, Texas A&M University, College Station, Texas, USA

Katherine Wayne, Instructor, Department of Philosophy, Carleton University, Ottawa, Ontario, Canada

Zipporah Weisberg, Research Associate, Animals in Philosophy, Politics, Law, and Ethics (APPLE), Department of Philosophy, Queen's University, Kingston, Ontario, Canada

INTRODUCTION

Christine Overall

Fueled in part by a mounting awareness of the mistreatment, exploitation, and misappropriation of animals as sources of food, clothing, entertainment, work, and research material, animal ethics is generating growing interest both within academia and outside it. This book focuses on ethical issues connected to a group of animals who play an extremely important role in human lives: companion animals. Companion animals are both vulnerable to and dependent upon us. What responsibilities do we owe to them, especially since we have the power and authority to make literal life-and-death decisions about them? What kinds of relationships should we have with our companion animals? What might we learn from them about the nature and limits of our own morality? How should we (re)create our lives with them?

There are many commonplace assumptions about companion animals. For example, most people probably hold at least some of the following beliefs: that those who do not choose to live with pets have no moral responsibilities to them; that there is nothing wrong with pedigree-breeding or merely permitting animals to reproduce; that it is important to feed meat to our animals; that using canines as guide dogs or service dogs is morally unproblematic; that sex with animals is nothing but a bizarre perversion unrelated to ordinary human sexual behavior; and that in a lifeboat situation of extreme scarcity, it makes complete sense to sacrifice a dog rather than a human being. *Pets and People: The Ethics of Our Relationships with Companion Animals* challenges all of these assumptions, and many more.

This book is comprised of the work of philosophers from Canada, the United States, Australia, the United Kingdom, and South Africa. Some chapters are by senior well-known philosophers and some are by more junior philosophers who are helping to develop the field of animal ethics. The contributors write from a variety of philosophical perspectives, including utilitarianism, care ethics, feminist ethics, phenomenology, and the genealogy of ideas.

Pets and People is divided into two parts. The first examines the nature of our relationships to companion animals, the foundations of our moral responsibilities to them, what our relationships with companion animals teach us, and whether animals themselves are ethical beings (chapters by Jean Harvey, Cynthia Townley, Antonio Calcagno, Maurice Hamington, Gary Varner, Kathryn Norlock, and Bernard Rollin).

The second part explores specific ethical issues related to crucial aspects of companion animals' lives. The topics include breeding, reproduction, sterilization, cloning, adoption, feeding, training, working, sexual interactions, longevity, dying, and euthanasia (chapters by John Rossi, Katherine Wayne, Jennifer Parks, Jessica du Toit and David Benatar, Tina Rulli, Josh Milburn, Tony Milligan, Zipporah Weisberg, Chloë Taylor, Christine Overall, and Michael Cholbi).

The best way to indicate the scope, goals, and content of this book is by means of a discussion of three significant words in its title: "pets," "relationships," and "companion animals."

"Pets"

"Pet" is probably the term employed by most people to refer to the animals who share their homes. I use that word in the book's title because it is both familiar and obvious. But although in common parlance we often refer to "people and their pets," I have chosen to place "pets" before "people" to indicate both the book's philosophical focus and the importance of the animals whom we call our pets.

What exactly is a pet? "Pet" can be a term of endearment, and in most cases its use reflects genuine love and attachment. Nonetheless, the word is not unproblematic, and some of the contributors to this anthology choose not to use it at all.

To start, we could define a pet, perhaps perversely, as an animal whom meat-eating human beings would, for moral reasons (and other things being equal, that is, absent extreme conditions of famine), regard as unthinkable to eat.[1] Indeed, there is often an outcry in North America when dogs, for example, are used as food in some Asian countries, yet from the vast majority of North Americans there is no similar outcry when pigs, cows, or chickens are eaten—even though some pigs, cows, and chickens are occasionally treated as pets. This difference in reactions raises questions about the nature of the distinction between pets and non-pets, and why many people eat other animals who happen not to be classified as pets.

Pets are, uniquely and virtually by definition, not *consumable* items *because we do not eat family members*,[2] the beings who share our homes and lives. Significantly, the many meanings of "pet" include "[a]n indulged, spoiled, or favourite, child"; "[a] person who is indulged, spoiled, or treated as a favourite, esp. in a way that others regard with disapproval," and "[a]n animal (typically one which is domestic or tame) kept for pleasure or companionship." A pet is also "[a] sweet, obedient, or obliging person."[3] Thus to call an animal a "pet" simultaneously expresses both fondness and condescension. It suggests a hierarchical relationship of a particularly insidious kind, in which the animal so labelled is both singled out for special favor and also expected to be submissive and obsequious.

Indeed, the label "pet" implies dependency; the pet is "kept," which means that she is maintained and supported at the whim of the person by whom she is kept. Consider one of the standard questions between individuals getting to know each other: "Do you keep any pets?" Pets are certainly loved—the adjectival version of "pet" is defined as "[s]pecially cherished; for which one has a particular fondness or weakness; favourite; (also) particular"[4]—but the concept suggests they are maintained (and *retained*) at the favor of the persons to whom the "pets" belong. (Here the analogy that comes to mind is a "kept woman," whose food and shelter are supplied by someone who expects sexual services in return.)

To be kept implies being used by or being in the service of those who do the keeping. But under what circumstances, if any, is it justifiable to use companion animals for entertainment, work, therapy, comfort, commercial benefit, or even sex? In her chapter, "Companion and Assistance Animals: Benefits, Welfare Safeguards, and Relationships," Jean Harvey opens the book with a critique of the still-prevalent view that animals may be put to a variety of human uses, provided only that their welfare is protected.

Numerous kinds of animals are compelled to play the role of pets, including gerbils, hamsters, fish, birds, rabbits, lizards, turtles, skunks, pigs, and many others. Whether it is justified to "pet-ify" (to coin a term) all of these animals is questionable, since many of them are by nature not constituted to be the in-house companions of human beings, and so to force them to be pets is to mistreat them and likely cause them suffering, all in the interests of the personal gratification of human beings.

By contrast, contemporary dogs and cats have been created and modified through millennia of breeding practices to facilitate their lives with human beings. And indeed, except for those who are feral, most dogs and cats seem to *want* to live with us. They are also the two main types of nonhuman animals with whom human beings in the West choose to share their homes. For example, the Canadian Animal Health Institute reports that in 2014, Canadians were living with at least 7 million cats and 6.4 million dogs (Canadian Animal Health Institute 2015). The Humane Society of the United States (2015) quotes statistics from the American Veterinary Medical Association indicating that in 2015, 79.7 million American households had a pet of some kind; these included 163.6 million dogs and cats.

For all these reasons, the particular emphasis of this book is on dogs and cats. Nonetheless, even for these animals, there are legitimate questions about the practice of "keeping" pets. One question is whether it is morally justifiable for human beings to continue breeding them, and/or to allow or facilitate their reproduction; perhaps cats and dogs should be encouraged to gradually die out by preventing them from procreating. For example, legal scholar Gary Francione famously claims, "[W]e should not continue to bring more animals into existence so that we may own them as pets" (Francione n.d.).

Questions about feline and canine procreation are dealt with in several chapters of this book. In "Our Whimsy, Their Welfare: On the Ethics of Pedigree-Breeding," John Rossi presents and supports the case specifically against pure-breeding companion animals. In "Does Preventing Reproduction Make for Bad Care?," Katherine Wayne argues that a commitment to our cats' and dogs' flourishing is consistent, under certain conditions, with taking steps to prevent them from reproducing. From a feminist care perspective, Jennifer Parks contends that commissioning a clone of one's beloved dog or cat, after his death, is not justified ("'Lassie, Come Home!': Ethical Concerns about Companion Animal Cloning"). But Jessica du Toit and David Benatar go further: in "Reproducing Companion Animals," they argue that there are three strong reasons not to create any more companion animals at all. And in her chapter, "For Dog's Sake, Adopt!," Tina Rulli defends the existence of a duty to adopt companion animals instead of creating them.

Whatever one's perspective on pet reproduction, one might also wonder whether the very practice of having pets can be morally justified. After all, keeping pets requires that the animals' behavior be restricted in certain ways, that some of their inherent inclinations be modified in order for them to fit in with human customs, and that their interests sometimes be subordinated to those of the people with whom they live.[5] Our relationships with cats and dogs thus also raise important questions about when and under what circumstances we are justified in setting limits to their independence. In this volume, several chapters respond to these questions. In "A Two-Level Utilitarian Analysis of Relationships with Pets," Gary Varner makes a general case on consequentialist grounds for keeping pets. In "The Animal Lovers' Paradox? On the Ethics of 'Pet Food,'" Josh Milburn explains and offers a resolution to the moral paradox of feeding animal companions with the flesh of non-companions. Ideas about animal discipline are explored in "The Ethics of Animal Training" by Tony Milligan, who provides a genealogy of theories about the scope and justification of molding animals to meet human needs and desires. Two additional chapters also investigate the harms that particular forms of training can potentially generate. Zipporah Weisberg's chapter, "Animal Assisted Intervention and Citizenship Theory," discusses the recruitment of animals into therapeutic work with human beings, describing both the potential harms of such practices and how they can be avoided. Chloë Taylor's chapter, "'Sex without All the Politics'? Sexual Ethics and Human-Canine Relations," offers a feminist critique of the use of domesticated animals, especially dogs, for human sexual pleasure.

"Relationships"

Another crucial term in the title of this book is "relationships." There can be many kinds of relationships—ranging from exploitive, domineering, uncaring, and unjust, to supportive, loving, sensitive, and fulfilling. Like human-human relationships, animal-human relationships are complicated, and they can exemplify contradictory characteristics. Nonetheless, it seems safe to say that all human relationships with companion animals are unequal, and that fact must be taken into account. Although it may sometimes feel as if our cats and dogs have power over us, either because we love them so much or because their behavior is sometimes counter to our own desires and goals, we have almost complete power over the animals who live with us.

In her chapter, Jean Harvey argues that "the primary moral obligation we have with respect to companion animals is to develop, nurture, respect, and protect this relationship." Indeed, all of the contributors to this book seek to contribute to the extension of morally good relationships between human and nonhuman beings: relationships that adequately take into account the animals' own interests, needs, desires, and vulnerabilities, that are cognizant of the built-in inequality of human and animal, and that support the flourishing of both the animal and the human being.

At the same time, many of the contributors also explore what we, as human beings, can learn from our relationships with our companion animals. In "Building a Meaningful Social World between Human and Companion Animals through Empathy," Antonio Calcagno draws upon the concept of empathy to explain how we create our relationships with companion animals. Maurice Hamington ("Care, Moral Progress, and Companion Animals") argues that these relationships help us to develop our ability to be more caring moral individuals, and thereby contribute to the habits and skills needed for genuine moral progress. In "Ethical Behavior in Animals," Bernard Rollin shows how animal companions themselves model and demonstrate ethical behavior.

On the other hand, Kathryn Norlock, in "'I Don't Want the Responsibility': The Moral Implications of Avoiding Dependency Relations with Companion Animals," interrogates the moral implications of deliberately choosing *not* to live with companion animals. She urges people who do not live with companion animals to recognize what she suggests are their moral obligations to provide monetary, material, and sociopolitical forms of support to those who are caregivers of companion animals.

Two chapters focus on the endpoint of the human-companion animal relationship. My own contribution to the book, "Throw Out the Dog? Death, Longevity, and Companion Animals," argues that longevity for companion animals, as for human beings, is important: barring great suffering, a longer life is a better life, and we should not be insouciant about sacrificing animal lives for human lives. And in "The Euthanasia of Companion Animals," Michael Cholbi offers an account of when and why companion animals ought to be euthanized, and who is entitled to make the decision to end their lives.

"Companion Animals"

The third term in the title that warrants special discussion is "companion animals." It is widely used because it seems to be a respectful alternative to "pets" and does not carry the hierarchical connotations of that word. In his chapter, Gary Varner stipulates that a companion animal is a pet who has "significant social interaction with its owner and would voluntarily choose to stay with the owner, in part for the sake of the companionship," a definition that incorporates a recognition of the agency of companion animals. Still, one might have doubts about the appropriateness of the term "companion animal." In human interactions, a companion is usually someone who has chosen to be with us, but dogs and cats in fact have little real choice about the human beings whose lives they share. Perhaps "companion animal" misleadingly implies a kind of equality between human being and animal that does not exist.

Katherine Wayne suggests a different criticism of the term "companion animal." Her main concern is that it is "at best, misleading and painfully naïve to call animals of those kinds who are abandoned, neglected, or otherwise mistreated 'companion animals,' given that they have been denied companionship" (personal communication, January 22, 2016). Her point is that while animals such as dogs and cats are seen as archetypal companion animals, thousands of dogs and cats never acquire that status in any literal sense: they live as feral animals, or they die, unwanted, in shelters or on the street. To call all dogs and cats "companion animals," then, is to discount the reality of what many cats and dogs experience.

I believe Katherine Wayne is correct. "Companion animals" should not be applied to all cats and dogs, but only to those fortunate enough to live their lives as part of a human household. The reality of the lives of feral cats and dogs, and of those who are not adopted or are abandoned, must be recognized for what it is: these animals are not companions, not through any fault of their own but because human beings have failed to act on their own moral responsibilities. Hence the importance of companion animal adoption, as Tina Rulli argues, and of acknowledging responsibilities to dogs and cats even if we do not live with them, as Kathryn Norlock maintains.

In this book, the term "companion animals" is employed because it reflects the nature of the relationships between human and animal beings that many people—including the contributors to this volume—value and are seeking to promote. The idea that a dog or cat is a *companion* suggests the depth, value, and emotionality of the relationship. Indeed, as Cynthia Townley argues in her chapter, "Friendship with Companion Animals," the relationship can be legitimately interpreted as friendship.[6]

Yet as companions or friends, our relationship with a dog or a cat is unique. Dogs and cats live with us in our households. They are not companions whom we see only intermittently, friends from whom we part at the end of the day. Instead they are companions who go home with us, or who greet us when we come home. For that reason, many people think of their dogs and cats as not just companions but members of their family. Since they are not biologically related to us, these animals are like the relatives we acquire through marriage or marriage-like relationships (parents-in-law, siblings-in-law, stepchildren), or through the process of adoption. Indeed, we use the term "adoption" to describe the process by which many dogs and cats enter our lives.

Of course, not all human companions acquire their animal companions through adoption; sometimes a stray cat simply shows up in the backyard, is left on our doorstep, or is spotted by the roadside. But often we go through a formal process of picking out the animal, choosing it over other cats and dogs who are available. Some shelters and breeders also evaluate the potential human adopter for suitability.

In these respects, the creation of a relationship between human and animal companions is similar to the creation of a relationship between an adult and an adopted child. And indeed, some people analogize their dogs and cats to human children. This analogy is, perhaps, a good thing in that it may involve recognizing the individuality, needs, and interests of cats and dogs. But the child metaphor is also problematic, for three reasons. First, most human children eventually become the equals of their parents; they develop into fully functional adults and establish independent lives of their own. But our animal companions almost always live with us and depend on us in crucial ways for all their lives. Second, although human beings do feed and discipline their children, many of the choices we make for our companion animals—related to their reproduction, their work, and their death—are not usually choices we make or legitimately should make for our human children.

Third, as Tony Milligan points out in his chapter on training, the child metaphor fails to capture the fact that our companion cats and dogs do grow up to be adults of their species; they do not remain babies or children. So the parental metaphor is inapt given that dogs and cats outgrow puppy- and kitten-hood. Infantilizing an adult of any species fails to acknowledge the intrinsic value of the adult and its capacity for self-determination. Regarding one's feline or canine companion as one's child may be a manifestation of a kind of paternalism that is inconsistent with respect for the reality of the animal's existence. For these reasons, it seems preferable to regard the cats and dogs who share our lives as companions, rather than as children.

As I hope this discussion has shown, living with cats and dogs raises many complex and difficult moral issues. The contributors to *Pets and People: The Ethics of Our Relationships with Companion Animals* offer insightful perspectives on responsible decision-making for our companion animals. By encouraging careful thought about pets, these perspectives will help to make our relationships with dogs and cats both more just and more fulfilling for all concerned.

Notes

1. Of course, meat-eaters might also refrain from eating certain animals because of the animals' taste or ostensible lack of nutrition, or for reasons pertaining to the meat-eaters' religious or nationalistic commitments, or even out of fear of legal repercussions (if, e.g., consumption of an animal were outlawed by the state).

2. However, as I shall suggest later, the use of family metaphors for animals can also be problematic.

3. The word "pet" originally denoted "a hand-reared lamb" in Scotland and northern England, where it also meant "a spoilt or favourite child." The word came from Scottish Gaelic "peata," meaning "tame animal." *Oxford English Dictionary Online*, s.v. "pet," accessed August 3, 2016, http://www.oed.com.proxy.queensu.ca/view/Entry/141778?rskey=F11mER&result=5&isAdvanced=false#eid.

4. *Oxford English Dictionary Online*, s.v. "pet," accessed August 3, 2016, http://www.oed.com.proxy.queensu.ca/view/Entry/141778?rskey=F11mER&result=5&isAdvanced=false#eid.

5. Thus, some people speak of "house-breaking" their pets. Although it is obvious that animals who share homes with human beings must follow certain rules, just as the humans themselves do, the term "house-broken" suggests that the animal cannot simply be itself but must be reconstructed for the human being(s) with whom it lives.
6. In his chapter, Bernard Rollin gives several examples of genuine friendships between animals.

References

Harvey, Jean. 1999. *Civilized Oppression*. Lanham, MD: Rowman & Littlefield.

Canadian Animal Health Institute. 2015. "Latest Canadian Pet Population Figures Released." February 12. https://www.canadianveterinarians.net/documents/canadian-pet-population-figures-cahi-2014.

Francione, Gary. n.d. "Excerpt from *Introduction to Animal Rights: Your Child or the Dog?*" http://www.abolitionistapproach.com/faqs/#.Vowz6FLstLw.

Humane Society of the United States. 2015. "Pets by the Numbers." http://www.humanesociety.org/issues/pet_overpopulation/facts/pet_ownership_statistics.html.

THE NATURE OF THE HUMAN/ COMPANION ANIMAL RELATIONSHIP AND ITS ETHICAL FOUNDATIONS

COMPANION AND ASSISTANCE ANIMALS

BENEFITS, WELFARE SAFEGUARDS, AND RELATIONSHIPS

Jean Harvey

This chapter has to do with our moral responsibilities toward companion animals, although because of space and my own background, I focus on dogs and cats in Western societies.[1] My main goal is to assess one approach to the ethics of companion animals (which I call the "utilization with welfare safeguards" model) that emerges from the dominant historical tradition, and to point to an alternative account. Given space restrictions, I have separated out work on other recent positions[2] and selected for examination a view that is familiar in everyday thinking and the most prominent in institutional thinking (in scientific and medical research, and veterinary training, for example). Given the work that this appraisal involves, a full development of arguments in favor of the alternative position (which I believe is far more morally sound) would be the subject of another paper. I do, however, explain how it differs from the "utilization with welfare safeguards" model and how some of the moral dangers of that approach are avoided.

The Historical Legacy

Speaking of moral obligations owed directly to animals goes against the dominant tradition in Western thought, which traces from Aristotle through Aquinas to Descartes and Kant. It emphasizes the value of "self-controlled," rational subjects, who are thereby deemed to have intrinsic value and also moral standing: they are beings to whom obligations can be owed. It is held that animals lack reason and so also intrinsic worth and moral standing: we have no direct moral obligations toward them. Their value is merely instrumental, and their role in the natural order of things is to be of use to humans. Moral constraints on our treatment of them arise only because some obligations to human beings are involved.

This is greatly simplified, but so too is its non-academic, social legacy. Signs of this derivative conception of their moral status are easily found. We have discovered a correlation between cruelty to animals and later violence toward people, but when people call for tougher laws against animal cruelty on this basis alone, animal suffering has no inherent significance. It matters solely as an indicator of human suffering to come. For example, when Hurricane Katrina hit New Orleans, many people refused to vacate their homes when ordered to leave their companion animals behind. A US law now requires that provisions be made for the evacuation of both people and their animal companions (if emergency funding from the federal government is to be received), but the rationale given is that human compliance depends on it.[3]

The sense of entitlement in using animals for human benefit is immense and still largely unshaken. There is a growing awareness of the suffering involved in some uses of animals (although deeply resisted in medicine, science, and sport), but we can see the historical legacy in what I call the "default position." Most people do not question our general entitlement to make use of animals and offer no justification for it. Any concern raised has to do with some specific use.[4] Challenges to specific uses, though, whether because of the benefit's triviality or the animal's suffering, do not dislodge the conviction that, other things being equal, it is our prerogative to use animals for our benefit.

The "Utilization with Welfare Safeguards" Model

Given this settled conviction, welfare concerns can enter the scene as a proviso on this prerogative, what I call the "utilization with welfare safeguards" model. Such a proviso can come in weaker and stronger forms.

In his book *Rain without Thunder*, Gary Francione refers to "welfarists" whose main goal is "to ensure that animals, who are regarded as property under the law, are treated 'humanely' and not subjected to 'unnecessary' suffering" while still being used (1996, 2). He insightfully explains the disastrous moral implications of this approach (and why so many so-called animal rights activists have taken this same welfarist approach, at least for the foreseeable future).

This is a fairly weak form of the welfare clause, since accessing the various uses the animals serve takes precedence over eliminating welfare violations, although the violations are to be minimized. In this chapter, though, I will consider what seems to be a stronger and morally safer proviso, where animals can be used only if their full welfare (or, at least, as much as is within human reach) is sustained. It goes beyond reducing welfare infringement to the minimum needed in order to use the animal. Our longstanding practice of using animals continues, but now it must be morally combined with ensuring their welfare.

Selecting this approach for comment may seem odd when thinking of companion animals, but the model is more relevant than it first appears. I will consider "companion animals" in a broad sense, where the basic requirement is that the dog or cat lives with humans in a "home setting" at least most of the time.[5]

"Utilizing animals (with safeguards)" is a self-interested project; humans expect to gain from it. To phrase it more gently, there are benefits involved, but when we move from the language of "using" to that of "benefits," the heavily empirical disciplines (including medicine) contain plenty of material on "the benefits of having pets." When we add in a pervasive assumption in the same literature that these benefits are why we have "pets," we then have the self-interested motive that completes the package: we have the "utilization with safeguards" model applied to companion animals, but in the gentler form of "seeking benefits while ensuring welfare." In one fairly representative empirical study of pets, Sheila Bonas, June McNicholas, and Glyn M. Collis write,

> This high level of pet ownership [about 50%] persists despite many potential costs. In addition to the financial costs of food, veterinary care and other pet products, disadvantages of pet ownership can include: time spent caring for the pet; restrictions on lifestyle; daily hassles resulting from caring for and cleaning up after pets; worry due to destructive or anti-social behaviour of pets; emotional distress, e.g., on the death of a pet; and risks such as bites, allergic reactions and other zoo-noses. . . . Given this long list of potential costs, and that relatively few pets are working animals 'earning their keep' in a practical way, owners presumably perceive substantial benefits from pets to persuade so many to keep them. (Bonas, McNicholas, and Collis 2000, 209)

Since, it is claimed, having a pet must be in the human's interest, the benefits must outweigh the costs. What are these benefits?

> Pets may have functional roles . . . such as impression management (e.g. dogs as fashion accessories, or acquisition of a fierce dog to fit a macho image), or avocation (the pet as a diversion or hobby, e.g. those kept for breeding or competing in shows). However, most accounts of positive aspects of pet ownership focus on pet ownership as a social relationship with advantages arising from relationship-based concepts such as support and attachment . . . and protection against loneliness. (Bonas, McNicholas, and Collis 2000, 209)

Another empirical study emphasizes, in its list of benefits, promoting calmness, relaxation, and social interaction, but "above all, a pet provides an outlet for nurturant and care-giving behaviour. Through its various gestures of attachment, affiliation, and dependence, it provides its owner with a powerful sense of being valued and needed" (Council for Science and Society 1988, 37). In the report as a whole, the underlying framework is clearly the "utilization with safeguards" model. For example, the report's authors observe, "It is one of the moral assumptions of our society (and of many others) that a duty exists to protect the interests of animals, thereby setting limits on what may be done to them in order to satisfy human needs and desires" (Council for Science and Society 1988, 64). "It is evident from this study that the keeping of companion animals . . . satisfies human interests; it is not ordinarily contrary to the social or public interest and, in the absence of abuse, is not in itself contrary to animal interests" (Council for Science and Society 1988, 69).

Other examples in the social science literature are readily found. The "utilization with safeguards" model, then, can be captured in the gentler language of "seeking benefits while ensuring welfare," and it can be exemplified in various practical forms, depending on what the "use" (or "benefit") involves. There are, of course, many benefits to be gained by humans when this model is applied to companion animals in the broad sense specified earlier. The welfare of the dogs and cats is apparently ensured as well. However, the comments below point to a less rosy view of the model.

Dangerous Motives

"Utilization" is goal-oriented, and what is used in the process may, rightly or wrongly, be seen by the agent as merely instrumentally valuable. Adding in a self-interested motive is straightforward in the case of an individual: the person uses something or someone as a tool to achieve some personal advantage. Talking about motives takes more care when speaking about groups, particularly when members of one group utilize members of another group for their advantage.

If belonging to a certain group is an important part of who I am, I feel a kinship with others in that group and typically want them to thrive. When my self-conception as a group member is strong, threats or harms to other members feel deeply personal. Similarly, I can be especially delighted when others in the group receive some improvement in their situation. This role of group membership in one's self-conception can appear in various actions, responses to events, and ways of talking without being explicit in the person's mind. Even with no change in my own life, "we" have made headway if some in the group have received substantial benefits; "we" have been humiliated if some have been treated with contempt. There is a conception of "our interests" that refers to the collective interests of the group, but this does not mean interests shared by every member. If being a woman is important for Jill's self-conception, she may speak of its being "in our interests" to legally ensure maternity leave, even if she has never borne or adopted a child and is determined not to. Some of "our interests" are not literally self-interests of the individual speaking, but given the role of group membership, the paradox evaporates. When members of a privileged group with social power have a self-conception involving that group membership, they too are motivated to "promote their interests," and that motivation can function without self-awareness. Now add to the mix a long tradition of such a powerful group's members using members of another group for their own benefit, where these uses involve both intentional acts and also habitual actions that pass under the moral radar screen of the agents. There is, then, the motivation not only to promote individual self-interest by continuing this long tradition, but also to promote the interests of the group in the same fashion.

Where group membership is vital to my self-conception, furthering the interests of the group or a portion of the group is significantly analogous to classic, individual self-interest, even if I do not benefit in the easily visible sense. I am not simply a compassionate and caring observer, trying to do the right thing. When someone acts in the interests of the group she identifies with, there is a personal investment, so to speak, in what happens. The physical self may or may not be involved, but the sense of self, the self-conception, is.

The familiar dangers with any motivation that is akin to self-interest are, first, the inappropriate self-favoring at the expense of others, or here, favoring one's own group at the expense of another group (especially one used for "our" benefit), and second, the proliferation of "uses" of others, if indeed the others are in practice readily usable. Although the welfare proviso is intended to limit the kinds of uses made, the fact that utilization is in principle acceptable is itself a motivation for a never-ending quest to use the others in as many ingenious ways as possible, always providing the proviso can be met. There is a mindset of utilization at work. Such moral dangers increase when the group's interest being promoted does not involve me directly, since I am likely to be far less aware of any self-serving motivation here than in situations where the self-interest is purely individual, and I will probably be challenged less often by those around me, given the appearance of altruism. As with other group biases, a speciesist person is not crudely and blatantly selfish. These dangers arise when humans use cats and dogs for human benefit, if our membership in the group (humans) carries significant psychological weight for us.

Tacit Value Claims

Sometimes there is explicit "use" over and above simply living with the companion animal, for example, with assistance and therapy dogs (such as guide dogs) and police dogs (who often live with their "handlers" in a family setting). With such arrangements between a very powerful party (the humans) and a far more vulnerable party (the dogs), there is enormous scope for the abusive exploitation of the more vulnerable. Yet even with such explicit uses, surely the strong welfare proviso blocks such exploitation and ensures that the arrangement is morally sound?

A dog's welfare includes psychological as well as biological or physical matters. It is wrong to turn your dog into a permanently chained watchdog, since being permanently tethered and isolated are both contrary to a dog's psychological welfare. Not all morally dubious arrangements, though, involve clearly visible cruelty or neglect, and here a major vulnerability of the model surfaces. Recently the treatment of assistance dogs has been questioned. Serpell, Coppinger, and Fine (2000) point out that sometimes pups are raised in foster homes with a lot of family interaction and then moved to individual kennels for months in their final training stages. What does this dramatic change do to the youngsters? Serpell also notes that assistance dogs may have a series of human handlers during their lives. Since the pups are selected for their sociability, they bond with their handlers. How emotionally painful, then, is such a series of moves from one human or family to another? These potential welfare concerns do not involve physical abuse. While we would likely describe months of isolation in kennels in final training as a straightforward welfare violation (although this is contested by the program's proponents), we might also wonder how many moves from one home to another also count.

Although the question seems to be straightforwardly empirical, it is not at all clear that it is, even though empirical facts are involved. To say that an animal's welfare is ensured is not to say that his quality of life could not be better, but rather to say that certain kinds of fulfillment that are in line with the animal's nature or *telos* (to use Bernard Rollin's term [2006, 99–101]) are ensured at a certain level, the level that enables that animal to thrive. To speak of a welfare violation is not to say that there are things that could be done to improve the quality of life that are not being done, but rather to say that others are responsible for things that bring the welfare level below that at which the animal's nature has a fulfilling expression. But the distinction between a fulfilling life experience and an already-fulfilling life that is further enriched rests on more than empirical facts. The distinction matters because the welfare proviso being considered should ensure the former of these two. It brings no commitment to the latter, nor would interventions that prevented only "further enrichment" be "welfare violations."

The misery experienced by a permanently tethered dog is so transparent that just about anyone without a preconceived agenda will agree that it is a welfare violation. The dog cannot fulfill her nature, especially her psychological and social nature, even minimally in that condition. She cannot have a good life experience that way. But agreement on the more transparent and extreme cases does not change the point that "a fulfilling life experience" is value laden: it is roughly a way of living that is in line with the animal's *telos* and that is therefore stimulating, psychologically satisfying, and rewarding in ways and to degrees that result in a "good" life experience. What if a dog permanently wears a bark-control collar (which sends an electric shock to the dog whenever she barks)? When people focusing on welfare issues disagree as to whether this is a welfare violation, it is not because they disagree that it causes some pain every time it is activated. They disagree on what constitutes a good life experience for a dog. (There are, of course, other kinds of disagreements, where the reference to welfare issues is rejected as relevant to the question of whether a dog should be subjected to such a device.) In thinking of a good, fulfilling life experience, people can usually conceive of one that is better, so a judgment has to be made as to when the level is high enough to count as good. The further away from the basics and the extremes we go, the more that differences in "standards" emerge even if the empirical facts are agreed upon.

Unclear Cases and the Momentum Problem

Disputes as to whether something constitutes a welfare violation, then, can take different forms. In some cases it is indeed the empirical facts that are uncertain, but in others there is a conflict of value judgments (as to what constitutes a "good" or "fulfilling" life experience for the animal). Consequently, there is a broad scope for dispute in any but the most obvious and extreme cases, and when this occurs, the momentum is overwhelmingly in one direction: to assume that all is well and to go ahead with the proposed use of the animal. This "momentum problem" is a corollary of arrangements with the general features in question, namely, the parties have unequal power over the arrangement, the more powerful have an unquestioned presumption that they are entitled to make use of the less powerful, and the architects of the arrangement have something akin to self-interested motives (at least at the group level). There will always be this momentum in one direction if there is no clearly visible neglect or abuse. The onus to prove the case will always be on whoever challenges the specific arrangement.

Complex Uses and Benefits: "No Ability" and "Lost Ability"

Companion animals (in the broad sense explained above) may provide sophisticated benefits requiring extensive prior training or simpler benefits requiring no complex training. Given the focus on dogs and cats in this book, the sophisticated benefits are usually provided by dogs.

When used for complex purposes, the young dog is valued insofar as she is suited to the use. A fair question, then, is whether the program organizers should take any responsibility for dogs who turn out to be unsuited for the intended use (the "no ability" cases). What should happen to the youngsters taken from shelters or bred for the program or accepted as donations, who prove unsuitable somewhere in the process? According to the model under discussion, utilization is qualified by the welfare proviso, but this in itself says nothing about those not utilized. With some kinds of uses, like police work, the number of young dogs who are successful in the training program can be as low as one in twenty. What of the remaining nineteen? Usually they would be good companions (with no sophisticated use involved), but whose moral responsibility is it to ensure their adoption?

There are reasons for thinking the program organizers should be involved. While the animals in question are not "serving the purpose" of, say, being a police dog, the only way the organizers locate the one suitable dog in twenty is by having full access to all twenty for varying time periods. Police websites in Britain indicate that the pups are raised in a family setting until 10–18 months or even 12–24 months old. They are then taken from that setting for the initial, formal training lasting 8–14 weeks. Guide-dog organizations in the US indicate that the pups are raised in a family setting until 22–26 months old and then enter 4–6 months of formal training, followed by about 4 weeks of working with their selected sight-impaired guardian. Presumably, in both cases the formal training period is one where unsuccessful dogs are screened out, which means that many rejected dogs are already adults: for American guide dogs, well over two years old, and for police dogs in the UK, well over a year and sometimes over two. For shelter dogs, the older they are, the slimmer the chances of adoption. So if rejected dogs go to a shelter, their time in the program badly hurts their chances of a long-term home. It is not clear that the programs save even one life which otherwise would be lost, since successful guide or police dogs are sociable and intelligent, just the kind of pup likely to be adopted out of a shelter anyway. Refreshingly, some program organizers do help to adopt out the ultimately rejected dogs. In the US there is even a waiting list for these "second career" dogs, which is a very different outcome from that awaiting them in local animal shelters.

The second point in this section concerns dogs who are no longer able to serve in their sophisticated service roles (the "lost ability" cases). Since they will no longer serve that purpose, the utilization with safeguards model, strictly construed, says nothing about them. What, though, ought to happen at this point? For highly trained, special-use companion dogs, the most vulnerable time, physically and psychologically, is when they acquire a chronic or serious illness or reach their senior years. Removing them from their home and closest humans at this time of frailty is painful for a deeply bonded dog. It is indeed taken as a serious issue by some of the organizations involved. Retired guide dogs in the US, Canada, and the UK often continue to live with their handlers or related family members, but if impossible, the program organizers find a caring home. Police dogs too quite often continue living with their handlers. Sampled police websites in these countries indicate this trend, and if living with their handler is not possible, the police units make every effort to find a home with someone experienced with ex-police dogs (who can otherwise have problems adjusting to a non-working life).

It seems, then, that whether or not the two groups of dogs—the unsuited and the retired—fall under the model we are considering, the organizations involved believe they have some obligations toward them. There are, though, practices not described on the organizations' websites, but made public by incensed critics. For example, while retired police dogs in the US often continue to live with their handlers, most police departments withdraw all financial support at that time. So at a stage when a dog is more likely to develop a chronic but treatable illness, veterinary bills become the responsibility of the handler or new adopter. It is easy to find news items where the policy produces public outrage. Some departments have even made use of the policy by "retiring" a young police dog precisely in order not to have to pay a hefty veterinary bill for a treatable injury or illness; this practice may result in euthanasia.

Such a policy (of ending concern for the dog's welfare as soon as she can no longer serve the special purpose) comes very close to the most ruthless interpretation of the model, where concern for welfare is tightly connected with being utilized. I say "very close" because most American police departments do try to ensure that the dog has a caring home (often with the dog's human partner) in standard retirement situations, but there the concern typically ends. Clearly, both police departments and individual handlers accept the model on some reading or other, agreeing that using police dogs is morally acceptable and that (at least while working) the dogs' welfare should be ensured, but the unrelenting tie between most departments' welfare provision and the dogs' continuing to work is a morally objectionable practice to many human partners and members of the general public. I think this criticism is justified, but why? The account offered below of our primary moral obligation to companion animals will provide an answer to this and some other questions.

Simpler Uses and Benefits

This issue of dogs and cats who, strictly speaking, are not covered by the "utilization with safeguards" model also arises for the more usual cases of companion animals, those serving no elaborate purpose. In his chapter on companion animals in his powerful book, *Animal Rights and Human Morality*, Rollin's list of benefits humans derive from having dogs includes several of this simple kind: "a playmate for and protector of children," "a friend," "an exercise mate, a contact with nature for urban people, an invaluable source of friendship and company and solace for the old and the lonely," and "an inexhaustible source of pure, unqualified, and total love" (2006, 289–90).

If we translate the model's description into its gentler form—"seeking benefits while ensuring welfare"—then companion animals are indeed sometimes acquired to secure some benefit: "If you're going to go jogging at all hours, get a dog to take with you." "If we keep getting mice, we'd better get a cat." "You should get a cat. They've found it helps lower your blood pressure." "If you're worried about break-ins, why not get a dog?"

As already seen, literature in the empirical sciences often embodies a much broader assumption that portrays the practice of having "pets" as generally motivated by human self-interest. Interestingly, when Rollin rejects the historical tradition, he introduces the idea of a "contract" between companion animals and humans, which again suggests a self-interested motive on the part of humans. He writes, "One may choose to see the human relationship to the dog as involving something like a social contract," and he claims that "the dog evidences in countless ways its fulfillment of the contract with humans." Yet "we are systematically violating the contract and the fundamental rights of the animals who are party to it—the right to life of the animals and the actualization of their *telos* [i.e., the satisfaction of the physical, behavioral, and psychological interests that constitute their nature]" (2006, 289).

Rollin argues plausibly that animals "exhibit behaviors that qualify as agreements, both with humans and with each other," even if they are unable to affirm linguistically what they are doing (54). What I see as the biggest threat, though, to the notion of a contract here, at least, one that is morally sound, is the huge difference in power between the two parties. Dogs cannot reflect on proposed arrangements, foresee their practical implications, raise concerns, or propose revisions. Humans are the ones who decide on the arrangement, and the scope for "non-agreement" on the part of the dog may be all but non-existent. Even speaking of a consensual exchange of benefits here seems a bit strained. In virtually every respect, humans are in control. If the two items—the benefits the dogs provide and their welfare provision—are interdependent (one key element of a "contract"), then perhaps it is better described as "humans seeking benefits for themselves while ensuring the animals' welfare, with the compliance of the animals involved."

If so, it shares in the vulnerabilities already explained: the potentially dangerous motives of group membership, the tacit value judgments that are hard to secure, the momentum problem, and at least some situations that parallel the sophisticated skills' "no ability" or "lost ability" cases. A dog intended to be a playmate for the children feels comfortable only with adults (the "no ability" analogue) or no longer has the energy to play with the youngest child (the "lost ability" analogue).

Nothing in a standard contract protects either party beyond the specified, mutually beneficial arrangement. With literal contracts between humans and with the philosophical notion of a social contract, the motive is assumed to be self-interest. Is it reasonable, then, to honor the commitment made in the "contract" beyond the time when the benefits are being received from the other party, or where the expected benefits were never received? This question arises here as with more complex "uses" of companion dogs, and my response points to an alternative basis for our obligations to companion animals.

My target is not Rollin but the model itself, since it functions extensively in Western thinking (sometimes with weaker forms of the welfare proviso), being visible in just about every moral justification of sophisticated uses of companion dogs and in a goodly portion of the thinking about companion animals providing simpler benefits. For Rollin himself, though, the vulnerabilities the notion of "a kind of contract" involves can be avoided, since the moral validity of the two animal rights he specifies (the *prima facie* right to life and the actualization of their *telos*) depend on no contractual arrangement. Rollin argues for them directly in earlier sections of the book, and if successful, the obligation to respect those rights is independently grounded. In his book as a whole, this does seem to be his position. For reasons given later, I think Rollin may perhaps sympathize with the priority I place on the relationship between animal companions and their people.

Our Primary Obligation to Companion Animals

Whether the benefits are complex or not, whether planned for or not, when dogs and cats live with humans, in nearly every case they form deep bonds with them.

Contrary to the stereotype, this is as true of cats as of dogs if—and it is an important "if"—they are allowed to do so.[6] There is something disturbing about the often-heard claim, "He's not a pet. He's a guide dog." A distracted guide dog is indeed unsafe for the human, but the quote is misleading since just about every dog (and cat) living with a human is a companion animal (a "pet")—at least, from the animal's perspective—whether or not he serves some special purpose. It is part of the nature of most dogs and cats (yes, cats) to give love and loyalty to the human companion. As with anyone who loves, it makes them vulnerable—to the hurt of not being loved at all, to being manipulated, exploited, or traumatically abused or abandoned.

The nature of this relationship is central to the ethics of companion animals, or at least dogs and cats: the deep and abiding affection the animals give and seek, the profound emotional and physical vulnerability they face because of it, and the blunt fact that humans in general control the relationship and have the power either to treasure or betray their animal companions.[7] Such a loving, loyal, and respectful relationship on the part of humans is compatible with careful guidance and supervision, given some of the risks the animals are exposed to. Love and respect are not laissez-faire attitudes; they are attitudes of engagement, but very different from that of seeing someone as useful or beneficial to have around.

So the position I point to as the alternative to the "seeking benefits while ensuring welfare" model is that the primary moral obligation we have with respect to companion animals is to develop, nurture, respect, and protect this relationship. Given space restrictions, I cannot develop it fully here, but I will indicate some basic points. If we treasure the animals and the relationship, we will of course care for their physical and psychological welfare. The model I am critiquing also requires this, but when we place the loving relationship center stage, there is a far more proactive engagement called for, and this is a major difference.

The goal takes us beyond welfare provision, beyond even standard "tender loving care," to a relationship that deepens over the companion animal's lifetime, long after a good relationship has been established. The question is not whether this relationship is good, but whether it is the best it can be. The proactive attention and involvement are at a different level from that needed to keep a good relationship stable, and this is as true for the relationship between a human and her animal companion as it is for the relationship between parent and child or between spouses.

With the "simple benefits" group of companion animals—dogs and cats living at home and serving no special purpose—we can find plenty of examples of the model's functioning (and some were given earlier), but we can also find rejections of the model. One feature that many human companions of cats and dogs choke on is seeing "receiving and giving affection or love" as benefits to be aimed for in a self-interested fashion. I quoted earlier from a social science study: "Above all, a pet provides an outlet for nurturant and care-giving behaviour. . . . [I]t provides its owner with a powerful sense of being valued and needed." This kind of writing strikes many who live with animals as bizarrely out of touch with the nature of the bond. The magic of a loving relationship is chillingly absent. It will be objected that it is a quote from a social science text, but perhaps part of the point is that some things are not aptly described in such language. The other part of the point is that authentic love does not see the loved one as a means to an end, or in this case, two ends: receiving love and providing a vehicle for expressing love. Love values the loved one for who she is in herself; the focus is on the one loved, not the love received, and it is a kind of cherishing that has commitment as its heart.

Self-Interested Motives?

Many human companions also reject the sweeping, self-interested motivation that is sometimes presumed to hold. Adopting a cat, dog, or baby is a voluntary act, but neither that nor expecting it to be rewarding establishes a motive of self-interest. Adoptions in emergencies or of a second or third shelter animal are often actually counter to self-interest. Someone unexpectedly faced with an abandoned and injured cat in desperate straits may step in and provide a loving home, although inconvenient and costly, if the alternative is certain death at the local shelter. The same is true for many adoptions of additional animals from overcrowded shelters: the question is more "Can we provide a good home for one more?" than "Wouldn't it be nice to have a third dog?"

"Lost Ability" Cases and the Gratitude Argument

Strictly speaking, the "utilization with safeguards" model says nothing about companion dogs and cats who fall into the "no ability" or "lost ability" categories. With complex uses, the general public has often been the voice objecting to financially abandoning the animals who can no longer serve the purpose, but on what grounds? When the US police departments find homes for their retired dogs but refuse to provide further financial support, the objection usually heard is the charge of ingratitude. They have made use of the dogs for years, so ensuring their welfare is morally owed to them for life in return for all the benefits received. An analogous argument can be given for companion animals providing simpler benefits. The older, frailer cat who lives in quiet contentment but with little energy and initiative for making affectionate contact does not deserve to be abandoned after all the years of loving company he has provided. Anyone but a shockingly ungrateful person will cherish him in these later stages.

It is a tempting argument, but although the animals are no longer expected to provide the benefits, it nonetheless places the benefits received at the heart of the justification. So if this move rescues some companion animals from abandonment, it is the "lost ability," not the "no ability," group. Also, if the response is tied to benefits received in the past, does this mean that the measure of the grateful response may justifiably vary according to how successfully the companion animal provided those anticipated benefits, how valuable the benefits were, for how long they were provided, and so on? Does the refusal to abandon the animal in his senior years depend, then, on past achievements, so that the right to loving care and support in his frailer years must be earned? Clearly, if we think this way, it is not the relationship pointed to above.

If, on the other hand, our primary obligation is to respect, nurture, and protect the loving relationship between the companion animals and their humans, then they are to be treasured as much when elderly and a bit wobbly and confused as when young, vibrant with health, and eager to be the children's playmate. Providing sought-after benefits is not a moral precondition for being cherished throughout their lives.

With cases like police dogs, perhaps we refer to gratitude because those we are urging to do something are not, and cannot reasonably be expected to be, in a loving relationship with the animals. Police departments benefit greatly from police dogs, but it is the handler, not the administrators, who lives in a close relationship with the dog. The public's demand that police departments provide financial support for retired dogs cannot rest on the claim that the administrators are or should be in a lasting relationship of love with the dogs and that withholding such provision violates that relationship. Even so, appealing to gratitude is an uneasy line of support, given the role of benefits received.

Keith Burgess-Jackson argues that people who bring animals into their lives thereby acquire special responsibilities toward them (1998, 161), and this point, together with the one in this paper about our primary obligation toward animal companions, provides a sounder route. Although the police dog does not live with the administrators, they take the initiative in acquiring the dog, and this brings with it special responsibilities toward that particular animal. They know the close relationship that develops between dog and handler and the challenges the dog faces when retired to a non-working life. They also know that if the older dog is injured or sick, she will look to her human partner for comfort and help. The handler in fact is bailing them out of a morally unsatisfactory situation (where a dog the administrators have acquired is no longer wanted by them) and all at a difficult transition time for the dog. On my account, the close relationship between dog and handler is at the center of what is morally owed to her, and although the department's administrators are not directly involved in the relationship, they do acquire the dog, and the least they can do by way of resulting moral involvement is to actively support that close relationship, for example, by providing stress-reducing financial support for predictable medical expenses.

Implications for "No Ability" Cases

There are also implications for the "no ability" dogs and cats. If the primary obligation is to provide a setting in which the animals will thrive in a deep, committed, and long-term relationship, then there is indeed a moral basis for guide dog organizations' and police departments' taking an active role in finding loving homes for the dogs who are unsuited for their special purposes, especially since their time in the program has disadvantaged the dogs in this respect.

For companion animals in the more usual sense—those serving no sophisticated purpose—"no ability" cases are those where the adopted animal does not provide the anticipated benefits. If developing the relation between the animal companion and her humans is the foremost goal, missing the expected benefits is not a morally decisive reason for reassessing the adoption. You think the cat will spend time playing with the children, but she prefers to lie quietly with the parents. You expect the dog to enjoy jogging with you, but he prefers a sedate walk with your spouse. If you adopted in order to secure these benefits—the "utilization with safeguards" model—reassessing the adoption will seem reasonable. If, however, the benefits are expected but not the reason for the adoption, if developing a deep relationship of love is the priority, then disappointment about the expected benefits should not threaten the adoption. While expecting the relationship with the adoptee to be rewarding, a mature adopter will expect some difficulties, confusions, and adjustments. It is not a straightforward, self-interested, pleasure-seeking exercise any more than adopting a child is, and the wise adopter knows that a wonderful and rewarding relationship is unlikely to develop if approached in a self-interested spirit by the more reflective and powerful party. The relationship rests on valuing the animal companion as intrinsically precious, and this provides a very different perspective on the notion of expected benefits.

In *Animal Rights and Human Morality*, Rollin claims that "in the past fifty or so years, dogs (and to a lesser extent, cats and other species) have become valued not only for pragmatic, economically quantifiable purposes, but for deep emotional reasons as well. These animals are viewed as members of the family, as friends, as 'givers and receivers of love' . . . ; and the bond based in pragmatic symbiosis has turned into a bond based in love" (2006, 292). The contrast is the one explored in this paper, between a mutually beneficial "kind of contract" between humans and dogs (which, being under the control of the humans involved, can be described as a gentler version of the "utilization with safeguards" model) and a bond "based in love." For Rollin himself, there are so many allusions to the special bond between humans and at least dogs that I think he may be sympathetic to the priority placed on it here. He speaks of dogs as "an inexhaustible source of pure, unqualified, and total love" (290), and refers to "the mystical bond that can unite humans and animals" (291–92). He clearly treasures the loving relationship between humans and companion animals.

More Radical Implications?

Nearly all dogs and most cats living from a very early age with caring and loving humans enter into loving relationships and thrive in them. They become affectionate companions who bask in the security of the relationship, relish the affection, and develop into fascinating and wonderful individuals. The joy and deep sense of security dogs and cats find in the relationship is mirrored in the quiet comfort felt when close to their human companions, the delight they show when playing with them, the loving greetings with which they welcome them, the affectionate presence offered to their sick or despondent humans, the way in which they heal more quickly or die more peacefully in the arms of their human companions, and the grief they feel when they lose their people.

Hundreds of thousands of dogs do not live as companion animals. Some are "purely working dogs," at least from the perspective of the humans. (It is far from clear that such dogs never themselves enter into a loving relationship, giving their hearts and loyalties to non-reciprocating humans who treat them like decently maintained machines.) Given the many ways in which dogs in general and many cats display their happiness, delight, and sense of deep comfort in a lasting and loving relationship with their humans, a case can be made that being animal companions is part of their evolved nature, their *telos*, as Rollin calls it, and if so, it has radical and far-reaching moral implications.

For example, except for the very occasional case where a pup cannot enter into such a loving relationship or is unhappy in it, there should not be any "purely working dogs." If the work cannot be accomplished if the dog enters into a companion role, so much the worse for the work. That the work is beneficial to humans establishes nothing morally, just as the work of human slaves being beneficial to their "owners" establishes nothing morally. In both cases it begs all the important questions to claim that the recipients of the benefits are so special, so superior in value that their benefits are worth the suffering or deprivation of the animals or slaves. There are also implications for dogs and cats in research labs, veterinary training, sports, and more, and for other animals whose evolved nature includes entering into and fully thriving in such relationships, but here I can only nail the flag to the mast and develop the points another time.

Conclusion

The claim that being animal companions is part of the evolved nature of nearly all dogs and most cats is not the only reason for objecting to the use of animals in contexts like scientific research and some sports, but it has in itself significant implications. The "utilization with welfare safeguards" model, even under the gentler formulation of "seeking benefits while ensuring welfare" (an apparently strong version of the welfare proviso), is not as morally sound as it first appears. We should move away from its focus on the "benefits" dogs and cats bring to humans. Instead we should highlight and explore the relationship of loving inter-action that cherishes the animals for the wonderful individuals they are, a rela-tionship that develops over the lifetime of the animals and that calls for far more time and energy, and a far more proactive kind of involvement, attentiveness, and reflection, than does a basic and stable warm and caring relationship. The moral obligation to develop such a relationship with our animal companions (with dogs and cats at least) and possibly to enable dogs in general and most cats to enter into such a relationship provides a morally more secure basis for an ethic of compan-ion animals.

Notes

1. I refer to nonhuman animals as "animals." Unfortunately the chapter would become unreadable otherwise.
2. E.g., Martha Nussbaum's capabilities approach (2006, 325–407).
3. See the Pets Evacuation and Transportation Standards Act of 2006, where it states that in order to receive funding from FEMA (the Federal Emergency Management Agency), a jurisdiction's emergency plans must make provision for the evacuation of pets. As is stated in the summary, "This bi-partisan legislation is necessary because Hurricane Katrina has clearly shown that when given a choice between their per-sonal safety or abandoning their household pets, a significant number of people will choose to risk their lives in order to remain with their pets. It is now clear that we must require that jurisdictions have plans in effect to deal with their pet-owning populations as a matter of public safety."
4. Even leading advocates of the traditional view occasionally object to a specific use, not because of the animal suffering as such, but because the human benefit is trivial. See Kant's distinction between sport and vivisection (1963, 240–41).

5. I say "home setting" for simplicity, but the relevant closeness can be found in less paradigmatic modes, e.g., a cat living with a homeless person, a dog living in a close relationship with his human companion out on the range.
6. People with a fixed stereotype of a cat as solitary and independent often miss the cat's attempts to move into a closer relationship, interpreting all approaches in material terms (as seeking food or physical warmth, or wanting to go out), and neither offer nor respond to nudges for physical affection—in effect training the cat not to seek such a connection. The preconception of the more powerful party defines the relationship.
7. Some cases fall outside of this general claim, e.g., when a family dog suddenly and apparently inexplicably attacks a family member. Nothing in the chapter undermines one's right to self-defense.

References

Bonas, Sheila, June McNicholas, and Glyn M. Collis. 2000. "Pets in the Network of Family Relationships: An Empirical Study." In *Companion Animals and Us: Exploring the Relationship between People and Pets*, edited by Anthony L. Podberscek, Elizabeth S. Paul, and James A. Serpell, 189–208. Cambridge: Cambridge University Press.

Burgess-Jackson, Keith. 1998. "Doing Right by Our Animal Companions." *Journal of Ethics* 2 (2): 159–85.

Council for Science and Society. 1988. *Companion Animals in Society*. Oxford: Oxford University Press.

Francione, Gary L. 1996. *Rain without Thunder*. Philadelphia: Temple University Press.

Kant, Immanuel. 1963. *Lectures on Ethics*. Translated by Louis Infield. New York: Harper & Row.

Nussbaum, Martha. 2006. *Frontiers of Justice: Disability, Nationality, Species Membership*. Cambridge, MA: Harvard University Press.

Pets Evacuation and Transportation Standards Act. 2006. H.R. 3858. 109th Cong. https://www.govtrack.us/congress/bills/109/hr3858.

Rollin, Bernard. 2006. *Animal Rights and Human Morality*. 3rd ed. Amherst, NY: Prometheus.

Serpell, James, Raymond Coppinger, and Aubrey H. Fine. 2000. "The Welfare of Assistance and Therapy Animals: An Ethical Comment." In *Handbook on Animal-Assisted Therapy: Theoretical Foundations and Guidelines for Practice*, edited by Aubrey Fine, 415–32. San Diego, CA: Academic Press.

2 FRIENDSHIP WITH COMPANION ANIMALS

Cynthia Townley

Animals seem to be friends with each other. Many people with a regular routine of dog-walking know the playmates their dogs prefer, and can identify those that just do not get on. Within multi-pet households, patterns of conflict and affiliation often arise between animals of the same or different species. Horses show definite likings and dislikings for one another, and primatologists observe ape friendships that are distinct from family bonds and hierarchical ordering (de Waal 2005). So animals themselves appear to engage in friendship-like relationships.

On the face of it, Western anglophone culture seems to accept that people can be friends with companion animals. Relationships with companion animals are significant in many people's lives and documented in photographic books (Darcy 2014), memoirs (Rowlands 2008), as well as many private physical or virtual photo albums. Human friendship with animals is easy to observe and is a common theme in fiction and poetry (Oliver 2013; Auster 1999; Hornung 2010). It may be conceded that for some of us, and at some times in life, an animal friend can provide better comfort and companionship than the humans around us. Consider a person with dementia, for whom humans are discomfortingly unfamiliar, or a hospital patient (Haggard 1985). To a child in a bereaved family, sometimes the best comfort comes from an animal friend.

Taken literally, the familiar saying "a dog is man's best friend" raises interesting philosophical questions about how to understand such relationships. Philosophers who consider animals to be fully or partially excluded from friendship would see the claim that some people count an animal companion as their true best friend as clearly mistaken. While the term "friend" is commonly applied to relationships with nonhuman animals, the strict concept of friendship, properly understood, applies only to humans. On this full exclusion view, the apparent friendship observed within and between members of different animal species, including human-animal friendship, is not the real thing. If friendship has various kinds, a partial exclusion view would be that animals might be capable of some but not all forms (Jordan 2001; Frööding and Peterson 2011). Consequently, on this view, animals would lack the capacity for the kind of friendship that matters most to people, and so the relationship with an animal would not be "true best friend," but some more limited, shallower, perhaps less valuable connection. Arguably either version of this mistake—ascribing to non-human animals any capacity for friendship, or ascribing to them the capacity for the highest form of friendship—would involve inappropriate anthropomorphism, or a faulty ascription to the nonhuman party of characteristics that are in fact absent.

Others might accept that the "best friend" claim could be true in some cases, but would consider it unfortunate that some people have their strongest relationships with companion animals: such lives would be considered relationally impoverished. Even if such a friendship were possible, it would be second-rate in some sense. The person would have a "best" friend, but not the best possible or best kind of friend. Here, the claim would not be mistaken, but the state of affairs would be unfortunate.

In this chapter, I will argue for the possibility of an animal as a friend in the strongest sense. This does not mean that this possibility is always available. Certain kinds of friendship may be sustainable only under certain cultural and material conditions. My experience is limited to middle-class life in an affluent anglophone country (Australia) where many households include companion animals, and while I have no doubt that friendships exist in all human communities, I do not know whether all human communities are conducive to friendships with animals. So the claims here are not intended to be universal—I concede that the conditions for possible relationships may be different elsewhere. But I think this is a contingent matter, like other circumstances that may enhance or discourage possible trajectories of friendships. For example, human-human friendships can use technology to transcend physical distance. It is hard to imagine a friendship maintained via the internet or phone if one party cannot use those tools, so this would typically be unavailable to friendships between members of different species. But friendship presumably predated both analogue and digital literacy, so the use of technology seems more of an incidental feature of some friendships than an integral requirement. Friendship across geographic distances, genders, generations, cultural or religious differences, and species may all be differently patterned, and at least some of these patterns accommodate friendship with non-human animals.

Pets, Friends, or Companions?

Some of the debate about whether an animal really can be any kind of friend with a human arises from how "friendship" is defined, and there is little consistency about how the term is applied (Hankin 2009). Even those who fully acknowledge the importance and depth of relationships with pets may still deny that humans can be friends with animal companions. For example, Tony Milligan (2009) discusses end-of-life decisions involving animals with great insight and sympathy, even seeing them as potentially instructive for human cases, but withholds the label "friendship" from relationships with companion animals. Milligan uses the terms "companionship" and "guardianship" in preference to "friendship" (106–117). Jeffrey Masson (1998) expresses a clear view that a dog can have the highest status as friend and even moral exemplar, but is indifferent to the label, often referring to a dog's "caretaker," which he considers equivalent to companion or friend. In contrast, Kristien Hens (2009) is prepared to call the relationship between a human and a canine companion a friendship, but in other ways seems to consider the relationship as less deep than Milligan does.

Hens and Milligan differ not only about the term "friendship," but also about important elements such as replaceability. To be replaceable means that a substitute could do as well, or nearly as well, in the same role. For example, I can replace my hairdresser; nothing inherent to the relationship seems to rule that out. But talk of "replacing" a son or daughter, for example in a case of infant death, seems to miss the significance of that unique individual, and would offer little comfort to a grieving parent. Another child may well be born, but this is not a matter of replacement. Hens says, "Within a relationship of friendship, there are again major differences: dogs are only for a short period of time in our lives, they are to some extent replaceable and they are at our mercy with regard to medical care and euthanasia" (2009, 8). Milligan sees the relationship with companion animals as precluding replaceability: "The concept of pet, which plays a role within a life that is enriched by a relation to a non-human other, is one which involves treating (valuing) these animals as unique and irreplaceable creatures" (2009, 406). Like Milligan, I see irreplaceability as inherent to the relationship of a pet and her person, or a person and her pet. That said, my household is one that includes animal companions, and my preference for a household of that shape predates and will likely extend beyond the lifespans of the cat and dog with whom I currently share a home. I anticipate that there will be a future dog or dogs in my life, but Chica is irreplaceable.

The kernel of truth in Hens's characterization of a pet dog as living "for a short time only" is that the different life expectancies of humans and dogs will most often mean that an individual human will have a series of animal companions. It is also true that a dog can have a series of human companions, and in some cases may choose to redirect its affection and loyalty to a new person. Human lives, too, can involve different sets of companions, due to major life changes such as parenthood or relocation. Yet making a new friend is not at all the same as replacing an old friend.

To sum up: Milligan does not consider pets to be friends, but he does think they are strictly irreplaceable, whereas Hens thinks they can be friends but allows for a degree of replaceability. The philosopher who recognizes a more demanding standard for the relationship is the one who chooses not to call it a friendship. Masson (1998) is happy to use the term "caretaker" as equivalent to friend, but Milligan sees an important difference between guardian and friend. And I agree with Milligan about the irreplaceability of pets, and the difference between the conception of a friend and the conception of a guardian or caretaker, but like Hens I find the label "friendship" entirely apt for at least some relationships between humans and dogs (and other interspecies combinations).

This brief exploration shows the difficulty of applying a term like "friendship" to an interspecies relationship. Friendship is understood in various different ways, and many views not canvassed here could be reasonably defended. The relationships between pets and their people are likewise highly variable. My own intuition is that conceiving of (human or nonhuman) friends as replaceable mischaracterizes friendship. The extent to which one considers a companion (human or nonhuman) as replaceable is the extent to which one is talking about something other than friendship. Replaceability seems antithetical to the loyalty that friendship involves. If I were to have Rover put down before going on holiday, intending to replace him with a similar dog on my return, my attitude could not count as loyal, nor my relationship with Rover as friendship.

A person who relates to an animal in her care merely as a breeding machine or experimental subject, as disposable once it ceases to perform a particular function, is in a relationship that Milligan would consider outside the concept of pet, and that I would consider outside the concept of friendship. This does not mean all breeders or laboratory workers treat their animals callously. Arguably, though, the animal is treated as replaceable, and there is no loyalty to that particular individual. It seems unlikely that a human who cares for an animal in a laboratory or breeding setting would grieve for its death in the same way as for a pet.

Friendship in Philosophy

Two important philosophical approaches to friendship are Aristotle's classic account and Jeanette Kennett and Dean Cocking's "drawing" account (Aristotle

2000; Cocking and Kennett 1998). Both have the potential to include nonhumans as friends. Ultimately I argue that friendship with companion animals can meet the criteria presented in these philosophical accounts, and is as robust, valuable, and worthy of respect as any other friendship. This claim has more than mere academic interest. Recognizing the importance of friendship with animal companions has the potential to influence social policies. For example, housing regulations that customarily prohibit pets might be changed to a default that allows for or encourages animal companionship, or new policies may require building shelters for animals within or alongside emergency accommodation for humans.

Accounts of Friendship: Value, Virtue, and Influence

Aristotle's (2000) classic analysis of friendship distinguishes three ways that friendship can be grounded: pleasure, utility and advantage, and admiration and virtue. The pleasure of spending time with an amusing, charismatic, fun individual is the basis of some friendships. We can also befriend someone because of advantage and mutual benefit. Or, Aristotle claims, a third kind of friendship can be based on the recognition and admiration of virtuous character, so within the friendship there is mutual support for and encouragement of virtue.

In all cases of friendship, there is a concern for the other as well as for oneself. For example, if I share a ride with a fellow commuter, and our transport costs are reduced, this could be mere convenience, which would not be friendship, or it could include additional kindness or consideration such that it could count as friendship. Likewise, if I seek another's company, but my pleasure is at his expense, as I laugh at him but not with him, this lacks regard for the other, and hence is not friendship.

If the friendship is based mainly on pleasure or utility, it will most likely last only as long as those features remain present. The friendship may not persist if circumstances or locations change, or if more effort, even sacrifice, would be required to sustain the connection. Aristotle's highest kind of friendship involves liking what is good (in the Aristotelian sense of character and virtue) in the other party. Virtue-based friendship will frequently incorporate pleasure and advantage, but these are collateral effects, not the heart of the friendship. Arguably, this kind of friendship is more resistant to circumstantial change, as it is grounded in the durable virtuous character inhering in the individual, not in changeable external conditions. Its focus is on true goodness, not on personal rewards of pleasure or utility.

Cocking and Kennett offer an account of friendship that illuminates how friends provide reasons for one another, so that each friend draws the other to different ways of being in the world (Cocking and Kennett 1998). These reasons can be reasons for action—for example, my being motivated by my friend's interest in ballet or football to involve myself in attending to these things—and reasons for reflection, such as my response to my friend's opinion being affected by its source. I am more inclined to hear and consider a criticism or reproach voiced by my friend than I would be if the same content were presented by anyone else.

The "drawing" account is partially compatible with much of the Aristotelian account, although it is not a perfect fit. It could well be that friends are drawn together by mutual pleasure, advantage, or admiration, and that these factors play a part in how the friends respond to one another. There are important differences, though. For Cocking and Kennett, the most important reason for the mutual influence of friends is friendship itself. I will listen differently and be motivated more positively precisely because it is my friend who speaks, advises, or invites. By contrast, a strict Aristotelian account would not accept as true friendship the cases in which my friend leads me astray, because virtue or goodness is central to the highest form of friendship. For Aristotle, an excellent friendship must reflect and reinforce the virtuous character of both friends.

Like Cocking and Kennett, I accept that even friendship of the strongest and closest kind can be mixed and downright harmful (Cocking and Kennett 2000). A friendship can encourage greed and excessive self-indulgence, or harmful self-denial, for example. It does not thereby fail to be friendship. However, while the friendship may lead to or involve harmful activities, it cannot be part of the intention of the friends to harm one another or to damage the friendship—at most, such hostility can be a temporary attitude within a broader context of good will.

How Do Nonhuman Animals Fit These Accounts of Friendship?

Can a companion animal, a cat or dog, be a party to friendship as described above? One interpretation of the Aristotelian view is that we can have pleasure- and utility-, but not virtue-based friendships with nonhuman companions. For example, Jeff Jordan argues,

> Since one can play with a dog, enjoy being with a dog, communicate with a dog, share things with a dog, do things with a dog, trust and be trusted by a dog and take care of a dog, it certainly looks as though one can be a companion-friend with a dog. Further, there appears no obvious reason to deny that one could even establish a utility-friendship, or a

pleasure-friendship, with a dog. While it is true that one cannot establish a virtue-friendship with a dog, it does not follow that one cannot be a friend in any sense with a dog. (2001, 520)

Thus, Jordan defends a partial exclusion view: while animals cannot participate in the most moral kind of friendship, they nevertheless can be real friends of the other two Aristotelian kinds.

It is relatively easy to see mutual pleasure in human-animal interactions. The greetings between a dog and her person are an obvious example. Mutual benefit, too, seems fairly evident, although, as Mark Rowlands (2011) points out, without a degree of pleasure and admiration, utility alone would not be sufficient for friendship. Friendship involving admiration of virtue is the most controversial to apply to companion animals and their humans.

Animal companions also seem to satisfy Cocking and Kennett's account of being drawn to different ways of being in the world. The animals in my household, especially my dog Chica, definitely influence the patterns and habits of my life. I take different walks, at different times, than I would otherwise. I, for the most part willingly, accept the discipline and limits imposed by Chica's needs and expectations for daily early-morning walks. While the structure and discipline that my dog brings to my everyday life are a great benefit to me, I could often achieve these desired ends more conveniently and even efficiently in other ways. Over time, her needs and desires for exercise have become less well-aligned with mine, so I need to adjust to suit her. Chica does not directly offer me interpretations, criticism, or advice, but her approval and disappointment can be palpable, and our interactions can have a normative dimension.

My friendship with Chica involves co-production and co-construction of a shared (part of a) life. An important part of this mutual influence is the potential for reproach and rebuke if one or the other of us fails to sustain the expectations we have mutually established (Gilbert 1990) The normative aspect of our shared activity lies, in the words of Simon Lumsden, "between the space of causes and the space of reasons" (2008, 196). It can emerge as a pattern of shared expectations, in which two parties have the standing to call one another to account. This holding to account need not be verbal, and for nonhuman animals it clearly will not be verbal. When friends are attuned to one another, a glance or a gesture will often suffice to indicate when one has disappointed the other's expectations, or failed to uphold a tacit understanding or agreement. Dogs, wolves, and others can be observed navigating shared norms as they play together, for example, by using the "play bow" (Bekoff and Pierce 2009). Many human-dog relationships exhibit patterns of normative expectations (Haraway 2008).

Barriers to Friendship: Power, Intellectual Capacity, and Ethics

I will consider three philosophical objections to the claim that relationships between dogs and humans can be genuine friendships. The first objection is that an asymmetry of power precludes friendship, the second is based on different abilities to communicate and understand, and the third relates to moral capacity. I will consider power, cognitive capacity, and morality in turn, focusing on how in each domain, important differences can be accommodated within friendship.

While my dog influences my life, there are enormous differences between her power over me and mine over her. Humans can control the household, the quality and availability of food, the options for medical intervention, and even life and death decisions for pets. An animal companion cannot impose its will over the human in the same way. These differences in power and limits to reciprocity may be impediments to complete or genuine friendship (Tuan 1984). Humans have conceptual and communicative capacities that are beyond the comprehension of animals. For example, while Chica knows and expects that we will take a walk together every morning, I cannot let her know that next week I will be away and she will be staying in the dog hotel. A third source for an objection is that friendship has a moral dimension in which an animal cannot participate. This objection requires further consideration of the moral and normative issues briefly canvassed above.

Humans can exercise tremendous power over their household companions, just as they can over livestock or laboratory animals. The nonhuman may not choose what or when it eats, where and for how long it can exercise, whether it can breed, what kind of medical attention is available, and so on. The human makes decisions in all these domains. Does this inequality of power make friendship impossible? I think it depends on how the power is exercised.

Here, Masson's (1998, 18) term "caretaker" is instructive. I could take impeccable care of breeding or working animals as a professional role, a form of engagement that is very different from the mutual coordination of (part of) a shared life that is characteristic of friendship. This brings out a difference between the conceptions of caretaker and friend. I can be a caretaker of animals for various reasons, such as their capacity for work or breeding potential, as well as for their own sake, as in friendship. In the former cases, if the work or breeding capacity diminishes, then the priority given to their wellbeing does too, even to the extent that options like convenience euthanasia and replacement might be consistent with the caretaker role.

Even though there is a power imbalance, the attention and intention brought to the decisions can be highly sensitive to the nonhuman's wellbeing, her individuality, her own way. If there is no intention to respond to the animal's needs and evident preferences, and no adjustment or concession is made to the animal's point of view, then the relationship fails to be one of friendship. Likewise, a human relationship that lacked any give and take would fail to be friendship. If one individual seeks to act for the sake of her friend, and prioritizes knowing about and accommodating the interests and welfare of the friend, it seems irrelevant that one party has greater power and capability than the other. Stuart Spencer and colleagues (2006) claim that a dog is forced to exercise at the owner's whim. While this is possible, it is also possible that the human defers to the animal's preferences and interests.

It is plausible that, as Aristotle argues, we are concerned for our friends, not for our own sake but for the friend's sake. Many humans act for the sake of their animal companions and do not treat them instrumentally. The power to make decisions does not preclude non-instrumental treatment and genuine friendship. The pattern of early morning walks with my dog has emerged as part of our shared life in such a way that I do not get to vary it on a whim. I share with Chica an expectation that "this is how things work," and our normative practice means variations are disconcerting. We both abide by a shared norm.

Human friends with different capacities and resources may defer to each other in different ways in different domains. For example, if my time is more flexible than that of my (human) friend with young children, I might fit in with her schedule and suggestions for activities. The give and take required by friendship is not a perfectly calibrated balance, and in fact too much calculation and insistence on equality suggest something awry rather than a more ideal friendship. Likewise, I defer to my dog's express preference for an early morning walk, and I prioritize her wellbeing even when she does not express it. There is a level of paternalism or deciding on her behalf. But this is different from the power that a breeder or farmer wields over animals that are valued for their functions rather than as particular individuals.

To qualify as friendship, some of each party's actions need to be plausibly called other-regarding, for example, in expressing affection for or being accommodating to the needs or preferences of the other. We adjust to, prioritize, and even sacrifice for our friends—this is what loyalty requires. By these standards, humans and animals can be friends.

Cognitive capacity is the second major difference between humans and nonhumans that might be construed as an impediment to genuine friendship. Attention to the human capacity for abstract thought is commonplace in philosophy. Human linguistic animals have a special capacity for active and self-critical thinking, and other forms of cognitive complexity. My discussion is limited to the narrative understanding and communication that Milligan considers when he argues that the cognitive limits of nonhuman animals preclude fully-fledged friendship (2009). I suspect friendship is connected more closely to the companionship and affiliative behavior seen in many social animals than to sophisticated abstract analytic and conceptual thought. As discussed below, a morally deep relationship, whether between humans or across species, requires a level of mutual regard and reciprocity. The question at stake here is whether that reciprocity depends on the kind of conceptual linguistic understanding that seems peculiar to humans. In Milligan's view,

> This reciprocity need not be understood as cognitively demanding for the animal. An animal guardian may be well aware that their lifelong companion's appreciation of the companionship is of a restricted sort. I will suggest that this supports the use of a terminology of *companionship* rather than *friendship* and that the latter involves a more demanding requirement of mutual understanding (2009, 410).

According to Milligan, friendship requires a high level of mutual understanding, which includes the capacity for a "narrative" understanding of the other being. This means understanding her in light of her history as well as her current presentation, or understanding her life as a meaningful whole. This seems to be something that only linguistic humans can do. Milligan is probably right that humans can understand their pets whereas pets cannot understand their humans in this way. But does friendship depend on this capacity?

Human friendship can withstand degrees and domains of incomprehension: an atheist can be friends with a person of deep faith, even though each finds the other's perspective utterly opaque and alien. Insistence on a capacity to fully comprehend one's friends would likely involve too many implausible and controversial exclusions. My best narrative explanation of my (human) friend might be one she cannot recognize, which could be due to my misinterpretations or to her lack of insight or both. Given that it is hard to recognize and acknowledge all of one's own feelings, motivations, and reactions, the narrative interpretations between friends will be highly fallible. We are not perfectly transparent to ourselves or to others. Arguably, it is more important for friendship to tolerate the inevitable incompleteness, failures, and mistakes of understanding, than to insist that true friendship is sustained only by complete mutual knowledge of one another.

Much of our communication and interaction with both linguistic and nonlinguistic companions is nonverbal. The importance of language and explicit verbal content may be overstated, as friendship across linguistic barriers suggests. A look, a hug, a gesture, or a smile all can be significant in a way that a wordier response might not be. I can be friends with a person for years and might never know salient information about her past. It may be partially revealed to me over time or never disclosed. This is not to deny the significance of narrative understanding to many friendships, but to deny that it is a necessary or central feature of all friendship.

Admittedly, some things cannot be communicated to nonverbal companions, and are nearly impossible to communicate without words. It is difficult to communicate to my dog that I need to leave her in the boarding kennel in order to travel interstate or overseas. I do not think she can understand my promise to return and to bring her home again. I am quite sure she did not understand the prospect or implications, including quarantine, of our international relocation, nor can I assume she would have consented to it if she had understood.

So perhaps my dog and cat do not fully comprehend me, nor do I fully comprehend them. Yet I can observe the intensity of my dog's joy when we prepare to set out on a walk, and I am in no doubt about her disappointment when she has to stay behind. I am confident that we share a companionable contentment by the fire in the evening. Likewise, she is attuned to my mood, responding to my sadness, or disturbed if I am angry or distressed. The limitations of understanding and communication between friends do not impede friendship.

The third objection claims that nonhumans cannot participate in the right kind of moral relationship with humans to count as friends in the fullest sense. Jordan, as discussed above, accepts real friendship with companion animals, but restricts virtue-friendship to human-human friends. Steven Sapontzis argues similarly that "while many of their actions are virtuous, animals are not moral beings because these actions are not part of a moral life" (1980, 50). A moral life is understood by Sapontzis as a life in which a person is aiming toward some ideal (or morally better) individual or social way of life. The ability to reflect on how to close the gap between aspiration and achievement is needed for this "program of fulfilling an ideal" (50). Only human animals reflect in this way.

It seems uncontroversial that nonhumans do not display this kind of reflective moral thinking, character cultivation, and aspiration to live a good life. I suspect, also, that it is rare that humans engage in these practices. There are more cultural products for gourmet cooking and weight loss than for building character. The contents of self-help and self-improvement books generally are more pragmatic than moral—how to get ahead at work, live tidily, manage anxiety, become highly effective, find a partner, and the like. If the kind of morally directed effort described by philosophers were necessary for friendship, many of us would fail the test. My (human) friends and I talk more frequently and in more detail about our favorite beers and latest exercise regimes than we do about developing a virtuous character. So the moral life Sapontzis refers to seems marginal, rather than central, to friendships in my experience.

Ascribing moral virtues to companion animals may seem implausible, since humans can often provide explanations and justifications that animals do not. Yet we continue to call someone brave who insists that he did not think or reflect before dashing into the burning building. Likewise, empathy may be best expressed by gesture or silence rather than words. Much of our complex moral experience and emotions such as love are difficult to put into words, and impossible to express for at least some people sometimes. I think it would be indefensible to deny moral experience to humans who are inarticulate or not good with words. So if the observable conduct, presence, or action of an animal companion meets the standards we apply in the human case, it would seem preemptive to exclude her from the sphere of virtue.

Moral exemplars may achieve their influence without reflecting on and verbally recounting what they are doing and why. So animals are not in principle excluded from this role. Our connection to, close observation of, and caring about nonhuman animals can teach us about important values and virtues. Animals can exhibit compassion, bravery, and loyalty, as well as joy, tolerance, and forgiveness. Mark Rowlands admires Hugo, a Schutzhund, for his courage and "for the extraordinary tolerance, forbearance, kindness and gentleness he exhibits towards [his] two young sons" (2011, 78). He is happy to call Hugo a friend and hopes his admiration is returned. To that end, Rowlands ensures that his own conduct is "fair, consistent, calm, stable and when necessary, strict" (79). We can admire qualities we could share, and those that are beyond us, in other humans and in nonhuman friends. In Freya Mathews's words, "Emotional involvement with creatures who do not share our human goals and aspirations, our systems of values, enables us to gain an external perspective on those values. It enables us to appreciate how odd or arbitrary our human priorities might appear to non-human observers" (2007, 16). Some writers such as Masson have even argued that animals may be morally superior to humans. Dogs do not lie, they are loyal friends, and no other animal on the planet has engaged in the wholesale slaughter of its own species in the way that humans have done (Masson 2014, 50–65).

Like many attempts to separate humans from animals, these objections to friendship across species risk excluding too much by setting the bar too high. Most friendships are not highly intellectual, and the admiration and normativity they involve need not involve complex abstract thought. Friendship comes from the heart, not the head.

Conclusion

This discussion shows that the degree and kind of admiration, mutuality, and reciprocity that can arise between humans and nonhuman companions are similar to those between human friends. If asymmetry were to rule out friendship, few cases would be left. Human friendships need not improve our ethical behavior, so an excessively high moral standard for nonhuman friendships is implausible. It is true that some human friendships involve interpretations, discussions, and explanations of a kind that nonhumans do not participate in. Yet these practices can lead us morally astray as well as encourage virtuous attitudes (Cocking and Kennett 2000). Articulate discussions of human character might be malicious gossip, might feed insecurities, and might encourage arrogance or superiority. So a high level of verbal articulation and reflection through "talking about" both seem to be inessential and ambivalent features of friendship, not reasons to exclude the possibility of nonhuman friendship.

If the core constituents of friendship are pleasure, loyalty, admiration, and the co-construction of a shared life or part of life, where the participants are mutually responsive to shaping their activities together, then we can be and often are friends, even best friends, with nonhuman animals. We humans can and do admire, delight in, and shape our lives to fit our animal friends, just as we do with other friendships.

References

Aristotle. 2000. *Nicomachean Ethics*. Translated by Roger Crisp. Cambridge: Cambridge University Press.

Auster, Paul. 1999. *Timbuktu*. New York: Picador.

Bekoff, Marc, and Jessica Pierce. 2009. *Wild Justice: The Moral Lives of Animals*. Chicago: University of Chicago Press.

Cocking, Dean, and Jeanette Kennett. 1998. "Friendship and the Self." *Ethics* 108 (3): 508–27.

Cocking, Dean, and Jeanette Kennett. 2000. "Friendship and Moral Danger." *Journal of Philosophy* 97 (5): 278–96.

Darcy, David. 2014. *A Girl's Best Friend*. Sydney: Murdoch Books.

Frööding, Barbro, and Martin Peterson. 2011. "Animal Ethics Based on Friendship." *Journal of Animal Ethics* 1 (1): 58–69.

Gilbert, Margaret P. 1990. "Walking Together: A Paradigmatic Social Phenomenon." *Midwest Studies in Philosophy* 15 (1): 1–14.

Haggard, Ann. 1985. "A Patient's Best Friend." *The American Journal of Nursing* 85 (12): 1374–76.

Hankin, Susan J. 2009. "Making Decisions about Our Animals' Health Care: Does It Matter Whether We Are Owners or Guardians?" *Stanford Journal of Animal Law and Policy* 2 (1): 1–51.

Haraway, Donna. 2008. *When Species Meet*. Minneapolis: University of Minnesota Press.

Hens, Kristien. 2009. "Ethical Responsibilities towards Dogs: An Inquiry into the Dog-Human Relationship." *Journal of Agricultural and Environmental Ethics* 22 (1): 3–14.

Hornung, Eva. 2010. *Dog Boy*. New York: Viking.

Jordan, Jeff. 2001. "Why Friends Shouldn't Let Friends Be Eaten." *Social Theory and Practice* 27 (2): 309–22.

Lumsden, Simon. 2008. "Habit, Reason and the Limits of Normativity." *SubStance* 37 (3): 188–206.

Mathews, Freya. 2007. "Without Animals Life Is Not Worth Living." *Between the Species* 13 (7): 1–28. doi 10.15368/bts.2007v13n7.4.

Masson, Jeffrey. 1998. *Dogs Never Lie about Love*. London: Vintage.

Masson, Jeffrey. 2014. *Beasts: What Animals Can Teach Us about the Origins of Good and Evil*. London: Bloomsbury.

Milligan, Tony. 2009. "Dependent Companions." *Journal of Applied Philosophy* 26 (4): 402–13.

Oliver, Mary. 2013. *Dog Songs*. New York: Penguin.

Rowlands, Mark. 2008. *The Philosopher and the Wolf*. London: Granta.

Rowlands, Mark. 2011. "Friendship and Animals: A Reply to Frööding and Peterson." *Journal of Animal Ethics* 1 (1): 70–79.

Sapontzis, S. F. 1980. "Are Animals Moral Beings?" *American Philosophical Quarterly* 17 (1): 45–52.

Satz, Ani B. 2006. "Would Rosa Parks Wear Fur?" *Journal of Animal Law and Ethics* 1: 139–60.

Spencer, Stuart, Eddy Decuypere, Stefan Aerts, and Johan De Tavernier. 2006. "History and Ethics of Keeping Pets: Comparison with Farm Animals." *Journal of Agricultural and Environmental Ethics* 19 (1): 17–25.

Staatsa, Sara, Heidi Wallace, and Tara Anderson. 2008. "Reasons for Companion Animal Guardianship (Pet Ownership) from Two Populations." *Society and Animals* 16 (3): 279–91.

Tuan, Yi Fu. 1984. *Dominance and Affection: The Making of Pets*. New Haven: Yale University Press.

de Waal, Frans. 2005. *Our Inner Ape*. London: Granta Books.

3 BUILDING A MEANINGFUL SOCIAL WORLD BETWEEN HUMAN AND COMPANION ANIMALS THROUGH EMPATHY

Antonio Calcagno

In memoriam Jean Harvey, *amica*

What kind of relationship do we have with our companion animals? What facilitates this relationship, and does it help create a shared, common, meaningful world with our companion animals? In this chapter, I wish to examine the role that empathy plays in our understanding of companion animals. In particular, I draw upon the work of Edmund Husserl and Edith Stein on the question of *Einfühlung* or empathy, as this body of work has garnered wider attention over the last decade.[1] Scholars who have employed the foundational studies of Husserl and Stein on empathy generally agree that empathy works across species, that is, humans can carry out empathic acts that allow them to understand the minds of other animals: empathy permits human beings to understand the minds of animals through a kind of trading of mental places or an "introjecting" of themselves into the place of the other nonhuman animals, giving them access to the content of their minds but also facilitating an awareness of their emotional states, for example, whether animals are suffering or in pain. One can understand the mind of the other insofar as it is analogously similar to one's own mind and vice versa. Empathy as a conscious act, however, whether exercised between humans or between humans and animals, has limits: we can never know perfectly or identify completely with the mind of the other, be it human or animal.

Philosophers extend the intentional analysis of Husserl and Stein, arguing that if empathy is possible between humans and companion animals, we understand that animals do suffer, and hence they should be extended care and protections, because they are conceived as moral subjects who suffer like human beings.[2] Further questions also arise: How much like human beings are companion animals? And how similar is (or should be) their moral status to that of human beings? What does empathy suggest is owed to them?

If we pay close attention to Stein's analysis of empathy, however, we discover not only that empathy allows us to understand some things about other minds, including the minds of our companion animals, but also that empathy allows us to build a social world together constituted by a meaningful relationship of inter-subjectivity. In this social world, empathy allows us to share an understanding of history, ritual, play, and even language. What, then, would a common social world between humans and companion animals look like? Drawing on Husserl and Stein, I argue that a shared social world with companion animals would have to include the following elements: a shared sense of a built environment, a common language, which includes speech but also gesture and bodily expression, a shared value system, and a rich common affective life. Empathy is foundational for creating larger social worlds between humans and companion animals where particular bonds of meaning, shared space, value, and togetherness manifest themselves.

What is Empathy?

Though Husserl has a traditional and largely prejudicial Enlightenment view of animals as objects to be used or studied, he does remark at various places that empathy is possible across species, thereby tempering his own view of animals as simply objects in the world like other objects. Arun Iyer observes,

> Empathy, for Husserl, is not confined to beings that experience the world with an identical level of sophistication. Rather empathy can extend itself across species irrespective of their stage of intellectual development. Husserl actually claims that human beings can empathize with jellyfish. The analogical distance between the two empathizing subjects has no effect on the possibility of empathy.[3]

Dermot Moran notes that bodily movement is also required for us to understand how other animals experience the world:

> Other subjects—including some animals—turn or tilt their heads in order to see, reach out to touch, shrink in fear, and so on. Husserl does not address the limits of this apperceptive analogization. He does seem to think we could not understand a living organism without a sense of its self-movement as somehow—no matter how different physiologically—paralleling our movements. We can get a sense even of a jellyfish's propulsion through the water by watching its movements.[4]

Critics of empathy, including Martin Heidegger, have rightly pointed out that the phenomenological approach to empathy is anthropocentric, but work has been done to show that the classic distinction between higher and lower animals must not be read as speciesist. Christiane Bailey argues that the aforementioned distinction must not be read in terms of the difference between "primitive" and "higher order" animals, but as the phenomenological difference between familiar and unfamiliar animals.[5] Though acts of empathy deal with our own consciousness, this does not mean that we cannot understand what others are feeling, including our companion animals. There are limits to empathy; for example, it can never give us full and complete understanding of other minds, and it never allows us to experience, in an identical fashion, what others are feeling or living through: there is no fusion/identity of minds, or what phenomenologists and psychologists calls an *Einsfühlung*. Furthermore, the notion of higher- and lower-order animals, as developed in much of modern philosophy, must be bracketed here, especially when it comes to the discussion of the value or worth of animals; rather, we can compare differences in brain structure and complexity of development, thereby allowing us to speak of a wider- or focused-range of brain function relative to various animals, including ourselves and our companion animals.

So, what is empathy? Both Husserl and Stein conceive of empathy as a conscious act of mind in which one subject comes to understand the mind of another by analogously comparing what one experiences about the other with one's own understanding of oneself. For example, I can understand that another person is sad because when I first perceive the other's long face, subdued manner, and suffering voice, I inadvertently compare what I perceive with my own experience of sadness and I recognize the other's sadness as similar to my own. Stein describes this kind of analogizing as "bringing the other into relief," whereas Husserl calls it "trading places." Both phenomenologists would never claim that one feels the very same sadness as the other's: no identification with the other is possible. Rather, one experiences a sense or meaning that conveys an understanding of the other's sadness. But the sense (*Sinn*) achieved by empathy is not only a matter of cognition: it requires and is deeply conditioned by embodiment, indexicality of place or space, language, psychic affect, and values.

In order for empathy to happen, we need to explain how various layers of the constitution of human beings come to condition the ultimate achievement of cognition through acts of empathy, understood as the grasping of the sense of the conscious experience of another person. What, then, is an empathic act? Stein believes, as does Husserl, that empathy allows one to become inwardly aware and understand the consciousness of the foreign I. Stein believes that empathy, understood as an act, is an experiential act *sui generis* that is "primordial as present experience though non-primordial in content."[6] Empathy is not like any other act of consciousness. It is peculiar unto itself. One does not experience the consciousness of the other as one would the lamp resting on the desk next to the computer. Empathic acts are marked by a doubleness, a primordiality and a non-primordiality.

In order to explain what she means by the distinction between primordial (*Originarität*) and non-primordial (*Nicht-Originarität*), Stein gives the example of a man who is saddened by the death of his brother. Stein perceives the man's long face, his countenance, and the pain. But the objects of her perceptions, namely, the sadness and the pain, are not objects of outer experience, that is, they are not things in the world like a cat or an inkwell, and they are not given to her immediately, as I am to myself. She recognizes them in the other only by perceiving the other. They do not belong to the proper sphere of her own-ness. She does not experience the other's sadness as if it were her own actual sadness, identical with her own sadness. Stein says it is only when "I try to bring another's mood to clear givenness to myself, the content, having pulled me into it ... [that] I am no longer turned to the content but to the object of it, am at the subject of the content in the original subject's place" (*Emp.*, 10).[7] In an empathic act, I feel myself in the other's place. I know the experience of the other as my own because I have entered into or have found myself "living" the other's experience of pain. There is a kind of exchange that takes place; in a sense, the other's experience is transferred to me. What is primordial is the co-givenness of the other as other, yet my experience of the other's pain is always experienced non-primordially. "The other subject is primordial although I do not experience it as primordial. In my non-primordial experience I feel, as it were, led by a primordial one not experienced by me but still there, manifesting itself in my non-primordial experience" (*Emp.*, 11). Hence, empathy is described as led and not absolutely projected. Ultimately, empathy is basic for the understanding of intersubjective experience (*Emp.*, 64), including the intersubjective experience between humans and companion animals. For example, we can understand what our companion animals are experiencing insofar as we can make sense of and understand our own experiences that we judge to be similar to those of our companion animals. So, for example, we understand our own apprehension and anxiety when visiting the doctor. Likewise, when we see our companion animals behaving in an uncomfortable fashion at the veterinarian's office, we can right-fully understand their experience as similar to our own: we understand that our companions are feeling anxious and afraid.

What are some of the principal forms of empathy that humans and companion animals can share? Stein's descriptions start from more basic kinds of acts (e.g., the awareness of sense experience) and move to higher order (spiritual) acts like the understanding of another's motivations or reasoning, and they are much like the descriptions we find in Husserl's *Ideas II*.[8] Stein begins by outlining three basic ways in which empathy can be achieved: through sensation, emotion, and bodily expression. In the analysis of sensation, she begins with an analysis of the body. The living body (*Leib*) is not given to me by external perception; rather, the material body (*Körper*) is given to me in such a fashion, for when I turn my head and look at my hand, I see a hand extended in space possessing certain dimensions.[9] As long as I can see and touch, my material body is given to me as an object. "As long as I have my eyes open at all, it is continually there with a steadfast obtrusiveness, always having the same tangible nearness as no other object has. It is always 'here' while other objects are always 'there'" (*Emp.*, 42). But if I block out all perceptual sensation, external perception cannot give me my material body. For example, if I close my eyes and extend my arms in such a fashion that I can neither touch nor be touched, I do not perceive anything with my senses as I would if I were touching something. My material body is not given to me as an object that I observe. However, even if I do this sensuous experiment, I cannot deny the presence of my body as "my" living body. This living body perpetually belongs to me. It is given originally in perception.

The sensations of pain or cold are just as absolutely given as the experiences of willing, judging, and perceiving. Sensations, however, are peculiar in that they do not radiate from the I of consciousness as in acts of judgment, willing, and perception, insofar as sensations do not take on the form of a cogito in which the I turns toward an object. Sensation is localized in a certain space somewhere at a distance from the I. One can never find the ego in this space through reflection; nevertheless, this space is not an empty space. "All these entities from which my sensations rise are amalgamated into a unity, the unity of my living body, and they are themselves places in the living body" (*Emp.*, 42). Stein clarifies what she means when she claims that in sensation there is a distance between the ego and the space in which the sensation is localized in consciousness. This distance is mediated by the ego as the zero-point of orientation. In the cogito, the ego of the cogito is immediate, whereas in the sensation of coldness, the feeling of coldness is not rooted in the ego as the zero-point of orientation; it is rooted somewhere else like my foot, my leg, and so forth (*Emp.*, 43).

In addition to experiences of sensation giving one a sense of the lived body, Stein believes that sensations are not isolated events or moments. They also open up fields of sensation (*Emp.*, 44). Fields of sensation are more general experiences of the specifically sensed experience. For example, I may experience the hardness of the table against my body when I hit it. The sensation of hardness is localized in my body and in the table; however, in addition to this specific feeling of hardness being localized in my body, I also form a general concept of "hardness" by which I can judge other experiences (*Emp.*, 44–45). Hence, we know the specifically localized as well as the more general experience of hardness. Like Husserl, Stein affirms the connection between ego and body, but Stein also wishes to affirm a distance between them as well. In sensation, not only do I feel pain, but my foot also feels pain. There is a doubleness in sensation affecting both the I and the localized point of sensitivity.

The experience of the other's bodily sensation is achieved through analogy. What permits me to understand the other's sensations is an analogizing. I understand in my own experience of my own ego and its various lived experiences a certain sensation. I also know analogously the feeling of the other, including our companion animals, because of my own experience. I understand the other's experience with reference to my own similar experience. But my experience is not identical to the experience of the other and vice versa (*Emp.*, 59).

It is within this discussion of analogizing that Stein introduces and briefly describes another way, besides analogy, by which the ego apprehends the foreign consciousness of the other. She refers to empathic representation (*Emp.*, 57–58). Representational empathy refers to the way "fields of sensation" come to givenness. Hence, the only way the field of sensation called "pain" comes to be understood mutually without the pain being specifically localized in the living bodies of the ego or the other is through a re-presentation of the field of sensation from memory. The field of sensation is not being experienced by either party directly, "here and now," localized in space, yet they may understand what each means by the general experience of pain through a kind of recollection or re-presentation of their own field of sensation.[10] One can get a better picture as to what Stein intends by returning to Husserl, who makes the distinction between straight and oblique empathy.[11]

The aforementioned discussion of empathized sensations permits us to seize what our companion animals may be experiencing insofar as we analogically compare and introject our own sensations and analogically compare those of our companion animals with our own. Sensation allows us to experience ourselves as embodied, to feel specific sensations, like heat and cold, and it allows us to experience fields of sensations. If we accept Stein's account of empathy and if we also accept Husserl's clam that empathy can work across species, then presumably we do have access to the sensations of our companion animals as well. For example, we know that dogs and cats feel excessive cold and heat, much like we do, and we respond accordingly to alleviate the extremes of such feelings in our companion animals, trying to provide comfort to them.

Feelings and emotions are phenomena that also enable the ego to enter into the life of consciousness of the other, including our companion animals. Sensations are different from acts of reason (e.g., simple deductions) because sensation is localized at a distance from the conscious ego, whereas in acts of reason there is no such localization of the cogito other than immediately in ego consciousness. For example, a feeling of pain may be localized in my foot as well as in my consciousness of the sensation of pain. In the case of emotions and feelings, when they are experienced, not only do they have an object, but they also dwell and spring forth from the depths of the "I."

Not all emotions and feelings are the same, nor are they experienced to the same degree. There are also feelings and emotions that have other people as their objects. Such feelings include love, hate, and vengeance (*Emp.*, 101). One can feel these emotions and feelings to greater or lesser degrees, with greater or lesser depth.

Stein sees the theme of bodily expression as relevant to the discussion of empathy. Husserl also believes that bodily expression is a *phenomenon* that facilitates empathy (*Ideas II*, 247). The understanding of bodily expression is based on understanding the foreign body as "already interpreted" as a living body of an "I" (*Emp.*, 82). Bodily expressions often communicate various sensations and emotive states. The experience of a body as an I is a primary experience given to us immediately. In order to understand the other's bodily expression, I simply "project" my experience into it, thereby recognizing it as similar to my own. "I project myself into the foreign living body, carry out the experience already co-given to me as empty with its countenance, and experience the experience ending in this expression" (*Emp.*, 82). Here, empathy is described as projection, but recall that one is led first by the immediate presence of the other, led in such a way that one projects oneself into the other's place. Projection is never absolute.

The discussion of projection must be clarified. Before Stein can project herself back into the experience of the other, she has to have already recognized or understood the other's experience within her own sphere of immanence, namely, the sphere of the ego. The mere projection into the other (without reference to the ego as the zero-point of orientation) is not how acts of empathy are generally constituted. Husserl speaks more of analogical transfer than projection, but the sense in which Stein uses projection is in line with other descriptions of the analogization that takes place between the ego and the other. I understand the meaning of certain bodily expressions and what they may reveal about the other first through my own experience, which serves as the basis for understanding the experience of the other as expressed in body language. Hence, the experience of the other's joy as expressed in the other's smile is understood only as an expression of joy insofar as I am able to recognize such an experience within my own sphere of experience. There is a seizing of one through the other, an "*Ineinandergreifen.*"[12] I then perceive the expression of joy through the smile, as a given only after I see the similarity between my experience of a joyous smile and the experience of the other.

We often will draw from our experiences of emotions in order to understand what another may be similarly experiencing. When we see a change in our companion animal's habitual behavior—for example, a dog's sign of elation at the prospect of her early-morning walk suddenly becomes lethargy or fatigue—we can infer that our companion animal may not be well and that a visit to the veterinarian's office is in order. Empathy across species can only work insofar as we understand the behavior of various species, including expressive bodily gestures that communicate moods, emotions, sensations, and so forth. But these alone are not enough, at least not for Husserl and Stein: we need to be able to analogize our feelings of similar moods and affects in order to enter into the specific lives of our companion animals: empathy allows us to personalize and feel into the life of our companion animals rather than just permitting us to give objective descriptions of them.

The final distinguishing feature of Stein's description of empathic acts is her awareness of the significance of empathy for the constitution of our own person. Empathy is vital in that it helps us value ourselves. "By empathy with differently composed personal structures we become clear on what we are not, what we are more or less than others. Thus, together with self-knowledge, we also have an important aid to self-valuing" (*Emp.*, 116). In understanding the consciousness of another, including that of our companion animals, and because such understanding mostly refers back to the ego's own sphere of immanent awareness or consciousness, we see how we are unlike the other or how we are similar. We can see difference as well as similitude.

For example, in empathic acts concerning value, the very experience of value is very basic to our own value. When new values are acquired through empathy, one's own unfamiliar values become visible. If I experience industriousness in another person, I may see how lazy I have been in comparison to the other even though I understand what industriousness as a value means in my own, immediate egological sphere of concrete immanence. I may have known what it was to be industrious, but my valuing of that particular value changes when I see a new, greater degree of industriousness before me in the other. One sees how one lacked understanding or familiarity in the past now that a new value is acquired (*Emp.*, 116). Empathy, then, does not only concern understanding or inner awareness proper, but also may affect the shape of our lives by the values we accept or reject through empathy. Another example can be seen when we observe the attachments of our companion animals to certain pieces of furniture, toys, or the layout of a home. Animals value or care about these things, and when they are taken away or moved, they sometimes become distraught. Through analogization of empathy, we can understand what it is for our companion animals to care about and lose something that is valuable to them. In short, empathy is not only constituted, but also constitutes who we are vis-à-vis ourselves and others.

The innovation that Stein introduces here is that empathy explains our capacity to understand our own personal value and the personal value of another by the very fact that empathy makes the I stand in relief to the other. In other words, the very act of empathy itself makes visible such differences and facilitates an understanding of the values that we attach to the similarities and differences that are essential in the individual and communal lives of both the ego and the other. Empathy not only allows us to understand others and ourselves but also facilitates the sharing of values of the ego and the other.

Our Companion Animals

Let us assume that our companion animals are more familiar to us than other animals and that empathy is possible between us and them. What, then, can empathy achieve? Again, while there are numerous studies that show that empathy allows us to discover the moral status of our companion animals, which ultimately means that, as with us, it is morally wrong for them to suffer undue injury, harm, or pain, I believe that empathy does more than establish a moral community of understanding between human and companion animals. Empathy allows us to recognize that we share a world in common with our companion animals, and that this world is valuable and meaningful.

David Morris remarks that behaviorist accounts of animal life reduce animals' common life to a series of patterns, ultimately neglecting the relationship between the collective minds of animals and their bodily movements.[13] He convincingly demonstrates that humans can understand group behavior in animals, and that humans and animals share a sense of a built environment. Morris discusses how dogs, for example, build together a "friendly" environment. Though empathy is not discussed as facilitating the building up of the environment between dogs, empathy does allow us to understand dogs' group life and environments as analogously similar to our own collective lives. Morris observes,

> Gregory Bateson has argued that the rituals, for instance, that two dogs enact in meeting and greeting each other are not instinctual in the sense of being pre-programmed and automatic. The rituals are rather a matter of the two dogs expressively and intercorporeally determining the situation, and working out a shared world. Animals, Bateson asserts, cannot use negations. They cannot say 'I will not bite.' What they do, instead, is

act out a kind of *reductio ad absurdum*: they play at biting and fighting, for instance, in order to reveal to each other that 'it is biting that I am not doing.' In this way, they 'discover or rediscover friendship.' ... The crucial point is that to show that 'it is biting that I am not doing,' the dog must perform biting, whilst not actually biting. Performing biting that is not biting thus entails something like a behavioural 'as,' doing something that is not what it appears to be. But this behavioural 'as' requires another dog not to bite, and this means a dog who does not bite back. In this behavioural complex, biting appears as something other than a captivating dictate of instinct: the dogs behaviourally recognize biting as 'doing' 'friendship.' They likewise recognize each other's bodies as something more than a captivating pole of a dominate-or-submit instinct; they behaviourally recognize in each other a dominating body (a biting-fighting body) that is behaving as not dominating.[14]

Given what I have said about empathy across species and given the possibility of understanding animal group life in non-instinctual terms, through an understanding of sensation, emotion, and values, could one argue that empathy can allow us to establish an interspecies understanding of a shared built world that is both meaningful and valuable? I believe empathy can do so. Though one can rightfully ascribe a particular form or structure to the shared or group world of animals and of humans, there is also a shared world that we inhabit with our companion animals. We deploy our understanding of ourselves and our companion animals, understood both as individuals and as group members (mindful of the fact that not all humans and animals are social beings—some can be quite solitary), in order to develop a meaningful and valuable shared built environment. Some dog behaviors and our response to them simply imitate or repeat patterns in group life, for example, hierarchies in packs of dogs. We understand the behavior of a leader of the pack or a leader of a political party. But there exist points of encounter where both human and animal actually understand one another. Let us examine the example of play.

In play, communication and expression are possible and visible—and they are unique to the individuals involved, both human and animal. As animal studies become more focused and developed, the experiences of play have been more commonly observed.[15] The companion animals with whom we play and for whom we ensure the absence of pain and suffering through our protection and care develop unique bonds with us, their caregivers. When, for example, dogs play with their caregivers, they have a highly advanced language, which we see in their play with other dogs.[16] Humans learn to understand through empathy the body language and sounds of dogs just as dogs learn to understand our body language and some of our words or sounds. When caregiver and dog play together, they share a world and a space. The dog is familiar with its toys and routines just as humans are. The two together have a common play routine and understand how it unfolds and what can be expected. Moreover, there is pleasure in both humans and dogs as they play. Empathy can allow us to engage and understand the play of the caregiver and dog insofar as we can read and analogize across species experiences of pleasure (sensation), the delight of cooperation (emotion), and the value of friendship (the bond between caregiver and companion animals).

Dogs and cats are known to become stressed when their built environments with humans change or are dismantled. Our companion animals form habits (and attachments) just as we form habits, and habitual space is vital for the cats' and dogs' psychological wellbeing. Earlier in this chapter, we saw how Stein argues that empathy requires not only cognition but also a sense of embodied space and movement. Morris shows how embodiment and lived space are important for the group life of animals. The interactions between humans and dogs in play, for example, a shared home or couch or play area, show that a shared space and the understanding through empathy of its purpose for living and playing are both possible and essential. In shared play, an understanding of body language, sounds, and words communicates the various movements and gestures required for play. Moreover, empathy allows us to analogically comprehend how play is important and valuable for dogs, given the primary role of play for establishing certain bonds, including pack behavior and hierarchical relations, in their group lives as dogs. Caregiver and dog can play together, they form a unique community, but this community of play and understanding is dependent, in part, on the empathic understanding of humans that enables them to grasp the meaning or sense of play for dogs and for themselves. We have to be able to "trade places" with the dog in order to understand what is pleasurable or important (i.e., valuable), what is not pleasing, and what is delightful (the feelings of pleasure and delight are basic affective structures). This analogization constitutive of empathy requires communication and language, expressed through sound and bodily gestures.

Play can be understood as the extension of care we give to our companion animals, whom we value in personal terms. Care, understood in phenomenological terms, consists of a series of actions and behaviors that stem from the living out of certain values we hold dear. The understanding of value in others is rooted in empathy. We understand what it means for someone to care about something by analogically comparing what the other experiences or expresses with our own experience of care (here, care is understood as a value). The work of Olin E. Myers demonstrates how care for animals (and its underlying empathy) can be deployed in order to broaden children's care for nature and the environment:

> In addition to understanding animals' needs from a biological perspec-
> tive, the current study offers fresh insights for understanding other devel-
> opmental factors related to caring about nature. Our findings suggest
> that development in thinking about animal needs is not quite as linear
> as awareness of the needs of individual animals, then the needs of spe-
> cies, and finally the needs of ecosystems. For example, some children's
> early conceptions indicate a divergent, non-naturalistic anthropomorphic
> framework. Two additional non-scientific conceptions—one aesthetic
> and one psycho-social—appear in older children. In different ways, both
> may facilitate ecological understanding. Most importantly, these alternate
> developmental pathways encourage the affective and biocentric moral
> components of environmental caring.[17]

Remarkable in Myers's studies is the emphasis on embodiment and the shared space of an environment that is achieved by taking on the perspective of another, in this case, animals. Myers points out that the extension of care for the environment through education is rooted in a fundamental shift in perspectives, what Stein and Husserl would call an analogical trading of places or empathy.[18]

If we accept Myers's findings, one of the implications of his research is that empathy allows us to understand what it is to share a world and dwell in it together, not only with our companion animals but with all animal life and our environment.[19] Empathy with our companion animals, as Myers's work with children shows, can help foster a more caring environment for animals in general and care for the environment as a whole. This awareness requires as one of its fundamental constitutive elements an understanding of how we share and build a space together with other animals, a place in which human and nonhuman animals communicate and share emotions and certain values and care.

Notes

1. See, for example, the excellent volume *Phenomenology and the Non-Human Animal: At the Limits of Human Experience*, ed. Corinne Painter and Christian Lotz (Dordrecht: Springer, 2007).
2. Corinne Painter, "Appropriating the Philosophies of Edmund Husserl and Edith Stein: Animal Psyche, Empathy and Moral Subjectivity," in Painter and Lotz, *Phenomenology and the Non-Human Animal*, 97–115.

3. Arun Iyer, "Transcendental Subjectivity, Embodied Subjectivity, and Intersubjectivity in Husserl's Transcendental Idealism," in *Epistemology, Archaeology, Ethics: Current Investigations of Husserl's Corpus*, ed. Pol Vandevelde and Sebastian Luft (London: Continuum, 2010), 66–76, at 71–72. Though I do not agree with Husserl's view of animals, I do find his extension of empathy to animals very useful for this discussion.

4. Dermot Moran, *Husserl's Crisis of the European Sciences and Transcendental Phenomenology: An Introduction* (Cambridge: Cambridge University Press, 2012), 132.

5. Christiane Bailey, "Kinds of Life: On the Phenomenological Basis of the Distinction between 'Higher' and 'Lower' Animals," *Environmental Philosophy* 8, no. 2 (2011): 47–68.

6. Edith Stein, *On the Problem of Empathy*, trans. W. Stein (Washington, DC: ICS Publications, 1989), 10; hereafter parenthetically cited as *Emp.*

7. When Stein speaks of bringing to mind something given to consciousness, she is referring to an act of consciousness where one focuses on the content of what appears in consciousness in order to clarify the content's nature or essence. To understand what appears in consciousness, we make the content into an object that can be observed from the viewpoint of subjective consciousness, that is, the consciousness of an embodied I/ego or person.

8. Edmund Husserl, *Ideas Pertaining to a Pure Phenomenology and to a Phenomenological Philosophy. Second Book: Studies in the Phenomenology of Constitution*, trans. R. Rojcewicz and A. Schuwer (Dordrecht: Springer, 1990); hereafter parenthetically cited as *Ideas II*.

9. The material body refers to the body as perceived as having extension in space; that is, it is perceived as occupying a certain amount of space and having certain dimensions. The lived body is the experience of my own body, as I live or experience it as my own body. Here, the body is not observed like an external object; rather, the body is experienced from within one's own embodiment. In early phenomenological literature, the foregoing distinction was understood as external versus internal perception.

10. Reiterated empathy or reflexive sympathy is not connected with the field of sensations, but is merely an empathizing that takes place with already-experienced empathic experience. For example, my brother and I felt great joy at the birth of our new nephew. We understood each other's feeling of joy. When we recollect this memory in present circumstances, we both experience the joy of that day. The joy we experience together and understand in common is drawn from a re-presented or recollected past experience of empathy—hence the phrase, an "empathy of empathized acts" (*Emp.*, 18).

11. Edmund Husserl, *Zur Phänomenologie der Intersubjektivität: Texte aus dem Nachlass. Erster Teil: 1905–1920*, in *Husserliana: Edmund Husserl—Gesammelte Werke*, ed. Iso Kern (Den Haag: Nijhoff, 1972), 13:401–2.

12. Edith Stein, *Einführung in die Philosophie* (Freiburg: Herder, 1991), 219.
13. David Morris, "Animals and Humans, Thinking and Nature," in *Phenomenology and the Cognitive Sciences* 1, no. 4 (2005): 49–72.
14. Ibid. 60–61.
15. See the work of the Memorial University Canine Research Unit at http://dogs-body.psych.mun.ca/cru/Canine_Research_Unit_2016/CRU_Home.html.
16. Lydia Ottenheimer Carrier, Amanda Cyr, Rita E. Anderson, and Carolyn J. Walsh, "Exploring the Dog Park: Relationships between Social Behaviours, Personality and Cortisol in Companion Dogs," *Applied Animal Behaviour Science* 146, no. 1–4 (2013): 96–106; see also http://dogsbody.psych.mun.ca/cru/CRU_Summer_2014/Publications_files/M.S.c%20talk%20summer%202014-website%20short%20refs.pdf.
17. Olin E. Myers, Jr., Carol D. Saunders, and Erik Garrett, "What Do Children Think Animals Need? Aesthetic and Psycho-social Conceptions," in *Environmental Education Research* 9, no. 3 (August 2003): 305–25, at 323.
18. Ibid.
19. Olin E. Myers Jr., Carol D. Saunders, and Erik Garrett, "What Do Children Think Animals Need? Developmental Trends," *Environmental Education Research* 10, no. 4 (November 2004): 545–62.

4 CARE, MORAL PROGRESS, AND COMPANION ANIMALS

Maurice Hamington

While fair play in animals may be a rudimentary form of social morality, it still could be a forerunner of more complex and more sophisticated human moral systems. But perhaps more important, if we try to learn more about forgiveness, fairness, trust, and cooperation in animals, maybe we'll also learn to live more compassionately and cooperatively with one another.

—MARC BEKOFF[1]

My dog friend, Bella, growls as we play a game of tug of war with a rope and a plush toy disk. If I had confronted a growling animal in another context, I might be concerned for my safety. However, Bella and I know this is play. Bella is wagging her tail. Her mouth is open. She is breathing hard and making quick darting motions. We have a lot of physical contact with one another, and it is all in good fun. If she wanted to, Bella could hurt me, and I could hurt Bella in this rough-housing, but neither of us will, except by accident, and we both know it. We are in a zone of playful comfort that anyone who lives with dogs recognizes.[2] Bella is clearly enjoying herself. The activity is not instrumental. We are not using the play to get any future benefit or reward but simply enjoying the moment. Bella belongs to a different species than I do, but we have an understanding. We do not share a common narrative language, and yet we communicate. This common understanding was developed over time until we have come to trust and respect one another. This respect prevents each of us from harming the other. There is a context of care. Bella and the other companion animals that I have lived with have helped me develop habits of care and responsiveness. These caring habits have ontological, epistemological, and ethical implications. They are not just indicative of my behaviors with animals; they also influence who I am, how I come to know others, and how I respond to others.[3]

The thesis of this chapter is not only that companion animals are vital to human moral development of care, but also that care as learned and exhibited in companion animal relationships provides the habit and skill needed for moral progress. This moral development is achieved not in an instrumental or exploitative relationship with companion animals but within the context of authentic care.[4] In other words, the argument is not so much that we learn care from animals, but that we learn skills of care from our rich and mutually beneficial *relationships* with animals that feed our imagination and make moral progress possible.

What is Care Theory?

The basic concept in care ethics as I develop it is the caring relation. Life itself starts in such a relation. The caring relation is an empirical reality, not a theoretical construct.

—NEL NODDINGS[5]

In this section, I briefly describe care theory and then focus on its embodied and performative aspects, in order to demonstrate that care is particularly well suited to understanding our relationships with companion animals. Evidence is mounting that, contrary to the traditional notion that competition, assertiveness, and cunning are the principle reasons for human flourishing, it has been care and compassion that have served to help humans survive and thrive, so much so that Jeremy Rifkin refers to humans as *Homo empathicus*.[6] The literature on care ethics has only a three-decade history. Although relatively young when compared to the history of rule-based, consequence-based, or virtue-based ethics, care theory has captured the imagination of numerous philosophers and political theorists as both nimble and liminal enough to engage the reality of a postmodern world.[7]

Care ethics describes a relational approach to morality that values emotion, context, and reciprocity rather than abstract systems of principles or formulas of utility. Care resists such abstraction. Care engenders a moral ideal. Providing care represents an aspiration that is not always met in relationships. Furthermore, the caring ideal is not formulaic in its application. One cannot prescribe the proper manifestation of care in advance of knowing the particular individual and circumstances involved. Caring requires listening and attentiveness, thus suggesting an emergent normativity: a notion that right action emerges from context rather than from predetermined or abstract rules or moral calculus. This does not mean that care is purely subjective, however. Rather than definitively prescriptive, care is guided by several contours or trajectories. One of these guides is responsiveness. Care is responsive to the needs of the other and thus entails deep and active listening, or what Nel Noddings describes as "engrossment."[8] Another and related guideline is an acknowledgement that humans are fundamentally relational; thus actions are never isolated transactions but rather occur in a web of relationships. Care is also guided by motivational displacement, or imaginatively and sympathetically understanding the standpoint of others. Taken together, these moral guides situate care as neither relativistic nor normative in an *a priori* sense.

Since the early 1990s, Carol J. Adams and Josephine Donovan have been applying care ethics to understanding human relationships with animals, although not companion animals exclusively.[9] Adams emphasizes the similarities and synergies between the oppression of women and the oppression of animals.[10] Both Adams and Donovan view animal care ethics as superior to traditional rights-based or utilitarian-based approaches, which are based on individuality rather than relationality, and which tend to confront animal welfare from an aggregate or species approach rather than from particular relationships with particular animals.[11]

My work takes care theory in a slightly different trajectory than those described above, in that I explicitly contend that care is embodied: care is understood and delivered through the body in large and complex ways as well as in small and simple ways.[12] Our bodies have tacit yet rich knowledge of care through muscle memory and visceral understanding. For example, the body can learn the nuances of how to deliver a comforting hug, or demonstrate attention and concern through eye contact and facial expression, or use the voice to communicate understanding. When these skills are underdeveloped, there can be discomfort and awkwardness in circumstances where care is called for. Usually, these embodied habits of care are enacted without extensive forethought. Performing "embodied care" does not describe a natural ability but rather a natural capacity that requires exercise and development. Like other natural capacities, attention and practice can improve care. Also like other natural capacities, we can attain proficiency and habituation with significant work and thought. We are not born able to walk, but we are usually born with the capacity to walk given the proper development and practice. Eventually, walking becomes habit. Some people further develop the ability to walk into running with great skill. Similarly, our bodies are built with the capacity to care, as evinced by our ability to focus attention on others, learn about them, sympathize, and act to meet their needs. However, the capability of caring exists on a continuum, and proficiency only comes with development and effort.

The notion of care as embodied is the foundation for understanding it as a performative activity. Judith Butler famously developed a performative theory of gender identity based on the notion that gender is neither fully natural nor fully socially constructed.[13] For Butler, gender is created by a series of iterative choices and performances that coalesce into a dynamic sense of identity. This identity can evolve, but it is not simply determined by biology or social forces. According to Butler, we help recreate our gender identity every time we make choices to act and display ourselves in a particular way, even though certain choices are strongly reinforced or discouraged by social norms. Similarly, I contend that our caring moral identity is created through our performances of care in our relationships with other beings. Care is a series of actions taken in the world—in time and space. Caring involves agency because caring is always a choice we make, but it is a constrained choice. There are always social forces that impede or promote our caring activities. Describing care as performative is a method for capturing the negotiation of personal agency within social constraint. Because as embodied beings we are both subjects (we have agency and will) and objects (we can perceive and reflect upon ourselves in time and space), we engage in care while simultaneously observing ourselves performing care. Witnessing ourselves care and thematizing the experience creates an iterative feedback loop that contributes to constructing our self-identity. What is a caring person other than someone who repeatedly demonstrates care? This is the ontological dimension of care. I participate in creating my identity, but my efforts confront social norms. The character of my caring identity is not an innate quality, nor is it the product of assent to a set of abstract ethical principles. My caring identity is a negotiation of will and social forces.

Care has sustained both human civilization and mammalian species. Frans de Waal, although not explicitly a care theorist, has repeatedly argued that the basis of human morality in evolutionary terms lies in the empathetic relationality observed in animals.[14] Thus, when we engage our companion animals, we are in a sense interacting with individuals who possess the building blocks of our own morality minus the abstract notions of ethics that society has constructed. In *The Bonobo and the Atheist*, de Waal gently (and caringly) implies that although there is nothing to be gained by antagonism between atheists and theists, religious morality has likely run its course:

> The big challenge is to move forward, beyond religion, and especially beyond top-down morality. Our best-known "moral laws" offer nice post hoc summaries of what we consider moral, but are limited in scope and full of holes. Morality has much more humble beginnings, which are recognizable in the behavior of other animals.[15]

De Waal is arguing for a fresh way to look at morality that is more embodied, social, and relational than traditional approaches. Our caring performances in the context of our relationships with our companion animals exhibit this kind of morality. Although marked by routines, caring relationships with companion animals are largely devoid of mutually agreed-to rules, rights, or moral calculus. Rather, these relationships are guided by need and response.

To summarize, I suggest that care is both an embodied and a performative activity that influences who we are. If this is the case, then ethical development cannot be a strictly cognitive endeavor. Caring habits and behaviors need to be attended to and fostered in rich, varied, and meaningful ways. Because moral identity is an iterative process, rich opportunities to care can help form our sense of caring self and provide the structures and schemas of caring habits that can be applied to new and unfamiliar circumstances. Such opportunities can come through deep and varied relationships with other humans and through imaginative engagement of stories such as in theatre or novels; it can also develop in relationships with companion animals. Relationships with companion animals not only provide rich opportunities to habituate flexible care structures of responsiveness; they offer the imaginative character that can contribute to moral progress as well.

Habits of Touch and Imagination

To touch is to share. This sharing takes place as a trace, a detour, an erring. When I touch you I do not contain the experience within a preconceived narrative. To touch is to open us to a story we have not yet heard, to an unworked work, a narrative without a beginning and an end.

—ERIN MANNING[16]

Given the embodied and performative dimension of care, in this section I discuss two specific and interrelated ways that caring relationships with animals contribute to enriching human moral development, which lays the groundwork for informing moral progress: habits of touch and imagination. Because companion animals tend to live in close proximity to their companion humans with regular interaction, many habits of interaction form.

Habits, as conceived by John Dewey, provide a framework for understanding the structure of caring embodied relationships. For Dewey, habits are not simply rote movements. He describes habits as

> that kind of human activity which is influenced by prior activity and in that sense acquired; which contains within itself a certain ordering or systematization of minor elements of action; which is projective, dynamic in quality, ready for overt manifestation; and which is operative in some subdued subordinate form even when not obviously dominating activity.[17]

Habits are robust structures of activity involving mind and body that are both open-ended and recursive. A simple example involves doorknobs, which come in many different shapes, colors, sizes, heights, and resistances to turning.

Nevertheless, our body has captured the habit of doorknob-opening such that we simply make the muscle adjustments to accommodate the differences. Even something as simple as doorknob-opening involves a collection of micro-habits tied together in a structure of responsiveness to our environment. Habits are adaptive. Dewey refers to them as "an acquired predisposition to *ways* or modes of response, not to particular acts."[18] Habits can exist without our giving them much thought but gain in significance and power if coupled with reflection. Attending to and reflecting on the habits we have with companion animals can bring forth insight and fodder for imaginative extension to other relationships.

Let us consider the habit of touch we have developed with companion animals. Here, I am limiting the discussion to common companion mammals such as dogs and cats, with which we can have rich, tactile relationships. For example, at times Bella will sidle up next to me and lean her body into me. I do not know specifically what Bella is communicating at those moments, but I perceive this as a positive act. At these moments, my body has habits of receiving and responding to Bella's touch with my own acknowledging touch. The interaction is characterized by comfort and tenderness. Physical habits can range from simple to complex while entailing various levels of depth of understanding and connection. Adapting some habits to new contexts takes more attention, reflection, and imagination than others. Care engages a multiplicity of habits, including habits of touch. Touch is a crucial dimension of care that humans experience from infancy.[19] We can communicate many aspects of care as well as accentuate vocalized expressions of care through habits of touch.[20] As described above with Bella, touch can indicate reassurance, love, and a tacit sense of caring.

Although social mores regarding touch wax and wane, North American tactile sensibilities include norms governing the range of appropriate touch between individuals. Combined with individual differences in comfort with touch, these tactile restrictions have resulted in truncated opportunities to develop the habits and skill in tactile interaction. Although there are also variances in regard to their comfort with touch, companion animals generally do not maintain social restrictions on touch. Therefore, often companion animal bodies are much more available for tactile interaction. These tactile interactions are not all the same and require habit adaptation, or what Gene Myers refers to as accommodation to the bodies of animals.[21] This accessibility does not mean that there are ways that companion animals should not be touched, but these varied opportunities for touch with companion animals mean that rich tactile habits can be developed that in many cases can be translated into diverse human interactions. Such habits of touch are not to be confused with a straightforward application of the same movements across species, such as petting. However, the superstructure of the habit of touch as a method of communicating care, for example, can be imaginatively applied to new contexts. In other words, our relationships with animals can facilitate a comfort with embodied interaction.

One of the unique aspects of the human experience with companion animals is that a robust relationship[22] usually occurs within the proximity of a household but without the benefit of an extensive narrative dimension. Correspondingly, a rich tactile relationship between humans and companion animals develops. Touch becomes a major aspect of communication and the affective relationship. Care, love, happiness, and playfulness are expressed through contact initiated by either animal or human when we consider cat and dog companions. Within the proximity of this relationship, habits of tactile interaction develop.

A second and perhaps more complex habit of care built upon tactile habits that exist in human relationships with companion animals is anthropomorphism. Although anthropomorphism is often invoked as a human error of self-centered projection onto nonhuman animals, it can also be viewed as an effort at imaginative understanding of the interior motivation and will of animals in the absence of straightforward narrative explanation.[23] The challenge of alterity, the presence of others and other minds that we cannot know because we can never be those others, is exacerbated in human-animal relations because of the absence of language. Thomas Nagel describes the challenge of trying to understand what it means to be a bat:

> Our own experience provides the basic material for our imagination, whose range is therefore limited. It will not help to try to imagine that one has webbing on one's arms, which enables one to fly around at dusk and dawn catching insects in one's mouth; that one has very poor vision, and perceives the surrounding world by a system of reflected high-frequency sound signals; and that one spends the day hanging upside down by one's feet in an attic. In so far as I can imagine this (which is not very far), it tells me only what it would be like for *me* to behave as a bat behaves. But that is not the question. I want to know what it is like for a *bat* to be a bat. Yet if I try to imagine this, I am restricted to the resources of my own mind, and those resources are inadequate to the task. I cannot perform it either by imagining additions to my present experience, or by imagining segments gradually subtracted from it, or by imagining some combination of additions, subtractions, and modifications.[24]

As Nagel suggests, we are limited to the resources of our own mind, and this limitation is manifested in anthropomorphism. Thus anthropomorphism is a rational endeavor by humans to understand animal behavior and will be based on human perceptual evidence, but that does not mean that the interpretation is correct.

Bekoff and de Waal independently describe the efficacy of an informed anthropomorphism.[25] This informed anthropomorphism can be viewed as an attempt at honing habits of imaginative understanding across species, habits that are facilitated by our interaction and careful reflection. In describing observations of dog-human play, Alexandra C. Horowitz and Bekoff find an important function in the anthropomorphizing effort:

> The observed, successful bouts of human-dog play represent, in effect, brief dialogues between humans and their anthropomorphized companions; anthropomorphism is the explanatory lubrication, which these dialogues require, between visible behaviors and the seemingly inaccessible internal states of the animal. Anthropomorphizing thus is involved in perpetuating a satisfying pet relationship.[26]

Horowitz and Bekoff's anthropomorphizing is neither sentimental nor overly anthropocentric, but reflects an authentic effort at understanding the companion animal's behavior as a reflection of their will and internal state. Such efforts develop habits of imaginative caring. They are opportunities to hone skills that can be applied to other beings—not to habitually map a conclusion onto another individual but to iterate the practices and efforts needed to effectively explore the context and needs of another being. Accordingly, caring relationships with companion animals can spur better caring with humans.

To summarize, the caring relationships we have with companion animals help us to develop habits of care, including habits of touch and complex habits of imaginative understanding in part through anthropomorphizing. If these habits are part of an authentically caring relationship, then they are tools of responsiveness. As habits, they are open-ended and widely adaptive and thus can inform our relationships with humans as well.

Care, Companionship, and Instrumentality

My contention is that our relationships with companion animals teach us about caring in robust ways. Such a claim can smack of an instrumental relationship. Is this just another way to exploit animals for human gain? Certainly, within a traditional liberal individualistic identity that undergirds modern capitalist society, it could appear so. However, if one takes the fundamental relationality of human beings seriously, then learning care from animals is anything but a parasitic relationship. In care theory, the relationship is central not only to morality, but to identity and epistemology as well. Although a modernist approach desires to place acting, knowing, and being in separate categories, they are not discrete in the gestalt that constitutes the human condition. Having a relationship with a companion animal is adding to my identity just as much as it is adding to my companion's.

Although the sum is greater than the parts, when it comes to identity, I am ultimately made up of my relationships.[27] Each relationship not only teaches me something, but also contributes to who I am. These changes and additions can be subtle or profound. The more meaningful the relationship, the greater potential impact it has on who I am. When I live in a household with another being, as is the case with companion animals, I make myself vulnerable to adapting who I am to this relationship, particularly if there is trust and respect in the relationship. Of course, some people enter into abusive relationships with their companion animals, but such relationships can hardly be called caring. Someone may claim that he or she is caring for an animal by using corporal punishment, for example, but that does not meet the standards for responsiveness and growth we have laid out for care.

Companion animals both live in continuity with us and are not us at the same time. This is the paradox of care. I am able to make a connection with the other because of our shared existence as embodied beings—and I thus often sympathetically understand some of what the other is going through—but at the same time, the other represents an alterity that I can never own; the other thus stands outside of me. If I accidently step on Bella's paw, I do not have to wonder whether it hurts. Even though Bella is a member of a different species, I can grasp her pain as manifested by a yelp and a cowering movement. There are other times, for example, when we are at a park, and Bella barks at me. I try my hardest to understand. She is wagging her tail, and it seems to be a friendly bark. However, I am not sure if she wants me to throw a stick, run, or do something else. At these moments, Bella reminds me that we are different and that I cannot completely understand her. However, analogously, this lack of complete understanding is the same with all caring relationships. Even with the benefit of language, I do not always know exactly what other people need or want. If I want to offer care, I have to attend to them and endeavor to understand their circumstances and desires with the best habits of care that I have acquired, realizing that the others will always be alterities, others whose difference I must respect.

Bella's actions compel me to attend to her in ways that humans do not. The answers do not always come easily, although over time routines provide an equilibrium of understanding. For example, I know that Bella likes to eat several times a day but seems to prefer our presence in the house when she eats. However, I do not know why she takes a small morsel and eats it first some six feet from her bowl, prior to going back to the bowl to consume the rest of her meal. The reason for this habit is unclear to me, but I respect this habit and let it be.

Respect is an under-theorized aspect of care. There are some who raise concerns about the potential for paternalism in care relationships, but authentically caring does not allow for running roughshod over respect. Whether the relationship is with other humans or animals, sometimes we must make decisions. In a caring relationship though, those decisions take into account the expressed needs of the other. As Rita Manning describes,

> Caring does not require that we simply accede to the wishes of the one cared for. Rather, we should respond in the interest of the one cared for, insofar as furthering that interest is compatible with our abilities and where this response sustains the network of care that connects us. In doing so, I should be sensitive to the relationship, and open to the possibility of compromise and accommodation.[28]

There really is no authentic responsive caring for companion animals without some respect for the one cared for.

Names are another sign of respect. Companion animals are universally named. These names are imbued with meaning. Having a name signifies a being who can be cared for; this explains why laboratory workers engaged in animal experimentation or vivisection avoid naming the animals they work with. A name also signifies a will that must be respected. "Bella wants to go outside." "Bella wants to go for a walk." "Bella wants some love." These statements all suggest the acknowledgement of an embodied will. Although caring sometimes means denying another being's will, it does mean taking that will seriously and responding to it.[29]

What I have attempted to convey in this section is that the fact that companion animals can teach us much about caring does not imply that the relationship is strictly instrumental. The relationship is instrumental in the way that any caring relationship is, in that we learn from one another what it means to care. Companion animals have the added "advantage" of requiring a greater range of our attentiveness because we cannot fall back on linguistic narrative. This "limitation" makes companion animals better teachers for certain aspects of caring. For this reason, I am inclined to agree with Jean Harvey in seeing instrumentality as compatible with a caring or loving relationship:

> The other part of the point is that authentic love does not see the loved one as a means to an end, or in this case, two ends: receiving love and providing a vehicle for expressing love. Love values the loved one for who she

is in herself; the focus is on the one loved, not the love received, and it is a kind of cherishing that has commitment at its heart.[30]

Companion Animals, Moral Progress, and Ethical Veganism: Dogs Versus Dogmatism

In this concluding section I argue that companion animals facilitate the skills necessary for responsiveness in caring, and caring is an essential building block for human moral progress. In other words, we need animals to reach our moral potential. This is a challenging argument from a number of standpoints. First of all, there is the question of whether morality can progress at all. There are many who believe that human morality has in fact regressed. Precision of word choice and agreed-upon meaning are crucial for this discussion, so I will explicate how I am referring to "progress" in this discussion.

By "moral progress" I am describing a social environment that exhibits greater caring than the present context. Not only would such an environment have caring institutions with commensurate policies and practices such as in the classic conception of the welfare state, but also its members would have an abiding, albeit fallible, commitment to caring. I want to make it clear that such progress would not describe a fixed utopia or a definite path. This moral progress can loosely be described as a world where we take better care of one another personally, socially, and politically, recognizing the dangers of paternalism and the overreach of power. Furthermore, this kind of progress is marked by widespread participation. Jane Addams used the term "lateral progress" to describe a broad-based social improvement.[31] Caring moral progress will carry little weight if it is a limited achievement of a few individuals. Rather, the vision here is of a pervasive valorization of care.

What happens when morality is centered on caring relationships? Moral progress is reconstituted as better responding to the needs of others. New questions arise to promote moral progress. How can we listen better, be more responsive?[32] How do we take better care of one another? Moral progress thereby becomes centered around relational and emotional skill development. The requisite skills include understanding the needs of others and how to contribute to their care. Experiences, practice, and habits then become the stuff of moral progress. As members of a community value care and learn the habits and skills to effectively understand others and deliver responsive care, the community progresses. In care, moral progress is achieved with keener ability, willingness, and effectiveness at responding to the needs and circumstances of others.

This is where companion animals come into play. Companion animals challenge us to enter into caring relationships without the benefit of narrative exchange. Given the lack of symbolic interaction, humans must become far more attentive to touch, vocalizations, and bodily movement to understand the disposition and needs of our companions. Simply asking someone what their needs are is an important habit of care, but being attentive to nonverbal cues of need is another skill. Care is hard work, and the gulf between species makes the work harder. However, care changes the rules of moral progress to mitigate the differences.

Moral progress means moving beyond existing social norms. It involves attention, reflection, imagination, and ultimately risk. To progress morally means sometimes acting in ways that society has not yet accepted, and there may be social discipline for challenging existing norms. Imagine the risk of being a slavery abolitionist in the mid-nineteenth century or a gay rights activist in the mid-twentieth century. In his major work on moral progress, Peter Singer claims, "Knowledge alone will not resolve the conflicts built into ethics . . . but knowledge may clear up the confusion that surrounds ethics so that we can see, dimly, the way forward."[33] Our relationships with companion animals not only provide us with knowledge regarding the affective caring dimension of proximal relationships; they can also provoke us to reflect and attend to that knowledge in a manner that can spur new action and growth.

If we allow them, companion animals can challenge our moral imaginations to push us toward an important, albeit controversial, form of moral progress: ethical veganism. Bella is part of my family. We make sure she is taken care of and provided with not just life's necessities but also stimulation, playtime, and affection. As a nonhuman mammal, she has taught us a great deal about caring. So did our other companion animals before Bella: Magic, Snoopy, and Woodstock. I have some understanding of their joy in living. However, through my imagination, our relationship is also thought-provoking beyond the proximity of my family unit. If I can be in a caring and meaningful relationship with a dog, what about with a cow, chicken, or pig? What about the pain and suffering they experience if I consume meat? What makes some animals companions and other animals protein sources?[34]

The moral value of being an ethical vegan can be comprehensively argued elsewhere. Despite the pervasiveness of carnivorous traditions, it is difficult to dispute how compelling the rationale to be vegan is, given what the consumption of animals causes in pain and suffering, as well as the degradation it inflicts on our bodies and environment. Living in rich relation with animals focuses attention and makes concrete the reality of the lives of animals and how they experience a variety of emotions. Social standards prevent many people from investigating the source and implications of consuming animal products. In the *Apology*, Plato, through Socrates, famously described the unexamined life as not worth living. Perhaps attending to our relationships is similarly vital for a rich existence.

Examined companion animal relationships can enrich the caring potential of those involved in them.

This chapter has emphasized that caring is not just an emotion but also a thoughtful responsiveness to need. Ideally, if morality is in part understanding the cause and effect of our actions on others, there comes a time when living with companion animals causes a thoughtful person to reconcile what they eat with who they share their lives with. The dogmatism that "I must have my meat" or "I cannot give up cheese" or "I love the feel of leather boots" is challenged by an honest look into a dog's eyes. I can touch their bodies and imagine their pain to expand my circle of caring to other embodied beings.

Notes

1. Marc Bekoff, *The Emotional Lives of Animals* (Novato, CA: New World Library, 2007), 109.
2. Cynthia Willett describes friendly play as providing "a training ground for a concretely situated reciprocity that binds selves-in-community" (*Interspecies Ethics* [New York: Columbia University Press, 2014]), 75.
3. It is because I view care ethics as having both ontological and epistemological elements as well as moral ones that I prefer the term "care theory" to the term "care ethics." Nevertheless, I view this work as an extension of the care ethics scholarship, albeit a radical one. For those unfamiliar with care ethics, there are many outstanding resources. For a quick overview, see the "Care Ethics" entry in the *Internet Encyclopedia of Philosophy* (http://www.iep.utm.edu/care-eth/). The works of Nel Noddings provide a clear introduction to this field.
4. I use the term "authentic care" to distinguish between care subjectively defined by the caregiver (e.g., in colonialism) and care that is truly responsive, contextually based, and driven by the caring relationship (as described in the development of the moral ideal in care scholarship).
5. Nel Noddings, *The Maternal Factor: Two Paths to Morality* (Berkeley: University of California Press, 2010), 28.
6. Jeremy Rifkin, *The Empathic Civilization: The Race to Global Consciousness in A World in Crisis* (New York: Jeremy P. Tarcher/Penguin, 2009), 43.
7. Care ethics was born out of women's experience and feminist theory in the 1980s, and although the influence of care ethics has moved beyond feminist scholars, the significance of gender is undeniable. The social construction of care as feminine has certainly contributed to the devaluing of care as explicative of human survival as well as ethical analysis.
8. Nel Noddings, *Caring: A Feminine Approach to Ethics and Moral Education* (Berkeley: University of California Press, 1984), 17.

9. Josephine Donovan and Carol J. Adams, eds., *Beyond Animal Rights: A Feminist Caring Ethic for the Treatment of Animals* (New York: Continuum, 1996); and Josephine Donovan and Carol J. Adams, eds., *The Feminist Care Tradition in Animal Ethics* (New York: Columbia University Press, 2007).

10. Carol J. Adams, *The Sexual Politics of Meat: A Feminist-Vegetarian Critical Theory* (New York: The Continuum Publishing Company, 1990).

11. Donovan and Adams, *Beyond Animal Rights: A Feminist Caring Ethic for the Treatment of Animals*, 15–16.

12. Maurice Hamington, *Embodied Care: Jane Addams, Maurice Merleau-Ponty, and Feminist Ethics* (Urbana: University of Illinois Press, 2004); and "Learning Ethics from Our Relationships with Animals: Moral Imagination," *International Journal of Applied Philosophy* 22, no. 2 (2008): 177–88.

13. Judith Butler, "Performative Acts and Gender Constitution: An Essay in Phenomenology and Feminist Theory," *Theatre Journal* 40 (1988): 519–31.

14. Frans de Waal, *Primates and Philosophers: How Morality Evolved* (Princeton, NJ: Princeton University Press, 2006), 181.

15. Frans de Waal, *The Bonobo and the Atheist: In Search of Humanism among the Primates* (New York: Norton Press, 2013), 240.

16. Erin Manning, *Politics of Touch: Sense, Movement, Sovereignty* (Minneapolis: University of Minnesota Press, 2007), 13.

17. John Dewey, *The Middle Works of John Dewey, 1899–1924*, ed. Jo Ann Boydston, vol. 14, 1922, *Human Nature and Conduct* (Carbondale: Southern Illinois University Press, 1988), 31.

18. Dewey, *Human Nature and Conduct*, 32.

19. In his wide-ranging study, Matthew Fulkerson describes the emotional and therapeutic significance of touch for humanity (*The First Sense: A Philosophical Study of Human Touch* [Cambridge, MA: The MIT Press, 2014]).

20. See, e.g., Maurice Hamington, "Tactility, Care Ethics, and Patient Relations," in *Ethics and Phenomenology*, ed. Mark Sanders and J. Jeremy Wisnewski (Lanham, MD: Lexington Books, 2012), 167–84; and Maurice Hamington, "A Father's Touch: Caring Embodiment and a Moral Revolution," in *Revealing Male Bodies*, ed. Nancy Tuana, William Cowling, Maurice Hamington, Greg Johnson, and Terrance MacMullan (Bloomington: Indiana University Press, 2002), 269–88.

21. Gene Myers, *The Significance of Children and Animals: Social Development and Our Connections to Other Species* (West Lafayette, IN: Purdue University Press, 2007), 82.

22. Describing human-companion animal relationships as robust is something of an understatement. A study by Nickie Charles confirms what many people describe: companion animals are often considered family; see "'Animals Just Love You as You Are': Experiencing Kinship across the Species Barrier," *Sociology* 48, no. 4 (August 2014): 715–30.

23. Theoretical debate over the efficacy of anthropomorphism is rich. See, for example, Robert W. Mitchell, Nicholas S. Thompson, and H. Lyn Miles, eds., *Anthropomorphism, Anecdotes, and Animals* (Albany: SUNY Press, 1997).

24. Thomas Nagel, *Mortal Questions* (New York: Cambridge University Press, 2012), 169.

25. Bekoff, *The Emotional Lives of Animals*, 122–26; de Waal, *Primates and Philosophers*, xvi.

26. Alexandra C. Horowitz and Marc Bekoff, "Naturalizing Anthropomorphism: Behavioral Prompts to Our Humanizing of Animals," *Anthrozoös* 20, no. 1 (2007): 32.

27. In feminist theory, a relational ontology is sometimes described with the notion that we are all "second persons." See Annette Baier, *Postures of the Mind: Essays on Mind and Morals* (Minneapolis: University of Minnesota Press, 1985); and Lorraine Code, *What Can She Know? Feminist Theory and the Construction of Knowledge* (New York: Cornell University Press, 1991).

28. Rita Manning, "Caring for Animals," in *Beyond Animal Rights: A Feminist Caring Ethic for the Treatment of Animals*, ed. Josephine Donovan and Carol J. Adams (New York: Continuum, 1996): 105.

29. In the United States, 4-H Youth Programs represent a hollow form of care. Young people are encouraged to care for farm animals and often end up treating them like companion animals, including naming them and forming attachments. However, the animals are inevitably sold for slaughter, thus tragically terminating the caring relationship. Such programs force children to alter and limit their understanding of empathy (Colter Ellis and Leslie Irvine, "Reproducing Dominion: Emotional Apprenticeship in the 4-H Youth Livestock Program," *Society and Animals* 18, no. 4 [2010]: 21–39).

30. Jean Harvey, "Companion and Assistance Animals: Benefits, Welfare Safeguards, and Relationships," *International Journal of Applied Philosophy* 22, no. 2 (2008): 171. See also Harvey's contribution to this volume.

31. Jane Addams, "A Modern Lear," in Jean Bethke Elshtain, *The Jane Addams Reader* (New York: Basic Books, 2002), 163–76.

32. Willett makes a similar claim about the potential for relationships with animals to spur moral progress in particular ways: "Response ethics may serve to urge humans to respond to the alterity of animals and animal suffering" (*Interspecies Ethics*, 9).

33. Peter Singer, *Expanding the Circle: Ethics, Evolution, and Moral Progress*, 1st ed. (Princeton, NJ: Princeton University Press, 2011), 168.

34. In *Why We Love Dogs, Eat Pigs and Wear Cows* (Newburyport, MA: Conari Books, 2011), Melanie Joy explicitly tries to get the reader to extend the relationships we have with companion animals to our perception of other animals.

5 A TWO-LEVEL UTILITARIAN ANALYSIS OF RELATIONSHIPS WITH PETS

Gary Varner

When it is understood simply as the view that *the right thing to do is whatever will maximize aggregate happiness,* utilitarianism is easily parodied and dismissed for failing to match everyday persons' intuitions about a range of cases, including lying, breaking promises, and punishing the innocent. And as far back as John Stuart Mill, people have worried that, by focusing on cost/benefit calculations, "utilitarianism renders men cold and unsympathizing" ([1861] 1957, 25), and thus unfit for loving relationships and good friendships. Someone whose relationships with others are at every moment consciously mediated by calculations about what would maximize aggregate happiness certainly does not seem like a good candidate friend or lover, or, for that matter, a good companion for a pet.

The utilitarianism that Mill was describing, however, is caricatured when it is understood simply as the view that you ought always to do whatever you think will maximize aggregate happiness under the circumstances. In this essay I illustrate how a more nuanced version of utilitarianism that descended from Mill—the "two-level" utilitarianism of the late twentieth century philosopher R. M. Hare (1919–2002)—provides a nuanced perspective on our relationships with each other and with our animal companions, one that mirrors the complex and varying relationships that people in different positions have to the animals most commonly kept as pets. It also provides a useful framework for understanding how, when, and why the standards for those relationships embodied in our laws, codes of professional ethics, and our shared "common morality" should change over time.

The Principle of Utility, ILS Rules, and Pragmatism

For present purposes, I will stress just three things about Harean two-level utilitarianism. (For a more detailed treatment, see Varner 2012.) The first is that it does endorse "the greatest happiness principle" as its ultimate ethical principle. But the second is that a utilitarian needs a system of rules for the conduct of everyday life, a system of rules many of which will be decidedly *non*-utilitarian. One reason that a utilitarian needs such a system of non-utilitarian rules is that a world full of people whose relationships were at every moment mediated by conscious calculations about what would maximize aggregate happiness would be a world without the selfless love that most people find to be one of the greatest sources of human happiness. So although it sounds ironic, a utilitarian—who thinks that ultimately the right thing to do is to maximize aggregate happiness—has good reason to train herself and others not to think like a utilitarian all of the time.

Something like this is what Mill had in mind when he said that a utilitarian needs "secondary principles" or "corollaries from the principle of utility" that "admit of indefinite improvement" ([1861] 1957, 31). In his capstone work, *Moral Thinking: Its Levels, Method, and Point* (1981), Hare called these "intuitive level rules," and he gave several more reasons that a utilitarian would need to rely on them. One is that extremely detailed information would often be needed to fully work out the utility calculus, and real-world humans usually do not have all of the relevant information. A related reason is that real-world humans have limited data-processing abilities and make mistakes. A third is that humans are inclined, as Hare put it, to "cook the data" in favor of self-interest; that is, to fool themselves into thinking that what they happen to want to do is what will also maximize aggregate happiness (38). The fourth and final reason that Hare mentioned for a utilitarian needing "secondary principles" is for use in the moral education of young children (35).

Hare argued that the rules in this system must have certain features. First, for purposes of early moral education, some of them need to be relatively simple to formulate in words. And to combat our tendency—even as adults—to "cook the data" in favor of self-interest, many of these rules must be learned in a way that produces both a habitual disposition to judge in accordance with them, and also diffidence, hesitance, or wariness about violating them. For these reasons, Hare spoke interchangeably of intuitive level "principles" or "rules" on the one hand, and "habits of thought," "dispositions," or "motivations" on the other, and he spoke of all those as being "absorbed" or "inculcated" as much as being "taught." In that vein, I refer to intuitive level rules as being "internalized" rather than "learned" or "accepted."

I use the expression "ILS rules" to refer to the rules in such an intuitive level system. The acronym seems appropriate because in aviation it stands for the "instrument landing system" that pilots use to approach a runway when weather prevents them from seeing it, and for a Harean utilitarian, the intuitive level system of rules functions as a kind of "moral autopilot." In the same way that an instrument landing system has to be reprogrammed to find runways as some airports are closed and new ones are built, ILS rules must be updated over time, as our understanding of the world we live in changes. And, Hare emphasized, since people in modern societies play various different roles in which they face different kinds of moral challenges, ILS rules will be clustered in several different subsystems.

One subsystem of ILS rules I refer to as "common morality," by which I mean a community's shared system of moral commitments. Some authors use the term "common morality" more narrowly, to refer to a smaller number of moral commitments that are found in all human societies, but Hare described what I am calling common morality as changing across generations. As such, it must consist of a larger number of moral commitments that are generally shared by the members of a given society at a given time in its history. Obviously there are issues associated with individuating societies and their corresponding common moralities, and with just how universal agreement about a norm has to be within a society for it to count as part of the common morality. For present purposes, however, I will not pursue those issues here.

From a Harean perspective, statute laws and other legally binding standards are another type of ILS rules that also reflect shared normative commitments, but laws contrast with common morality in important ways. Laws are normally written down in documents that are agreed to be their official repositories, while the common morality of a modern society typically has no canonical statement. And while there are official, formal processes for working out ambiguities in legal standards and amending them over time, there typically are no such processes for interpreting the standards of common morality and amending them over time. Indeed, of the rules of common morality, Hare said that one may have internalized ILS rules that one cannot adequately formulate in words. I would add that it is hard to say exactly how the rules of common morality change over time. This is because there is no formal process for amending them, and a wide range of factors contributes to changes in common morality over time: popular literature, film, television, and art; political discussions in the press, on radio and television, and around dinner tables; church authorities', celebrities', and public intellectuals' pontifications; blog posts, viral videos, iconic posters, and photographs; and on and on.

Another important category of ILS rules is codes of professional ethics. These differ from both common morality and statute laws in that they are seen as binding only on a proper subset of a community, namely members of the profession in question. From a Harean perspective, this narrower focus is required because people in different roles face different kinds of moral challenges in the normal course of their lives, and this is why codes of professional ethics both differ in substantial ways and have some overlap. For instance, many codes of professional ethics discuss things like plagiarism, co-authorship, and so on, because many different professions engage in scholarship. On the other hand, most codes of professional ethics say nothing about non-combatant immunity and the conduct of high-speed chases, because professionals other than soldiers and police do not normally engage in combat and high-speed chases. Like laws, however, codes of professional ethics are normally written down in canonical form, and there are formal processes that professional organizations use for interpreting them and amending them across time.

For a Harean two-level utilitarian, there are still some roles that explicitly utilitarian thinking (which Hare referred to as "critical level" moral thinking) should play in our lives. One is to guide the interpretation and amendment of ILS rules over time. For a set of ILS rules is better to the extent that it would increase aggregate happiness if internalized by "the target population" (be that all the members of a society or some subset of professionals), so in interpreting and amending ILS rules, a Harean utilitarian engages in explicitly utilitarian reasoning. Hare said that explicitly utilitarian moral thinking is also required in new or very unusual cases that ILS rules cannot be designed to cover, and when ILS rules conflict, although there are reasons to believe that such cases will be rarer than might first appear. Hare also recognized that in some cases that existing ILS rules *are* designed to cover, there may be times when one should, after some careful and explicitly utilitarian thinking, act contrary to those rules because *both* (a) it is clear that doing so will maximize aggregate happiness under the circumstances, *and* (b) the person justifiably believes that he or she can trust their judgment that (a) is true. Hare emphasized that in such cases, one has not properly internalized the ILS rule in question unless one feels some guilt or at least disquiet about acting contrary to it. Critics have thought that this "self-effacing" quality of the principle of utility raises serious questions about the coherence and plausibility of two-level utilitarianism, but any thorough treatment of that issue is beyond the scope of this essay, so suffice it to say that here again, there are reasons to believe that such cases will be rarer than might first appear (for more, see Varner 2012, §§4.7–4.9).

The third thing I want to stress about Harean two-level utilitarianism is that it has a pragmatic bent. For each generation finds itself immersed in a society with a set of institutions and practices defined by the system of laws, codes of professional ethics, and common morality that it has inherited from previous generations. The questions for each generation are, What changes to those sets of ILS rules would improve things, and which changes can we effect in our lifetimes? A Harean utilitarian advocates changes in ILS rules on the grounds that the changes will help increase aggregate happiness of all those affected, but the starting place is the system of rules that we have collectively inherited from the previous generation.

Justifying the Institution or Practice of Pet-Keeping

When it comes to any institution or practice that our generation has inherited, the first question to ask is whether or not its existence is justifiable, and why. If it is not justifiable, then we should work toward abolishing it. If it is justifiable, however, we then ask, second, how it should be governed by us collectively as a community, both formally through our laws and codes of professional ethics, and informally, through our less clearly codified common morality. When we are asking about an existing practice or institution, this second question takes the form of asking how our existing ILS rules relating to it should be modified. In this section, I address the first question: is the institution or practice of pet-keeping justifiable from a utilitarian perspective? I argue that it is justifiable, because three empirical considerations suggest that both pets and people can benefit from it. In the next section, on the assumption that pet-keeping should not be abolished, I illustrate various approaches to modifying the practice in order to increase its contribution to aggregate happiness.

It will help me both to articulate the empirical considerations that support pet-keeping from a utilitarian perspective, and to discuss modifications to the ILS rules governing it, if I first introduce three stipulative definitions. In a 2002 essay entitled "Pets, Companion Animals, and Domesticated Partners," I adopted Deborah Barnbaum's (1998) analysis of the concept of pet as any entity that meets four criteria, according to which

1. A pet's keeper feels affection for it (although not necessarily vice-versa),
2. A pet leads a very different life than its keeper,
3. A pet lives in an area significantly under the keeper's control, and
4. A pet depends on its keeper to have various important interests met.

I then introduced the following stipulative definitions:

A *companion animal* is a pet that receives the affection and care owners typically give to pets, but also has significant social interaction with its owner and would voluntarily choose to stay with the owner, in part for the sake of the companionship.

A *domesticated partner* is a pet that works with humans fairly extensively in ways that emphasize and exercise the pet's mental and/or physical faculties fairly extensively and in healthy ways.

A *mere pet* is a pet that is neither a companion animal nor a domesticated partner.

In terms of the above categories, I can now describe some empirical considerations that support pet-keeping from a utilitarian perspective. The first is that even if we are talking about what I would call "mere pets,"

1. *There is some evidence that keeping pets improves people's lives.*

Scientific interest in the health effects of pet-keeping arose in the 1970s when a graduate student studying the effects of social conditions and isolation on heart disease was surprised to discover a statistical correlation between heart-attack recovery rates and pet-keeping (Serpell [1986] 1996, 97–100). A subsequent study found that calm interactions lower both humans' and dogs' blood pressures and were accompanied by significant increases in neurochemicals associated with relaxation, suggesting that a surge in neurochemicals causes the drop in blood pressure (Odendaal and Meintjes 2003, 298 and 299). On the other hand, a recent review of the available research notes that other studies have failed to replicate such findings and concludes that "the scientific evidence has not yet delivered a clear verdict on the existence of such benefits," although they note that "studying the health effects of pet ownership is extremely challenging, and it may not in fact be possible to design and conduct the definitive study that will finally settle this debate" (Sandøe, Corr, and Palmer 2016, 53–54). So while it would be premature to conclude that physical and mental health benefits to human pet-keepers have been scientifically *demonstrated*, there are reasons to think that pet-keeping can improve humans' lives in various ways. And the fact that pet-keeping has been nearly ubiquitous in human societies for several thousand years (the exceptions being medieval times and early-modern Europe, according to Sandøe, Corr, and Palmer [2016, 21]) suggests that humans at least *think* it is beneficial or enjoyable.

The second empirical consideration that supports pet-keeping from a utilitarian perspective is this:

2. *That many animals kept as pets fit my stipulative definition of a "companion animal"—one that has significant social interaction with its owner and*

would voluntarily stay for the companionship—is prima facie evidence that they have better lives because of the relationships they have with their human keepers.

The large majority of animals kept as pets in contemporary affluent nations are dogs and cats, which appear to bond readily with humans. We know all too well, of course, that human beings sometimes choose to stay in dysfunctional relationships because they see no viable alternative, and a cat or a dog that has lived its entire life with certain humans probably does not see any alternative. At least with regard to cats and dogs, however, because they have been domesticated for thousands of years, it would seem that some form of cohabitation with humans is their "natural habitat," and concerns about dysfunctional relationships can be addressed by various adjustments in our common morality, laws, and professional ethics as illustrated in the following section. What other species readily meet my definition of a companion animal I cannot say, but consideration #2 applies to any that do.

The third empirical consideration that supports pet-keeping from a utilitarian perspective is this:

3. For pets that meet my stipulative definition of a "domesticated partner," behavioral problems, which are the leading cause of strife in humans' relationships with pets, can be more effectively controlled, and humans' relationships with them tend to be more satisfying, than with pets that do not qualify as "domesticated partners."

Studies have found that "behavior problems"—meaning pet behaviors that human owners find bothersome—account for as many as 20 percent of pets surrendered to shelters, and "the number one way to prevent behaviour problems, in the case of dogs at least, is proper education of both the dog and owner through training" (Sandøe, Corr, and Palmer 2016, 133). Cats are more challenging to train, of course, but owners can certainly teach them simple behaviors that help cats and their owners live well together in a domestic setting. For most cats, the average person can teach them to desist when told "no," to come on command, to enter a carrier for a treat, and so forth.

The increasing popularity both of dog parks, where owners can let their dogs run free but can also legally work with them "off lead," and of agility courses, where owners work intensively with their dogs in ways that exercise both body and mind, suggests that contemporary dog owners are increasingly cultivating domesticated partnerships with their animals. Relatedly, while I do not know of any studies on the subject, my *hunch* is that people who work with dogs in complex ways, from basic obedience training through racing agility courses, probably enjoy their relationships with their dogs more than people who do little or no training of them, just because their relationships with those dogs are "richer." And, of course, the members of one category of domesticated partners, service dogs, benefit their human keepers and others in diverse ways, including helping the visually and hearing impaired and the physically disabled, locating people buried in rubble, anticipating seizures, and so forth.

From the three empirical considerations discussed in this section, I draw three conclusions. The first is that the practice of keeping pets is *justifiable* from a utilitarian perspective. I say "justifiable" rather than "justified," because from a Harean perspective, each generation needs to ask anew what modifications to make to the ILS rules that they have inherited from their ancestors. There are obvious downsides to the practice of pet-keeping as we have inherited it. When I say that pet-keeping is *justifiable* from a utilitarian perspective, I mean only that the empirical considerations discussed in this section suggest that it can, at least under certain circumstances, improve the lives of both the humans and the animals involved. We have in fact inherited the practice of pet-keeping in the various forms that it now takes, and the question for our generation is what modifications of the current practice—modifications achievable in our time—will tend to increase the aggregate happiness of the humans and the animals involved. That is the subject of the next section.

The second conclusion I draw is that although keeping "mere pets" may sometimes be a good thing, it is generally better to keep companion animals than to keep mere pets. Keeping a "mere pet"—one that would not choose to stay for the sake of companionship—could still be a good thing, if the animal is from a species that will not bond with a human, as long as its life in captivity is better than life in the wild would have been. If an animal is capable of enjoying a companion relationship with its owner, however, then it can both live a better life than it would face as a mere pet (or in a feral state, since dogs' and cats' "natural habitat" is some form of cohabitation with humans) and also enjoy the interactions with its human keeper(s) that animals unsuited to being companion animals normally shun.

The third conclusion I draw is that it is generally good for pet-keepers to develop, to the extent practicable, a domesticated partnership with their companion animals. Other than dogs, the only commonly kept pets that I can think of with whom humans regularly develop sophisticated domesticated partnerships are horses (and maybe some birds and rodents). As I indicated above with regard to cats, however, the average person can usually train them in some basic ways that facilitate domestic cohabitation, and that will apply to varying degrees for some other species.

Modifying the Institution or Practice of Pet-Keeping

From a Harean utilitarian perspective, there are three approaches to modifying the practice of pet-keeping as we have inherited it. These correspond to the three types of ILS rules described above:

1. Laws,
2. Codes of professional ethics, and
3. Common morality.

In this section, I will describe examples of each; then, in the final section, I will discuss two additional considerations that arise from taking a Harean perspective on our relationships with pets.

Laws

An obvious way to change the practice of pet-keeping would be through legislation at the various levels of our government. Two-level utilitarians like Hare typically hold that laws should be less broad in scope than common morality. Famously, in *On Liberty* ([1859] 1956), Mill argued on utilitarian grounds for keeping "the private sphere" immune to government regulation, because the cost of allowing people to make bad decisions about their own lives is outweighed in the long haul by their having the freedom to experiment with new lifestyles. When it comes to pets, however, bad decisions of pet-keepers can significantly harm their sentient charges, so some legal restrictions on pet ownership seem called for.

Obvious examples are laws against neglect and "cruelty," which are uncontroversial in modern societies. However, attending to the distinctions that I have drawn between companion animals, domesticated partners, and mere pets suggests some further refinements to consider. For an incredible diversity of animals that are kept as pets are ill-suited to being true companions, and in the case of some, providing them with a life in captivity that is better than they would live in the wild can be a tall order.

Catherine Schuppli and David Fraser (2000) have proposed classifying various species in terms of their appropriateness as companion animals and as what I would call "mere pets." Based on answers to twelve questions about the animals' welfare, the welfare of humans, and risks to the environment, they conclude that animals in their two most appropriate categories include domestic mice and golden hamsters, as well as most dogs and cats ("as long as they are procured from known and responsible sources" [367]). They place "exotic pet species" such as the green iguana in their category of animals "that have complex or demanding requirements needing skillful and knowledgeable owners" (366, table 2), and they place "dangerous species such as venomous snakes and large cat species" and "species whose requirements (e.g., for normal social behavior) cannot reasonably be met in captivity" into an "unsuitable as pets" category (and they place some dog breeds in this category) (367).

Their framework suggests options for fine-tuning existing laws to better reflect the different welfare-related considerations that arise with animals that are (and are not) suited to being real companions (as opposed to mere pets). For instance, "a municipality might choose to permit only species judged to fall into [their two most appropriate categories], or it might require licensing for species judged to fall into [their complex and demanding needs] category," perhaps coupled with an inspection system and other requirements as with falconry in the United States (368).

Codes of Professional Ethics

Another venue for effecting change in the practice of pet-keeping as we have inherited it lies in the codes of ethics of professions, and in the analogous official standards of organizations that influence pet owners' attitudes.

The case of purebred dogs provides a ready illustration. Two areas of concern that could be addressed by this means are the health effects of closed studbooks and the imposition of breed standards requiring ear cropping and tail docking. The notion of a "purebred" dog is usually tied to its lineage's being traceable in a studbook that was "established by including particular animals that were thought at the time to represent the best specimens of their breed, after which the studbook was typically closed" (Sandøe, Corr, and Palmer 2016, 15). With the first studbook published over 140 years ago, inbreeding has led to a variety of problems with phenotypes, such as English Bulldogs' partially obstructed airways, and with susceptibility to disease, such as King Charles Spaniels' high rate of heart disease (Sandøe, Corr, and Palmer 2016, 107–8). In some breeds, the official breed standard requires dogs' ears to be cropped and/or their tails docked. With regard to tail docking, this is usually true of those that were originally bred to work with humans in ways that would put them at risk of injury or infection if their tails were not docked, but that rationale is lost with regard to most contemporary purebreds.

The main breed-showing associations like the American Kennel Club (AKC) could have a significant impact on future generations of purebred dogs by removing requirements for tail docking and ear cropping from breed standards, and by allowing additional new bloodlines into various breeds' studbooks. The pragmatist bent of two-level utilitarian thinking that I mentioned earlier forces us to question just how likely it is that such changes are going to occur, however. I am not in a good position to judge, but I suspect that it is not likely that these reforms will emerge from the kennel clubs in the next generation. As far back as 1976, the American Veterinary Medical Association adopted a policy statement recommending that the AKC and other breed associations "delete mention of cropped ears or trimmed ears from breed standards for dogs," and in 2008 it expanded that recommendation to include tail docking (AVMA 2015), but the AKC has yet to follow that recommendation.

I can imagine, however, an alternate approach to improving the welfare of pet dogs that an organization like the AVMA or the Humane Society of the United States (HSUS) could advance via a program that recognizes a new dog breed, one that we might call the Certified Companion-Bred Dog (the names of officially recognized dog breeds are capitalized). From an initial breeding population of dogs who score well on various health measures, as well as tests of trainability and (lack of) aggression, only the highest-scoring offspring would be bred. In the famous Russian experiment breeding tameness into silver foxes, a combination of morphological and behavioral changes typical of domesticated animals emerged from a wild canid species in only 8–10 generations (Trut 1999, 164). This suggests that a special degree of "companionability" could be bred into dogs after selecting across a relatively small number of generations. Then an organization like the HSUS would create a studbook, allowing breeders and buyers to know that they are getting a dog from a lineage designed to work well as companion animals, and which are well suited to becoming domesticated partners. With this record keeping, the imprimatur of an organization like the HSUS, some media coverage, and maybe a trademark on "Certified Companion-Bred Dog," breeders could turn a good profit producing Certified Companion-Bred Dogs. The resulting breed would not have a uniform appearance, and so publicity surrounding it would also provide a new model of what "a good breed of dog" is, one focused on the dogs' health and their behavior with humans, rather than on how their appearance resembles some ancestral archetype.

Common Morality

The example of Certified Companion-Bred Dogs illustrates how, in the face of institutional inertia, a Harean utilitarian can still use creative modifications of some ILS rules to improve conditions for future generations of pets. When it comes to the final venue for changing ILS rules, however, the situation is complicated by some features of common morality that were mentioned earlier. These are the facts that there is usually no formal process for altering the rules of common morality, and that often people are not even capable of clearly articulating the ILS rules that they have internalized.

Still, I think that changes in common morality have a greater potential for effecting change than do changes in laws and codes of professional ethics. Just imagine, for instance, that a generation from now, our common morality will have changed so that almost no one thinks it appropriate to crop ears or dock tails for cosmetic reasons. If that change could be ensured by something we do now, then we would not need the AVMA to recommend it, because the AKC would change its breed standards in response to the shift in common morality. So it is worth considering the variety of factors that influence our common morality.

Earlier I mentioned the following: popular literature, film, television, and art; political discussions in the press, on radio and television, and around dinner tables; church authorities', celebrities', and public intellectuals' pontifications; blog posts, viral videos, iconic posters, and photographs; and so on. Usually no one can point to a specific work of art, news reporting, or event as *the* cause of a shift in common morality. Consider, for instance, the change in attitudes toward same-sex marriage in the United States. Before and after the Supreme Court's June 2015 ruling that legalized it nationwide, pundits and news reporters frequently noted how quickly the change had occurred in comparison to shifts in other major cultural norms: roughly speaking, attitudes toward same-sex marriage as measured in opinion polls flip-flopped across only 20–25 years. No one can say exactly what influences were at work, but surely the growing presence of gay musicians, movie and television characters, news anchors, and other public figures contributed to the "normalization" of same-sex marriage. If that is correct, then we must not underestimate the power of the entertainment industry to cause changes in our common morality.

Academics can point to "public intellectuals," who have successful careers in academia, but also influence public opinion on a large scale. An example related to animal ethics is Peter Singer's 1975 book, *Animal Liberation*. Like many who teach classes on related topics, I cannot say how many times someone has told me that reading it affected their thinking about animal ethics. Now in its fourth edition, the number of paperback copies of it in print has sometimes been used as a measure of the growth of the contemporary animal rights movement (see, e.g., Jasper and Nelkin 1992, 37–38), yet at the time he published it, Singer could not have predicted that it would influence so many people for so long. Of course

Singer has had very little to say about pets specifically, but the book's influence illustrates how a popular work on philosophical themes *can* help shift public attitudes toward animals.

What lesson emerges from these examples? I would say this: people in all walks of life can contribute to major changes in the common morality of the next generation, sometimes in big ways (e.g., with a book that makes a splash), but always in smaller ones (e.g., by serving as examples of certain lifestyle choices). Whether you are writing a book, making a movie, or just getting on with your job in a world that has not shared certain of your values up to now, you cannot fully predict what effect you are going to have, *so just get on with it!*

That said, what do *I* hope changes about the next generation's common morality with regard to pet animals? I hope that future generations will look askance at the keeping of what I call "mere pets" more than we do today, with only highly knowledgeable individuals keeping various kinds of "exotic" pets. I hope that future generations will take it as a given that when one keeps a pet that I would say qualifies as a true "companion," one also works at developing what I call "a domesticated partnership" with it, to the extent that its species is capable of that relationship.

What am I *doing* to contribute to these changes? Well, I publish books and articles on animal ethics in general and companion animal ethics in particular—although I am under no illusion that they will be influential! I also teach about animal ethics in my college classes (although I carefully avoid advocacy in my teaching). And in my private life, I do chat people up on the subject a bit, and I work on my relationships with the two cats that I currently keep as pets. One of them grew up feral in my neighborhood and showed up expecting to eat on my deck (at a very cautious distance from me) and ready to deliver a litter of kittens. A couple of years after I "took her in" (which initially meant *trapping* her in my house), she now desists when told "no," she comes on command, she goes into a cat carrier to get her meals, and she stays off the kitchen countertops (at least while I am around). That is something of an accomplishment with a feral cat taken in as an adult, and I hope that my training her to at least some extent sets an example in the area of "earnestly working on a domesticated partnership."

Two Additional Considerations

I also hope that in the future, pet-keepers will be less inclined to think of their companions as "replaceable" than I get the impression that they now do, but let me first describe the second of the two additional considerations that I said

I would close with, one that will be found unpalatable by many readers. I have stressed that from a Harean perspective, because people in various roles can face very different challenges, they should sometimes internalize quite different sets of ILS rules. The most obvious example is the one I used earlier, that of members of different professions embracing different codes of professional ethics, but a related consideration is that people relating to the same species of animals in different ways (e.g., as pet-keepers, search and rescue trainers, veterinarians, animal control officers, farmers, medical researchers, et al.) should sometimes internalize different sets of ILS rules.

A broader version of the same implication is that people in societies with different, deeply entrenched cultural traditions cannot be expected to change overnight. My impression is that Westerners currently find it a curiosity that Hindus will not eat cattle, but an abomination that Koreans eat dogs. From a Harean perspective, however, the latter practice is (pardon the expression) "on all fours" with the former: each reflects a common morality that a generation has inherited from its ancestors. In both cases, the ILS rules in question are open to revision by the current generation, but in each case the changes that the current generation can make are limited by pragmatic considerations that a two-level utilitarian must acknowledge. Similarly, as long as eating a particular species and performing medical research on a particular species are accepted practices in a given society, it will be appropriate for certain professionals to internalize different ILS rules regarding their relationships with animals that are in other contexts kept as pets.

I can now end on what I consider a brighter note, by returning to a theme that was introduced at the beginning of this essay: the persistent worry that taking utilitarianism seriously will render one "cold," calculating, and unfit for loving relationships and good friendships. As I stressed earlier, there are a number of good reasons for thinking that a real-world utilitarian *needs* a system of what Hare called "intuitive level rules," the internalization of which disposes one *not* to think like a utilitarian during the moment-to-moment management of many interpersonal relationships. I believe that should also apply to the relationships we have with our companion animals.

The studies on blood pressure and neurochemicals suggest that we benefit from *loving* animals in some of the same ways that we benefit from loving other humans. But loving another sentient being requires you not to think of it as "replaceable" the way everyone and everything is when you are doing explicitly utilitarian thinking. I am disturbed when I hear pet owners say that they immediately "replaced" a beloved pet with another animal from the same breed. I think that it would be better if we thought about our animal companions who are to some extent what I call "domesticated partners" in something like the way we think about a deceased human partner:

> I will always miss my special friend whom I have lost, but one day I will meet a new friend, who need not look anything like my old friend, and could not have replaced my old friend while she was alive. In time, though, my new friend and I will bond in a special way, and we will cultivate a trusting relationship based on a kind of mutual respect and mutual accommodation, a relationship that will enrich both of our lives in a healthy way, until one of us dies.

I hope that some such attitude takes hold of our psyches in coming generations—and I say that as a sincere convert to (two-level) utilitarianism!

Acknowledgments

Christine Overall and Clare Palmer provided helpful feedback on this essay, although I was not able to address all of their concerns here.

References

American Veterinary Medical Association (AVMA). "History of Policy on Ear Cropping and Tail Docking of Dogs." https://www.avma.org/KB/Policies/Pages/Ear-Cropping-and-Tail-Docking-of-Dogs.aspx. Accessed November 27, 2015.

Barnbaum, Deborah. 1998. "Why Tamagotchis Are Not Pets." *Thinking: The Journal of Philosophy for Children* 13 (4): 41–43.

Hare, R. M. 1981. *Moral Thinking: Its Levels, Method, and Point.* New York: Oxford University Press.

Jasper, James M., and Dorothy Nelkin. 1992. *The Animal Rights Crusade: The Growth of a Moral Protest.* New York: The Free Press.

Mill, John Stuart. (1859) 1956. *On Liberty.* Indianapolis: Bobbs-Merrill.

Mill, John Stuart. (1861) 1957. *Utilitarianism.* Indianapolis: Bobbs-Merrill.

Odendaal, J. S. J., and R. A. Meintjes. 2003. "Neurophysiological Correlates of Affiliative Behaviour between Humans and Dogs." *The Veterinary Journal* 165 (3): 296–301.

Sandøe, Peter, Sandra Corr, and Clare Palmer. 2016. *Companion Animal Ethics.* Oxford: Wiley Blackwell.

Schuppli, C. A., and D. Fraser. 2000. "A Framework for Assessing the Suitability of Different Species as Companion Animals." *Animal Welfare* 9 (4): 359–72.

Serpell, James. (1986) 1996. *In the Company of Animals: A Study of Human-Animal Relationships.* New York: Cambridge University Press.

Singer, Peter. 1975. *Animal Liberation: A New Ethics for Our Treatment of Animals*. New York: Avon Books.

Trut, Lyudmila N. 1999. "Early Canid Domestication: The Farm-Fox Experiment." *American Scientist* 87 (2): 160–69.

Varner, Gary. 2002. "Pets, Companion Animals, and Domesticated Partners." In *Ethics for Everyday*, edited by David Benatar, 450–75. Boston: McGraw-Hill.

Varner, Gary. 2012. *Personhood, Ethics, and Animal Cognition: Situating Animals in Hare's Two-Level Utilitarianism*. New York: Oxford University Press.

6 "I DON'T WANT THE RESPONSIBILITY"

THE MORAL IMPLICATIONS OF AVOIDING DEPENDENCY RELATIONS WITH COMPANION ANIMALS

Kathryn J. Norlock

Philosopher Jean Harvey argues for a moral obligation to develop relationships of "loving interaction" with animal companions, "and possibly to enable dogs in general and most cats to enter into such a relationship" (2008, 175; also in Chapter 1 in this volume). Her recommendation to enable relationships offers a striking contrast to the reasons some people report for not having a companion animal in their homes. For example, in a study of the 45 percent of Canadian households that do not have dogs or cats (Perrin 2009, 49), main reasons reported include "I don't want the responsibility" (58 percent) and "I travel too much/they don't fit my lifestyle" (41 percent).[1]

I sympathize with the intuitions reflected in the survey responses. I believed for years that if I acquired one of these animals then I would have responsibilities to them, and therefore, if I had no relationship with a pet, I would have no such responsibilities. In retrospect, I think I committed the error of denying the antecedent and believing that in doing so, I could deny the consequent. It is clearer to me now that it does not follow from avoiding a closer relationship that one has no responsibility to dogs and cats available for adoption. To be petless is not the same as to be free of responsibilities to would-be companion animals in communities with a supply-and-demand imbalance in dog and cat populations.[2] In this chapter I draw attention to the nature of the relationships between humans and companion animals, with an eye to clarifying the responsibilities of petless people to unhoused animals and their caregivers. The responsive capabilities of petless individuals may vary, but we can at least reflect on the implications of our choices for the communities in which we live, and the sorts of communities in which we expect to live.

The petless people responding to the polls above demonstrate some awareness that individual adoption of a dog or cat will create a particular, concrete *dependency relation* between at least two specific relata with specific obligations, and a sense of the consequent *secondary dependence* of pet owners as caregivers. I clarify my use of these concepts below, building on Eva Feder Kittay's (1995) account of human-human dependency relations and secondary dependence. I extend her account to cover human-companion animal relationships in a way that she may not have intended, but that evidently applies to pet owners. I then argue that many non-owners also have palpable, but indefinite, dependency relations with dogs and cats that they could adopt but do not. Indefinite dependency relations avoid the secondary dependence of the caregiver, but they yield duties to current caregivers of not-yet-adopted dogs and cats, as well as to the dogs and cats themselves; in other words, in avoiding the secondary dependence of pet owners, the petless increase the caregiving burdens of any others who are currently caring. In order to live up to a moral obligation like the one Harvey identifies, to enable dogs and cats to enter into loving relationships, those who do not care for companion animals may bear responsibilities toward those who do, as well as to the animals themselves.

I focus on dogs and cats in this chapter, not just because they are paradigmatic companion animals, but because Harvey is persuasive that dogs' and cats' capacities for love and loyalty to their human owners are morally important. Dogs and cats with capacities for such affectionate bonding, whose natures and very existences are partially due to human actions, make a moral demand on those humans with the power to do something about the conditions in which these animals live and love. The moral obligations of those of us who refrain from incurring particular relationships with dogs and cats are correlative with the power of persons like me, that is, those with what Harvey (1999) elsewhere called "interactive power" (43–44), the power to take the initiative in and direct the course of a relationship. I connect Harvey's points about interactive power to my application of Kittay's dependency critique, to show that those of us who refrain from incurring particular relationships of dependency rely on caregivers in our communities and regions to fulfill the moral and social demands that an abundance of companionable animals makes on the community. As Kittay suggests, dependency relations are to some extent inevitable (and can be value-neutral or even desirable), but they give rise to problems in a sociopolitical context in which the fact of dependency is ignored or deplored; these problems include the neglect of secondary dependents. Since avoiding a particular relationship with one dog or cat increases our obligations in other sorts of relationships with companion animals and their caregivers, those without pets who yet possess interactive and sociopolitical power ought to provide monetary, material, and socio-political forms of support to caregivers of companion animals.

It may not be obvious that the owner of a dog or cat exists with the animal in a dependency relation. Kittay describes a dependency relation as a relationship between a dependent, that is, one who "requires care," who is "unable either to survive or to thrive without attention to basic needs," and a caregiver or "dependency worker" who provides this care (1995, 8). Kittay's conceptions of dependency (1995, 2002) include ranges and types of dependency. A dependent is "inevitably dependent" (1999, x) or "utterly dependent" (1995, 8) to the extent that she relies on a caregiver for "basic needs" (1995, 8) or "basic life functions" (2002, 260); a caregiver is a "derivative" (1999, x) or "secondary" (1995, 12) dependent insofar as her dependency is not inevitable but "derivative of the care of dependents" (1999, x) or constituted by the social arrangements in which care is provided (1995, 12). "The dependency worker acquires a dependence on others to supply the resources needed to sustain herself and the dependents who are in her charge" (1995, 12).

I suggest that this relationship applies quite directly to the relationship domesticated dogs and cats bear to pet owners. Whether or not an individual dog or cat could fend for itself when an owner ends care-provision, it seems clearly the case that the practice in which many pet owners engage, of locking companion animals inside houses most days with only the food and water that the human chooses to supply, renders a dog or cat dependent upon that human for basic needs. Dogs and cats who have food and water may survive, but not thrive if other basic needs are not met as well, including their capacities for affectionate bonding, for love and loyalty; it is an irony of the results of human domestication efforts that cats and dogs were domesticated in part because of their desirability as loyal and affectionate companions, and these desirable qualities are also basic needs that dogs and cats present in dependency relations.[3]

Arguably, the application of Kittay's account admits of ambiguity with respect to what it means to be inevitably dependent or secondarily dependent, since companion animals are not utterly helpless, and since it is not clear that secondary dependence is the dependence of caregivers only. However, the ambiguity as to which type of dependency we are discussing is not an obstacle to identifying companion animals as dependents of *some* sort. And it is possible that the dependency relation of dogs and cats to human owners is *both* inevitable *and* derivative from social arrangements. Consider that, to an extent, this is a dependency that is human-caused; as economist Joshua Frank argues, "Humans have a certain responsibility for the welfare of companion animals. Dogs . . . have been bred for thousands of years to serve our needs. They have therefore ceased being truly 'wild' animals and instead become dependent on humans for survival" (2004, 108). Cats have been bred for less time, but in many regions cats are the largest "input" (Hamilton 2010, 279) into shelters, and studies in North America and the United Kingdom refer to their cat populations as a crisis.[4] Although breeding choices and shelters are the result of social arrangements, in a material and undeniable sense, dogs and cats inevitably live or die by the decisions of humans who care for them (or do not).

Further, dependency relations have moral import in the social contexts in which caregivers operate; caregivers can become secondarily dependent or derivatively dependent themselves, in virtue of social arrangements, as the moral demands upon them from being caregivers of dependents are made easier with supportive social structures, or more difficult with obstacles built into social structures. In human-human dependency relations, the secondary dependence of caregivers is readily recognized. For example, parents with newborn children or adults with disabled parents are derivatively dependent upon social arrangements providing medical care (or not), parental and family leave (or not), and accessible services for varieties of bodies.

Although Kittay did not include human-animal relationships among dependency relations, it is also the case that caregivers of animals face a number of social arrangements that make their tasks easier or more difficult. Someone who has worked in animal husbandry may find that caring for farm animals is made easier or harder depending on governmental systems regulating veterinarians, corporate structures that offer or limit available feed, and the willingness or resistance of neighbors to honor clean water practices. Those who have taken in companion animals know that they are vulnerable to the presence or absence of humane societies and shelters, the fee schedules of veterinarians, the availability of insurance to cover the fees, and the affordability of food and medicine for animals. In short, not only is it the case that domesticated animals are dependent upon those who own them, but by entering into dependency relations, pet owners become vulnerable as well. So a complete picture of dependency relations is one in which one who can give care is in a relationship with a dependent who creates obligations to care, and those obligations result in some new or further vulnerabilities of the caregiver.

Kittay argues further that the provision of bare survival does not fully meet the moral demands of a dependency relation. Dependents call upon caregivers for positive care, not just an absence of cruelty or interference (2002, 260). She argues, and I agree, that the newborn baby and the disabled parent arrive with vulnerabilities and capacities to thrive, and these require active support and provision of goods, not just avoidance of harms. When my sister leaves her infant in my supervision, I am in a dependency relation with my nephew; if he stops crawling, then suddenly spits up and cries, it is not sufficiently responsive of me to refrain from crossing the room and harming him. I care for him: I clean him and comfort him, and I later spread a fresh blanket on the floor so he may crawl again. I work to create conditions for his thriving.

I should note that in so describing dependency relations, Kittay mainly addresses only human relationships with other humans. She argues that nonhuman animals do not require the sort of positive care that humans require, "the full-blown sort," and she suggests that "for nonhuman animals, it may be sufficient to invoke the principle that harm inflicted on them is wrong because of what it does to those who do the injury" (2002, 272); animals may do just as well in the absence of cruelty. Elsewhere, I have argued against this view (Norlock 2004). I suggest it is more accurate to see companion animals as dependents requiring positive care in their dependency relation with human caregivers. The social and individual relationships that humans cultivate with companion animals combine to render companion animals dependent upon humans for positive care and not just an absence of cruelty. They are moral patients whom humans have gone to lengths to encourage to affectionately bond to us, through our historical breeding practices (as these come to influence the natures of the companion animals we bring into being), ongoing commercial reproduction, animal control policies, and sheltering provisions generally, and the particular relationships incurred by individuals in concrete contexts. Further, some breeds of dogs, in particular, are distinctively vulnerable, or sicklier than other breeds. This too is a legacy of some deliberate and some accidental endeavors, with the result that it is entirely up to humans whether or not to meet companion animals' needs as members of particular species, or to enable their capacities to thrive.

So far, I have discussed the relationships of dogs and cats to humans in both general and specific terms. Generally, organizations of humans set or support many of the social arrangements regarding such goods as the availability or affordability of pet food, accreditation in veterinary medicine, and social policies regarding animal control and kill- or no-kill shelters. More specifically, when an individual decides to acquire a dog or a cat, she calls a new and distinctive concrete relationship into existence, especially one in which, to use Harvey's term in *Civilized Oppression* (1999), she has almost all the "interactive power" (43–44), that is, the power to take the initiative in a relationship, to begin or end it, and to set its terms. Harvey refers to interactive power as "a major part of assigned direct power in positions of responsibility" (1999, 43). If one calls a dependency relationship like this into existence, by acquiring a companion animal with a social and emotional nature, then one therefore has the power and the responsibility to navigate that relationship, to maintain it, even to end it, if that is what is called for in the service of the flourishing of the one cared-for, based on its nature. Ending the relationship may not sound as if it serves the relationship, but consider those who have chosen, after some deliberation, to give an animal to another household when the owner cannot afford to feed it, or to opt for their animal's euthanasia rather than its continued persistence in a bad state. Although pet owners disagree, some have argued that the decision to give a companion animal away, or request its death at the hands of a compassionate veterinarian, is made in order to avoid a decrease in their pet's flourishing.[5]

These aspects of dependency relations—the inevitable dependency of companion animals, and the consequent vulnerabilities of their caregivers to social arrangements—are the reasons that I have never adopted a dog or cat myself. As I said at the outset, it seemed to me that if choosing a relationship to a companion animal entailed obligations to its wellbeing, then no relationship meant I had no responsibilities. For years, I saw this as even praiseworthy, especially since it meant the sacrifice of a desire to have a pet. (Look how good I am not to have a pet, despite wanting one!) Instead of being a neglectful owner, or a forgetful one, or a wicked one, I am no owner at all, avoiding special responsibilities. As Harvey says, "People who bring animals into their lives thereby acquire special responsibilities toward them" (2008, 173) because a companion animal and its human owner have a relationship of a "huge difference in power between the two parties" (169). Rejecting any model of a pet-owner relationship as contract-like, she says, "Dogs cannot reflect on proposed arrangements, foresee their practical implications, raise concerns or propose revisions. . . . In virtually every respect, humans are in control" (169).

Additionally, control over these relationships is not limited to the humans who house companion animals. Harvey goes well beyond discussion of interactive power within particular relationships when she identifies our primary obligation to companion animals. Describing the natures of dogs and cats as at least partly constituted to "give love and loyalty to human companions," she argues that "as with anyone who loves, it makes them vulnerable—to the hurt of not being loved at all, to being manipulated, exploited, or traumatically abused or abandoned" (2008, 170). Due to such animals' "deep and abiding affection, the profound emotional and physical vulnerability they face because of it, and the blunt fact that humans in general control the relationship and have the power either to treasure or betray their animal companions," Harvey concludes that "the primary moral obligation we have with respect to companion animals is to develop, nurture, respect, and protect this relationship" (170, 171). In short, her model requires that "we place the loving relationship in centre stage," calling for "a far more pro-active engagement" with such relationships. Her critique of alternative models of human-nonhuman relationships notes, "The magic of a loving relationship is chillingly absent. . . . Love values the loved one for who she is in herself; the focus is on the one loved, not the love received, and it is a kind of cherishing that has commitment at its heart" (171).

Harvey is persuasive that philosophers of moral theory, especially in European and American traditions, have neglected love's moral importance. Bearing in mind Harvey's conclusion that the primary moral obligation we have with respect to companion animals is to develop, nurture, respect, and protect this relationship, I appreciate anew her different description of the appropriate attitude: "Love and respect are not laissez-faire attitudes; they are attitudes of engagement" (171). It is not sufficient to the moral tasks Harvey outlines to refrain from owning a companion animal when one is not prepared to positively support its thriving; my commitment to refrain is still rather preoccupied with human benefits, namely, avoidance of my own failure to engage, my secondary dependence, and my time commitment, at the expense of animals who are already constituted to love and be loved, but lack a companion role or a home.

In light of Harvey's arguments to see our primary obligations to companion animals more clearly as relationships with love-capable beings, I have come to think my petlessness implies a view of animal companions as having bodies that I know are constituted for love and affection, which is precisely why I avoid the moral demands that such bodies bring. Mine is not demonstrative of Harvey's recommended attitude of engagement, and rather bespeaks an attitude of wishing to avoid costs to myself by entering relationships. It is an avoidance of already-existing demands, already-existing dependents currently capable of relationship and currently living in shelters in my region. This is an implication I am not comfortable with, and suggests that my attitude is not appreciative of the realities of what millions of households actually do, by taking attitudes of engagement and sheltering animals.

The unavoidable fact that Harvey so effectively features is that while I avoid all the concrete relationships I want to avoid, those animal bodies with loving natures already exist. Their existences pose some challenges where dog and cat populations constitute problems for communities and the agencies and animal shelters that work within communities. Not all communities have the same problems; the expectation of unowned and roaming cats and dogs in an area may be accompanied by indifference toward unowned animals' effects on humans or other animals, as well as a lack of interest in animal welfare.[6] But I do not live in such a community, nor do most, nor do I think it is ideal that some may. The International Companion Animal Management Coalition points to good reasons to manage unowned and roaming cat and dog populations, including where the welfare of the cats and dogs is compromised, where they "present a public health risk to humans, either through the transmission of zoonotic disease (e.g. rabies, toxoplasmosis) or contamination of the environment (through

urine, faeces), . . . where cats pose a significant threat to wildlife through preda-
tion," especially birds, and where there is risk of human-animal conflict, especially with dogs, and conflict between owned and unowned dogs and cats, to the
detriment of the wellbeing of both.[7] As Francis Hamilton, a former owner of a
clinic that sterilized feral cats in an effort to decrease animal euthanasia, observes,
"Governmental agencies and shelters are charged with controlling the animal
overpopulation problem"; he unequivocally states that the costs and burdens of
doing so are a problem for the municipalities and for the individuals who must
work to manage the input (especially of cats) (2010, 277).

Activists such as Nathan Winograd argue that "overpopulation" is an inac-
curate depiction of the problem in the United States, since there are enough
households in the country to house every animal (2007, 161–62). However, as
blogger Leslie Smith (2013) argues regarding Winograd's "repeated assertion
that overpopulation is a myth," whether or not to call the problem one of overpopulation is beside the point. "The fact is, we have too many animals who need
homes—some with looks or behaviors or years behind them that are not considered desirable by a fair portion of the animal-acquiring public. And that's a
problem" (2013). She and other authors note that while a cursory look at the
numbers suggests that homes outnumber homeless animals, people looking for
companion animals tend to acquire them from friends, family, neighbors, and
breeders rather than shelters, and they tend to acquire young and able kittens
and puppies. Roaming cats and dogs present problems as sometimes homeless,
sometimes ill, and sometimes surrendered (owned but no longer wanted) beings,
and these problems must be handled by someone.

The concerns of practitioners like Hamilton, Smith, and Winograd reveal
that Harvey's arguments for attention to human relationships with animals are
not, therefore, limited in application to dyadic, individualized dependency relations. Like Kittay's arguments that caregivers become secondarily dependent
upon the wider society when social arrangements are obstacles to their caring
labors, Harvey's arguments imply some moral recommendations regarding wider
relationships between humans and animal companions generally. This is clearest
in her consideration (2008) of cases of former service animals with "lost ability"
and would-be service animals determined to have "no ability" (173–74). Here,
she considers the situations of service animals put to sophisticated, complex uses
for human benefit, especially police dogs and guide dogs. She notes that police
dogs can outlive their usefulness to their trainers and employers, and are routinely retired from duties and from any monetary or material support just at an
age when they may be most likely to need it. She notes that guide dogs and therapy dogs are selected from groups of dogs trained for the purpose, with selection
rates as low as one in twenty trained dogs successfully placed.

What happens, Harvey asks insistently, to the other nineteen? What becomes of dogs with a lost ability (such as retired police dogs or elderly guide dogs), or no ability (such as dogs not selected after training), when the human-centered motivation for the relationship is not present, when they are not service animals and will only be companion animals? While I was patting myself on the back for adopting none of them, guaranteeing my success at non-creation and therefore non-violation of particular dependency relationships, Harvey's injunction to cultivate an attitude of engagement indicates that in avoiding particular relationships with any one of these no-longer-service, now-companion animals, we neglect attending to the changed but pre-existing relationships with these currently living and love-capable dogs. She concludes, "We should highlight and explore the relationship of loving interaction that cherishes the animals for the wonderful individuals they are. . . . The moral obligation to develop such a relationship with our animal companions (with dogs and cats at least) and possibly to enable dogs in general and most cats to enter into such a relationship provides a morally more secure basis for an ethic of companion animals" (2008, 175).

Turning to Kittay's *dependency critique* clarifies that a pressing ethical task for petless people may be to attend to the needs of those who provide animal care in our stead, for the sake of both workers and their charges. Kittay offers a dependency critique of societies predicated on liberal ideals of equality, arguing that "by construing society as an association of equals, conceived as individuals with equal powers," one neglects "the condition both of dependents and [of] those who care for dependents" (1995, 11). Populations of dogs and cats as a civic, social, relational, and moral problem for communities are destined to be invisible in such liberal polities, because material dependencies, in a socio-political arrangement organized along principles of social cooperation among equals, are ignored or deplored, and if they are recognized as unavoidable, they "are sustained by a social organization that creates a secondary dependence on those who care for dependents" (11). Not coincidentally, dependency workers then tend to be undervalued and underpaid. In the case of animal care, they also tend to be women.[8] (This too seems not coincidental.)

The dependency worker is so situated that "her responsibilities lie with another who cannot survive or thrive without her ministrations. Her attention is directed to another's needs; even her understanding of her own needs are enmeshed with the needs of a vulnerable other whose fundamental wellbeing is entrusted to her. And yet, within a liberal doctrine of society as a contractual agreement between equals, she should be an autonomous individual" (Kittay 1995, 11). The realities of the tasks of care-workers are difficult in "an economy" built on the presumption "that each will assume a share of the burdens and each will claim her own share of benefits" (12).

The salience of Kittay's observations is demonstrated by the high turnover of employees in animal shelters (Rogelberg et al. 2007; Lopina et al. 2012) and the evidence of their high rates of burnout and stress (Ferrari et al. 1999), as well as "compassion fatigue" (Rank et al. 2009), a "secondary-traumatic stress disorder" (Figley 1995, 7–8) that can lead to depression and suicide. One can see why a historical sociopolitical legacy endowing only (some) humans with rights, expectations of medical care, and a presumed capacity for love could lead to a political sphere in which veterinarian price schedules are unpredictable, euthanizing and no-kill shelters are overcrowded and under-funded, and dogs and cats become sources of stress, heartbreak, or aggravation for underpaid workers, rather than a relational and publicly embraced responsibility. If we take rather more seriously that, whether or not we each individually wish to have the responsibility of a privately owned dog or cat, some caregivers elsewhere are providing the positive care that love-capable dogs and cats require, then those of us who do not own dogs or cats in regions with these groaning social supports can at least attend to the requests for secondary support of the caregivers serving in these dependency relations.

However, the dependency critique enjoins us to take seriously the actual circumstances of the political and social situations currently in place. The responsibilities and the real expenses of providing positive care for dependents are not trivial for all the members of a region that benefits from others' caregiving to dogs and cats. Estimates suggest that dogs cost over a thousand dollars a year to house well; cats cost about a thousand a year but live longer, and these are not trivial amounts for all non-owners.[9] Nor could all easily afford the monetary support that caregivers in shelters and animal control agencies may need. I return to Harvey's concept of interactive power to clarify that our obligations depend upon the extent of our interactive powers. Members of communities with burdened shelter populations bear the responsibilities to provide political, financial, and social support to caregivers in the public and non-profit spheres when they can.

Those of us who can afford to take in companion animals, and do not, are already exercising our interactive power when we refuse to initiate dependency relations. Instead of seeing this as an individual and unencumbered consumer choice, we can further exercise our interactive power to navigate our already-existing relationships with sheltered animals and their caregivers by—depending on which of these capabilities we each have—adopting or fostering a dog or cat, centering the local shelter's concerns in community affairs, donating money, prioritizing shelter funding in political and non-profit gatherings, volunteering our time, donating wish-list items that are usually easy to find on shelter websites, and speaking and writing to "encourage all pet parents to spay and neuter their dogs and cats" (The Dodo 2015), to assist in breaking the breeding cycles that contribute to the stresses on animals and workers in shelters.

In early work on human oppression of other humans, Harvey suggests that those of us who can issue a "power-backed refusal to engage" possess "systematic and morally inappropriate control embedded in relations that are morally unacceptable" (1999, 53). I hope I have shown reasons for holding a parallel argument to be true of some of us who shove the responsibility for companion animals off on those we do not think of as providing labor we refused. Given that the direct monetary costs are too high for some, I should add that the reluctance of community members living in constrained circumstances may amount to a refusal to engage in dependency relations with companion animals, but theirs is not a power-backed refusal. On the contrary, the choice to refuse a potentially loving relationship with a companion in the absence of wealth is arguably a loss to those without more monetary options. The rest of us who live in communities and regions structured to offload the responsibility without compensating the caregivers have more work to do, however, to explore all of our relationships with love-capable animals and their caregivers. Living up to our obligations to provide indirect support to caregivers in dependency relations would achieve Harvey's "morally more secure basis for an ethic of companion animals."

Notes

1. Primary reasons cited by companionless Americans in a similar survey included veterinary and general expenses, travel, "no time," and the burdens of cleaning up (especially after a cat). See American Humane Association (2012, 19).

2. Indeed, I cannot find evidence of communities without any shelter population problems. In what follows, I will rely on the statements and statistics provided by those with expertise in shelter population problems. I enjoin readers to determine whether or not their community has imbalances in supply and demand with respect to dogs and cats, or at least to speculate whether roaming animals in their community are managed by someone.

3. Of course, as Jared Diamond (2002, 700) points out, there are many reasons for domestication: "Especially instructive are cases in which the same ancestral species became selected under domestication for alternative purposes, resulting in very different-appearing breeds or crops. For instance, dogs were variously selected to kill wolves, dig out rats, race, be eaten, or be cuddled in our laps. What naive

zoologist glancing at wolfhounds, terriers, greyhounds, Mexican hairless dogs and Chihuahuas would even guess them to belong to the same species?" My point is not that all owners of cats and dogs equally desire their pets to actually need affection and loyalty; rather, I am arguing that whether or not one currently desires an animal to present these moral demands, dogs and cats are dependents in part because they have been cultivated by humans to thrive when their capacities for love and loyalty are realized.

4. See, for example, Canadian Federation of Humane Societies (2012); for similar information in the UK, see RSPCA (2014). Information from the USA is available from many sources, and best summarized by the American Humane Association (2013) Pet Fact Sheet, which estimates that fifty million cats are feral or roaming community cats, and notes, "Recent regional and national trends suggest that the intake and euthanasia numbers are increasing in U.S. shelters, unlike dogs where intake and euthanasia numbers are decreasing and trends are more positive." The Humane Society (2013) observes another part of the problem; 30 percent of shelter dogs are reclaimed by their owners, but only 2 to 5 percent of shelter cats are reclaimed by owners; see their US shelter and adoption estimates for 2012–13, "based on information provided by the (former) National Council on Pet Population Study and Policy."

5. It is possible to imagine a change in the relationship, such that the companion animal is currently thriving and the human is not; a study of owners' reasons to relinquish pets in the UK indicated that almost 5 percent cited the owner's illness (Diesel, Brodbelt, and Pfeiffer 2010), and a broad report in the US noted the citation of caretakers' personal issues (Coe et al. 2014), which can include the grounds that they will not be able to care for them in the future due to a caretaker's illness or new financial stresses. Even then, I suggest the animal is still being surrendered for the animal's sake, as its future thriving is perceived to be endangered.

6. See International Companion Animal Management Coalition (2007, 2010) for helpful discussion of what factors must be considered in saying that a community does or does not have a dog or cat population requiring management.

7. See International Companion Animal Management Coalition (2007, 2010); in both publications, ICAM attentively notes that roaming animals can include owned as well as unowned animals; for brevity I occasionally use "roaming" to refer to the larger category of "roaming and unowned" cats and dogs.

8. For example, in Canada, 80 percent of employees in animal care, animal control, and pet grooming are women (Statistics Canada 2011). In the UK, the sector is estimated to be 87 percent women (National Careers Service 2015). In the US, women are estimated to be 70 percent of sector employees (Bureau of Labor Statistics 2015). Volunteers are not counted in these statistics, and tend to be reported as also likely to be women (Davis 2013, 9–10; Neumann 2010, 363).

9. See Perrin (2009, 51, table 6).

References

American Humane Association. 2012. "Keeping Pets (Dogs and Cats) in Homes: A Three-Phase Retention Study." http://www.americanhumane.org/aha-petsmart-retention-study-phase-1.pdf.

American Humane Association. 2013. "U.S. Pet (Dog and Cat) Population Fact Sheet." http://www.bradfordlicensing.com/documents/pets-fact-sheet.pdf.

Bureau of Labor Statistics. 2015. United States Department of Labor, *Occupational Outlook Handbook*, 2014–15 edition, Animal Care and Service Workers. Last updated December 17, 2015. http://www.bls.gov/ooh/personal-care-and-service/animal-care-and-service-workers.htm.

Canadian Federation of Humane Societies. 2012. "Cats in Canada: A Comprehensive Report on the Cat Overpopulation Crisis." http://cfhs.ca/files/cfhs_catreport_english_1.pdf.

Coe, Jason B., Ian Young, Kim Lambert, Laura Dysart, Lea Nogueira Borden, and Andrijana Rajić. 2014. "A Scoping Review of Published Research on the Relinquishment of Companion Animals." *Journal of Applied Animal Welfare Science* 17: 253–73.

Davis, Rebecca. 2013. "Understanding Volunteerism in an Animal Shelter Environment: Improving Volunteer Retention." College of Professional Studies Professional Projects. Paper 54. http://epublications.marquette.edu/cps_professional.

Diamond, Jared. 2002. "Evolution, Consequences and Future of Plant and Animal Domestication." *Nature* 418 (6898): 700–707. Last updated August 8, 2002. http://www.nature.com/nature/journal/v418/n6898/full/nature01019.html.

Diesel, Gillian, David Brodbelt, and Dirk U. Pfeiffer. 2010. "Characteristics of Relinquished Dogs and Their Owners at 14 Rehoming Centers in the United Kingdom." *Journal of Applied Animal Welfare Science* 13 (1): 15–30.

The Dodo. 2015. "How to Help." Last updated April 13, 2015. https://www.thedodo.com/how-to-help-animals-1089583102.html.

Ferrari, Joseph R., Michelle M. Loftus, and Julia Pesek. 1999. "Young and Older Caregivers at Homeless Animal and Human Shelters: Selfish and Selfless Motives in Helping Others." *Journal of Social Distress and the Homeless* 8 (1): 37–49.

Figley, Charles R. 1995. "Compassion Fatigue as Secondary Traumatic Stress Disorder: An Overview." In *Compassion Fatigue: Coping with Secondary Traumatic Stress Disorder in Those Who Treat the Traumatized*, edited by Charles R. Figley, 1–20. New York: Taylor and Francis.

Frank, Joshua. 2004. "An Interactive Model of Human and Companion Animal Dynamics: The Ecology and Economics of Dog Overpopulation and the Human Costs of Addressing the Problem." *Human Ecology* 32 (1): 107–30.

Hamilton, Francis E. 2010. "Leading and Organizing Social Change for Companion Animals." *Anthrozoös* 23 (3): 277–92.

Harvey, Jean. 1999. *Civilized Oppression*. Lanham, MD: Rowman & Littlefield.

Harvey, Jean. 2008 (reprinted in this volume). "Companion and Assistance Animals: Benefits, Welfare Safeguards, and Relationships." *International Journal of Applied Philosophy* 22 (2): 161–76.

Humane Society. 2013. "US Pet Ownership and Shelter Population Estimates." http://www.humanesociety.org/issues/pet_overpopulation/facts/pet_ownership_statistics.html.

International Companion Animal Management Coalition. 2007. "Humane Dog Population Management Guidance: International Companion Animal Management Coalition." http://www.icam-coalition.org/downloads/Humane_Dog_Population_Management_Guidance_English.pdf.

International Companion Animal Management Coalition. 2010. "Humane Cat Population Management Guidance: International Companion Animal Management Coalition." http://www.icam-coalition.org/downloads/ICAM-Humane%20cat%20population.pdf.

Kittay, Eva Feder. 1995. "Taking Dependency Seriously: The Family and Medical Leave Act Considered in Light of the Social Organization of Dependency Work and Gender Equality." *Hypatia* 10 (1): 8–29.

Kittay, Eva Feder. 1999. *Love's Labor: Essays on Women, Equality and Dependency*. London: Routledge.

Kittay, Eva Feder. 2002. "When Caring Is Just and Justice Is Caring: Justice and Mental Retardation." In *The Subject of Care: Feminist Perspectives on Dependency*, edited by Eva Feder Kittay and Ellen Feder, 257–76. Lanham, MD: Rowman & Littlefield.

Lopina, Erika C., Steven G. Rogelberg, and Brittany Howell. 2012. "Turnover in Dirty Work Occupations: A Focus on Pre-entry Individual Characteristics." *Journal of Occupational and Organizational Psychology* 85 (2): 396–406.

National Careers Service. 2015. "Job Profiles: Animal Care Worker." https://nationalcareersservice.direct.gov.uk/advice/planning/jobprofiles/Pages/animalcareworker.aspx.

Neumann, Sandra L. 2010. "Animal Welfare Volunteers: Who Are They and Why Do They Do What They Do?" *Anthrozoös* 23 (4): 351–64.

Norlock, Kathryn J. 2004. "The Case for Our Widespread Dependency." *Social Theory and Practice* 30 (2): 247–57.

Perrin, Terri. 2009. "The Business of Urban Animals Survey: The Facts and Statistics on Companion Animals in Canada." *The Canadian Veterinary Journal* 50 (1): 49. http://www.ncbi.nlm.nih.gov/pmc/articles/PMC2603652/.

Rank, Michael G., Tracy L. Zaparanick, and J. Eric Gentry. 2009. "Nonhuman-Animal Care Compassion Fatigue." *Best Practices in Mental Health* 5 (2): 40–61.

Rogelberg, Steven G., Charlie L. Reeve, Christiane Spitzmüller, Natalie DiGiacomo, Olga L. Clark, Lisa Teeter, Alan G. Walker, Paula G. Starling, and Nathan T. Carter. 2007. "Impact of Euthanasia Rates, Euthanasia Practices, and Human Resource

Practices on Employee Turnover in Animal Shelters." *Journal of the American Veterinary Medical Association* 230 (5): 713–19.

RSPCA. 2014. "Tackling the Cat Crisis: A Collaborative Approach to Neutering." http://www.rspca.org.uk/ImageLocator/LocateAsset?asset=document&assetId=1232734779317&mode=prd.

Smith, Leslie. 2013. "The No Kill Newsletter: Pet Overpopulation Is a Myth." Dogtime. com. http://dogtime.com/dog-health/general/17225-the-no-kill-newsletter-pet-overpopulation-is-a-myth.

Statistics Canada. 2011. Occupation—National Occupational Classification (NOC) 2011 (691), Class of Worker (5), Age Groups (13B) and Sex (3) for the Employed Labour Force Aged 15 Years and Over, in Private Households of Canada, Provinces, Territories, Census Metropolitan Areas and Census Agglomerations (table). 2011 National Household Survey. Statistics Canada Catalogue no. 99-012-X2011033. http://www12.statcan.gc.ca/nhs-enm/2011/dp-pd/dt-td/Index-eng.cfm, last modified 2014-03-04.

Winograd, Nathan J. 2007. *Redemption: The Myth of Pet Overpopulation and the No Kill Revolution in America*. Almaden Books.

7 ETHICAL BEHAVIOR IN ANIMALS

Bernard E. Rollin

To the memory of Jean Harvey, scholar, friend, and animal advocate

In the past fifty or so years, companion animals have become valued not only for pragmatic, economically quantifiable reasons but for deep emotional reasons as well. These animals are viewed as members of the family, as friends, as "givers and receivers of love" as one judge put it; and the bond initially based on pragmatic symbiosis has turned into a bond based on love (personal communication, a south Florida animal lawyer, 2005).

Humans need love, companionship, and emotional support, and they need to be needed. In today's world, a companion animal can be one's psychic and spiritual salvation. Divorce lawyers repeatedly tell me that custody of the dog can be a greater source of conflict in a divorce than is custody of the children! An animal is someone to hug, and hug you back; someone to play with, to laugh with, to exercise with, to walk with, to share beautiful days with, to cry with. For a child, the dog is a playmate, a friend, someone to talk to. The dog is a protector; one of the most unforgettable photos I have ever seen shows a child of six in an apartment answering the door at night while clutching the collar of a two-hundred-pound Great Dane, protected.

But a dog is more than that. In New York and other big, cold, tough cities, it is a social lubricant. One does not talk to strangers in cities, unless he or she—or preferably both of you—is walking a dog. Then the barriers crumble.

With this new role for animals in human life, where they serve as our friends, it is appropriate to rethink how we view their abilities. In particular, we must be prepared to attribute capacities to them, beyond those we have traditionally acknowledged. In particular, the concept of "friendship" requires some morally based and selfless reciprocity on the part of those engaged in friendship relationships. Doubtless many who live with animals and observe their behavior in a sympathetic manner are prepared to acknowledge the conceptual possibility of friendship between animals and humans. Most of these people would further probably be willing to talk about friendship between animals such as dogs, who live together and play with one another on a regular basis. Even most skeptics would doubtless acknowledge that such relationships—i.e., with humans or with other dogs—could be "hardwired" (to use current jargon) from an evolutionary perspective as an "evolutionary strategy" for maximizing survival and success.

On the other hand, there is no reason for dogs and other animals of different species to cooperate. What evolutionary advantage to the dog could come from befriending a turkey (as we will shortly illustrate)? And even more so, what advantage would accrue to the turkey? Furthermore, why would a dog who was abused, unappreciated, and unloved, rented out to construction sites for the first eight years of his life, ever bond with a human being late in his life (as we will again shortly illustrate)? Yet the answers to these questions were provided to me by the best canine teacher I ever had, who also showed me that animals, philosophers notwithstanding, can behave ethically.

Let us now illustrate with some autobiographical examples of what appear to be animal moral and friendship behavior, before returning to our philosophical discussion. It is worth noting that ordinary common sense, as illustrated in ordinary language, has no compunctions about attributing to animals the components necessary to call something "moral behavior" and "friendship."

A few years after my wife and I moved to Colorado from New York City, we realized a long-time dream of ours and purchased a rural property, ten miles from town, situated on the shore of a large public lake. Our nearest neighbor was half a mile away, and we were too often visited by groups of urban gang members looking for trouble and a remote place to party. At this point in my career, I was beginning to travel extensively in order to lecture, and I was uncomfortable leaving my wife alone in such a remote location. It dawned on me that a guard dog represented a reasonable solution to my concerns, and I began to look for one. One day, I answered an advertisement in a local newspaper, offering a guard dog to the first person who would pay the animal's kennel fee. My wife and I visited the kennel to meet the dog and the owner. It turned out that the man, an outlaw biker, had acquired the eight-year-old adult dog as compensation for some manual labor, and rented the dog out to junkyards and construction sites. It was evident that there was no bond between the dog and the owner—each feared the other. The dog was in the kennel because the owner's wife and two little daughters were in constant fear of the dog. The owner's wife took my wife aside and begged her not to purchase the dog, saying that he was a monster and could not be trusted. The owner would raise his hand in a threatening way and tell the dog to lie down. In turn, the dog would bare his teeth and snarl.

I thought the dog, Blitz, would be perfect for our purposes. My wife wisely had reservations, but was somewhat comforted by the fact that the dog would live outside in a doghouse, secured by a long, heavy chain. Over the next few months, we bonded with the dog by paying him a good deal of attention, though heartbreakingly he did not know how to play. He gradually learned to chase a ball. Eventually, his favorite game became picking up a hard rubber handball and offering it to my wife. When she would reach for it, he would bare his teeth, snarl and withdraw the ball as she jumped.

One summer day, as I was outside playing with the dog, I saw something walking up our quarter-mile driveway. I had no idea what it was, but it had a blue head and a red, pulsating snood. My wife shouted, "That is a turkey! Hold the dog!" I did so, and the turkey continued to advance. Shortly thereafter, one of my neighbors drove up the driveway looking for his turkey. He then took the bird home.

The next day, the turkey was back, this time lying curled up, pressing against the dog in the sun, with no apparent hostility between them. I called my neighbor, and he said, "The hell with it! Keep him, seeing as how he and the dog seem to be pals!" Over the ensuing weeks, the relationship intensified, with the dog allowing the turkey to share his house and then his meals. It soon became second nature around my house—the dog barking, the turkey gobbling in response. When the dog was asleep, the turkey would warn him of intruders by gobbling. One day, I noticed the turkey sleeping *on top of the dog*. They eventually became inseparable. I have photos of me mowing the lawn, the dog following in my steps, the turkey following the dog.

The relationship between these animals grew and deepened. About a year later the dog developed degenerative spinal disease, so that his back legs were paralyzed. He and the turkey remained inseparable. I used to come home four or five times a day to move and clean Blitz, as he could not walk. The turkey stayed with him. One evening when my wife and I came home from late-evening grocery shopping, we opened the car door and a giant Malamute jumped in. Our amusement became horror when we saw that his muzzle was bloody. We followed a trail of blood and feathers into the backyard, where the dog lay. There, between his forepaws, was the turkey, torn open but still alive. He had come to his friend for protection after being attacked, and the shepherd had kept the Malamute away by snarling and growling, as he did while we watched. Though the turkey eventually died of his injuries, I will never forget that paralyzed dog bravely protecting his companion, crossing species boundaries and training boundaries to protect what must be called his friend.

It is worthwhile reflecting upon this incident. In terms of hardwired behavior, the turkey should surely have been viewed by the dog as prey, as something to kill and eat. In terms of learned behavior, the turkey should have been viewed by the dog as an intruder to be repelled and attacked. In no way should the dog have tolerated sharing food and a sleeping place with the turkey. In no way should the turkey have sought protection from the dog. Impossible! Yet it happened and remains in my mind as one of the most touching incidents I have ever experienced involving animals. Despite insurmountable species and training barriers, these animals became and remained friends, united by mutual concern and a sense of mutual obligation. Though deemed impossible by science, it happened, I lived through it, and I can never look at animals again as I have been led to think by science-oriented colleagues. Those animals were friends, in every sense of the word! And never again can I entertain agnosticism regarding animals possessing moral qualities and capabilities.

In a number of books and articles, I have deplored what I call "the common sense of science," or Scientific Ideology, which affirms that science is value-free in general and ethics-free in particular, that science must be agnostic about the knowability of consciousness in other humans, and a fortiori in other animals, and that mechanistic explanations are the only epistemologically valid explanations. Yet such skepticism is categorically unacceptable to ordinary common sense, and is also unacceptable to first-rate scientists such as Charles Darwin (1872) or Jane Goodall (1986). Indeed, stories of cross-species animal communication and friendships, such as my story of the dog and the turkey, are rife among ordinary people and popular science programs. And thank God we can still find and accept such thinking, which enriches our world view and gives us a sense of wonder and mystery!

To be fair, at least some members of the scientific community have begun to acknowledge the possibility of studying animal consciousness and even animal moral behavior. As a paradigmatic example, primatologist Frans de Waal (e.g., de Waal 2009) has demonstrated the presence of empathy and altruism in chimpanzees by showing that chimps given a food reward would rather share it with another chimp than keep it for themselves. More surprisingly, perhaps, rats have also been shown to display empathy and altruism. In a series of experiments, researchers have shown that rats will let other rats out of cages, even if releasing the others means they must lose some of their food rewards (Bartal, Decety, and Mason 2011).

While the number of such experiments continues to grow, animal mentation is far from being a dominant trend in science, and animal moral behavior even less so. These issues are typically not covered in biology textbooks or courses, despite their obvious significance to how we view animals. (Ethologist Marc Bekoff is a stalwart example of a biologist who never doubted animal thought or moral action, having authored numerous books dealing with animal consciousness, e.g., Bekoff, 2007.) Despite its sporadic presence in science, seeing animals as capable of moral action is very well-ensconced in ordinary common sense, particularly in its view of companion animals. My appeal to common sense is very similar to that of Aristotle, Hume, Moore, Wittgenstein, Reid, and many others. Common sense is based in the non-reflective manner in which we experience the world. It provides a metaphysical structure for dealing with reality. We cannot prove that objects endure when we are not perceiving them, but we are driven to believe that by common sense. We cannot know that other people have thoughts, perceptions, and feelings analogous to our own, but we could not function if we were not led by human nature to think that way. Logical positivists, who were hyper-empiricists and based their construction of reality only upon what could be experienced, nonetheless could not sustain such a view when it became clear that the reports advanced by other scientists and other people could not be experienced by us directly. If they had held to such a view, science would have been rendered impossible because we do not share the experiences of others. Indeed, it is common sense that tells us that there *is* an external world and a past, and that all was not created a minute ago along with us with all our memories.

The philosopher Steve Sapontzis (1987) made an intriguing point about putative moral behavior of animals. Sapontzis argued that whether animals are genuine moral agents or not, that is, whether they act freely (whatever that means) and out of some sense of right and wrong, their behavior often models for us the highest virtues such as loyalty, self-sacrifice, and maternal and devotional love. Consider the killdeer, a bird that will feign a broken wing in order to lead predators away from her helpless babies in the nest. Even if we doubt that the bird acts out of a conscious awareness of the right thing to do, we can still view her actions as exemplary and praiseworthy. A genuinely cruel Renaissance experimenter, Realdo Columbo, noted this early in the history of research on animals, when he eviscerated a near-term bitch, pulled out her puppies, and hurt them before the mother's eyes. Despite being in extremis, he reports, the mother did everything she could to bite him and protect the pups (Monamy, 2000).

In this chapter, however, we will hold animal behavior to a higher standard, and bring forth as evidence for animal moral behavior not only behavior that is *compatible with* moral praiseworthiness in the sense delineated by Sapontzis, but behavior for which the best explanation seems to be something like an awareness of right and wrong and a sense of reciprocity between animals of different species, as is the case in the story of the dog and the turkey. The fact that we cannot understand what highly sophisticated moral cognition is like in a non-linguistic being does not militate against our recognizing what appear to be patent examples of such behavior. When we have no reason to believe that a given behavior is hardwired, for example, because it is rare among animals of the type we are studying, or, alternatively, when we have good evidence that the behavior in question has not been inculcated into the animal by rote training, it is plausible to suggest that such behavior is indicative of some moral sense.

In 1989, Jane Goodall told me a marvelous story of animal virtue.[1] There is an island off the coast of Africa that was purchased as a sanctuary for chimpanzees returned to the wild from circuses, zoos, and animal entertainment. One such animal was an old male, scarred and fractured from abusive trainers and handlers. The island is much favored by students of animal behavior as providing a chance to study and observe these animals under more or less natural conditions. On one occasion, a graduate student had docked his little boat and was walking around the island. Unfortunately, he blundered into a glade where a female chimpanzee was giving birth, surrounded by other highly protective females, who attacked the student and soon had him on the ground, biting and savaging him. The student would almost certainly have been killed had not the old male entered the glade and scared off the females, enabling the hapless investigator to return to his boat, and indeed, even escorting him there. As Dr. Goodall said to me, "If an animal who had experienced nothing but abuse from humans could nonetheless fight to save a human, how much more so are we obliged to protect them?"

I will restrict my account of animal morality to cases I have personally experienced, where the best explanation seems to be imputing something like a moral sense to the animal. Most of us do not interact with non-human primates, but we can find admirable, estimable, and morally exemplary behavior in animals with whom we are closer.

At the time my son was born, we had a cat, Mao, which my wife and I had acquired while living in New York City and which had moved to Colorado with us. The cat was devoted to us and to our dog, but she was very much a New Yorker in her behavior toward strangers—suspicious, surly, and often overtly hostile. We were genuinely concerned about how she would interact with the baby, having heard folktales and urban legends of old cats resenting new babies and smothering them, or scratching and biting. We watched them carefully and made sure the baby was never alone with the cat. One day, when the child was about a year old, we heard a loud meowing from the baby's room. Oddly, we heard two very different meows, which seemed to come from two different cats! We raced in and found the cat in the crib with the baby, curled up against him, holding a meowing conversation with the child. His first articulate word was in fact "meow"!

A few years earlier, a colleague of mine had acquired a foster child, developmentally disabled and afflicted with cerebral palsy. She had been through many agonizing surgeries aimed at helping her walk—all had failed, and she wore heavy, onerous, metal braces on her legs. While at my house, she spotted my horse and she grew animated, her eyes shining, her face smiling. Suddenly I had an idea—perhaps she would enjoy sitting on my horse, Raszam. She nodded with enthusiasm, and I put her on the saddle. Radiating happiness, she asked if she could ride. I hesitated. I had in fact gotten this horse for next to nothing from a womn who feared him, as he had refused to obey her and acted up every time she mounted. I had worked with him for a year and found him to be quite calm, needing only consistent direction and someone who would not be scared off when he acted up and danced. He was now quite reliable, and I had put many novice riders on him with no problems. But a disabled child?

Holding tightly to his halter, I nervously started to lead him forward. I need not have worried. My wife shouted, "My God, he's walking on eggs!" And it was true; he walked with care and deliberation we had never seen before or since. He followed me as a dog might—so much so that I was able to give the child the reins. Regardless of what she did, he followed me slowly and gingerly as her face radiated the joy of being mobile and high over everyone else. (Years later she remembered this vividly, even after she had been institutionalized.) In subsequent years, I learned from people who did riding lessons for persons with disabilities that many horses in fact picked up on the impairments and walked with exaggerated care.

Companion animals have become sources of friendship and company for the old and the lonely. Since the 1940s, following the pioneering work of Boris Levinson, dogs have served as vehicles for penetrating the frightful shell surrounding a disturbed child. They have been eyes for the blind and ears for the deaf. My friend, who was blinded in her fifties by a madman who put acid in store-bought eye drops, tells me unequivocally that she would have ended her life were it not for her guide dog. They have provided the comfort of touch to our most asocial and neglected persons. Many humane societies now bring dogs and cats to nursing homes, turning hopelessness into joy. In one extraordinary case, I watched a videotape of an old man who had sat stone-faced for twenty years in a nursing home, silent and expressionless. When a puppy was placed in his arms, he smiled for the first time in two decades, and spoke—"Pretty!" Through the efforts of the late Leo Bustad, veterinary dean at Washington State University, women inmates of a maximum-security prison in the Northwest began to train—and bond with—service dogs, and some were rehabilitated.

As my son grew, we witnessed many marvelous interactions with animals. As a toddler, we took him down to the lake directly adjacent to the property, to let him see it close up for the first time, accompanied by our female Doberman. As soon as we approached the water, she interposed her body between him and the lake, continuing to do so whichever way he tried to get around her, and despite generally being punctiliously obedient, would not desist even in the face of our commands.

I have always strongly believed that one should not keep a solitary horse, how-ever much space is provided to the animal. For this reason, shortly after acquir-ing my horse, one of my close friends, a veterinarian, began to keep her horses at our fourteen-acre property. She had three beautiful Morgan horses. April was her mare, and with April came Jubilee, April's colt, and Festus, April's brother. As is the case with all horses, the three had a rigid and well-established dominance hierarchy. Festus, a very large animal, was most dominant, with April next in line, and the colt was dead last. The hierarchy was diligently maintained by Festus, and was manifested in bite marks and kick marks primarily on Jubilee. Raszam even-tually assumed third-place after April. Once established, such hierarchies tend to endure.

One day, Raszam developed a condition of temporary blindness, colloquially known as "moon blindness." He could not see and could not locate his food or water. My wife and I watched in amazement as Jubilee, the lowest-ranking horse, began to nudge and guide Raszam to food and water, and, *mirabile dictu*, to pro-tect him from Festus. What was most extraordinary was how Jubilee would keep Festus away from Raszam, breaking the hierarchy, and would not eat his own food until Raszam had finished and no longer needed protection. This behavior occurred at every feeding for two weeks; Jubilee would even guide Raszam to the shelter that protected them from wind and rain and provided shade. Linda and I were deeply and profoundly touched by this deviant and selfless behav-ior, and she vowed that Jubilee would never want for a home. When Raszam's sight returned, things reverted to normal, and the old dominance hierarchy was restored, with Festus again moving to the top.

Jubilee's behavior during Raszam's moon blindness was a patent violation of normal horse behavior, allegedly "hardwired" into these animals. And obviously, his protective behavior toward Raszam was spontaneous and morally based, and not the result of any sort of training.

The anecdotes I have related regarding my dog, the turkey, and my horses are unlikely to appear in any scientific text of animal behavior. And virtually the entire history of philosophy denies to animals the ability to act morally. Yet, hav-ing experienced these events, it is *impossible* for me to deny the morality implicit in these behaviors. It is furthermore clear in my mind that we are dealing here with situations that qualify as friendship, not as "friendship," as those wishing to avoid the dreaded charge of "anthropomorphism" put it. I have in various venues argued that there is nothing wrong with soundly based anthropomorphism, and indeed that anthropomorphic locutions constitute the "best explanation" for a considerable number of such anecdotes.

Why would anyone believe that animals could not behave ethically and thus be incapable of what conceptually counts as friendship? The most pervasive reason would be a total denial of consciousness in animals of the sort posited by Descartes. For Descartes, animals were properly viewed as machines, as incapable of thought because they lacked language. It appears to me that such a claim is far too strong. If animals lack language and the syntactical manipulation of symbols that is entailed by language, it is clear that certain aspects of thought would be closed to them, while others would not be.

Human thought is irreducibly tied to language, which allows us ingress into modes of thought closed to animals. Humans can think in very abstract terms (e.g., mathematics and logic); in negative terms ("there are no dragons in the library"); in conditional terms ("if it does rain, we will hold graduation indoors"); in future terms ("I wish to retire in Iceland someday"); in universal terms ("all triangles have three sides"); in fictional terms (writing novels); and in counterfactual terms ("if Darwin had not discovered natural selection, someone else would have"). These are all made possible by being able to structure thought linguistically, which in turn allows linguistic syntax to transcend thought rooted in immediate experience. Clearly, animals cannot prove abstract mathematical theorems—but neither can most people!

I am not, of course, denying that animals can have short-term future expectations and projections. This is evidenced by the cat waiting outside the mouse hole, anticipating the mouse's appearance, and the dog waiting at the door for a walk. These limited future anticipations can be explained by associative learning. What I am denying is that animals can, for example, conceptualize accepting current major suffering in exchange for the possibility of an extended lifespan. This has major implications for the treatment of cancer in companion animals. There is no reason to believe that an animal can grasp the notion of extended life, let alone choose to trade current suffering for it. Thus animals appear to be unable to value life itself. But there are other modes of richer thinking that animals could be capable of.

What of moral behavior, and particularly the sort of reciprocity that friendship requires? According to Kant (1989), one of the most commonly invoked and taught philosophers of ethics, for behavior to be genuinely moral, it must be done freely out of awareness of and respect for a universal moral law. As we just saw, lacking syntactical ability, animals cannot formulate universal judgments. At best they can formulate restricted generalizations, such as "this fire is dangerous," rather than the more powerful claim "all fires are dangerous." or "if anything is a fire, it is dangerous." If animals are also incapable of forming the very abstract concepts of "moral law," "universal moral law," and "respect for the moral law," and furthermore incapable of rational freedom in choosing the moral law, it would of course be impossible for animals to exhibit moral behavior in Kant's terms (i.e., acting according to the categorical imperative, the rule whereby your action is to be conceived of as potentially a universal law).

Despite Kant's fairly esoteric technical account of morality, in his *Foundations of the Metaphysics of Morals* even he begins his discussion of ethics with an appeal to common sense (Kant, 1989). Such an approach is extremely sensible, because whatever metaphysical or scientific worldview one may hold, ethics is operative in the world given to us by ordinary experience and common sense. For example, even if I hold a solipsistic world view claiming that I can only be certain of the existence of my own mind, I must still deal with other people on the level of common sense. And, as Wittgenstein and other ordinary language philosophers demonstrated, the structure of a common sense world view is embodied in ordinary language, our way of coping with the world of our experience. Thus, it is reasonable to subject the examples of putatively moral behavior in animals to the test of ordinary experience and the common language we use to talk about such experience.

There is a clear sense of "free action" built into common sense and ordinary language. Consider Gilbert Ryle's (1949) famous example of the Smiling Bridegroom. If we are wondering whether a bridegroom is acting "freely," we should look at his facial expression. If he is smiling and acting comfortably, he is presumably acting freely. If, on the other hand, he is being prodded to move forward by a shotgun in the hands of his future father-in-law, he is probably not acting out of free choice. In other words, in ordinary talk "freedom" is opposed to overt compulsion, not to metaphysical determinism. In fact, such an insight is the basis for holding people responsible for their actions in our legal system! Courts have been extremely unwilling to accept metaphysical deterministic accounts (such as DNA or genetics) as mitigating responsibility. As Kant himself pointed out in his discussion of free will, we cannot *know* if free will is real, but *must act as if* it is.

What do common sense and ordinary language presuppose about animal action and freedom? Clearly, much of animal action is "hardwired," as when predators immediately give chase to fleeing animals who are prey. Some such behavior is inborn, as is submissive behavior. But a great deal of animal behavior is voluntary, in the same sense that we use the word "voluntary" regarding humans. When the dog picks up a ball, as opposed to a stuffed animal, and offers it to a human, that is plainly voluntary. When a large dog plays gently with a small kitten, that is also voluntary, and indeed overrides inborn predatory programs. When a small child accidentally sticks a finger in the dog's eye and the dog does not attack, that too is voluntary, especially if the dog's forbearance is not the result of deliberate training. Without a repertoire of actions that are chosen to fit a given set of circumstances, animals could not survive, and it is appropriate to call what is chosen "voluntary," and what common sense would call "free" as opposed to hardwired or learned through repetitive conditioning.

In some cases, watching dogs choose is hilarious. I have seen videos of dogs left in a room with a tray of appetizers and a hidden camera. One can see the dog deliberating, watching for the owner, making a decision, and snatching the food. If one puts a microphone in the room, watches the animal, and yells "No!" when the dog moves toward the food, the dog will slink back in a "guilty" manner.

Presumably for Kant, as for Descartes, animals are definitely not free, because they lack linguistic abilities and therefore are not rational. This, of course, is never proven. In the commonsense ordinary notion of freedom, labeling some animal behavior free or voluntary and some not is non-problematic, no more problematic than so labeling human behavior! (In both cases, of course, such judgments are not infallible.)

It is clear that animal behavior does not follow Kant's requirement that moral actions be done "out of respect for the moral law alone." It is also quite clear that for Kant, if one derives pleasure from a moral action, for example, enjoying social status for charitable donations, the action is probably not moral, for one might perform it simply for the community status or pleasure in giving to charity, and not solely out of respect for the moral law (Kant 1989). Motives other than respect for the law make putatively moral actions suspect. In fact, Kant remarks that there may never have been a purely moral action in all of human history, because there could well be other motivations than respect for the law.

Of course, such a position completely undercuts Kant's position as in any way a plausible account of ethics. If ethical action is an inherently unattainable goal, what is the value of Kant's account? Perhaps we ought to allow common sense to direct us to other features constitutive of moral action. If so, it is hard to see how one could deny the potential morality of animal behavior if such behaviors have other positive sources, such as affection for the object of such behavior. We allow, in ordinary language, for calling actions of people not done out of respect for the moral law "moral"; why have stronger criteria for animals?

One of the features of our understanding of moral actions in people is the element of selflessness, kindness, or generosity that typifies such actions. If I offer to carry your groceries because I know that you tip very well in such circumstances, we would not call that moral, but rather self-interested, behavior. On the other hand, when Jubilee bucked the established equine dominance hierarchy to help Raszam, that seems to be a paradigmatic case of selflessness, with Jubilee risking a beating to help the blind horse and expecting nothing in return. Similarly, in the case of Blitz sharing his food and lodging with the turkey, there was nothing materially advantageous to the dog, except perhaps solidification of his friendship with the bird. Clearly this dimension exists with animals. In fact, part of the dog's friendship with and moral behavior toward the turkey was Blitz's sacrificing an easy meal for the sake of sharing with what we must call his "friend."

Being in a moral relationship with another being also entails an element of reciprocity. Even as the turkey benefits in terms of warmth by lying with the dog, it is reasonable for the dog to expect the turkey to allow the dog to huddle with him. Even more dramatically, given the turkey's expectation that the dog would protect him, one could reasonably expect that the turkey would, as far as possible, protect the dog. And indeed, when a person or animal crossed into the animals' territory, and the dog would display threatening and attack behavior, so too did the turkey, essentially putting himself at risk.

Numerous other aspects of what we call "moral behavior" in humans are illustrated in the anecdotes we have related. For example, many of the stories indicate what must be called "kindness" manifested in the animals' behavior. Jubilee taking care of Raszam, while risking being abused and losing a meal, would truly be called both selfless and kind.

Many thinkers have described morality in terms of a social contract. Carl Cohen (1986), for example, in his unequivocal defense of biomedical research on animals, has made this claim. In this article, Cohen accuses me of ignoring the fact that morality depends on a social contract between parties wherein it operates, and that animals do not enter into social contracts. Both of these claims are false. I specifically addressed this point in 1980 in my first book on animal ethics (Rollin 1980). The key point in a response to Cohen is that we do indeed have many social contracts with animals.

The housedog that suffers pummeling and abuse from a heedless child, yet does not even growl or snap at the child, is, through its actions, respecting the contract it has with humans. This is similarly the case with horses who exaggeratedly make heroic efforts to avoid stepping on a fallen rider. It is again the case with hugely powerful animals, such as elephants, who do the bidding of humans. (If the reader wishes to conceptualize what the world would be like if this were not the case, he or she should read Arthur Machen's powerful book, *The Terror* [1917], which depicts what occurs when animals stop participating in the social contract.) Indeed, animals who are unwilling to participate in the social contract could do great damage by opting out.

Thus far, I have attempted to show that certain animal behaviors are very similar to what we call moral behaviors in humans. To be sure, we have very little idea of the mechanisms underlying such moral behavior in animals, but we have very little idea of these mechanisms in humans! In a metaphysical sense, we have little understanding of "free will" in humans—for example, we have no clue how we can be free in a deterministic universe. But if we focus on the voluntary, uncoerced sense of freedom, we see free will equally in animals! Indeed, many if not most of the features of moral action we find in humans are illustrated plainly in the anecdotes presented here.

In the case of humans, the possession of language helps us understand how we can assert universal judgments of morality. In animals, we have seen that there is no way to apprehend or assert universal judgments. But we do know that animals can make limited *generalizations*—"fire is dangerous" if not "all fires are dangerous;" "edible" versus "not to be eaten." We also know that this ability extends to realms we call moral. Thus animals may have an inborn sense of other animals who can be seen as "kinfolk," that is, other animals they trust and care for (for example, children, parents, and siblings). It seems explanatory to suggest that, for unclear reasons, this sense can on occasion be extended to others, as my dog did with the turkey, and Jubilee with Raszam. This is not to suggest that such ethical extension is hardwired or inborn. Precisely why it occurs is fertile ground for further study.

I can, however, offer no explanation of why such behavior occurs only sporadically. Suffice it to say that in the cases where such behavior does occur, it seems reasonable to assimilate it to moral behavior in humans, which is also by no means universal. We must also recall that our lives with animals are replete with such instances, although they are generally less dramatic than the stories I have told. Every time a dog tolerates abuse from a child, or refrains from stealing a child's food, we are witnessing a ubiquitous, but unnoticed, example of moral behavior in our lives. When we recognize this, both we and the animals are better off for the realization, and our view of the world is greatly enriched.

Finally, it is worth remarking that if animals are capable of moral behavior, it is plausible to suggest that they are also capable of immoral behavior. In ordinary language, we speak routinely of "bad dogs." An animal trained to coexist with other companion animals who gratuitously attacks the other animals after learning through training the unacceptability of such behavior, can be said to be acting "immorally," just as we say of a child who acts similarly toward peers or siblings.

Note

1. Goodall, Jane, personal communication to author, 1989.

References

Bartal, Inbal Ben Ami, Jean Decety, and Peggy Mason. 2011. "Empathy and Pro-Social Behavior in Rats." *Science* 334 (6061): 1427–30.

Bekoff, Marc. 2007. *The Emotional Lives of Animals: A Leading Scientist Explores Animal Joy, Sorrow, and Empathy—And Why They Matter*. Novato, CA: New World Library.

Cohen, Carl. 1986. "The Case for the Use of Animals in Biomedical Research." *The New England Journal of Medicine* 314: 865–69.

Darwin, Charles. 1872. *The Expression of the Emotions in Man and Animals* (reprinted). New York: Greenwood Press, 1969.

De Waal, Frans. 2009. *The Age of Empathy: Nature's Lessons for a Kinder Society.* New York: Rivers Press.

Goodall, Jane. 1986. *The Chimpanzees of Gombe: Patterns of Behavior.* Boston: Harvard University Press.

Kant, Immanuel. 1989. *Foundation of the Metaphysics of Morals.* Translated by Lewis White Beck. Library of Liberal Arts. New York: Liberal Arts Press.

Machen, Arthur. 1917. *The Terror.* New York: Robert M. McBride Co.

Monamy, Vaughn. 2000. *Animal Experimentation: A Guide to the Issues.* Cambridge: Cambridge University Press.

Rollin, Bernard E. 1980. *Animal Rights and Human Morality*, Part One. Buffalo, NY: Prometheus Books.

Ryle, Gilbert. 1949. *The Concept of Mind.* London: Hutchinson's University Library.

Sapontzis, S. F. 1987. *Morals, Reason, and Animals.* Philadelphia: Temple University Press.

LIVING WITH COMPANION ANIMALS

136 | LIVING WITH THE COMPANION ANIMALS

OUR WHIMSY, THEIR WELFARE

ON THE ETHICS OF PEDIGREE-BREEDING

John Rossi

Pedigree-breeding (used interchangeably here with "pure-breeding") is the practice of selectively breeding animals so as to produce, and then maintain, distinct species sub-types, commonly known as breeds. These breeds are usually defined by a combination of distinct physical appearance, ancestry, and (sometimes) behavior. Pedigree-breeds of multiple species have been developed, including companion animals and livestock. Well-known examples of dog breeds include the English Bulldog, Golden Retriever, Beagle, and German Shepherd; well-known cat breeds include the Persian, Siamese, and Maine Coon. Pedigree-breeds were (and are) created and maintained through inbreeding within a closed subpopulation of animals. When an animal shows desirable physical or behavioral characteristics, it is bred with another animal that shows the same characteristics and/or that is expected to produce offspring showing these characteristics. This process of breeding related individuals continues as breed characteristics are "fixed" and as the breed population expands, and continued propagation of the breed over time then occurs within a "closed" subpopulation of the species, that is, a population that (generally) does not introduce new genetic variation from individuals outside of it (Rooney and Sargan 2009; Gough and Thomas 2004).

Pedigree-breeding can be contrasted with outbreeding (used synonymously in this chapter with "mixed-breeding"), in which the animals that are mated to each other are unrelated or very distantly related. Though pedigree-breeding is a form of selective breeding, it is not synonymous with selective breeding: animals may be bred with any number of selection goals, such as improved health, and such selection need not entail the creation or continuation of pedigree-breeds.

Thus my target in this chapter is pedigree-breeding specifically and not selective breeding more generally.

Historically, humans developed pedigree-breeds of dogs for two main purposes: work and entertainment. Work-related purposes include hunting, guarding, and herding; entertainment-related purposes include aesthetics and fighting (Farrell et al. 2015). Pedigree-breed cats seem to have been uniformly developed for aesthetic purposes. Today, most purebred companion animals are not used for work purposes, and the decision to specifically seek out a particular breed (as opposed to a mixed-breed), while sometimes based on temperament, often appears to be based partly or wholly on aesthetic enjoyment, a term that I understand to include both sentimental attachment to a particular breed and the hobby of breed showing. There are presently hundreds of dog and cat breeds in existence (Farrell et al. 2015; Gough and Thomas 2004). It is not known how many of the eighty-three million dogs and ninety-five million cats kept as companions in the US are pedigree-breeds, but the Humane Society of the United States (HSUS) estimates that 25 percent of dogs in shelters are pedigree-breeds (HSUS 2014). If this statistic is taken to reflect overall companion-animal composition, then there are approximately twenty million pedigree dogs in the US.

It has long been known in veterinary medicine that pedigree-breeds of dogs and cats suffer from "breed-associated diseases," which are diseases seen exclusively in one or more breeds, or for which pure-breeds are at an elevated relative risk as compared to mixed-breeds. Veterinary textbooks often devote substantial space to such breed-associated diseases, with some textbooks being entirely devoted to them (e.g., Gough and Thomas 2004), and the diagnosis and treatment of such diseases are a routine part of veterinary medical practice. Concern about the adverse welfare effects of breed-associated diseases has been building for some time, with a sharp uptick in recent years due to increased media attention to this problem. Despite this, the ethical defensibility of pure-breeding seems to be assumed by most parties to the debate. Here I offer an argument against the pedigree-breeding of companion animals: not only has pedigree-breeding caused harm to companion animals, but in addition it seems unavoidable that it should do so as compared to "mixed-breeding" or "outbreeding" (when properly undertaken). Further, the harm caused by pedigree-breeding cannot be defended on any reasonable view of animals' moral standing, since the human interest in pedigree-breeding is morally insignificant. While most of my discussion focuses on dogs, the arguments elaborated below apply to pedigree-breed cats and to other species of companion animals as well. There appear to be no philosophical defenses of pedigree-breeding in the literature, so in considering this issue I have tried to anticipate and respond to what I think the major arguments might be.

Breed-Associated Disease: A Very Short Overview

The first step in my argument will be traversed the most quickly: my claim is that pedigree-breeding produces comparatively more disease than outbreeding. As a historical claim this seems almost indisputably true, and I strongly suspect that it is true of necessity.

Pedigree-breeding causes disease in two ways. First, the various physical attributes for which we have selectively bred dogs and cats—large heads; excessive skin folds; short, stubby legs; corkscrew tails; short, "smushed" faces; distinctive coats; and so on—can directly cause disease or predispose the animal to disease. One recent review classifies these as "conformation-related" diseases and identifies a total of eighty-eight distinct conformational attributes in the top fifty UK breeds of dog causing or predisposing animals to disease (Asher et al. 2009). An example of a conformation-related disease in dogs is Brachycephalic Airway Obstruction Syndrome (BAOS), seen in brachycephalic ("short-faced") breeds such as English Bulldogs and Pugs. In BAOS, a constellation of common anatomic features in the animal's upper airway makes it difficult for them to breathe comfortably; these features are a direct result of selection for these breeds' characteristic facial appearance. At the milder end, BAOS can result in uncomfortable breathing and exercise intolerance. At the more severe end, BAOS can result in respiratory distress, loss of consciousness, and occasionally even death, either spontaneously or because of euthanasia (Gough and Thomas 2004; Lodato and Hedlund 2012).

The second mechanism underlying breed-associated disease arises from the fact that pedigree-breeds are created and maintained through inbreeding in a closed population. It is well known that inbreeding increases the chance of an individual's developing recessive genetic diseases, and this has been seen with pedigree-breeds. A recent review identified over three hundred breed-associated inherited diseases in dogs that were not conformation-linked, that is, that were due to the tendency of pedigree-breeding to cluster disease-causing genes. These diseases include heart defects, skin problems, cancers, neurologic diseases, and many others. By definition, these are diseases for which pedigree-breeds are at an increased risk as compared to mixed-breeds (Summers et al. 2010; see also Gough and Thomas 2004).

This is not the place to discuss in detail the welfare impacts of breed-associated diseases or their risk assessment, but two important points will be made. First, though the severity of breed-associated diseases is variable, they often impose a substantial welfare burden on affected animals, in terms of discomfort, pain, impaired functioning, and early death (Rooney and Sargan 2009; Gough and Thomas 2004). Second, many breed-associated diseases occur commonly. In some cases we can base this judgment on prevalent data, but since these data are often unavailable, in other cases the judgment is based on the clinical experience of many veterinarians, including my own when I was in practice. We also know that relative risks for breed-associated diseases are often significantly elevated in pure-breeds compared to mixed-breeds. Further, when mating two purebred animals, knowledge of the parents' ancestry and genetics, as well as the anticipated anatomy of the offspring, will sometimes give us more specific reason to think that breed-associated disease will occur. These points are worth emphasizing because some stakeholders have called for more research on the incidence and prevalence of these diseases before action is taken. According to the argument presented in the next section, additional research would be helpful but not necessary.

Two further notes are in order. First, the availability of medical and surgical treatments for breed-associated diseases does not compensate for or nullify the added harm associated with pedigree-breeding. Treatments are not always available, and are often of variable efficacy when available. Treatments (e.g., surgery) often add morbidity to an animal's condition, and even if a condition is corrected, it does not make up for the welfare cost imposed by the disease before it was treated. And, perhaps most importantly, treatment is often not pursued.

Second, some commentators (e.g., Jeppsson 2014) have argued that pedigree-breeding is desirable on health grounds as compared to outbreeding because pedigree-breeds sometimes receive the added benefits of additional health screens and/or selection against health problems. But this argument is misleading, because it conflates the question of whether pedigree-breeding increases disease with the question of what quality medical care we choose to provide to pedigree- versus mixed-breed dogs. There is no reason why we cannot or should not provide outbred dogs with the same quality of medical care that is sometimes provided to pedigree-breed animals.

An Argument against Pedigree-Breeding

Pedigree-breeding causes significant and avoidable harms to animals. These harms are avoidable because they would not occur, or would occur to a lesser extent, in a general outbreeding scheme. This avoidable harm cannot be justified on any reasonable assumptions about animals' moral standing.

My (unargued) starting point is that essentially all moral theories recognize and grant significant weight to a principle of non-maleficence as concerns other humans, which holds that we ought not to harm others and should keep unavoidable harms to a minimum. Allowable harms tend to be very limited, including, for example, harms committed in defense of one's life and safety or small harms imposed by the state in the service of an important public health goal (e.g., required vaccination)—but not much else. Notably, perpetrating harms upon others for one's own personal benefit (e.g., financial benefit, sexual gratification, entertainment) is generally considered unjustified, especially when the harms in question are not trivial. Even committed utilitarians—whose preferred theory might seem to sanction various harms to individuals if such harms maximize population welfare—often expend much argumentative effort in attempting to preserve the stringency of non-maleficence, for example, by appealing to indirect effects or by adopting rule-utilitarianism.

Second, powerful arguments have been provided for granting many sentient animals' interests equal moral consideration (EC) to humans' interests (e.g., DeGrazia 2002), and certainly most mammals, which would include many species of companion animals. This means not only that these animals' interests should be given equal moral weight to comparable human interests, but also more generally that it is wrong to morally "discount" animals' interests. Such arguments are motivated by the claims that sentient animals have interests and thus moral standing; that species per se is a morally arbitrary characteristic according to which to assign moral standing; and that other possible criteria for morally discounting animals' interests, such as their lesser intelligence, inability to use language, inability to form contracts, or inability to robustly participate in the "moral community" (however this is defined) all fail for one reason or another. Usually these arguments fail because they also have the consequence that certain members of the human community do not deserve equal moral consideration of their interests, a conclusion that most persons find counterintuitive and unacceptable. In addition, arguments against EC run into other difficulties. For example, our special obligations to other persons with whom we have close relationships are invariably positive in nature; the lack of a close relationship does not relax the stringency of our negative obligations in human-human morality, so it is unclear why it should do so in human-animal morality, as the "moral community" argument often holds (see DeGrazia 2002). If we accept EC, as I think we should, then we can only justifiably harm animals in the very limited kinds of scenarios in which similar harm would be justifiable to other humans. Pedigree-breeding does not even come close to meeting the test of stringency we impose on allowable harms to other humans: it causes harm that is nontrivial and easily avoidable, and does not serve a vital human interest (e.g., individual self-defense or safeguarding the welfare of the entire community). Thus pedigree-breeding is not justifiable on an EC view.

It might be observed that not all pedigree-breed animals suffer from breed-associated disease, and while this is true, it does not affect the moral conclusion. What matters from the standpoint of a person creating more purebred animals is *ex ante* risk, not *ex post* harm. As with other risky decisions (e.g., drunk driving), a lucky good outcome does not negate the fact that the decision, when it is undertaken, is riskier than another decision that one could have made (driving only when sober, mating mixed-breeds instead of pedigree-breeds). Further, the appropriate frame of ethical analysis is not merely (and probably not even primarily) with individual breeding decisions; it is with the avoidable harm inherent in perpetuating a breed as a whole. Two pedigree-breed animals can only be mated if the breed as a whole is maintained, and as long as some members of the breed are affected by breed-associated disease, then pedigree-breeding causes avoidable harm. Furthermore, the preceding discussion shows that the EC-based conclusion against pedigree-breeding does not depend on the harms of breed-associated disease's being frequent or severe (though they often are); the strength of our obligation of non-maleficence to companion animals is sufficiently high that harm in general will not be permissible unless for very important reasons.

I might rest my case with the argument from EC, but it will be useful to show that pedigree-breeding is not justifiable on any plausible version of an unequal moral consideration (UC) view, either—especially since many readers might be inclined toward such a view. According to UC views, animals' interests deserve some moral consideration, but less so than humans' interests. UC views might take a number of forms, but the most plausible form is the sliding-scale view, according to which a being's level of moral considerability is a function of its mental complexity. At the top of the hierarchy stand humans, who deserve full moral consideration. As one moves "down" the phylogenetic scale, animals of progressively lesser cognitive, affective, and social complexity are granted progressively lesser moral consideration (DeGrazia 2002). According to the sliding-scale view, the permissibility of harming an animal will depend on three things: (1) the degree of harm involved, (2) the animal's place on the sliding scale, which will determine how much moral weight we give to this harm, and (3) the significance of the human interest that is being advanced by harming the animal. It has already been argued that the harms of breed-associated diseases are often significant and that they occur frequently. As concerns the issue of moral standing, common companion animals, such as dogs and cats, possess relatively complex mental lives—not as complex as those of some other nonhuman animals, including numerous primate species and dolphins, but complex enough that we can reasonably expect that our companion animals will sit fairly high on the scale of moral considerability. This means that strong reasons will have to be provided to justify harming them.

Pedigree-breeding does not seem to serve a significant human interest. In fact, in the vast majority of cases it seems to serve a trivial interest, namely an aesthetic interest, and not of the deep kind that we might associate with art, but rather of the more shallow kind that we associate with "fancying" something, which can reasonably be described as entertainment. This conclusion seems rather obvious to me, but in conversation with some veterinarians and breeders I have encountered substantial resistance to the preceding claim. It is argued that persons who take an interest in pedigree-breeds sometimes devote significant time, money, and energy to breeding, showing, and general "breed fancying." They may even base their careers and personal identities on it and form deep attachments to a particular breed. Are *their* interests in pedigree-breeding morally significant? I would answer "no" for several reasons.

First, we should resist the view that something qualifies as a significant human interest simply in virtue of being proclaimed as such. This view implausibly collapses all critical distance between what we value and what we ought to value. Even more implausibly, it also prevents us from making judgments of the relative importance of interests, but we do this sort of thing all of the time: we do not view things like having adequate food, shelter, and medical care, or an ability to exert some measure of control over our lives, as of similar importance to getting a new TV or even accepting a job with a slightly shorter commute.

Second, while human interests in entertainment and the development of hobbies are of some moral significance at the *categorical* level—after all, who would want to live a life devoid of leisure pursuits?—there are many alternative ways to satisfy these interests apart from pedigree-breeding. Since taking animals seriously means that we should look for ways to avoid conflicts between our interests and theirs (see Zamir 2007), we should look for ways other than pedigree-breeding to satisfy our interests in entertainment and hobby-building. Some persons might press by asserting a significant interest in pedigree-breeding *specifically*, arguing that it provides something irreplaceable to their lives, which would be impoverished without it. But it just seems very unlikely, to this author at least, that such persons would not be able to find equivalent satisfaction in other activities. Some of the perceived significance in the human interest in pedigree-breeding likely stems from the meaningful relationships that persons form with individual animals of a specific breed, but such meaningful human-animal relationships can and do often exist with mixed-breed animals as well.

This perceived significance might also arise from the way in which some people build a personal identity around one or more of such breeds. Once a specific personal identity is formed, it might seem daunting to contemplate giving up something crucial to that identity, as though a part of oneself would be lost. However, reflection on the complexity and variety of human interests and hobbies suggests to me that a significant part of the value of many hobbies lies in building a person's identity, apart from the value of the specific hobby/interest in question. Many (though certainly not all) hobby-based interests do not in themselves appear to have much intrinsic moral significance. They are enjoyed and serve the larger human need for entertainment, purposive activity, and the formation of a personal identity. However, many persons are interested in many things, with the intensity of interests waxing and waning over time. An identity built around one interest may instead be built around another. What is more, hobbies often have instrumental value, for example, because they allow people to find support in a community, but again such value can be served by any number of hobbies.

Further, even if we accept the claim that some persons' lives would genuinely be impoverished by the elimination of pedigree-breeds, this only holds true of persons who have previously built a personal identity around such breeds. Were we to do away with pedigree-breeding, future persons would never develop such an interest in the first place and would develop other interests instead. Nothing of independent moral value would appear to be lost in this scenario (if anything, it would be morally preferable on account of the harm that pedigree-breeding causes and its implicit commodification of animals); rather, all that would be lost would be *someone's particular interest in pedigree-breeding*. Thus, any loss to human interests entailed by the elimination of pedigree-breeding would be transient.

Finally, it might be argued that the moral significance of human interests is a function not just of their strength for the persons who hold them, but also of the *kind* of interests that they are. For example, we might discourage a person's development of certain interests, such as an interest in psychologically manipulating others or engaging in an environmentally destructive hobby, not just on the grounds that these activities result in harm to others, but also on the grounds that our own moral development is hindered by the adoption of such interests, *exactly because* of their consequences for others. Said another way, *we should not be the kind of people* who develop such interests. While UC views do justify comparatively more harms to animals than EC views, the purpose for which we are harming animals still matters very much to the justification of such harm. Harms perpetrated to advance an important social goal, such as curing a disease, might sometimes be justified on a UC view, but pedigree-breeding does not serve an interest this important. Further, in the case of research, someone who harms an animal does so only as a means to the larger end of a social benefit that is otherwise unobtainable (or so at least the scientists conducting the research tend to assume), but in the case of pedigree-breeding, the harms are a function of the ends themselves. These differences between the harms of research and those of pedigree-breeding help to show why an interest in the latter might be negatively evaluated from the standpoint of moral virtue, even on a UC view allowing some harms to animals.

The preceding discussion has focused on pedigree-breeding as an aesthetic interest; what of pedigree-breeding for other purposes, such as herding, hunting, or other sport? The first thing to say regarding these other uses of purebred animals is that they are far less common than the keeping of such animals for aesthetic purposes. Second, some such uses—particularly sporting—can be subsumed under entertainment and so require no further argument. Activities such as hunting and herding might at one time have served a significant human interest, but since humans no longer need to rely on either hunting or animal agriculture more generally (even though many choose to utilize the products of the latter), this significance can no longer be claimed. At most, this need might justify the keeping of some herding animals in non-industrialized pastoral societies relying on animal agriculture, but for all intents and purposes it would still result in the abandonment of herding breeds.

In sum, we have a number of reasons to conclude that the human interest in pedigree-breeding is not morally significant, which means that pedigree-breeding is not justifiable on a plausible UC view.

Is Pedigree-Breeding Inherently Risky?

Might pedigree-breeding be reformed to the point where it does not impose additional harm as compared to outbreeding? Probably not. Breeding for less extreme physical appearances can mitigate conformation-related diseases, but as long as we are breeding for physical conformation, it seems likely that *some* conformational disease will continue to occur, especially since it cannot always be anticipated how physical conformation will produce disease. As concerns genetic disorders, breeding within a closed subpopulation will always increase the risk of disease. Occasional outcrossing and backcrossing can reintroduce some genetic variability into a breed, and limiting the number of times that a sire can be bred (in order to reduce so-called "popular sire syndrome") has also been recommended and would be helpful. However, the norm of pedigree-breeding in closed populations will still reduce genetic diversity as compared to the norm of outbreeding.[1] Similarly, the aggressive use of genetic tests for pre-mating screens could help reduce the transmission of disease-causing genes, but such tests are only available for a small number of genetic conditions, and this is unlikely to change soon. Further, the maintenance of pedigree-breeds entails that when new disease-causing alleles emerge through mutation, they will be more likely to produce disease in the animal population.

There are also pragmatic factors to consider. If the preservation of a breed is deemed important, then tradeoffs will likely have to be made between removing animals from the breeding pool on account of their carriage of disease-causing genes, and not further reducing already-small effective breeding population sizes (Bateson 2010). Similarly, the availability of various screening tests and breeding strategies to reduce disease does not mean that they will be routinely and aggressively used. Any discussion of the ethics of pedigree-breeding needs to acknowledge not only what is possible, but also what is likely. If a nontrivial percentage of breeders will be tempted to "cut corners" (e.g., for economic reasons), then the question of whether breed-associated disease can in principle be eliminated will be moot. Since pedigree-breeding itself seems to represent a kind of commodification of animals, and since animals are classified as property and are used in economic transactions (i.e., they are bought and sold), such corner-cutting seems likely.

To avoid misunderstanding, the preceding discussion is not meant to suggest that mixed-breed animals never develop disease (they do) or that mixed-breeding is always ethically unproblematic (it is not). For example, close inbreeding of mixed-breed dogs (as might occur, for example, in "backyard breeding") will tend to produce the same kinds of genetic disease that we see with pedigree-breed animals, and this is ethically problematic. But the difference between the two is that mixed-breeding can be maintained without inbreeding while pedigree-breeding cannot. Similarly, mixed-breeding can be maintained without selecting for the kinds of conformational attributes that produce disease, while pedigree-breeds would cease to exist if not for their unique appearance.

The Objection from Non-Identity

One objection to my argument against pedigree-breeding is the "non-identity problem" (Palmer 2012). According to this objection, the purebred animals that we create are not harmed, *even if* they experience more disease than outbred animals. This is because the definition of "harm" is to make an individual worse off than they otherwise would have been, and when we bring individuals into existence (as we do when breeding pedigree dogs and cats), they have no prior state of welfare with which to compare their present existence. In other words, these animals cannot be worse off than they previously were, because they previously did not exist.

The non-identity problem has a significant record of discussion in moral philosophy as concerns reproductive ethics and our obligations to future generations; it has also been raised as a potential rebuttal to welfare-based criticisms of pedigree-breeding (Palmer 2012). I will not respond in detail to this problem here, partly because an adequate response would be lengthy, and partly because other authors have advanced potential solutions to this problem. I will, however, briefly sketch my favored response.

First, I embrace the claim that we do not harm or wrong individuals by failing to bring them into existence, but we can both harm and wrong individuals by bringing them into existence under certain conditions. There are numerous ways to make sense of this claim, one of which is that nonexistent individuals have no interests and thus cannot be harmed, benefited or wronged, while the individuals that we bring into existence do have interests and therefore moral standing. Thus the way in which our reproductive decisions affect the interests of the animals we create has moral salience and demands moral justification, while our failure to bring individuals into existence does not affect their (nonexistent) interests and thus does not require moral justification.

Second, I hold that pedigree-breeding harms the animals that we create as compared to the level of welfare generally enjoyed by outbred animals (again restricting our focus to genetic and conformational disease). This comparative judgment appeals to a "species norm," but this norm is not offered in an essentialist sense, nor in a purely descriptive statistical sense describing "average" species welfare at any given time. Rather, "species norm" as understood here is the historical baseline from which we departed when we created pedigree-breeds, a baseline that is still approximately represented by the average health of mixed-breed animals. Pedigree-breed dogs and cats are the result of a process by which domesticated dogs and cats were intentionally bred by humans to accentuate certain morphologic or behavioral features, inadvertently resulting in an increased tendency toward disease. This process is reversible, and furthermore, to reverse it we need only to refrain from a particular course of action: the course of action whereby we perpetuate pedigree-breeds. Against this baseline we can make sense of the judgment that our breeding practices have resulted in harm, and will continue to do so should we keep them up.

Strictly speaking, it is true that the purebred animals we create are not *themselves* made worse off by their creation, so how can we say that they are harmed? I believe that this core aspect of the non-identity problem is best approached by inquiring after the moral significance of the concept of harm. Both the non-identity problem and some solutions to it (e.g., the so-called "impersonal solution"; see Palmer 2012 for discussion) *presuppose* a certain conception of harm, rather than arguing for it. This conception of harm is temporal in nature: an individual must exist on "both sides" of a putative harm in order to say that it has been harmed. That is, the individual must exist beforehand, so that we have a "baseline" of its welfare with which to compare its future welfare after the putative harm occurred; this temporal comparison allows us to say that the individual has been made worse off. Since most of our moral decisions concern individuals who already exist, this temporal conception makes sense: by harming them, we typically make them worse off than they formerly were or otherwise would have been had we not acted.

But why is *this* important? The most plausible answer seems to me to be that morality is centrally concerned with the welfare of others, and the concept of "harm" is a way of making sense of our own agency and the way that our decisions affect the interests of sentient others. Said another way, "harm" is not a metaphysical concept describing something that exists in the world independently of human experience or judgment. Rather, it is a *pragmatic* concept that we employ in moral decision-making. This being the case, showing that our decisions have made others worse off than *they* otherwise would have been is sufficient to demonstrate harm, but it is not necessary. Rather, we need only show that our decisions have decreased the welfare of the sentient others affected (and perhaps also created) as compared to alternative courses of action. To insist otherwise appears stipulative and question-begging.

The Best-Interest Objection

A second potential objection to my argument against pedigree-breeding acknowledges that it results in harm (unlike the objection from non-identity), but goes on to argue that it is in the pedigree animals' best-interest, all things considered, to be brought into existence. This is because pedigree dogs and cats are brought into existence *because* they are pedigree animals, and their increased risk of disease is the "price of admission" to (we are assuming) a good-quality life; thus our creation of breed-associated disease is morally permissible. Though he does not address the issue of pedigree-breeding, Tzachi Zamir provides a general basis for this kind of argument:

> Well-kept pets are a source of joy to their owners, live a much better life than they would have lived in the wild, and, as far as I can tell, pay a small price for such conditions. . . . The [owner-pet] relationship is not fully paternalistic since, unlike with children, one is not merely a guardian acting with only their interests in mind but is also acting with the interest of preserving the relationship as such. Many morally problematic, invasive owner actions, such as limiting movement, sterilizing, or declawing, are conceptualized (and sometimes justified) in this light. (2007, 97–98)

Though Zamir states that the owner-pet relationship is not based only on what is in the animal's best interest, the argument presented in this passage seems to amount to this claim, albeit in two steps: (1) The life of a domesticated companion animal is better from the standpoint of its welfare than the life of a wild animal; (2) certain actions that harm companion animals in the immediate sense will nonetheless be morally justified because they preserve the owner-pet relationship, which is necessary to the keeping of domesticated animals, thus allowing for their enjoyment of a quality of life that is better than that of a wild animal.

Let us assume, for the purposes of this discussion, that claim (1) could be satisfied for the species of animals under consideration. Whether claim (2) justifies pedigree-breeding depends on just how we interpret the idea of being "necessary" for the preservation of the relationship between owner and companion animal.

On a strict interpretation, an action would be necessary to the preservation of the relationship between owner and animal if this relationship *could not plausibly exist* were it not for the action in question. This kind of necessity clearly does not apply to pedigree-breeding: many people can and do develop stable, mutually beneficial, long-term relationships with mixed-breed animals. Furthermore, some physical and behavioral characteristics of specific breeds, such as aggressive tendencies or a predisposition to disease that is costly to treat, would (other things being equal) seem to jeopardize the human-animal bond more than they promote it; people prefer specific breeds of animals in spite of these things and not because of them.

On a broader interpretation, an action would be necessary to the preservation of the relationship between owner and animal if *a particular person would not maintain the relationship were it not for this action*. For example, a person might decide that s/he only wants a dog with cropped ears or a cat that is declawed, and if these actions are not undertaken then s/he will relinquish the animal. Since it is better for the animal to be well cared for, it might be argued that it is in the animal's "best interest" to be subjected to these procedures, as it preserves the human-animal relationship. Analogously, it might be argued that pedigree-breeding is morally justified because a particular person's predilection for a particular breed increases their sentimental attachment to the animal, thus strengthening the human-animal relationship (something like this argument has been put to me in conversation).

As my use of scare-quotes indicates, I am skeptical that this kind of argument can be justified. Zamir also seems to agree, insofar as he labels as "unproblematically immoral" actions that "cause pain and possible complications to the pet without benefiting the animal (e.g., tail docking and ear cropping)" (2007, 98), even though these might strengthen the owner-pet relationship. The question is "why?" and the simple (and, in my view, correct) answer is that if we assume that nonhuman animals deserve equal moral consideration, then it will not be permissible to harm them outside of very limited circumstances. One such possible circumstance is if we are interested in providing the best possible life for an animal. If we grant claim (1), then it would be better from the standpoint of an animal's life if that life were a domesticated life. If we also grant a further, seemingly uncontroversial claim—that the "best possible life" for a companion animal will be reasonably bounded at what does not *substantially* set back the interests of the owner (e.g., by seriously jeopardizing the owner's safety)—then some animal-harming actions might be justified if they are necessary to avoid infringing upon a very important interest of the owner, if the extent of harm to the animal is not too great, and if there are no less harmful alternatives.

Even granting some controversy and fuzziness around the previous argument (e.g., what counts as a "substantial" interest for the owner?), we can see that it would not justify pedigree-breeding, because in the case of pedigree-breeding we have a less harmful and clearly viable alternative: outbreeding. Furthermore, whatever interest a person might have in a specific pedigree-breed does not seem to come even close to the level of importance that would justify the harms of breed-associated disease. On an EC view, it is not the owner's interests that assume primacy, but rather the animal's interests. Harms to companion animals would be permissible only to the extent that they are necessary to the human companion's being *reasonably able* to provide the superior (we are assuming) quality of domesticated life. A serious threat to one's own welfare counts as affecting what a person is reasonably able to do; a preference for a particular breed does not.

This conclusion also seems to hold on any reasonable UC view of companion animals' moral standing. Such a view would still ascribe significant moral importance to animals' interests, and in order to justifiably set back their interests we would need to be able to show that a significant human interest is being advanced and that there is no less harmful alternative to meeting this interest. Pedigree-breeding seems to satisfy neither criterion.

Conclusion

I have argued here that pedigree-breeding causes avoidable harm to animals, and that this harm is not justifiable on either EC or UC views of animals' moral status. It is not justifiable on UC views because the human interest in pedigree-breeding does not rise to the level of significance required to justify nontrivial harms to animals like dogs and cats. Pedigree-breeding is not justifiable on EC views because only the most important reasons (e.g., self-defense) could ever justify harm to animals on this kind of view. Pedigree-breeding can be reformed to cause less harm to animals, but it seems unlikely that it can be reformed to the point that it causes no added harm as compared to outbreeding. Even in a less harmful formulation, and even as practiced on other species of companion animals, it seems doubtful that pure-breeding will be justified on a UC view, since the harm is easily avoidable and does not serve a significant human interest in almost any case, and since the interest served by pure-breeding in most cases (entertainment) can easily be met through other avenues. Thus, on the argument presented here, pedigree-breeding should not merely be reformed, but abandoned.

Note

1. Here it is important to distinguish between inbreeding as a practice and inbreeding as a description of a breed's lack of genetic variability. Some recent reviews have identified a few breeds that are relatively healthy despite being heavily inbred (see Farrell et al. 2015). It is speculated that the deleterious disease alleles in these breeds developed after domestication of the dog but before the establishment of the breed. Regardless, these findings do not controvert the claim that inbreeding increases genetic disease. Once a deleterious gene mutation arises, the practice of inbreeding will produce more diseased individuals than the practice of outbreeding. An inbred breed that has avoided this outcome has only been lucky—to date.

References

Asher, Lucy, Gillian Diesel, Jennifer F. Summers, Paul D. McGreevy, and Lisa M. Collins. 2009. "Inherited Defects in Pedigree Dogs. Part 1: Disorders Related to Breed Standards." *The Veterinary Journal* 182 (3): 402–11.

Bateson, Patrick. 2010. *Independent Inquiry into Dog Breeding*. Suffolk, UK: Micropress Ltd.

DeGrazia, David. 2002. *Animal Rights: A Very Short Introduction*. New York: Oxford University Press.

Farrell, Lindsay F., Jeffrey J. Schoenebeck, Pamela Wiener, Dylan N. Clements, and Kim M. Summers. 2015. "The Challenges of Pedigree Dog Health: Approaches to Combating Inherited Disease." *Canine Genetics and Epidemiology* 2 (3). doi: 10.1186/s40575-015-0014-9.

Gough, Alex, and Alison Thomas. 2004. *Breed Predispositions to Disease in Dogs and Cats*. Oxford: Blackwell Publishing.

Humane Society of the United States. 2014. "Pets by the Numbers." http://www.humanesociety.org/issues/pet_overpopulation/facts/pet_ownership_statistics.html.

Jeppsson, Sophia. 2014. "Purebred Dogs and Canine Wellbeing." *Journal of Agricultural and Environmental Ethics* 27 (3): 417–30.

Lodato, Dena L., and Cheryl S. Hedlund. 2012. "Brachycephalic Airway Syndrome: Management." *Compendium: Continuing Education for Veterinarians*. August, E1–E6.

Palmer, Clair. 2012. "Does Breeding a Bulldog Harm It? Breeding, Ethics and Harm to Animals." *Animal Welfare* 21 (2): 157–66.

Rooney, Nicola, and David Sargan. 2009. *Pedigree Dog Breeding in the UK: A Major Welfare Concern?* West Sussex: RSPCA.

Summers, Jennifer F., Gillian Diesel, Lucy Asher, Paul D. McGreevy, and Lisa M. Collins. 2010. "Inherited Defects in Pedigree Dogs. Part 2: Disorders that Are Not Related to Breed Standards." *The Veterinary Journal* 183 (1): 39–45.

Zamir, Tzachi. 2007. *Ethics and the Beast: A Speciesist Argument for Animal Liberation.* Princeton: Princeton University Press.

9 DOES PREVENTING REPRODUCTION MAKE FOR BAD CARE?

Katherine Wayne

Spay and neuter campaigns represent one of the more hopeful and friendly faces of animal advocacy to the public, and have been widely successful in convincing self-proclaimed animal lovers that sterilizing one's animal companion should be a given. Typically non-threatening to the core, such campaigns feature smiling celebrity endorsements, or cute (if occasionally risqué) posters.[1] When serious, they appeal to the public's sympathy for homeless animals and indignation toward irresponsible owners, whose failure to sterilize their animal companions perpetuates the unmanageable populations that ostensibly guarantee consistently overflowing shelters.[2] While spay and neuter campaigns may also invoke concern for the health and general wellbeing of one's companion animal, consideration of the potentially sterilized animal himself is not typically emphasized. This is unsurprising, given the serious risks of mainstream sterilization methods.[3] Nevertheless, spay and neuter campaigns enjoy widespread success and support among the general public, companion animal caregivers, and animal activists alike.[4]

In this chapter I examine the tenability of that support, and the justifiability of preventing reproduction in companion animals more generally, from an animal rights framework that espouses relational obligations.[5] My proposal for how to interpret the duty of care in regard to reproduction centers on an analysis of the relationship between reproduction and flourishing for companion animals and humans. I conclude that good care for companion animals may be compatible with preventing them from reproducing. Preventative efforts are not, however, unconditionally acceptable; for one, they must not reinforce instrumentalizing attitudes and practices concerning companion animals.

Characterizing the Human-Companion Animal Relationship

Companion animals' lives are pervasively regulated by their human caregivers. We make decisions about, and so impose restrictions on, virtually all of our companion animals' behaviors, from their most basic functions such as eating, excreting, and vocalizing, to activities such as exercising, learning, playing, and giving affection. While flexibly and multiply realized,[6] the necessity of such forms of regulation is seldom denied or unrecognized. While most of these forms of regulation are, as Jean Harvey observes (2008, 164–66), susceptible to slipping into forms of domination and instrumentalization disguised as paternalism, regulation *can* involve facilitating companion animals' flourishing within the confines of an asymmetrically dependent relationship and the interspecies community at large. Human caregivers know that their companions must, for instance, develop social skills and enjoy play opportunities in order to thrive; neglecting to present such opportunities typically consists in bad care. It would be at least equally egregious to actively *prevent* a companion animal from pursuing such opportunities for some instrumentalizing reason, such as wanting to keep all his love and affection to oneself. Without proper socialization, companion animals are vulnerable to deprivations such as diminished access to public spaces and fewer opportunities to give and receive affection.

Thus we fail our companion animals in a painfully obvious way when we prevent them from pursuing activities like socializing, where both the activity itself and its fruits contribute enormously—and visibly—to companion animal flourishing. If reproduction makes a comparable contribution to companion animal flourishing, it will be comparably misguided to prevent our animal companions from reproducing. Perhaps because reproduction is not viewed as a good in the same way that receiving affection or nutritious food might be, the question of whether preventing reproduction is a breach of the duty of care is relatively murky. I argue that resolving this issue demands consideration of the prior questions of whether preventing reproduction will reliably hinder flourishing, and whether the freedom to pursue reproduction is at least *prima facie* desirable. Before taking up those questions, I briefly examine the traditional debate surrounding the ethics of reproduction for companion animals, and how it has been monopolized by an unproductive opposition between welfarists[7] and abolitionists.[8] I suggest that neither of these camps offers a tenable analysis of the considerations at stake in negotiating reproductive issues in our companion animals. And while the recently advanced relational account of human obligations to domestic animals supplies a more plausible direction for thinking through these issues, it is not clear that it can also supply a satisfying resolution.

Welfarism versus Abolitionism

Welfarism typically focuses on animals' entitlements not to be subjected to unnecessary harm, not to be treated cruelly or callously, and most generally, to have their welfare interests taken seriously. Animals' rights to be treated humanely, however, are couched in terms of their appropriate service to humans, in that constraints on particular forms of treatment derive from a foundational acceptance of animals' resource and property status. When it comes to animals' reproductive capacities and behaviors, then, it is unsurprising that welfarists take the appropriateness of full human control for granted as well. The reproduction of all domestic animals is heavily regulated, and for companion animals, this typically means endorsing sterilization wherever "appropriate" breeding programs are not in place. Yet, as previously noted, mainstream methods of sterilization are associated with significant risks as well as potential health benefits; for instance, castration in male dogs significantly increases risks of several types of cancer (Palmer, Corr, and Sandøe 2012, 158–59). Routine sterilization is therefore not easily justified through appeal to individual health considerations. Conversely, common welfarist reasons in favor of sterilization tend to rely on impoverished accounts of animal agency and human accountability. These reasons include making the animal less prone to undesired behaviors (and therefore more likely to be adopted, kept, and well cared for), reducing companion animal overpopulation, and reducing frustration in individual animals (who would not be able to fulfill every desire to reproduce). Only the last reason elides an instrumentalizing view of companion animals.

In sum, spay and neuter programs are not generally enacted for the good of the sterilized animals themselves. Perhaps this is already explicit; welfarist campaigns have made it plain that reasons to sterilize concern the "pet *population*"—and not, as many owners may have mistakenly surmised, *your pet* (nor, in most cases, any individual pets at all). Jean Harvey's claim that the "welfare with safeguards"[9] model surreptitiously encourages a view of animals as resources—in the companion animal case, of affection, entertainment, and general human well-being— also applies to the case of companion animal reproduction. Companion animals' potential interests will always fall short of being worthy of protection when other countervailing considerations, particularly those pertaining to human interests, are presented.

Self-identified animal rights defenders, on the other hand, may reasonably be expected to fervently defend companion animals' individual rights to freedom from human infringement on basic functions like reproduction. While respecting individual rights does not in principle comprise respecting a right to bring new beings into existence, prohibiting reproduction as a matter of course, through highly invasive measures no less, seems clearly at odds with a strong animal rights position. It is generally taken for granted that individuals have at least a negative right to reproduce, in the sense of not having their reproductive activities infringed on.

Yet some of the most ardent animal rights supporters insist that it is at least permissible, if not obligatory, to prevent companion animals from reproducing. Gary Francione claims that "The recognition that animals have a right not to be treated as the property of humans would most certainly mean that we should stop bringing domesticated nonhumans into existence, and this would include dogs and cats. . . . Sterilization programs, although not ideal, are consistent with the abolitionist approach" (2010, 79–80). This endorsement of sterilization is deeply puzzling. For one, as strong animal rights defenders and devoted anti-speciesists, abolitionists frequently invoke the (unfortunately named) argument from marginal cases (AMC) to show how protecting the interests of all humans with inviolable rights rationally requires similar protection for nonhumans with similar interests.[10] Restricting entitlements to protection on the basis of species alone relies on a morally arbitrary distinction to justify differential treatment in relevantly similar contexts. Yet on the issue of reproduction, publicly proclaimed abolitionists apparently demonstrate a rare agreement with welfarists, whose claims they otherwise tend to dismiss as toothless if not outright counterproductive. Why is this?

Abolitionists' support for companion animal sterilization rides on the idea that holding a right presumes having a relevant interest. Domestic animals, abolitionists argue, do not have an interest in continuing their existence as a kind:[11] while the pervasively exploitative and often brutal systems of animal use and animals' legal property status are to blame for their ongoing wrongful treatment, remedying that injustice will fail to transform domestic animals into the sorts of beings who have an interest in perpetuating their existence. Their lives are deemed essentially unlivable because of the severely and inexorably dependent character of domestic animal life—even the best-off companion animals are deeply unfortunate creatures.[12]

Those who call for the deliberate extinction of the animals whose lives could be most radically improved by the very emancipatory measures abolitionists support can be referred to as "extinctionists." According to extinctionists such as Leila Fusfeld, sterilization becomes not merely permissible but obligatory in light of domestic animals' essential defectiveness: "The right to a true freedom from enslavement equates to a right not to be brought into existence" (2007, 262). Extinctionists claim that animal rights advocates cannot coherently endorse animal rights to bodily integrity and sexual freedom because the appropriateness of bestowing such rights hinges on the subjects' relevant interests. While its denigration of animal lives is both implausible and morally troubling, the extinctionist proposal retains the virtue of acknowledging the self-interested motives undergirding that familiar and palatable welfarist call to "spay and neuter your pets" in the context of supporting ongoing use of companion and other domestic animals. Nevertheless, and most pertinent here, extinctionism can only be made sense of with a deluded understanding of both what would be possible if domestic animal emancipation from property status were to be achieved, and the nature of cooperative relationships and their multiple realizations in interdependent society.

Community Membership

The third type of approach to reproductive ethics for companion animals that I will consider invokes what we can call the membership model of domestic animal rights, which is a branch of the group-differentiated approach to human obligations to animals and the human-animal relationship more broadly. I argue that, compared to welfarism and abolitionism, the membership model is equipped to supply a relatively appealing account of the human duty of care in relation to companion animal reproduction. The recent work of membership model proponents Sue Donaldson and Will Kymlicka (2011), Will Kymlicka and Sue Donaldson (2014), and Clare Palmer (2010, 2014) has ignited fresh debate concerning the precise limits and contours of human obligations to domestic animals as fellow moral and political community members. Yet they too remain torn and at times insufficiently clear on how the demands of the duty of care feature in relation to companion animal reproduction.

Donaldson and Kymlicka (2011, 82–85) counter extinctionist claims by pointing out that asymmetrical power relations are ubiquitous and inevitable. Echoing, among others, disability scholars and rights advocates, they argue that dependence is an essential feature of life that is not intrinsically harmful or undesirable; rather, it is the denigration and exclusion of dependent ways of being that are harmful and misguided. While Donaldson and Kymlicka predictably reject the practice of routine sterilization for companion animals, they also recognize the normative significance of companion animals' inability to self-regulate their reproductive behavior, and concede that some restrictions on reproduction may therefore be required for companion animals (2011, 145).

Advocates of the membership model recognize that reproductive rights may justifiably be constrained, but only through appeal to the interests of the rightsholder herself rather than the community at large. Risks to sustaining membership in the greater community that creates the very possibility of mutually enjoyed interspecies living can justify limits on reproduction. Donaldson and Kymlicka argue that "With the citizenship model, restrictions can only be justified by reference to the interests of the individual, while recognizing that these interests include being part of a cooperative social project which involves both rights and duties" (2011, 147). And as Palmer has pointed out, systematic restrictions on reproduction, such as routine sterilization, are implausibly justified paternalistically, given that the benefits of sterilization are primarily directed towards others—specifically, their human caregivers and other domestic and community residents (e.g., native bird populations).[13] Appeals to individuals' interests to justify routine sterilization are perhaps inevitably dubious; even claiming that sterilization serves the individual by facilitating her continued membership in society requires circular reasoning, for it implies that a given intervention can be appropriate as long as it contributes to the individual's suitability for cooperative living. And surely the individual's interest in cooperative living depends on whether it will involve a harmful or rights-violating intervention.

On the whole, membership model supporters and others who take inviolable rights for animals seriously admit the difficulty of systematically restricting reproduction at all within a strong rights framework.[14] Yet they also balk at alternatives such as unfettered reproduction for companion animals or even generally prohibiting sterilization. Donaldson and Kymlicka have begun the process of teasing out the relevant considerations at play in carving out appropriate versus inappropriate regulative measures for domestic animals' reproduction; if cooperative relationships form the bedrock of a just interdependent interspecies society, it will follow that "where animals do not or cannot self-regulate their reproduction, the costs to others of having to care for and maintain their offspring could become prohibitive. In these circumstances, imposing some limits on their reproduction is . . . a reasonable element in a larger scheme of cooperation" (2011, 147). Regulating reproductive behaviors is perhaps justifiable in a rather pedestrian sense, in that restrictions of all sorts are required in a cooperative society. Moreover, such restrictions need not be highly invasive; while current regulatory methods are, at least in North America, typically limited to risky and permanent surgical interventions,[15] alternative contraceptive measures that are far less harmful and that minimize infringements on individual freedoms could be explored and implemented. Surely, if we can reasonably expect reproductive self-regulation in those capable of it, imposed regulation cannot be completely off the table for those who are not so capable.

Reproduction as Practice: Typical Versus Essential Features

There is an important distinction between reproduction itself and the activities that are associated with reproduction. An informed analysis of how reproduction itself contributes to flourishing is needed to establish conditions for an obligation to facilitate reproduction in companion animals. In order to determine the value of reproduction itself in terms of how it contributes to flourishing, I draw an analogy to the human case, and conclude that the reasons for valuing reproduction itself do not apply in the companion animal case (or any other case with relevantly similar features). I conclude that human caregivers and institutions are not, *as a matter of principle*, failing companion animals by not facilitating their reproduction, and that preventing reproduction in companion animals is therefore not, again in principle, in tension with fulfilling the duty of care to them.

Reproduction typically means bringing new beings into existence through particular methods, namely heterosexual activity.[16] It involves a number of physiological changes and processes within the female body (conception, gestation, and birth), and creates a particular relationship with the offspring, namely parenthood. But the essential and (practically) unique[17] feature of reproduction is that it involves *bringing new beings into existence*; the other features are contingent and may be independently expressed. In particular, reproduction is not necessarily tied to sexual congress or parenthood; each of these activities can be realized in the absence of reproduction (as can, of course, reproduction be realized in their absence). Attaching reproduction to sex and possibilities for fulfilment is misguided in the nonhuman case as well as the human case; doing so marginalizes animal homosexuality, non-reproductive sexual activity, and non-heterosexual amity or partnership (even same-sex parenting). Empirical findings in ethology corroborate this conceptual divide between reproduction itself and its associated pursuits (Balcombe 2009; Bagemihl 1999).

Given the separability of these dimensions of reproduction, it seems reasonable to consider these dimensions separately in regard to how they foster or hinder flourishing. If they in fact relate differently to companion animal flourishing, this distinction will shape the duty of care humans have to companion animals in regard to reproduction. More specifically, the compatibility of the duty of care with preventing reproduction will reflect this distinction.

Valuing Reproduction through Valuing the Self

In the human case, reproduction alone has been construed as a vital component of flourishing in several different ways, which correspondingly ground different potential reasons for protecting some strong form of entitlement to reproduce. Legal scholar Carter Dillard reviews a number of proposals for the foundation of a moral right to reproduce, and finds that three categories of values are typically invoked: autonomy/freedom, the value of new relations and of life itself, and the value of self-replacement. He rejects the first two categories of interests as possible foundations, most broadly because they either fail to capture what is worthy of protecting or neglect the other-determining nature of reproduction, and he argues that "rather than autonomy, new relations, or life itself, we need some objective value related or intrinsic to procreation, which our authorities can recognize as deserving of protection" (2010, 189).

While I find dismissal of relationship creation as a grounding value for the entitlement to reproduce unconvincing, I am generally sympathetic to Dillard's criticisms of these notions of the foundational value of reproduction. He rightly highlights the problem of deriving a right to reproduction from the intrinsic value of other-regarding relationships in a context where it is both possible and desirable to cultivate such relationships in myriad other ways. Partly because other ways of cultivating nurturing relationships, even parental relationships, are readily available without reproduction—for instance, through adoption and fostering—the intrinsic value of other-regarding relationships does not itself lend support to the right to reproduction. In fact, the normative force of that value may serve to *undermine* the entitlement to reproduce; Dillard is harsh but astute when he observes that "Mother Teresa is perhaps a better model of other-regarding love and nurture than most parents" (188).[18]

But Dillard ignores the possibility that procreation may be a *distinctively* desirable sort of relationship creation. Even if it is true that a duty to protect the right to reproduce demands "a value that cannot be fully promoted by other behaviors" (188), Dillard must show that the relationship creation involved in reproduction has no value distinct from other forms of relationship creation. At least some different kinds of other-regarding relationships (e.g., friendships, mentorships, collegiate relationships) hold distinctive, and arguably incommensurable, value. And each kind may contain distinctively valuable components that may themselves vary, in nature and combination, among individual instantiations of those relationships. For instance, one may view the value of the parenting relationship to contain the value of gestating and bearing a child conceived with one's mate. Whether or not such variations in valuation are equally legitimate remains an open question, but Dillard cannot yet justify rejecting the value of creating and sustaining other-regarding relations as potential grounds for a defeasible entitlement to reproduce.

When Dillard settles on the third category of interests that may ground a rights-protecting value of reproduction, and supports that way of protecting an entitlement to reproduce, he is more convincing. This category of interests concerns the value of self-replacement, "the unique and incommensurable value we find in the very act of creating another person. . . . The value is continuity, the constitutive aspect of our wellbeing that comes from defeating in some way the utter finality that death represents by creating a sufficiently comparable life" (191). In other words, it is because we value our own lives that we value reproduction.[19] To have a child is, paraphrasing Christine Overall's observation, to both create a new life and recreate one's own life (2012, 17); protecting this interest in doing so is important because "every person is sufficiently valuable as to be worth replacing" (183). Overall and Dillard agree that the centrality of reproduction to one's self-conception and the meanings we assign to reproduction both signify the deeply worthwhile nature of reproduction for humans, and confirm a strong relationship between flourishing and reproduction.[20]

Will this ground for valuing reproduction also serve to entitle companion animals to some right to reproduce, if not to facilitated reproduction?[21] It might be argued that reproduction cannot play an important role in companion animals' self-conception; unlike in the human case, having children is not something they look forward to, and not something they get depressed about if opportunities to reproduce are limited or foreclosed. There are several issues with this view. The first is that if we allow for retroactive assessments, a thing might be valuable to an individual whether or not she values obtaining that thing. But even if the individual must value the thing in question for it to count as valuable to her, I am not sure that the above assumption is fair;[22] an expanded notion of valuing that includes a sense of satisfaction and indirect appreciation seems an important part of a non-speciesist approach to the duty of care. It may be that companion animals do not "look forward" to the activities and experiences that encourage their flourishing, but they may experience deep satisfaction through them, and appreciate the goods that are afforded to them by virtue of participating in other activities (e.g., being taught to recognize boundaries within and outside the home so that free run of the house or walking in parks without restraints is possible). Perhaps more importantly, the argument from marginal cases reminds us to consider whether dependent humans' entitlements to pursue or to be afforded certain goods are presented as contingent on whether those individuals value that good in the traditional, cognitivist sense. Placing capacity-related conditions on entitlements and protections has led to dark places for both vulnerable humans and animals, so it seems desirable to place the burden of justification on those who wish to withhold protection from certain forms of infringement, at least if companion animals give some signs of enjoying, being satisfied by, or appreciating reproduction.

What signs might we look to? First, companion animals can and often do exhibit what looks like deep enjoyment from having and caring for offspring. Moreover, when companion animals are not sterilized, they often exhibit clear desires to engage in mating behaviors, and consequently frustration when this is disallowed.[23] Returning to my distinction between the essential and associated

dimensions of reproduction, however, it seems reasonable to interpret these
considerations (that companion animals often exhibit enjoyment in caring for
offspring, and interest in mating) in light of their detachability from reproduction itself. That is, perhaps supplying opportunities for nurturing others and for
sex, as activities associated with reproduction, would suffice to protect companion animals' interests. Do companion animals show any signs of valuing self-
replacement? I am tempted to suggest that any sentient being who demonstrates
a strong preference for continuing to live values self-replacement; surely the "utter
finality" of death and its repugnance apply equally to all of us mortals.

But even if self-replacement is a value for companion animals as well as for
humans, there is little hope for the corresponding translation of entitlement
to companion animals. Consider how, as Dillard explains, the value of self-
replacement is a *satiable* value (2010, 192–94), which means that it can be fully
satisfied. While some proponents of the value worry about how it could non-
arbitrarily be deemed sated, Dillard suggests that "the objective intrinsic value
of self-replication, of the continuity of human living that it represents, is met
upon self-replication"; consequently, once reproduction has occurred, "all other
things being equal, we cannot achieve, meet, or satisfy that particular value
again" (194). Dillard's view allows for a clear cutoff point for the foundational
value and interest to be considered realized. He thereby supplies a strong and
self-constraining reason to reproduce, which helps ward off concerns about how
protecting an interest in reproduction will uncontrollably exacerbate existing
population problems.

Clearly, self-replication is not satiable in the same way for companion animals.
Quite simply, companion animals cannot appropriately act on the value of self-
replacement through reproduction—they do not even have the option of having
human help to limit their reproduction in this way, because they reliably introduce multiple lives into existence in a single act of reproduction. Like humans,
companion animals contribute to an already-serious problem of overpopulation
when they reproduce, both by increasing the total population as well as by fore-
closing opportunities to alleviate suffering through caring for already-existing
individuals. Also like humans, companion animals may value the experience of
having and raising offspring; that experience may even represent an essential
component of flourishing for some of them. Unlike humans, however, not only
are companion animals generally less able to self-regulate their reproductive
behaviors; they are by nature unable to limit their reproduction in a way that is
consistent with the grounding value of reproduction itself.

If the value of self-recreation is the best candidate for establishing an entitlement to pursue reproduction, and this is partly because self-recreation is a satiable
value, and companion animals do not hold that value in its satiable form while

what they do value is not inextricably tied to reproduction, reproduction itself should not be considered an important element of flourishing for companion animals. It should then follow that facilitating reproduction is not necessarily required by the duty of care, and that preventing reproduction may be compatible with fulfilling the duty of care to companion animals.

Preferences and the Good in Relationships and Communities: Respecting our Companions

In this final section, I consider another potential way of establishing that compatibility. Recall that in an animal rights framework, there is a burden of justification for exposing individual animals to serious risks and harms in order to benefit or avoid harm to the community. As a mode of reproduction prevention, then, surgical sterilization is morally dubious—no matter how dire the suffering of other currently existing and homeless as well as future generations of companion animals may be. But even in cases where some intervention includes significant risk to the individual for whom we care, it may not always be best to presume that they would prefer to avoid that intervention. Moreover, given that flourishing requires good acts, a non-speciesist animal rights paradigm may even construe risky acts that benefit others as desirably encouraged by caregivers.

I illustrate these considerations by revisiting David Boonin's (2003) attempt to reconcile sterilization with a strong animal rights view. One of the possibilities that Boonin considers and rejects is that preventing reproduction in companion animals could be deemed preference-respecting, and therefore in line with an animal rights perspective (which is consistent with the membership model). Boonin considers the following scenario:

> Fluffy does not know that spaying her will prevent her from contributing to the already overcrowded population of unwanted kittens. So we cannot say that she desires to be spayed. But if she did understand this, one might argue, she would prefer to be spayed, just as if she understood the nature of feline leukemia [and was suffering from an advanced case], she would prefer to be euthanized. And so what might be called "preference-respecting spaying" might be consistent with acknowledging Fluffy's right to respectful treatment in just the same way that preference-respecting euthanasia is. (2003, 4)

Boonin rejects this possibility for two reasons. First, it is not clear what Fluffy (or let us call her Mary, to assist in taking her seriously) would desire, and unlike in the euthanasia case, there is no reason to count on her desires to go that way. Why should we assume that Mary would willingly undergo nontrivial harm in order to prevent harm to others? Second, if we think Mary does prefer to undergo this harm, it seems we have the option of doing a number of harmful things to Mary that would prevent harm to others, under the guise of preference-respecting.

I am not convinced by Boonin's first reason. While we have no reason to believe that Mary will prefer not to reproduce, we also have no reason to believe that she will prefer to act selfishly either. In a cooperative community, in fact, we ought to assume that members will generally wish to act in ways that are cooperative and prosocial rather than not—indeed, their freedom to do so is an integral part of their flourishing, and as such is an interest worth protecting. It would, to be sure, be unreasonable to assume that this prosocial impulse will consistently manifest itself in the deeper roots of the individual's desires; that impulse will not necessarily remove the desire to reproduce, nor create a desire not to reproduce. But it may strengthen a higher-order desire to avoid practices that are likely to create significant harm; when relatively low-cost opportunities to ensure avoidance of such practices are presented, those opportunities might be reasonably taken up. Moreover, if Mary's interests in sexual behavior, relationship creation, significant freedom of mobility, and bodily integrity can be protected, and her relevant wishes fulfilled, the majority of flourishing opportunities associated with reproduction will be realized. In these cases, Mary's caregiver will not be failing Mary by preventing her from reproducing.

Such considerations remind us that we are not obligated—or justified—to expect less of some individual simply because he is more dependent. We *are* obligated to be more vigilant regarding what we deem appropriate to ask of her and how we obtain it. We must be able to assure Mary that prevention efforts will be limited to interventions that do not involve serious or ongoing harm, and that other flourishing opportunities associated with reproduction such as nurturing relationships will be presented. I disagree with Boonin again here, because assigning some degree of preference for sacrifice does not remove caregivers' obligations to help avoid or reduce harm to Mary, or to promote her well-being. Preventing reproduction will therefore be justified only in a qualified sense. Those qualifications will hinge on how the particular mode of prevention affects the companion animal's flourishing in other ways; for instance, opportunities for sexual activity and nurturing relationships will be fostered, and certain preventive methods, such as isolation, will be prohibited. Conversely, non-invasive contraceptive measures will be vigorously researched, developed, and distributed. Looking forward, it falls on animal rights activists and scholars to focus on answering practical questions of how to provide companion animals with sufficiently diverse and rich opportunities for pursuing desired activities associated with reproduction. The duty of care will continue to demand, first and foremost, attention to the flourishing needs of our animal companions—not as isolated individuals or passive recipients of care, but as dynamic participants in a variety of relationships.

Acknowledgments

I wish to thank Christine Overall for inviting my contribution to this anthology, for her detailed and insightful comments on previous drafts, and for her excellent management of this project. I am grateful to the late Jean Harvey for beginning this important collection, and for the avenues she helped cultivate toward understanding the promises and challenges for loving relationships between humans and animals. I am honored to contribute to this discussion. The community of scholars and affiliates of the Department of Philosophy at Queen's University, particularly the APPLE group, has provided much helpful conversation about the ideas herein. And I wish to thank Guy Scotton for his perceptive and rigorous editing assistance. This research was supported by the Social Sciences and Humanities Research Council of Canada (SSHRC).

Notes

1. Bob Barker, self-described animal activist and former host of the popular game show *The Price is Right*, always finished episodes with a friendly reminder to "help control the pet population by spaying or neutering your pet." Some campaign posters' attention-grabbing calls for pet sterilization play on human sexual norms, such as one that prominently captions a cat photo with the word "nympho," and in the smaller print encourages owners to spay, given cats' uncontrollable urges.
2. Overflowing shelters are, however, the result of several factors, including absent or poor regulation and enforcement of companion-animal owner responsibilities. A recent CBC documentary that targets cat overpopulation, *Cat Crazed*, features Calgary's (now less rare) legislation of mandatory licensing of companion cats and discusses how it has drastically reduced stray populations and overcrowding at shelters.
3. In their review of these effects, Palmer, Corr, and Sandøe (2012) conclude that while some significant health benefits are associated with surgical sterilization procedures (particularly in female dogs), so are significant risks (particularly in male dogs). They conclude that routine neutering is not morally justifiable. Another review of these effects similarly concludes that the mix of welfare risks and benefits of surgical contraception demands individualized case-by-case consideration (Reichler 2009).

4. This is (at least) true of campaigns that target animals being adopted or assessed for adoptability, which are my focus in this article (as opposed to campaigns that target feral and semi-feral populations, which present a set of issues I am not able to explore here).

5. I limit my argument's application to cats and dogs in order to constrain the scope of this chapter and because it is these companion animals over whose reproduction human caregivers tend to deliberately exert the most influence.

6. E.g., dogs with very high energy levels should be offered multiple daily opportunities to run, whereas mellow or frail dogs may find even extended walks exhausting.

7. Variations of this label include new welfarists, reformists, and protectionists.

8. For a comprehensive outline of and representative debate between abolitionism and welfarism/protectionism, see Garner and Francione (2010).

9. Jean Harvey presents the "welfare with safeguards" model (and its purportedly "gentler" formulation as "seeking benefits while ensuring welfare") as a more demanding version of mainstream welfarism. Her critique of this model suggests that even demanding forms of welfarism, which permit animal use for human benefit only when the animal's full welfare is sustained, fail to reliably devote attention and respect to companion animals' interests (2008, 162–64).

10. See Evelyn Pluhar (1995) for a detailed account and defense of two versions of the AMC.

11. It may be argued that the apparent tension is not so great, because while abolitionists obviously view the lives of domesticated animals as tragically compromised, they nonetheless generally endorse the interest in continued existence of those already living. I do not have the space to explore this issue in detail, so I will simply note that I, like many others, am not convinced that this distinction dissolves the incoherence of advancing a non-speciesist rights paradigm that calls for the elimination of new rights-bearers.

12. Francione is the most visible and vehement defender of this view (e.g., 2007, 2010).

13. For instance, a great deal of concern has been voiced recently about the impact of cats' hunting of local bird populations. A corresponding image of cats as voracious killing machines has emerged that contrasts sharply with the general tenor of cats' ubiquitous online depiction as adorable and goofy, if occasionally (and amusingly) cold, objects of entertainment. The aforementioned documentary *Cat Crazed* effectively outlines the surprisingly fraught relationships among cats, the individuals and institutions responsible for them, conservationists, and popular media.

14. E.g., see David Boonin (2003). Palmer (2014) resists Boonin's suggestion that sterilization constitutes only a minor harm and therefore renders it justifiably imposed only in cases where doing so will result in great overall benefit (or harm aversion) for the community at large.

15. Both the American Veterinary Association and the Canadian Veterinary Medical Association characterize spay/neuter surgery as an important part of "responsible pet ownership" in their position statements.

16. This is a characterization that clearly does not apply to domestic animals in general; farmed animals most commonly reproduce through forced insemination by humans or machines.

17. I reserve the possibility of cloning for future discussion.

18. Note that this criticism is not exactly saying that foregoing reproduction to pursue nurturing relationships with existing others is more truly other-regarding. As Christine Overall explains, while choosing to reproduce is inherently self-oriented, it is not thereby inherently selfish (2012, 217). Rather, the criticism points out that the individual interest in pursuing other-regarding relationships might be not only adequately but better fulfilled by choosing against reproduction.

19. There are legitimate worries about this way of justifying entitlement to reproduction; I am unable to address them here and hope to do so in a future paper on the ethics of human reproduction. Thanks to the colloquium audience members at Queen's who pointed out the complications of using this value as a way of justifying reproduction, as opposed to cloning, and who pushed me on the inherent difficulties of justifying procreation through the value of self-re-creation.

20. But neither is committed to claiming that reproduction is always morally desirable or even permissible.

21. Most broadly, facilitating reproduction involves creating or fostering conditions under which reproduction is more likely to take place, or is easier for the individual to pursue herself, in a way that aims to protect the individual's other relevant interests (e.g., safety). In the companion animal case, reproduction will typically require facilitation (e.g., through supplying safe opportunities for her to engage in mating behavior during fertile periods). Thus if there is an entitlement to reproduce for companion animals, facilitating reproduction will likely be included in the duty of care.

22. Perhaps the underlying concern is that attributing such features to animals would be anthropomorphizing. As Kristin Andrews has pointed out, however, anthropomorphism charges typically work from pre-empirical assumptions about what features animals can have, and tacitly construe the features in question as uniquely human (2011, 470–73).

23. Ethological findings again cast doubt on the common reading of such expressions as merely adaptive/reducible to instinctive, evolutionary mechanisms (e.g., Balcombe 2009).

References

Andrews, Kristin. 2011. "Beyond Anthropomorphism: Attributing Psychological Properties to Animals." In *The Oxford Handbook of Animal Ethics*, edited by Tom L. Beauchamp and R. G. Frey, 469–94. New York: Oxford University Press.

Bagemihl, Bruce. 1999. *Biological Exuberance: Animal Homosexuality and Natural Diversity*. New York: St. Martin's Press.

Balcombe, Jonathan. 2009. "Animal Pleasure and Its Moral Significance." *Applied Animal Behaviour Science* 118 (3–4): 208–16.

Boonin, David. 2003. "Robbing PETA to Spay Paul: Do Animal Rights Include Reproductive Rights?" *Between the Species* 13 (3): 1–8.

Dillard, Carter. 2010. "Valuing Having Children." *Journal of Law and Family Studies* 12 (151): 151–98.

Donaldson, Sue, and Will Kymlicka. 2011. *Zoopolis: A Political Theory of Animal Rights*. Oxford: Oxford University Press.

Francione, Gary. 2007. "Animal Rights and Domesticated Nonhumans." *Animal Rights: The Abolitionist Approach* (blog). January 10. http://www.abolitionistapproach.com/animal-rights-and-domesticated-nonhumans/.

Francione, Gary. 2010. "The Abolition of Animal Exploitation." In *The Animal Rights Debate: Abolition or Regulation?*, edited by Gary Francione and Robert Garner, 1–102. New York: Columbia University Press.

Fusfeld, Leila. 2007. "Sterilization in an Animal Rights Paradigm." *Journal of Animal Law and Ethics* 2: 255–62.

Harvey, Jean. 2008. "Companion and Assistance Animals: Benefits, Welfare Safeguards, and Relationships." *International Journal of Applied Philosophy* 22 (2): 161–76.

Kymlicka, Will, and Sue Donaldson. 2014. "Animals and the Frontiers of Citizenship." *Oxford Journal of Legal Studies* 34 (2): 200–19.

Overall, Christine. 2012. *Why Have Children? The Ethical Debate*. Cambridge: MIT Press.

Palmer, Clare. 2010. *Animal Ethics in Context*. New York: Columbia University Press.

Palmer, Clare. 2014. "Companion Cats as Co-Citizens? Comments on Sue Donaldson's and Will Kymlicka's *Zoopolis*." *Dialogue: Canadian Philosophical Review* 52 (4): 759–67.

Palmer, Clare, S. Corr, and P. Sandøe. 2012. "Inconvenient Desires: Should We Routinely Neuter Companion Animals?" *Anthrozoös* 25, supplement 1: 153–72.

Pluhar, Evelyn. 1995. *Beyond Prejudice: The Moral Significance of Human and Nonhuman Animals*. Durham: Duke University Press.

Reichler, I. M. 2009. "Gonadectomy in Cats and Dogs: A Review of Risks and Benefits." *Reproduction in Domestic Animals* 44, supplement 2: 29–35.

10

"LASSIE, COME HOME!"

ETHICAL CONCERNS ABOUT COMPANION ANIMAL CLONING

Jennifer Parks

A beloved pet is much like a family member. The unique life-enriching bond, the love and companionship—a truly special pet provides us a unique sense of comfort and life-enriching fulfillment which is nearly impossible to extend beyond your pet's natural lifespan. until now.

—VIAGEN PETS 2016

A friend of mine, Marcia, lost her beloved companion, Marcus, after his protracted battle with cancer. Marcia nursed him at home and was able to be with Marcus at the end of his life, holding him in her arms as he died. Her deep sense of loss was all-consuming, and for a very long time she was unable to overcome her grief.

Marcia's companion was not her husband or partner, but her companion animal of eleven years. That the description *sounds* like one that could be about human relationships tells us something about the depth and significance of human-companion animal connections: for many human beings, their relationships with their furry companions are the most significant ones of their lives. Indeed, so deep are these connections that some individuals have pursued the option of cloning their companions in the hopes of recreating the special relationship they once had.

This chapter concerns the novel practice of cloning companion animals and the ethical concerns it raises. My approach differs from previous approaches (see Fiester 2005a, 2005b) in that I wish to focus on the relational and care aspects of the practice. To date, the few ethical analyses of cloning companion animals have addressed the practice by considering it from Kantian or utilitarian frameworks, treating issues of harms to the "surrogate" females that are required to carry the clones, or the duty to support already-existing homeless and harmed animals. While these concerns are important, I will argue that in the area of cloning companion animals any rich analysis needs to address the relationships involved and the way the practice may result in emotional exploitation, capitalizing on the deep connectedness that people feel to their animal companions (specifically, for my purposes, dogs and cats). Adopting a feminist ethic of care, I will advance a moral argument against the practice and suggest that pet cloning is a morally risky practice because it instrumentalizes the human-companion animal relationship and treats as fungible the very relationships that are deemed to be so special and unique as to be worthy of being reproduced. I will consider objections to my position that challenge the idea that the marketing and practice of companion animal cloning exploits persons in any unique way, since arguably many of the options made available on the market (such as expensive cars) are at least as exploitative of relationships with others (for example, by convincing someone that in order to protect her children from harm, she ought to buy a very expensive vehicle that is marketed as being the safest on the market). Additionally, with regard to the high cost of pet cloning, defenders of the practice point out that it is no different than an individual spending money on other expensive luxury items, and if we are not willing to prevent people from spending money on other luxury items, then we have no grounds for preventing them from spending it on cloning their dog or cat.

As I will argue, the paradox of companion animal cloning is that the human's depth of feeling and relationship, and the experience of her beloved pet's uniqueness and irreplaceability, drive the very practice of trying to recreate that relationship. The practice is morally problematic because it treats these relationships with particular others as though they are easily refashioned, and it wrongly suggests that the loss associated with a pet's death can be overcome by a simple act of replacement.[1] While in a capitalist system those who supply animal cloning services may be legally free to do so, I will argue that they are *morally wrong* to do so, and that persons of moral integrity would not exploit these human/companion animal relationships, even if the practice is arguably well-intended. Before addressing these issues, let me first explain the process of cloning pets and address some of the general moral issues it raises.

What Pet Cloning Is and What It Involves

The technology to clone pets has only recently become available, and for that reason it is still a fledgling business. Indeed, the first commercially cloned pet, a cat named Little Nicky, was cloned in 2004 by Genetic Savings & Clone, and was commissioned by a Texas woman who paid a fee of $50,000. Prior to cloning companion animals, techniques in animal husbandry were developed that enabled the successful cloning of farm animals such as the now-famous Dolly the Sheep.

To create a pet clone, researchers harvest a mature somatic cell, such as a skin cell, from an already-existing animal in order to copy it.[2] They transfer the DNA of that animal's somatic cell into an egg cell that has had the nucleus removed; by removing the nucleus of the egg cell, the original animal's cell can be inserted and the genetic material from that donor animal can be recreated. Critics of pet cloning are morally disturbed by the number of pregnancies that adult female "surrogates" are required to endure in order to successfully achieve one live birth. In order to get to the stage of having the cloned embryos returned for implantation, the "surrogate" females may be first pumped with hormones and undergo an egg retrieval process to garner as many eggs as possible for the fusion process.[3] After that initial surgical intervention, the females face another intervention in being "primed" for embryo return by receiving hormone injections and undergoing another surgery to have the cloned embryos transferred. This process is repeated, again and again, in the hopes of having some of the embryos implant, though as ethicist Autumn Fiester notes, "The efficiency of animal cloning has typically been about 1 to 2%, so for every 100 embryos that are implanted in surrogate animals, about 98 of the embryos fail to produce a live animal offspring" (2005b, 331). Add to these concerns worries about the number of miscarried pregnancies and the resulting number of harmed offspring, and one can see why, from a purely utilitarian view, pet cloning is a morally questionable business.

Defenders of the practice, however, note that research animals are already subject to various forms of research and experimentation, and that the use of these dogs and cats in pet cloning may actually be a net gain for the animals, since it avoids other more painful and invasive forms of experimentation. Indeed, in embarking on the business of pet cloning, Genetic Savings & Clone (GSC) produced a set of practice guidelines intended as much as possible to protect the dogs involved from experiencing suffering and harm. As outlined by founder Lou Hawthorne, the guidelines included allowing the surrogates a minimum of two hours of play time per day, retiring the females from the project after eight months, and placing them in "loving homes" at the point of retirement (Hawthorne 2002b, 230). Their code of ethics also prohibited those involved in GSC's "Missyplicity Project"[4] from knowingly sharing information or techniques with those pursuing human cloning. Whether the harm caused to the dogs used in the Missyplicity Project was justified or not, Hawthorne's company was the first to institute a code of ethics surrounding their cloning practice.

Cloned Pets as Luxury Items

Another criticism faced by the practice of pet cloning is the cost: the fees paid by individuals who have commissioned the cloning have ranged from $50,000 to clone a cat to $155,000 paid by a couple to clone their deceased Labrador Retriever ("Florida Couple Clones Beloved Dog for $155,000" 2009). From a critical viewpoint, such expenditure seems like a gross misuse of resources when that money could be donated to the American Society for the Prevention of Cruelty to Animals to help reduce the pet population through spaying and neutering programs, or donated to animal shelters that care for homeless and abused animals. While I have some sympathy with those criticisms, they are handily answered by considering the other ways in which wealthy individuals spend their excess funds. As Hawthorne states, "Can anyone seriously argue that Porsche's new sports utility vehicle is really justified when millions are still starving? In a capitalist economy, consumer demand and the ability to fill it are all the justifications you need" (2002a, 243).

Hawthorne points out that companies offering pet cloning services are no different than other companies that offer luxury services: arguably, any such expenditures are wasteful and violate social justice concerns because rather than purchasing unnecessary luxury items, wealthy individuals could be putting their excess funds toward minimizing human or animal suffering by supporting programs to eliminate it. Yet I suspect that many wealthy individuals *do* contribute a certain portion of their wealth in service to the poor and needy, and to suggest otherwise may inaccurately represent them. In any case, any program that would dictate how people should spend their excess funds is doomed to failure, because it leads down a slippery slope that could potentially disallow something as mundane as purchasing a ticket to a movie when that money could be used to feed several starving African children.

Furthermore, as Fiester has noted in her work on animal cloning, defenders of pet cloning claim that the pet cloning industry will have a minuscule impact on the already-existing population of dogs and cats in need of homes. Even when perfected, the practice is likely to remain small, so even if all would-be pet cloners adopted an already-existing animal, it would not have "any measurable effect on the tragic numbers of animals euthanized" (Fiester 2005a, 335).

These defenses of the pet cloning industry are difficult to counter. I am not claiming that individuals should be barred from spending their money on pet cloning services, should that be where they want to put their resources. While it is disturbing to encounter persons who elected to spend over a hundred thousand dollars to clone a pet when there are children starving in the world or dying of easily preventable diseases like dysentery, the same is true of persons who choose to purchase extremely expensive cars or own three mansions. The pet cloning market opens up a new avenue for the wealthy to spend their money, but in itself it does not create the problem of social and economic inequality. I will not pursue this argument, although it is worth considering that by not having pet cloning as an option, individual pet owners might instead embark on a new relationship with an already-existing cat or dog that, while not recreating the relationship with their beloved deceased pet, may be equally if differently fulfilling and meaning-ful. Again, my emphasis here is on the *relationship* that is at stake, and not the pet itself. It is this issue of relationships to which I will now turn in considering what the practice of pet cloning means to our relationships of care.

Pet Cloning and Relationships of Care

In response to the question "Why clone pets?," critic Hilary Bok notes the following:

> Pet owners love their pets. When an animal one loves dies, the most natu-ral thing in the world is to want that animal back. Just as a parent whose child has died is unlikely to be comforted by the thought that there are plenty of other children waiting for adoption, most grieving pet owners are not consoled by the thought that they can always adopt another dog or cat. This is not because pet owners are unduly sentimental or confused about the differences between pets and children. It is because, like parents, they love individuals, and adopting another dog or cat will not replace the individual they have loved and lost. (2002, 235)

Bok eloquently identifies the reasons a person might consider cloning a cat or dog. Indeed, the stories surrounding individuals who have successfully cloned their pets give credence to her claim that, like parents, they "love individuals" and have deep connections to them. Consider, for example, the case of Joyce Bernann McKinney, a woman who lived a solitary farm life in North Carolina with an assortment of horses and dogs. McKinney's deep attachment to her pit bull Booger derived from the fact that he saved her life and aided in her recovery from an attack by her other pit bull, Tough Guy. As she recounts her story, when Tough Guy unexpectedly attacked her, she screamed for Booger's help, and Booger defended her by warding off the other pit bull, giving McKinney the chance to flee. The attack left her with severe injuries that required multiple surgeries and a long period of convalescence; during her recuperation Booger again assisted her by pulling off her shoes and socks at night, helping her in and out of the bathtub, and even turning doorknobs (Woestendiek 2010, 32–33). As McKinney states, "Booger taught me not to give up, not to feel sorry for myself. Booger made me feel like a whole person. . . . Booger taught me I could do anything I could do before—that I just had to figure out a different way to do it" (Woestendiek 2010, 34). It is fair to say that this beloved pet restored McKinney's sense of self, her ability to be a whole person, and that he gave her the resilience to manage the challenges she faced in recovering from the trauma. Other recent pet cloners share similar stories of deep attachment and sustenance of self in relation to their animal companions (Woestendiek 2010): it is unsurprising, then, that these individuals would turn to pet cloning in an attempt to revive their pets and the relationships that they so treasured.

A feminist relational approach to autonomy takes the individual as understandable in terms of her relationships with others, viewing human beings as primarily beings-in-relationship. Such an approach highlights the inescapable connectedness of selves and the degree to which our connections with others form our relationships, desires, aspirations, and our very identities (Barclay 2000, 52). Instead of understanding selves as "islands unto themselves," and processes of individuation as setting us apart from one another, relational autonomy sees selves as developing out of the relationships in which we are enmeshed. I argue that these identity-constituting relationships can include human-companion animal relationships, given the depth of feeling and the attachment that is often part of them.[5] Indeed, some humans (like McKinney) eschew relationships with other human beings and prefer to relate to animals because of the sense of comfort, acceptance, and unconditional love they receive from those relationships. It is often the case that human beings are not so accepting and loving, so it may be understandable that some human beings prefer to relate to animal companions.

This concept of the self as deeply relational fits within a feminist care ethic framework. According to care ethics, traditional Kantian and utilitarian moral frameworks overlook one of the most salient features of human moral life: the capacity for care and human relationship. "Care" involves seeing to the physical support and meeting the needs of self and others. It emphasizes the motivation to care for those who are dependent and vulnerable, and it is inspired by the recognition that, as Eva Kittay puts it, we are all "some mother's child" (1999, 23). Seen as more of a virtue or a practice than a moral theory in the vein of Kantian or utilitarian theory, care ethics emphasizes the importance to moral deliberation of emotion and the need to reason from particulars.

A care ethic framework thus serves to highlight an entirely different aspect of the pet cloning debate, which I argue is essential to understanding why it may be problematic. The practice represents as fungible the care relationships that are unique unto themselves and, thus, irreplaceable. This is not to claim that would-be pet owners do not appreciate that they are not getting an identical copy of their original pet; nor is it to claim that they are (or necessarily will be) dissatisfied with the pet that results. Rather, my concern is that by engaging in and encouraging such a commercial endeavor, pet cloning agencies are perverting and misrepresenting relationships of care to use them for commercial purposes.

The Exploitation of Pet Owners

In her article on pet cloning, Autumn Fiester (2005a) addresses concerns about exploiting human-animal companion relationships. She identifies the problem of pet cloners' self-deception regarding the cloned pet as a psychological, not a moral, issue, and she rejects the idea that they are exploited. Fiester claims that "if the customers don't feel betrayed or deceived (and indeed, they do not) and are satisfied with their investment and comforted by the clone's existence, then it is hard to get this psychological concern going" (39). She further claims that "the bereft pet owner might know full well that the clone will be nothing more than a genetic twin, and the decision to clone might be merely an attempt to preserve something important from the original animal, rather than resurrect it" (39). On Fiester's account, pet cloners are neither deceived nor exploited, since they may know full well what they are embarking upon and may be completely satisfied with the companion animals that result.

Contravening Fiester's account of exploitation, as philosopher Joel Feinberg has asserted, exploitation can be defined in such a way that the exploitee can both benefit from and consent to the arrangement. Feinberg states,

> Common to all exploitation of one person (B) by another (A) . . . is that A makes a profit or gain by turning some characteristic of B to his own advantage. . . . [E]xploitation . . . can occur in morally unsavory forms without harming the exploitee's interests and . . . despite the exploitee's fully voluntary consent to the exploitative behavior. (1988, 176–79)

I appeal to Feinberg's account of exploitation because he emphasizes that exploitation may not seem to harm the exploitee's interests and that it may occur with her/his voluntary consent. This fits within the context of pet cloning, where pet owners may seek out the services, give their consent to pursue the technology, and may not seem to experience a setback to their interests in doing so. Focusing on lack of psychological harm, as Fiester does, or emphasizing informed consent does not therefore settle the question of whether pet cloning may be an exploitative practice.

Such subtle exploitative aspects of pet cloning highlight the potential moral risks associated with it that are best revealed by a care ethics framework. The informed consent process may, indeed, remind pet cloners that the process will not result in a pet that appears or behaves identically to their original pet, yet on some level people want something back that was the same or else they would not pursue the practice in the first place, given the time, trouble, and cost that it involves. Some form of self-deception may be part of the process, given that grieving pet owners are paying to recreate something of apparent relational value. The possibility of disappointment, most likely to be directed toward the clone, is another moral risk that may not make pet cloning inherently morally wrong, but renders it of moral concern. From a care ethics perspective, the instrumental attitude toward these relationships (which may be transferrable to human relationships as well) is a kind of self-induced dehumanization that denies the uniqueness of our various human and animal relationships.

The technology to clone pets not only raises concerns about exploitation; critics have also avowed that it commodifies important human-animal relationships (Bok 2002). Yet these claims of commodification have been rebutted by defendants who point out that many goods and services offered within a capitalist system are marketed in such a way that they commodify relationships and encourage consumer behavior by playing off those relationships. It is to this criticism that I will now turn.

Why Commodifying Pets through Cloning Is a Form of Illegitimate Commodification

In her article on the ethics of egg donation, Bonnie Steinbock makes the following observation:

> To commodify something is to give it a market price. That in itself is not a bad thing. We could not buy our groceries or clothes or the morning paper if they did not have a market price. If some things should not be commodified, we need a rationale for this. This is not always forthcoming. (2004, 260)

Steinbock goes on to quote other commentators who claim that "[u]nfortunately, a great deal of the talk about 'commodification' has been clumsy and sloppy. The term has been used as a magic bullet, as if saying 'But that's commodification!' is the same as having made an argument" (260). Steinbock is right to suggest that merely claiming that a practice commodifies something is not a criticism unless one can argue that such commodification is illegitimate. I argue that pet cloning may be such a case of illegitimate commodification, as it serves to instrumentalize attachments that are supposedly beyond price, and puts a dollar value on the emotional vulnerability of those individuals who would consider cloning their dying or deceased animal companions.

As I noted earlier in this chapter, a care ethics framework highlights the value of relationships to our moral lives and the distinct ways in which we are affected by those with whom we are in relationships. Our feelings for the individuals (humans or animals) that are part of our web of relationships cannot be transferred or recreated by taking up a relationship with *another* human or animal. Such a fact creates a special moral obligation to respect the uniqueness of the relationships we have and to nurture and specially care for those with whom we are involved. Furthermore, these relationships are identity-constituting and allow for the possibility of human flourishing. Any system that undercuts these unique moral goods imperils those relationships, and this is a moral risk associated with the practice of pet cloning.

In her work, Margaret Radin addresses a concern about the degree to which the market has infiltrated areas of human life that were not heretofore subjected to market norms. As she claims, we cannot achieve a proper conception of human personhood and flourishing if certain aspects of life are in principle regarded as subject to being bought and sold. For Radin, when broadly understood, the term "commodification" includes not only actual buying and selling of something (commodification narrowly understood), but also regarding the thing in terms of market rhetoric, "the practice of thinking about interactions as if they were sale transactions," and applying market methodology to it (1987, 1866). Applying market norms to things renders them fungible, meaning they are replaceable with money or other objects. She claims, "A fungible object can pass in and out of the person's possession without effect on the person as long as its market equivalent is given in exchange" (1895). The practice of pet cloning, I argue, is one example where the market is intervening to illegitimately commodify and render fungible a relationship that should not be construed as such. Unlike the groceries or the morning paper to which Steinbock refers, the commodification of pet-human relationships does harm by regarding those relationships in terms of market rhetoric, applying principles of the market to them, and treating as fungible the unique relationships that prompt the cloning attempt in the first place. As Radin claims, "[W]e must reject universal commodification, because to see the rhetoric of the market—the rhetoric of fungibility, alienability, and cost-benefit analysis—as the sole rhetoric of human affairs is to foster an inferior conception of human flourishing" (1925).

Steinbock is correct that not all forms of commodification are morally wrong, and that we need a rationale for why something should not be commodified. In the preceding section, I have suggested that the technology of pet cloning is an example of illegitimate commodification because of the way it represents human-pet relationships and the impact it has on how we think and talk about the practice. In the next section I will address the concern that a care ethics approach to human/companion animal relationships might discriminate between animals on irrelevant moral grounds.

Are Animal Companions of Greater Moral Worth than Other Animals?

My emphasis in this chapter on a care ethics approach to cloning pets raises a difficult issue about how we assign moral value to others. In beginning my moral analysis by emphasizing the moral importance of relationship and care, and by underscoring the utter uniqueness of each relationship, I may seem to be suggesting that simply because we are in a relationship with them, our animal companions enjoy a higher status and moral value than other animals with which we are not in such relationships. To put the question bluntly, are our pets more deserving of care and concern simply because they are "ours," because we love them and view them as being special? The answer to this question is both yes and no.

Care ethics is appealing because it defends the value of our particular connections with our loved ones. I share a unique and special relationship with each of my beloved children, for example, and am especially attuned to their needs because as their mother I am especially well situated to identify and understand those needs. They belong to me, not in the sense that I *own* them, but because of our deep and longstanding mutual attachment. While I may enjoy and even love other children, I am not impartial about those to whom I owe special care and obligations. Indeed, should I be so impartial I would arguably be a terrible mother, since by definition good mothering (and good parenting) requires that I care about my children both passionately and with a deep personal investment. The same is true of my other relationships of care with my husband, my mother, my friends, and my pets: they are "particular others" to me and, thus, special. My obligations to them are unlike general obligations of care I may owe to other persons and animals.

Where companion animals are concerned, this means that the special treatment they receive from their humans is morally justified. Pet owners may be concerned about animals with which they are not in direct relationship, but they will nevertheless tend to shower their companion animals with special care and concern.[6] This does not mean that those with their "own" pets should not care about the welfare of all animals, but it does highlight a tension between animals within the same species that are subject to vastly different treatment. In his article "Human Morality and Animal Research," Herman Herzog clearly states the tension: "[T]here exists a peculiar situation in which treatment that is unacceptable for one category of animals is prescribed for animals of the same species that are of a different moral type" (1993, 340). Herzog is not claiming that we ought not to distinguish among these "moral types," but simply that human moral life is messy and complicated such that these sorts of moral complexities cannot be happily resolved. I agree with his account, which fits well with the care ethics framework from which my argument derives.

Care ethics does not suggest that those outside our web of relationships are of no moral consequence, and this is where the "no" arises in response to the question about whether we are justified in treating some (research) dogs badly and other (pet) dogs well. Having particular relationships of care does not absolve us of the responsibility to care for (and about) those who are outside our personal web of relationships; and, in fact, by virtue of having those personal relationships we should be able to see more readily that others have a unique moral value, whether they are "ours" or not. While care ethics requires us to care passionately about and especially for those who are in our lives, it does not mean we have no moral responsibility for those who are not. And, indeed, this is not the attitude one sees expressed by humans with companion animals: it is often the case that those with pets dedicate time and money to animal rescues and shelters, to help care for those animals that are not so happily situated in loving homes.

The Current Status of the Pet Cloning Industry

My moral concerns about the enterprise of pet cloning address it from a relational care ethics point of view, and extend both to those humans who commission the clones and to the pet clones themselves. But how viable is this industry, and should we be concerned that it is likely to grow, thus cementing the notion that our relationships are, indeed, fungible? While initially, in the early 2000s, entrepreneurs anticipated a market ripe for development, that market has not significantly grown over the past 10–15 years. In fact, Lou Hawthorne, CEO of BioArts International, published a notice outlining the reasons for which in 2009 BioArts International exited the pet cloning market. Hawthorne justifies this action by citing, among reasons, concerns about the "tiny market." As he states,

> In order to collect more data on the demand for dog cloning—and to promote our initial auction of cloning services—on May 30th, 2008 we announced the "Golden Clone Giveaway"—a contest with a grand prize of a free clone of the winner's dog. The media and blogosphere covered this announcement very thoroughly; we expected tens if not hundreds of thousands of contest submissions. We were astonished when just 237 people signed up for the giveaway. (Hawthorne 2009)

Hawthorne concludes, "Given how few people want to clone a dog when priced at zero, the market for dog cloning is at best a specialized niche. In a niche market, if one cannot capture a reasonably high price for each order, that market is not worth pursuing" (Hawthorne 2009). The fact that so few individuals applied for the cloning service "giveaway" may speak volumes about public perceptions of the value and pursuit-worthiness of cloning pets. In her work, Fiester notes 2004 polling data indicating that 64 percent of Americans "believe that animal cloning is morally wrong" (2005a, 329). Perhaps this reservation about the practice is why so few people are entering the pet cloning market; perhaps the "price point" is too high for most individuals to even consider it; or perhaps more people recognize that not just their beloved pets, but the relationships they had with those pets, are not capable of being recreated or that they ought not to be recreated.

Whether or not BioArts decided on any *ethical* grounds to withdraw from the pet cloning market may be a debatable point, especially given Hawthorne's claim that there are other more lucrative avenues that the company may pursue. However, given my ethical concerns about the way pet cloning may exploit and commodify relationships, and the way in which it allows market norms to invade relationships of care, the fewer companies that are engaged in this technology, the better. In the end, the practice of pet cloning may wither on the vine due to these market concerns (too few parties interested in purchasing the technology; too small a profit margin to justify the practice), and if that is the case, then we avoid the moral risks I have enumerated in this chapter. While we wait for these market-based considerations to take their toll, pet cloning companies like ViaGen Pet Services or Sooam Biotech Research Foundation—if they truly believe that pets hold a "special place in our lives" and are "part of the family"—would desist from offering cloning services.

Conclusion

I conclude by reiterating what I am *not* attempting to establish in this chapter. While I have emphasized the way in which a concept of relational autonomy and a care ethics framework help to better understand the moral harms of pet cloning, I am not arguing that the kinds of concerns addressed by utilitarian or Kantian theories are misplaced. On the contrary, those approaches to the pet cloning debate highlight concerns that must be taken very seriously. I am also not claiming that humans who elect to clone their pets are morally bad, since the desire to do so arises from the most understandable response to the loss of a loved one. Furthermore, I am not suggesting that those who countenance spending enormous sums of money on cloning their animal companions should be barred from doing so, since such an argument requires us to critique any number of ways that individuals elect to spend their wealth.

What I *am* arguing, however, is that cloning companion animals leads to erroneous thinking about the meaning and value of relationships, which does damage to our understanding of ourselves and those with whom we stand in relationship. The moral harms associated with the practice of pet cloning are, furthermore, transferable to our attitudes and beliefs about other relationships in which we are engaged, including human relationships. Expanding markets into the affective area of human life is morally problematic because it renders fungible those relationships that should be seen as unique, and it allows market norms and attitudes to bleed into them. It also sidelines important human emotions such as grief and loss, and represents a refusal to countenance our finitude, as both human and non-human animals. This is an undesirable implication of the practice that has been poorly acknowledged by the scientists and bioethicists who have been working in this area, and that I argue renders the practice unethical.

Notes

1. Notice I am not claiming that humans are necessarily trying to recreate the pet itself—they may recognize clearly that the cloned animal is not identical to its predecessor—but that humans are trying to recreate the relationship, which by virtue of its specificity cannot be reproduced.
2. Note that somatic cells must be harvested while the animal is alive, so that they can be stored for later use after the animal has died. For more information on animal cloning, see National Human Genome Research Institute (2015).
3. In his writing on his company's pet cloning practice, Lou Hawthorne claims that they do not do egg retrieval processes on their female surrogates. As he claims, "Although we at GSC have spayed some dogs in estrus to obtain mature eggs for study, we do not routinely use egg donors, much less hormonally stimulate them. We obtain most of our eggs from spay clinics, which GSC underwrites financially. Our approach not only avoids use of egg donors but also improves the pet overpopulation problem" (2002a, 244).
4. GSC's first pet cloning venture involved the attempt to clone founder Lou Hawthorne's dog, Missy, hence the name of the research program: the "Missyplicity Project."
5. I argue that this depth of feeling and attachment is not unidirectional, but is also reciprocated by companion animals. Accounts of pets that have found their way home from thousands of miles away, that have risked their lives to save their human companions, or that have showed grief over the deaths of their loved ones all suggest that dogs and cats are able to reciprocate in the human-nonhuman animal relationships. Whether this reciprocation is entirely equal may be debated, but not all human-to-human relationships are equally reciprocated, either, if one considers parents' connections to their infants, toddlers, mentally disabled children, or elderly

parents with dementia. See Eva Kittay (1999) for an excellent account of reciprocity in connection to relationships of care.

6. One does not have to think long to come up with examples of such care and concern: the money humans spend on their pets to accessorize them, to offer them specialized health care, and to purchase high-quality food and treats is clear evidence of this special treatment.

References

Barclay, Linda. 2000. "Autonomy and the Social Self." In *Relational Autonomy: Feminist Perspectives on Autonomy, Agency, and the Social Self*, edited by Catriona Mackenzie and Natalie Stoljar, 52–71. New York: Oxford University Press.

Bok, Hilary. 2002. "Cloning Companion Animals Is Wrong." *Journal of Applied Animal Welfare Science* 5 (3): 233–38.

Feinberg, Joel. 1988. *Harmless Wrongdoing*. Oxford: Oxford University Press.

Fiester, Autumn. 2005a. "Creating Fido's Twin: Can Pet Cloning Be Ethically Justified?" *Hastings Center Report* 35 (4): 34–39.

Fiester, Autumn. 2005b. "Ethical Issues in Animal Cloning." *Perspectives in Biology and Medicine* 48 (3): 328–43.

"Florida Couple Clones Beloved Dog for $155,000." 2009. CNN, January 29. http://www.cnn.com/2009/LIVING/01/29/cloned.dog/index.html?eref=ib.

Hawthorne, Lou. 2002a. "Hawthorne's Rebuttal." *Journal of Applied Animal Welfare Science* 5 (3): 243–46.

Hawthorne, Lou. 2002b. "A Project to Clone Companion Animals." *Journal of Applied Animal Welfare Science* 5 (3): 229–31.

Hawthorne, Lou. 2009. "Six Reasons We're No Longer Cloning Dogs." BioArts International. http://www.bioartsinternational.com/press_release/ba09_09_09.htm.

Herzog, Herman. 1993. "Human Morality and Animal Research." *American Scholar* 62: 337–49.

Kittay, Eva Feder. 1999. *Love's Labor: Essays on Women, Equality, and Dependency*. New York: Routledge.

National Human Genome Research Institute. 2015. "How Are Animals Cloned?" Last modified May 11. https://www.genome.gov/25020028/#al-6.

Radin, Margaret. 1987. "Market Inalienability." *Harvard Law Review* 100: 1849–937.

Steinbock, Bonnie. 2004. "Payment for Egg Donation and Surrogacy." *The Mount Sinai Journal of Medicine* 71 (4): 255–65.

ViaGen Pets. 2016. http://www.viagenpetservices.com/.

Woestendiek, John. 2010. *Dog, Inc.: The Uncanny Inside Story of Cloning Man's Best Friend*. Avery: New York.

11 REPRODUCING COMPANION ANIMALS

Jessica du Toit and David Benatar

Free from human intervention, most companion animals would copulate and produce offspring.[1] Given that companion animals tend to have (relatively) short gestation periods, as well as litters rather than singletons, the natural course would be prolific procreation, even if mortality rates would also be high.[2]

In many cases humans mediate this reproductive activity by selecting the animals' mates in order to breed animals who have the traits that humans desire. Sometimes this breeding is on a relatively small scale, but other times the breeding is on a large commercial scale.

Breeding companion animals as well as allowing them to breed is controversial. In this chapter we shall consider three kinds of argument for an alternative course of action, namely, preventing companion animals from reproducing, usually by sterilizing them. We begin with more controversial arguments and progress to one that should have the broadest appeal.

Anti-Natalist Arguments

One set of arguments does not apply exclusively to companion animals, but more generally to all sentient animals, including humans. These are the so-called "anti-natalist" arguments, according to which coming into existence is either so risky or so harmful that we should desist from bringing sentient beings into existence. One implication of these arguments is that breeding animals is wrong.

There are a number of anti-natalist arguments. They cannot be presented in full here, but we shall outline some of them.[3] The "asymmetry argument" claims that there is an important axiological asymmetry between benefits and harms, such that coming into existence is always a harm. According to this argument, (1) the presence of harm is bad and (2) the presence of benefit is good, but while (3) the absence of harm is *good* even if that good is not enjoyed by any being, (4) the absence of benefit is *not bad* unless there is a being for whom this absence is a deprivation.

If there is this asymmetry, which we may call the "basic asymmetry," then it follows that coming into existence has disadvantages but no advantages relative to never existing. The disadvantages are all the bad things that befall the animal who comes into existence. These include, but are not limited to, pain, suffering, frustration, dissatisfaction, and, on some views, death. Companion animals, or at least the luckier ones, also have good things happen to them. Lucky dogs, for example, are fed, tickled, loved, and played with. However, while all this makes a dog's life better, these goods are not an advantage over never existing. If there is no feeding, tickling, loving, and playing because there is no dog, then there is no deprivation and it is not bad. It follows that bringing an animal into existence harms that animal.

The usual response to this conclusion is to deny the basic asymmetry that leads to it. There are various ways of doing this. One could claim that absent benefits are bad even when no being is deprived of those benefits. Alternatively, one could claim that absent harms and benefits are neither good nor bad, precisely because there is no being for whom these are bad or good.

However, these claims come at considerable cost. This is because the basic asymmetry is the best explanation for a number of other widely endorsed asymmetries. For example, it is widely agreed that while we have a reason—even a duty—to desist from bringing into existence a being who would have a life of suffering, we have no reason—much less a duty—to bring into existence beings who would, by the usual standards, have a good life. This asymmetry is best explained by the basic asymmetry. If one thinks that absent benefits are bad, then one *does* have a reason to create a being who will enjoy those benefits. And if one thinks that absent harms and benefits are neither good nor bad, then one cannot say that it is good to avoid bringing into existence a being who would suffer.

The asymmetry argument implies that animals, like humans, are harmed by being brought into existence. This is not sufficient to show that it is wrong to breed animals or to allow them to breed. If the harm of being brought into existence were a minor one, it might still be possible to defend the practice of breeding animals or not sterilizing them. One might defend the practice by appealing, for example, to the benefits to humans of companion animals.

However, the harms of existence are considerable. This is true for all sentient beings, but our focus here is only on a subset of those beings—companion animals. To be sure, many such animals suffer less harm than do the vast majority of animals who are reared for human consumption. The harms are nonetheless more substantial than people typically recognize.

Consider the restrictions on companion animals' freedom. These are very severe in the case of many companion birds and rodents as well as other mammals who are caged. These animals effectively have a lifetime of incarceration, perhaps with occasional furloughs. This must be enormously frustrating. Other companion animals, such as dogs, are often not caged. However, their movement is restricted by closed doors, house walls, garden fences, and leashes. This frustrates their ability to pursue, among other things, the scents and sex they seek. It also leads to separation anxiety when their companion humans leave them. If they are left for long periods, boredom can result. Humans also restrict animals' freedom with regard to what and how much they eat. Dogs, for example, regularly beg for food that is withheld from them.

The claim is not that restrictions on the freedom of companion animals are all unwarranted. They are often justified by the welfare of the animals. Many companion animals would stand a high chance of being harmed if they had unrestricted movement. They would be killed by predators or motor vehicles, for example. Thus, given the existence of these animals and the dangers of the surrounding environment (even if that environment is humanly constructed), it is often indeed best, all things considered, to restrict companion animals' freedom in some ways, but not in others.[4] However, animals typically do not understand this, and we need to recognize that their lives include significant frustration as a result. This is very relevant when we are considering whether these animals should be brought into existence at all.

It is easy to underestimate just how often companion animals feel the frustrations, anxiety, and boredom just described. These are daily experiences and, at least in some cases, may last for large portions of the day.

Consider too the other hardships in companion animal lives. For example, cats are often declawed to prevent them from doing damage to the home interiors to which they are confined. Although it is a minority of cats who are subjected to this treatment, it is not a small minority. Approximately 25 percent of cats in the United States are declawed.[5] Besides the obvious pain associated with the surgery, the thwarting of natural feline behavior must be frustrating.

Many dog breeds are subjected to tail "docking." This is sometimes performed by means of a tight rubber band, which prevents blood supply to the remainder of the tail, causing it to necrose and slough off. More commonly, however, the tail is removed surgically by means of a blade or scissors. This is typically done without anesthesia or analgesia. The best available evidence suggests that this is painful to the puppies on whom it is performed, despite their early stage of development.[6]

Some animals are subjected to ear cropping and to "de-vocalizing," the latter designed to prevent them from barking or meowing.

There is more. Companion animals, such as dogs and cats, are typically wrenched from their mothers and littermates while they are young. They are then inserted into a new and initially bewildering environment. This is not a lifelong problem, but it is nonetheless an unpleasantness that must be considered when thinking about how much bad there is in the lives of these animals.

Arguably worse, and usually longer-lasting, are the ravages of ageing and disease. Just like humans, they go blind and deaf. They develop skin diseases, arthritis, dysplasia, or any of a number of cardiac, endocrine, gastrointestinal, urological, or dental diseases. They become paralyzed or epileptic, contract infections and become infested, and suffer malignancies. It should go without saying that this is merely a partial list.

The lifespans of companion animals are generally much shorter than those of humans. The periods of decrepitude are therefore shorter, although not proportionally to the lifespan. Many companion animals are spared the worst by euthanasia, but they endure significant decline before euthanasia becomes clearly the right option.

Even the luckiest companion animals will experience at least some of the above. Matters are still worse for the unlucky ones. Millions of dogs, cats, and other animals who should be companions to humans are in fact neglected or abused by members of our species. The full spectrum of this abuse is appalling. Animals are left chained and alone in disagreeable conditions. They are starved, beaten, mutilated, burnt, and killed.

There is a tendency for people to think that their companion animals' offspring will have good lives. Those who think this should be aware of the pervasive optimism bias that characterizes our species. Humans tend to think that things are better than they really are. There is ample evidence of this[7] and it cannot be ignored.

However, even if one thought that *some* companion animals lead good lives, it would still be the case that any animal brought into existence would stand a high chance of suffering significant harm at some stage in its life. One problem with breeding is that those who accept the risks of breeding are not those who will be the primary victims of whatever harm results. Instead, the breeder assumes the risk for the beings who will be brought into existence.

Nor are the risks minor. Any animal brought into being stands a very high chance of succumbing to serious harm at some point. Either it will be cut down in its youth, perhaps by an accident, or, if it lives long enough, it is likely to suffer from the decline and decrepitude that characteristically precedes death in old age.

The harm that will befall those animals brought into existence provides us with strong reason to desist from bringing them into existence by breeding existing animals. Does it also provide us with similarly strong reason to prevent existing animals from breeding? In the absence of long-term animal contraception, the means we have for preventing animals from breeding are either restricting their access to mates or sterilizing them. Preventing animals from mating adds to their frustration and makes the quality of these animals' lives worse. Sterilization avoids that problem, but surgery comes with some risks as well as postoperative discomfort that also diminishes the quality of that animal's life, albeit for a limited period.

Although sterilization does carry some costs for the animal sterilized, our choices are stark. Either we inflict this limited harm on existing animals or we allow many more suffering animals to be created. We cannot leave the choice to the reproducing animals. Because they are not able to make the decision themselves, we, as their custodians, need to decide.

Abolitionist Arguments

A second kind of argument against breeding companion animals and allowing them to breed with one another is one that calls for the eventual abolition of the institution of keeping companion animals. According to these "abolitionist" arguments, while humans should continue to care for the companion animals already in existence, they should desist from allowing any more of these animals to come into existence. This is because abolitionists think that there is something morally problematic about the category "companion animals." The purported problem would not be entirely avoided by shifting from *owning* companion animals to merely *keeping* them. The only ethically defensible means of bringing an end to the institution of keeping companion animals is by desisting from breeding them and by sterilizing those already in existence.

In what follows, we shall consider two abolitionist objections, namely what we shall call the "property objection" and the "dependency objection." In order to consider these objections on their own merits, we shall make no assumptions about the soundness of the anti-natalist arguments.

The Property Objection

As far as the law is concerned, companion animals are the personal property of the humans who keep them. The humans are the *owners* of those animals. However, humans as well as our legal systems distinguish companion animals from *in*animate items of property in that they recognize that humans ought not to treat companion animals in certain ways and that they owe at least some duties *directly* to these animals.[8]

While many people may find the present situation satisfactory, there are some who object to it. For example, Gary Francione acknowledges that existing legal systems offer *some* protection for companion animals' interests, but he insists that they are unable to offer *sufficient* protection for the interests of these animals.[9] Thus, he thinks that while humans ought to continue to care for those companion animals who *already* exist, they ought not breed these animals or even allow them to reproduce with one another.[10] We shall refer to this view as the "property objection."

Our ceasing to breed companion animals, when coupled with our preventing them from reproducing with one another, would eventually result in the extinction of these animals. Thus, the property objection is by no means uncontroversial, and there are numerous responses to it. One might, for example, agree with Professor Francione that the legal status of companion animals raises some serious moral questions, but think that we would be permitted to breed companion animals and to allow them to reproduce with one another *if* their legal status changed such that they were no longer viewed as property.[11]

The problem with this response, however, is that the legal status of companion animals is unlikely to change any time soon. Far too many people still regard animals as property, thus making imminent legal change unlikely. There is little reason to think that these attitudes are going to change in the short term. If breeding continues, many generations of animals will continue to have the status of property. Thus the property objection cannot be met by a glib appeal to the prospects of a changed legal status.

Another possible response to the property objection is to say that having the legal status of property need not harm companion animals, if those who keep these animals do not accept the law's view of those animals as property. That is to say, humans who do not regard their companion animals as property, but rather as sentient beings who are due everything that such a being is morally due, would not harm the animals in their care.[12] Thus, it might be thought that such humans may permissibly breed their companion animals or allow them to breed on condition that they ensure that the resultant offspring will be kept by humans with the same attitude.

However, while companion animals need not suffer any harm as a result of their being owned, they might nonetheless be *wronged*, just as one would wrong human beings by owning them, irrespective of how well they were treated. In other words, "property" is simply not an appropriate category in which to place human beings. To place *any* human being in the category of property is to impugn the moral status or intrinsic value of that human being and thus to wrong him or her. Similarly, it might be said that to place a companion animal in the category of property is necessarily to impugn the moral status or intrinsic value of, and so to wrong, that animal. This is because, with regard to being owned, there is no morally relevant difference between, for example, very young children or severely cognitively impaired humans and (most of) those animals who tend nowadays to be kept as companions. Young children, severely cognitively impaired humans, and companion animals are all sentient, and none are autonomous. Thus, even if they suffer no harm as a result of their being categorized as property, their being categorized in this way can nonetheless be said to wrong them. This remains true irrespective of how well they might be treated by their respective humans.

In response to this argument, it might be said that it is necessary to distinguish between a companion animal's (a) being wronged by the law and (b) being wronged by the humans in whose home it is kept. With regard to (b), it is necessary to distinguish furthermore between a human's (i) accepting or endorsing the law's categorization of companion animals as property and (ii) rejecting the law's categorization of companion animals as property.

Given that the law categorizes companion animals as property, they are clearly wronged by the law. However, it is our view that they are wronged by the humans in whose homes they are kept *only if* those humans accept or endorse the law's categorization of companion animals as property. Those humans who reject the law's categorization do not share the law's wrongful attitude and thus they own their companion animals merely in the technical, legal sense. Therefore, *they* do not wrong their companion animals by "owning" them.

One issue remains. Even if humans who reject the current legal status of animals do not themselves wrong their companion animals, they remain the "keepers," "custodians," or "caretakers" of those animals. (The same would be true of more humans if the legal status of animals changed and they were no longer legally property.) To be a keeper, custodian, or caretaker of a companion animal is much like being the (legal) guardian of a child, for example. In the same way that the guardian of a child is charged with caring for and safeguarding the interests of that child, the keeper, custodian, or caretaker of a companion animal is charged with caring for and safeguarding the interests of his companion animal. The question, then, is whether our continuing to bring companion animals into existence would be morally permissible if we merely kept and did not own them (or owned them only in a technical legal sense). This question brings us to the second abolitionist objection.

The Dependency Objection

According to Gary Francione,[13] even if the legal status of companion animals were changed so that they no longer fell into the category of property, humans would nonetheless have a moral obligation to ensure that no more companion animals were brought into existence. This is because he thinks that there is something inherently wrong with *keeping* pets and not merely with owning them. But what could be wrong with keeping companion animals if we are good keepers, that is, if we never fail to care for and safeguard the interests of those animals?

In Professor Francione's view, the inherent wrongfulness has to do with the fact that companion animals are domesticated animals. Domesticated animals are much more docile and trusting than the wild animals from whom they descended. While this renders them better suited to living with, or in close proximity to, humans, it also renders them less effective predators and too trusting to be successful in evading (other) predators. (There are packs of feral dogs, but life for them is typically "nasty, brutish, and short.") The consequence is that domesticated animals are almost entirely dependent on humans for the satisfaction of their fundamental needs and desires.

To be so dependent on another is to be in a position of extreme vulnerability. And to find oneself in this position is to run a very high risk of leading a short and miserable life. For this reason, Professor Francione deems it morally indefensible to place, or allow another creature to be placed, in such a position. Given, then, that our continuing to bring or allow domesticated animals to be brought into existence is to place or allow these animals to be placed in such a position, he thinks that we ought not to continue to do these things. Thus, he thinks that we ought to take steps to bring an end to the practice of keeping companion animals.[14]

In responding to this objection, we shall restrict our attention to kind and caring keepers alone. Although it is true that these keepers' animals are at their mercy, they are precisely the kind of keepers who can be relied upon to satisfy their pets' needs and desires (to the greatest extent possible). Thus, if the dependency objection is to make any sense in these cases, it must be because even if the relevant animals' needs and desires are met, it is morally unconscionable that companion animals are so dependent on their respective keepers.

To appreciate why this might be so, it might help to imagine a hypothetical situation in which someone began to breed genetically altered chimpanzees who are ill-suited to living in the wild, but well-suited to living with, or in close proximity to, humans. Those domesticated chimpanzees would have mental capacities equivalent to those of wild chimpanzees. They would, however, be much less aggressive and more docile, for example, than their wild relatives. Since they would therefore be unable to live independently of humans in the human world, the domesticated chimpanzees would be perpetually dependent on humans for the satisfaction of their fundamental needs and desires. Is there something morally problematic about creating a breed of such chimpanzees?[15]

While some might see nothing wrong with doing so as long as humans satisfy their needs and desires, others might have the intuition that it is morally problematic to choose to bring into existence a creature who will be perpetually dependent on another for the satisfaction of its fundamental needs and desires, even if it will be well cared for.

Thus, we are left with a clash of intuitions. What can be said in the face of these conflicting intuitions and the absence of any clear way of choosing between them? Some might argue that since proponents of the dependency objection are making the claim that certain actions are wrong and wish to change people's practices, they must bear the burden of proof. Since they have not been able to provide a compelling argument, however, it might be thought that we are entitled to dismiss the dependency objection.

However, others might reject the idea that proponents of the objection bear the burden of proof. In this case, the clash of intuitions that we are faced with would imply that the cogency of the "dependency objection" simply cannot be evaluated. Although it would be preferable to resolve this matter, it is entirely possible that there is no resolution available (at least at present). If that is the case, we should not artificially impose or stipulate one. Thus it is unclear whether, on the basis of the dependency objection, it is wrong to continue to breed companion animals and allow them to reproduce with one another. Fortunately, we do not need to reach a conclusion about the dependency objection in order to determine whether breeding companion animals and allowing them to reproduce with one another is permissible. There are other excellent practical reasons for thinking that these practices are wrong.

Harm Prevention Arguments

One such reason is rooted in the fact that there are far too many companion animals who are brought into existence but never homed, or homed for a short while before being abandoned or discarded. Indeed, the Humane Society of the United States estimates that there were approximately 6–8 million dogs and cats who entered animal shelters between 2012 and 2013.[16] The United Kingdom's Royal Society for Prevention of Cruelty to Animals (RSPCA) estimates that during 2013, 245,590 animals entered its shelters.[17] Australia's RSPCA estimates that between 2011 and 2012, over 100,000 cats and dogs were taken into their shelters.[18] And in Canada, shelters took in an estimated 150,000 cats and dogs during 2013.[19] Only some of these animals are rehomed. Millions are eventually killed.[20]

Thus, breeding companion animals contributes to the large number of such animals who are condemned to lead short and miserable lives. Even allowing animals to reproduce typically increases the number of unwanted animals. Sometimes it has this effect directly because the particular animals who are born end up being abandoned or killed. On other occasions the effect is indirect because although those particular companion animals are homed, their existence reduces the "demand" for other, existing animals who have been abandoned or will be killed.

According to Wayne Pacelle,[21] the President and Chief Executive Officer of the Humane Society of the United States, just under 25 percent of all dogs in American households come from shelters or rescue groups. Thus, just over 75 percent of dogs in American households come from pet stores, puppy mills, and small-scale breeders, for example.

Supporting "puppy mills" (by purchasing animals from "pet" stores) is an especially egregious moral wrong. This is because almost all puppy mills treat their dogs—especially the breeding females—atrociously. The dogs tend to be confined to crowded, squalid cages (which are sometimes so small that the animals cannot stand upright inside them), and deprived of human affection and the opportunity to play and exercise. As a result, many of the dogs who come from puppy mills suffer from a variety of (very serious) physical and emotional conditions.[22]

In the face of this, there is a very powerful argument that existing companion animals should be adopted before more are bred. The practical effect of this, as things currently stand, is that no individual should breed companion animals, and everyone should sterilize animals in his or her care in order to avoid the birth of more animals who will either be killed or who will doom other animals in need of adoption.

Of course, if the companion animal population eventually decreased such that the demand for these animals exceeded the number of them *already* in existence, then there would no longer be *this* reason for thinking that we ought to desist from breeding such animals and to prevent them from reproducing with one another. Whether breeding companion animals would then be permissible would depend on whether the anti-natalist and abolitionist arguments are sound.

Either way, we would have excellent reason for thinking that it is wrong to breed *some* companion animals and to allow *some* such animals to reproduce with one another. Here we are thinking of so-called "purebred" or "thoroughbred" companion animals, who tend to be plagued by various diseases and disorders. This has much to do with the fact that they have been, and continue to be, bred to conform to specific human standards. In some cases, the standards have some functional goal. For example, the very low carriage of Dachshunds allows them to enter burrows with relative ease. This makes them well suited to hunting badgers and rabbits, the purpose for which the breed was originally intended. In other cases, the standards are merely aesthetic and then often arbitrary and bizarre. Either way, this is problematic because conforming to these standards is closely associated with an assortment of abnormalities.[23]

For example, dog breeds with protruding eyes are prone to ulceration and irritation of the eye.[24] Large and giant breeds of dog are predisposed to bone tumors and hip and elbow dysplasia as a result of their body size or their fast growth rate.[25] Small breeds of dog—especially those with short legs—often suffer from dysplasias and patellar dislocations.[26] Dogs bred to have unnaturally short noses and flat faces are highly susceptible to varying degrees of upper airway obstruction.[27] There are also many disorders associated with wrinkled skin or excessive skin folds. These include skin fold dermatitis, which is caused by friction between the skin surfaces. This in turn leads to ulcers, infections, and the discharge of pus and fluid.[28] One final example of many possible further ones is that breeds with screw-tails or curly tails are predisposed to spina bifida, which can involve tremendous suffering for the affected animal.[29]

The problem is exacerbated in those breeds where the quest for meeting breed standards leads to the overuse of popular sires. This overuse results in greatly attenuated gene pools and, thus, a very high degree of inbreeding.[30] This inbreeding further explains why diseases and disorders that can be inherited are especially common in thoroughbred companion animals.[31]

Since these conditions usually have a profoundly negative effect on the quality of life of those who suffer from them, we should desist from actively breeding animals who stand a significantly elevated chance of suffering from these conditions.[32]

Conclusion

There are innumerable joys that come from sharing one's life with a companion animal. As a result, many humans treasure their relationships with their dogs and cats. Indeed, for many humans, their relationship with their companion animal is one of the most rewarding relationships in their life. But despite the great value that we attribute to these relationships, we should not lose sight of the important arguments against breeding more companion animals.

Two of the arguments that we have considered—the anti-natalist and the abolitionist arguments—are categorically opposed to all breeding of companion animals. The harm prevention argument, on the other hand, is a conditional one (except in the case of "thoroughbreds"). According to this argument, until such time as the demand for companion animals exceeds the number of these animals already in existence, we should desist from breeding more of these animals and from allowing them to reproduce with one another, even though we should also care for those companion animals who already exist. However, given how many millions of unwanted animals there currently are, we are nowhere near that point. Thus, as things stand, all three arguments converge on the conclusion that reproducing companion animals is wrong. The case against breeding companion animals is significantly overdetermined.[33]

Notes

1. This chapter is the product of a close collaboration. David Benatar wrote the first section. The second section is adapted from Jessica du Toit, "Is Having Pets Morally Permissible?," *The Journal of Applied Philosophy* 33 (2016): 327–43, and is used here with permission. This chapter in turn was adapted from a master's thesis written by Jessica du Toit under David Benatar's supervision ("Human-Animal Relationships," The University of Cape Town, Cape Town, South Africa, 2013). The third section and conclusion of the chapter were jointly conceived, with Jessica du Toit writing the first draft and revisions made by both authors.

2. One-year mortality rates in feral dogs have been found to be around 95 percent. L. Boitani and P. Ciucci ("Comparative Social Ecology of Feral Dogs and Wolves," *Ethology, Ecology & Evolution* 7 [1995]: 58) say that a number of studies have found this.

3. For a fuller account, with a focus on human reproduction, see David Benatar, *Better Never to Have Been: The Harm of Coming into Existence* (New York: Oxford University Press, 2006).

4. Companion animals are often restricted well beyond the level that can be justified. See Clare Palmer and Peter Sandøe, "For Their Own Good: Captive Cats and Routine Confinement," in *The Ethics of Captivity*, ed. Lori Gruen (New York: Oxford University Press, 2014).

5. Gary Patronek, "Assessment of Claims of Short- and Long-Term Complications Associated with Onychectomy in Cats," *Journal of the American Veterinary Medical Association* 219 (2001), quoting the American Pet Products Manufacturers Association, *1999/2000 APPMA National Pet Owners Survey* (Greenwich, Conn: American Pet Products Manufacturers Association, 2000).

6. P. C. Bennett and E. Perini, "Tail Docking in Dogs: A Review of the Issues," *Australian Veterinary Journal* 81 (2003): 208–18.

7. This evidence is reviewed in Benatar, *Better Never to Have Been*, 64–69.

8. Among other things, various animal welfare laws prohibit the unnecessary killing, torturing, maiming, starving, and under-feeding of companion animals, and require that these animals receive adequate veterinary or other medical attention whenever necessary.

9. Gary Francione, *Animals, Property and the Law* (Philadelphia: Temple University Press, 1995); *Animals as Persons: Essays on the Abolition of Animal Exploitation* (New York: Columbia University Press, 2009).

10. Francione, *Animals as Persons*, 13; "'Pets': The Inherent Problems of Domestication," *Animal Rights: The Abolitionist Approach* (blog), July 31, 2012, http://www.abolitionistapproach.com/pets-the-inherent-problems-of-domestication/.

11. The notion of the permissibility of breeding companion animals and allowing them to reproduce with one another, should, both here and at later points in this section, be understood to be very restrictive. That is, it should, for example, be understood to refer to the permissibility of breeding only those companion animals for whom we can provide a good home.

12. There might be some sense in which they would still be *vulnerable* to harm—it would not be illegal to harm them in some ways—but in another important sense even those beings who have full legal status are vulnerable to harm. They are vulnerable to harm by those who violate the law. Of course, there is legal recourse in the latter cases, but that is often no consolation. A murder victim is not brought back to life merely because his or her assailant is brought to account.

13. Francione, "'Pets': The Inherent Problems of Domestication."

14. In "'Pets': The Inherent Problems of Domestication," Francione says, "But if there were two dogs left in the universe and it were up to us as to whether they were allowed to breed so that we could continue to live with dogs ... [I] would not hesitate for a second to bring the whole institution of [pet-keeping] to an end."

15. It might be suggested that breeding permanently dependent humans is a better analogy and that our intuitions are clearly against such a practice. However, one confounding variable with this case is that the cognitive capacities of the bred humans would be stunted relative to the species-norm; this might explain our opposition to it.

16. Wayne Pacelle, *The Bond: Our Kinship with Animals, Our Call to Defend Them* (New York: William Morrow, 2011), 197. See also the Humane Society of the United States' fact sheet entitled "Pets by the Numbers," January 30, 2014, http://www.humanesociety.org/issues/pet_overpopulation/facts/pet_ownership_statistics.html.

17. See the UK RSPCA's fact sheet, "Facts and Figures," http://media.rspca.org.uk/media/facts.

18. See RSPCA Australia's "National Statistics 2011–2012" report, https://www.rspca. org.au/sites/default/files/website/The-facts/Statistics/RSPCA%20Australia%20 National%20Statistics%202011-2012.pdf.

19. See the Canadian Federation of Humane Societies' report, "Animal Shelter Statistics 2013," http://cfhs.ca/athome/shelter_animal_statistics/.

20. Of the 6–8 million cats and dogs who entered shelters in the United States between 2012 and 2013, only some were deemed sufficiently healthy to be adopted. Of those cats and dogs, approximately 2.7 million were killed. RSPCA figures obtained from the UK for the past five years show that 46 percent of the total number of animals who entered the charity's shelters were killed. While some of the animals killed were killed for their own sakes, many of them were killed because there was simply no room for them in shelters (Nick Craven and Lynne Wallis, "Revealed: RSPCA Destroys HALF of the Animals That It Rescues—Yet Thousands Completely Healthy," *The Daily Mail* (online edition), January 8, 2013, http://www.daily-mail.co.uk/news/article-2254729/RSPCA-destroys-HALF-animals-rescues--thousands-completely-healthy.html. During 2011, Australia's RSPCA killed approximately 38,900 of the 108,000 dogs and cats who entered its shelters (see RSPCA Australia's "National Statistics 2011–2012" report). And in Canada, it is estimated that 46,000 of the 150,000 dogs and cats who entered shelters in 2013 were killed (see the Canadian Federation of Humane Societies' report, "Animal Shelter Statistics 2013").

21. Pacelle, *The Bond*, 204.

22. Pacelle, *The Bond*, 206–7.

23. Asher et al., "Inherited Defects in Pedigree Dogs. Part 1: Disorders Related to Breed Standards," *The Veterinary Journal* 182 (2009): 402. Interestingly, conformational breed-associated defects were recognized as early as 1868 by Charles Darwin, who hypothesized that muscular defects in Scottish deerhounds were related to their great size (ibid.).

24. Ibid. 406; Advocates for Animals, "The Price of a Pedigree: Dog Breed Standards and Breed-Related Illness," 2006, 9, http://www.onekind.org/uploads/publications/price-of-a-pedigree.pdf.

25. Asher et al., "Inherited Defects in Pedigree Dogs," 406; Advocates for Animals, "The Price of a Pedigree," 14.

26. Asher et al., "Inherited Defects in Pedigree Dogs," 406; Advocates for Animals, "The Price of a Pedigree," 13.

27. Advocates for Animals, "The Price of a Pedigree," 10.

28. Asher et al., "Inherited Defects in Pedigree Dogs," 407; Advocates for Animals, "The Price of a Pedigree," 12.

29. Asher et al., "Inherited Defects in Pedigree Dogs," 409.

30. Summers et al., "Inherited Defects in Pedigree Dogs. Part 2: Disorders That Are Not Related to Breed Standards," *The Veterinary Journal* 183 (2010): 40; Pacelle, *The Bond*, 218.

31. Elaine A. Ostrander, "Both Ends of the Leash—The Human Links to Good Dogs with Bad Genes," *The New England Journal of Medicine* 367 (2012): 637–38.

32. Even those who, because of the non-identity problem (see Derek Parfit, *Reasons and Persons* [Oxford: Clarendon Press, 1984], Part IV), would deny that the animals brought into existence are harmed, could still recognize that worse outcomes result from breeding "thoroughbreds" than from alternatives.

33. We dedicate this essay to the memory of Ben du Toit (December 4, 2004 to December 14, 2014), an animal who was the best of companions.

12 FOR DOG'S SAKE, ADOPT!

Tina Rulli

People may be familiar with the view that we should adopt our animal companions from rescue organizations rather than purchase them from breeders. Animal welfare groups urge people to "Opt to Adopt!" or to "Adopt, Not Shop!" The imperative is to rescue an existing dog or cat in need of a new home rather than buy from a breeder. Buying from a breeder, whether it is buying an existing animal or one that is not yet born, is supporting a practice of creating new animals (hereon, just "creating them"). But why create more animals when there are so many out there in need of good homes already? Each year animal shelters in the US see a new 7.6 million companion animals come through their doors.[1] Despite the familiarity of the pro-animal-adoption view, there is little to nothing in the philosophical literature on the ethics of adopting our animal companions rather than creating them, nor is there anything defending the other side. What is the merit of this argument?

A look at the recent and emerging literature on the ethics of adopting children rather than procreating may be illuminating. The choice of adopting animal companions (rather than creating them) and the choice of adopting children (rather than procreation) are not entirely analogous. But the similarities and differences are instructive.

I explore the case of a duty to adopt our animal companions rather than commission their creation, leveraging the literature on the duty to adopt rather than procreate children. First, I draw comparisons: if there is a plausible duty to adopt children based on the duty to rescue, then there should likewise be a plausible case for a duty to adopt animal companions. I consider and reject the objection that animals cannot be the proper subjects of duties of beneficence. Next, I discuss the difference between a duty to adopt animal companions *simpliciter* and a duty to adopt *rather* than create. I focus primarily on the latter.

I then consider potential differences between the duty to adopt children rather than procreate and the duty to adopt our animal companions rather than create them. There are several ways in which the animal duty to adopt is especially compelling, given the problems with breeder practices. Next, I explore reasons people might have for choosing to buy their pets from breeders rather than rescue organizations. None justify that choice.

A Duty to Adopt Animal Companions: Comparison with Human Adoption

The first major similarity behind both human and animal adoption arguments is the view that adoption is a morally worthy activity because it helps an existing being in critical need of a new home and family. In contrast, procreation of children or paying someone to breed one's pet creates a new life with needs. But there are millions of existing children and animal companions who could benefit from adoption. Why create a new life to give scarce resources to when there are existing lives already in need of them? This is the main question that gives a duty to adopt in either case its moral force. An existing individual (human or nonhuman) will be badly off if it is not rescued, while a potentially existing individual is not worse off if she is not created. She is in no way at all. So adoption of existing children or animals is morally urgent; it meets a serious, critical need. Creation of individuals, if it is a benefit to them at all, is not urgent.[2] Not conferring the benefit does not result in any harm. The basic idea behind a duty to adopt humans or animals is the same: we should place moral priority on benefiting existing beings in critical need rather than create more needy beings.

The small literature on a duty to adopt children grounds the duty in the more familiar duty to rescue, which states that we should provide life-saving benefits to people when it is of no morally significant cost to ourselves to do so.[3] The initial analogy between rescue and adoption is compelling. Children in need of adoption are vulnerable moral innocents, in no way responsible for their plight. The benefit they need—that of a stable family, with loving parents—is critical. It will greatly impact their lives for the better, and its absence will greatly harm their lives. Without stable families, even when in an institutional setting, children may lack basic nutrition and medical care. They may be subject to neglect and abuse. Children without stable, familiar caretakers are at risk for psychological and emotional deficits, including an impoverished ability to form secure emotional attachments.[4] The prima facie case for a duty to adopt based on a duty to rescue is solid—children in need of adoption have a critical need that others can meet.

Proponents of a duty to adopt then argue that the costs of adopting rather than procreating are not morally significant enough to outweigh the good of rescuing through adoption. For instance, though adoption is financially costly, proponents of a duty to adopt note that its sum is easily minimized in context when considered against the large amount of money required to raise a child from infancy to adulthood.[5] Many people who cannot easily procreate choose very expensive artificial reproductive services (such as in vitro fertilization) whose costs and logistical difficulties easily swamp those of adoption.[6] Many people can muster up the resources when they want to. Also, though some adoptions can be expensive, there are less expensive alternatives to adopting. Finally, many people can afford adoption despite its costs.

Duty-to-adopt proponents also consider the "intrinsic costs" of adoption, including the failure to maintain the biological and genetic relationship between parent and child. Elsewhere, I investigate the reasons for desiring a genetically-related child and argue that these reasons do not defeat a duty to adopt children, as they are too trivial in weight, or are improper under a normative conception of parental interests, or they fail to distinguish genetically-related children from adopted ones.[7] The strategy is to show that children in need of adoption can generate a prima facie case for a duty to rescue through adoption, and then to show that costs associated with adoption, as compared to those of procreation, do not defeat the duty.

One could make a similar case for a duty to adopt animal companions based on the duty to rescue. After all, dogs and cats are in no way responsible for their plight. They are vulnerable and needy victims of a broken animal welfare system, negligent past-owners, or tragedy. Adoption gives them a critically needed benefit—that of a loving family—which will greatly improve their lives. Lack of that benefit will greatly harm their lives. Un-adopted animals and animals deemed unadoptable are routinely euthanized in shelters or left on the streets to fend for themselves. An astronomical 2.7–3.7 million are euthanized each year in the US.[8] The odds of survival for an animal entering a shelter are depressingly low. Though 35 percent of dogs and 37 percent of cats entering shelters are adopted, 31 percent of dogs and 41 percent of cats will be euthanized.[9] Even if any particular animal has a good chance of being adopted, the longer she stays in the shelter, the more room she takes up that could go to another animal, who will be killed for lack of space. There is a strong prima facie case for a duty to adopt companion animals.

Might one object to the animal adoption argument based on the duty to rescue on the grounds that animals are not the proper recipients of obligations of beneficence? One might deny that animals have any moral rights.[10] This putative lack of animal rights is what allegedly permits us to eat them, to perform invasive research on them, and to hold them captive. One might think: if animals have no right against us that we not harm them in these ways, then surely they have no right that we aid them.

Obviously, one could respond by arguing that animals indeed do have moral rights. But we need not sort out the issues with rights to defend the claim that animal lives can be the proper sources of a duty to rescue.[11] For one, it is not at all clear that, even in the human case, someone having the duty to rescue must depend upon someone else having a right to be rescued. Imagine the following case: there are five children at risk of drowning in a pond. You can save one of them at little cost to yourself, but only one of them.[12] You clearly have a duty to rescue a child. But if the duty to rescue is grounded in a rights claim of the child, then if one child has a right to be rescued, so do the other four. For they are all similarly situated. But then no matter which child you rescue, you violate the rights of the four you did not rescue. It seems implausible that in rescuing a child and doing the best you can do, you violate four children's rights. One might amend the view: each child has a right that you consider her equally among others in deciding whom to rescue. But this right alone will not explain why you have a duty to rescue anyone in the first place. It is a right to be considered as a beneficiary of the duty, not grounds for the duty itself. We still need an explanation of the duty to rescue. Rights are not helping.

This should not trouble us, for there are better explanations of the duty to rescue. It is an especially urgent obligation of beneficence that arises when an agent is in a position to respond to and potentially prevent another being from coming to grave harm. The beneficiary need not have a right to be rescued for an agent to have a duty to rescue; the beneficiary only need have morally relevant and urgent interests. Nonhuman animals do: they are sentient, have needs, have interests, and can suffer harms. For these reasons, it is implausible to deny that we have general, positive obligations to animals. It would be morally heinous if one refused to free a dog whose paw was stuck on the railroad tracks, at risk of being struck by an oncoming train, if one could easily do so. Further, that we have obligations of beneficence to animals is intuitively supported and acted upon. Where else does the iconic image of a firefighter rescuing a kitten stuck in a tree come from? Our cities support rescue organizations. From an early age, children rescue lost puppies and kitties, or nurse to health a squirrel or a bird that has fallen from a tree. Given the intuitive support for the claim, it would prove too much to deny the possibility for a duty to adopt animals by rejecting a duty to rescue them.

Plausibly, a general obligation of beneficence to animal companion species is augmented by the special obligations we may have to domesticated animals. As Bernard Rollin says, "The dog, in short, has been developed to be dependent on us; that is at the basis of our social contract metaphor."[13] Human beings are responsible for the domestic dog and cat (as well as other animals, including those we use for agriculture and medical research), who are uniquely vulnerable and dependent upon us. Millions of such animals are homeless, neglected, or in desperate need due to our creation and continuation of their kind. We are collectively responsible for their plight in a way that we are not responsible for the plight of wild animals (although, of course, we may be responsible for the latter's plight for other reasons—for example, due to our contribution to environmental degradation).[14]

The duty to adopt companion animals may be specific to companion animals because of their nature. As a type, they are benefited by being adopted—that is, by being given shelter and companionship with humans. Adoption may not be best for most wild animals, though they may be benefited by rescue more generally (and rehabilitation and release). This may seem obvious or trivial upon mention, but it is important. A duty to adopt is a specific kind of rescue—sharing a family, bringing a being into your circle of intimates, offering companionship. It is morally notable that we may have this duty to enter into special relationships with specific kinds of animals who can share this social bond with us. Indeed, by their very nature—one created by us—they depend upon it.

Like the duty to adopt children, a prima facie case for a duty to adopt animal companions is strong. But it is only the first step. Proponents of the duty to adopt animal companions must show that the prima facie duty to rescue is not defeated by other interests we might have in creating rather than rescuing our pets.

To Meet a Need Rather Than Breed

But let me first say something about the duty to adopt *rather* than to create. In the case of human adoption, it is plausible that there is a duty to adopt rather than create, not a duty to adopt *simpliciter*. That is, not all people have a duty to adopt children; instead, people who want to become parents have a duty to adopt rather than procreate. The reason is as follows: most of us think that while there are obligations of beneficence, we are sometimes permitted to not provide assistance to others so that we may pursue our most important personal projects. Morality recognizes moral permissions to fail to do the most beneficent act. Most of those who oppose a duty to adopt rather than create will do so by appealing to this moral permission. But if there are moral permissions to do less than the best, then presumably people have a moral permission to not become parents, for becoming a parent is a time-intensive, expensive, and all-consuming kind of project.[15] If there is a duty to adopt, it is prospective parents who are the best candidates for holding that duty—those who want to have children anyway. The question, then, is whether the cost of adoption is too high for those who want to become biological parents.

Having a companion animal is less demanding overall than being a parent to a human child. Perhaps, then, there is a duty to adopt some companion animals, even for those who, though they have no strong aversion to it, do not particularly desire to have a pet. Having a cat live in one's home would not drastically change one's life or inhibit one from pursuing her valued and morally protected projects (untreatable cat allergies aside). Of course, a duty to adopt animal companions, under any reasonable, normative interpretation of the duty, would include being kind and compassionate to them and making sure their welfare and social needs are met. Having a dog may be considerably more demanding than having a cat in this way. (Still, I think it is a mistaken belief that cats "are not social" and do not need attention.) But those with extra means could hire a dog-walker, for instance, while they are busy at work, or a pet-sitter for when they go on vacation. Then, perhaps, those of us who have the means to do so should adopt several companion animals insofar as we can provide them a much-needed critical benefit, without unduly burdening ourselves, even if we do not desire to do so.

As a quick aside: how many companion animals must we each adopt? The answer may depend on the additional burden to us, our families, and our existing animal companions in adopting each additional pet. Will having one more animal companion be too costly, putting the weekly grocery budget on the line? Would it cause strife among our existing animal companions? After all, once you adopt, you may have special obligations of care to your existing animal companions that constrain your general obligations of beneficence to animals that are not your own. So the answer to "how many?" is complex and must be decided case by case, taking into account additional burdens to oneself and to the others already under one's care.

A general duty to adopt animals faces a challenge. Americans spend nearly $60 billion a year on their pets (this includes food, veterinary care, and other services).[16] Can we really say that there is a duty to adopt animal companions when the resources used to do so could be donated to do more good elsewhere?[17] This is a formidable challenge to a general duty to adopt animal companions.[18] It may be that this duty is trumped by our other duties of beneficence. The challenge's success depends on what the moral value of animal lives is in comparison to human lives. It depends on whether there are more efficient ways to save lives (animal or human) by donating money rather than adopting. (Regardless, we should distinguish between adopting an animal companion—and providing for an animal's physical and social needs—and spending frivolously on our pets.

Americans spent $350 million on pet costumes for Halloween in 2014.[19] It may be either obligatory or permissible to rescue animal companions, but not permissible to spend lavishly on them.[20])

Perhaps there is a duty to adopt animal companions only on the assumption that we in fact have moral permission to spend some of our resources on participating in and experiencing the distinctive relationship one can have with an animal companion (rather than spend that money on something that promotes more good). But even if we do not have such permission, even if it is all things considered wrong to have pets at all because it is a waste of precious resources, we might have an obligation to do the wrong thing in a less bad way. If you are going to have a pet, then you should adopt, not shop. The argument for a duty to adopt rather than create is relevant even for those who think it is wrong to have pets. For this reason, I need not settle whether there is a general duty to adopt animal companions *simpliciter*. I will focus on the comparative duty: we should adopt rather than create our animal companions.

Important Differences

There are some distinctive issues raised by the duty to adopt animal companions rather than create them that do not arise with human adoption. These differences will reveal the duty to adopt animal companions to be especially compelling. For one, the duty does not require people to sacrifice experiences deemed by many to be intrinsically valuable—such as the experience of pregnancy or giving birth—as would a duty to adopt rather than procreate children.[21] In this way, the duty to adopt animal companions is less burdensome and thus comparatively stronger, on this dimension, than the duty to adopt children.

Second, the existing arguments for a duty to adopt children do not assume that procreation is a bad thing. They make the comparative claim that adoption is yet a better thing and that the costs of adoption, for many, do not outweigh its comparative benefit. It may, as a matter of fact, be the case that procreation is bad. Procreation imposes risks on the child who will be created and harms on third parties.[22] The success of these anti-natalist claims would strengthen the argument for a duty to adopt, for procreation would not be just comparatively worse than adoption; it would be wrong. But many people might not accept these arguments.

On the other hand, the case against animal companion creation is hard to deny. Most breeder practices are wrong or harmful, and supporting them makes one complicit in the harm. Most notorious are the "puppy mills" (there are "kitty mills" too), which are large-scale facilities where animals are bred en masse. Breeder animals are kept in small confines, often in wire cages for the entirety of their lives, and constantly impregnated.[23] Some never leave their cages; they have never set their paws on real grass.[24] They are deprived of normal socialization with their own kind or with humans and are often physically neglected and live in unsanitary conditions. When they can no longer reproduce, they are killed. Arguably, these breeder dogs do not even have lives worth living, insofar as the net harm in their lives outweighs the good. The breeders, preoccupied with profits, are not concerned with the health of the puppies and kittens being bred either. Many puppies and kittens from such mills have health problems.[25] People who purchase their animals from pet stores contribute to these unscrupulous breeding practices. This is no small problem. The American Society for the Prevention of Cruelty to Animals (ASPCA) estimates there are about 10,000 puppy mills in the US, though there is no federal recording of these practices.[26]

Of course, some breeders practice more ethical breeding. But all breeders are complicit in commodifying animal lives to some extent. As long as we permit animals to be bred for money, these conditions are inevitable; we incentivize unscrupulous people to cut corners so that they can increase profits. Tighter regulation could help, but the Animal Welfare Act in the US is notoriously under-enforced. Thus, there is a strong case to be made that, duty to adopt aside, it is morally wrong to support breeding practices. This strengthens the duty to adopt animal companions.

There is another argument against some breeding practices, though it is less straightforward. Many purebred dogs are bred for certain traits that are cosmetically desired but functionally impairing.[27] Or some breeds are simply so overbred that undesired, impairing traits arise incidentally. Take the English Bulldog, who is at risk for hip dysplasia, dermatitis, respiratory distress, and a shortened life, among other symptoms, due to overbreeding.[28] The harms of overbreeding could constitute an additional reason against purchasing one's pet from a breeder.

However, as Clare Palmer notes, this objection to pure-breeding animals faces the Non-Identity Problem.[29] Although, intuitively, many of us think it is wrong to bring into existence an animal who suffers from respiratory distress, we cannot explain in a straightforward sense how she is harmed. Since the traits are inherent to her breed, and thus to her genetic identity, there is no sense in which we can say that this particular dog could have existed in a healthier state. So she is not harmed compared to how she could have been. Given that she has a life worth living, she is not worse off existing with her impairments than not existing at all. The Non-Identity Problem is the tension between our strong intuition that creating certain impaired lives (that are worth living) is wrong and our difficulty in explaining exactly why. But if we can establish that breeding certain purebreds is wrong, then this would strengthen the duty to adopt in those cases.

Independent of that, we might ask whether the existence of domesticated animal companions is a good thing. Animal companions have their lives curtailed in quite a few ways, which may raise the question of whether we should continue to create them. Cats are safest when kept indoors, but this prevents them from exercising basic urges like hunting and chasing small prey. Are indoor house cats, though safe, horribly bored? It is best for our animal companions that they be spayed or neutered. We must literally cut away part of their nature for them to live with us. Given that some cats and dogs do already exist, we have strong moral reasons to ensure that they have good lives, even if neutered and indoors. But it may be altogether the case that we should support their kind going out of existence for the harms to them in constraining their lives in these ways.

Second, cats and dogs are carnivores. (Dogs can eat a vegetarian diet—this is yet another way in which we could subvert their interests.) Their survival requires harm to other animals.[30] Feeding already-existing carnivore companions may present little additional ethical concern, given the good to them, and on the assumption that they eat mostly the refuse of our own meat industry. (This is not true for outdoor cats, who wreak havoc on bird populations.) But there is reason against creating more carnivorous animals. The above factors might count against the creation of animal companions, further strengthening a duty to adopt rather than breed.

Finally, animal adoption is not controversial in the way human adoption can be, which is a fact that may comparatively strengthen the duty to adopt companion animals. Opponents of adoption worry about exploitation of birthmothers and human trafficking, for instance. People oftentimes emphasize these risks of adoption practices, while underemphasizing the harms to children in not being adopted. Nonetheless, these issues make human adoption a morally fraught issue. Animal adoption does not face widespread objections based on these concerns. Animals do not have strong, robust legal (and moral) ties to their guardians as do human children to their biological families. It is easier to identify animals in need of adoption and to make them available for adoption than it is to identify and make available children in need of adoption. In contrast, many children languish in institutional care, despite having existing biological families, because, although the families cannot care for them, they have not relinquished their legal ties either. But federal and state laws protect animals (some animals—the "cute" ones) from abuse, and, at least in theory, if not always in practice, authorities can intervene in a situation of abuse or neglect and terminate owners' rights much more easily.

In sum, there are distinctive issues related to the creation and adoption of animal companions that make the case for a duty to adopt rather than create especially compelling.

On Why So Many Shop Rather Than Adopt

If the arguments in favor of adopting rather than having our animal companions created are so straightforward, then why are they not followed in practice? What can be said for the other side—for those who think there is a prerogative to purchase from a breeder rather than rescue from a shelter?

The answer lies in our widespread treatment of animals as property, as objects for our own satisfaction rather than sentient lives with their own intrinsic worth. That we have the former basic orientation toward animals is evidenced by the fact that most people—including self-proclaimed "animal lovers," who love cats and dogs—eat and wear other kinds of animals.[31] People with means do it for their own convenience and pleasure, not out of necessity. Humans consume over fifty-six billion animals a year.[32] Our fondness for cats and dogs is the absolute exception, not the rule. We are not even consistent in our reverence for cats and dogs. Though most Americans would never think of eating them, many of us do quickly dispose of them when they become inconvenient to us. The proof is in the millions of animals abandoned on the street or relinquished to shelters. Though some of these relinquishments may be due to inevitable tragedy, many are the result of feeling inconvenienced by a creature deemed first and foremost to exist to serve our desires.[33] As a society, we endorse euthanizing abandoned animals by the millions rather than finding or funding some alternative. Palmer notes, "So, alongside the social recognition of cats and dogs as companions and family members lies the social treatment of them as expendable individuals that can be killed en masse at human will—or even whim."[34]

It is no surprise that our treatment of cats and dogs reflects our fundamental orientation toward animals as consumables. Many people treat dogs or cats as fashion accessories. Dogs, for instance, are status symbols or cultural signifiers. How many tough, pick-up-truck kind of guys would be seen carrying around a Yorkie Terrier in the backseat? We have all seen the photos of Hollywood actors toting in their designer purses a teacup-sized dog with a Swarovski crystal collar. We oftentimes want the cat or dog who reflects something that we value, much like other consumables. This is the primary explanation for why so many people choose to purchase their pet from a breeder rather than a shelter.

People seek an accessory, an animal who looks a certain way and signifies a certain kind of identity. I do not deny that we can come to deeply love our animals acquired for these reasons. Yet in many cases they are acquired in the first place because they complement our own self-images.[35] But this preference for purebred dogs from breeders cannot override a compelling duty to adopt instead. Morality does not let us ignore our obligations of beneficence for just any trivial preference.

Next, some people may prefer to buy from a breeder so they can "know what they're getting into." (There are similar defenses of procreation rather than adoption.[36]) Purebred dogs and cats are so meticulously bred that the personality types within a breed may offer more predictability than the average "mixed-breed" would.[37]

But a preference for a purebred does not rule out the option to adopt from a shelter. Twenty-five percent of the dogs that enter shelters are purebred.[38] There are also breed-specific rescue organizations. After all, many of the people who think they want a certain kind of dog end up abandoning them when they become adults and less cute or when they tire of taking care of them. The negligence of others means that people who strongly desire a purebred can satisfy that desire through rescue too.

Some people worry that shelter animals may have had some traumatic experiences prior to arriving at the shelter, and they may be concerned that these animals will have behavioral problems or unpredictable personalities due to their pasts. Concerns about behavioral issues are not insignificant to our decision about which pet to choose. But one cannot assume that all or most animals in shelters are there for behavioral problems. Many shelter animals are relinquished because their owners died or could no longer care for them (due to a move or loss of job).[39] The animals that are up for adoption are actually the select few. Recall that nearly half of animals who enter the shelter are euthanized. They are vetted for aggression and other behavioral issues. In fact, we can better predict an existing animal's behavior than we can that of an unborn puppy. Shelter staff or foster families who walk with and care for the animals every day become familiar with their personalities and are in a position to know whether any particular animal has behavior issues. Adult animals' personalities are developed, and adult dogs are usually housebroken. Finally, many behavior problems in cats and dogs are due to lack of training or education of their guardians.[40] If you are not dedicated to walking your dog, providing it obedience training, or cleaning your cat's litter box, you will have pet behavior problems regardless of whether you adopt or buy from a breeder.

There is a moral point to make, too. Yes, some animals have had trauma in their past. Some will find the shelter life itself traumatic. They might have behavior issues that will resolve only with a stable family and lots of loving care and training. But these constitute all the more moral reason for us to extend compassion to these dogs and cats and welcome them into our lives. It is really not all about us! The strong case for a duty to adopt requires that we justify our choice to buy from breeders instead. None of the above reasons justify that choice.

Conclusion

My focus has been on defending a duty to adopt animals rather than create them. The comparison with arguments for a duty to adopt rather than create human children, based on general obligations of beneficence, has been instructive. Just like human children, animal companions have interests and needs that can be the source of our duties to aid them by giving them the very thing they lack—a loving, stable family and long-term companionship. I have not explored the special obligations that arise post-adoption, though comparison to the ethics of human parenthood and adoption would be a fruitful expansion of the project.

Notes

1. "Pet Statistics," The American Society for the Prevention of Cruelty to Animals. Last accessed August 3, 2016. https://www.aspca.org/about-us/faq/pet-statistics.
2. Whether existence can be a benefit is a large and contentious debate in philosophy, but we need not delve into it here.
3. For a duty to adopt, see Rulli, "Preferring a Genetically-Related Child"; Friedrich, "A Duty to Adopt?" For the duty to rescue, see Singer, "Famine, Affluence, and Morality."
4. For a more detailed discussion and citations, see Rulli, "Preferring," 7.
5. Friedrich, "Duty to Adopt," 32.
6. Rulli, "Preferring," 6, n. 6.
7. Rulli, "Preferring."
8. The first statistic is from the ASPCA website, https://www.aspca.org/about-us/faq/pet-statistics; the second statistic is from 2008, from the American Humane Association post, "Animal Shelter Euthanasia," http://www.american-humane.org/animals/stop-animal-abuse/fact-sheets/animal-shelter-euthanasia.html?referrer=https://www.google.com/.
9. "Pet Statistics," ASPCA.
10. For instance, I think of Carl Cohen, "The Case for the Use of Animals in Biomedical Research."
11. Likewise, they do not need rights for us to be able to explain why it is wrong to harm them.

12. This response is inspired by Feinberg's discussion of imperfect duties, though our views about rights diverge; see *Harm to Others: The Moral Limits of the Criminal Law*, 143–46.

13. Rollin, *Animal Rights and Human Morality*, 220.

14. Burgess-Jackson mentions and then sets aside the issue of collective responsibility in "Doing Right by Our Animal Companions," 163–64; see also Palmer, "Killing Animals in Animal Shelters," 181–82.

15. See Rulli, "Preferring," 10.

16. "Americans Spent a Record $56 Billion on Pets Last Year," CBSNew.com, March 13, 2014, http://www.cbsnews.com/news/americans-spent-a-record-56-billion-on-pets-last-year/.

17. I recall a criticism along these lines when animal rights organizations tried to help rescue and relocate homeless dogs and cats during Hurricane Katrina in New Orleans.

18. A similar argument could be raised against the choice to become a parent—procreative or adoptive. A consequentialist might argue that we should spend the ¼ million dollars it takes to raise a middle-class American child and donate it to life-saving organizations instead. See Rachels, "The Immorality of Having Children." He targets procreative parents and does not discuss adoption.

19. Sarah Halzack, "Shoppers to Spend $350 Million on Halloween Costumes This Year—For Their Pets," *Washington Post*, October 29, 2014, https://www.washing-tonpost.com/news/business/wp/2014/10/29/shoppers-to-spend-350-million-on-halloween-costumes-this-year-for-their-pets/.

20. Burgess-Jackson makes this distinction, "Doing Right," 182, n. 69.

21. See Rulli, "Preferring," 25–28.

22. For the most famous anti-natalist argument, see Benatar, *Better Never to Have Been: The Harm of Coming into Existence*. See also Shiffrin, "Wrongful Life, Procreative Responsibility, and the Significance of Harm." For the harms of pro-creation to third-parties, see Young, "Overconsumption and Procreation: Are They Morally Equivalent?"

23. "USDA Urged to Improve Care Standards for Puppy Mill Dogs," Humane Society Veterinary Medical Association, September 21, 2015, http://www.humaneso-ciety.org/news/press_releases/2015/09/usda-care-standards-pm-dogs-092115.html?credit=web_id80597225.

24. Occasionally a video of an adult breeding dog from a puppy mill walking on grass for the first time goes viral on the internet. You need only do a quick internet search to see such videos.

25. "What is a Puppy Mill?," ASPCA, https://www.aspca.org/animal-cruelty/puppy-mills.

26. Ibid.

27. See Asher et al., "Inherited Defects in Pedigree Dogs. Part 1: Disorders Related to Breed Standards." For more on the ethics of pure-breeding, see John Rossi's chapter in this anthology.

28. Palmer, "Does Breeding a Bulldog Harm It? Breeding, Ethics and Harm to Animals," 159.
29. Ibid.
30. See the chapter by Josh Milburn in this anthology for more on the ethics of feeding companion animals.
31. In speaking of "our" attitudes, I will focus my observations on the average North American. Different animals have differing status depending on the culture or country. But with proper modification for these differences, my point applies widely. Most people worldwide eat and wear animals, though they may revere a particular species as an exception.
32. This figure is from the post, "Food," by the animal rights organization, Animal Equality, http://www.animalequality.net/food. It does not include fish or sea creatures. It is difficult to find any other type of organization that collects and reports this statistic.
33. Rollin catalogs the reasons for which people let their animals be "put to sleep." See *Animal Rights*, 221.
34. Palmer, "Killing Animals," 171.
35. Motivations to procreate human children are also usually self-, not other-, regarding. But children are less widely treated as consumer objects.
36. See Rulli, "Preferring," 15–24.
37. The idea of "mixed breed" is problematic. It treats purebreds as the original organism in a species, when in fact breeds are bred out of a species. Not all mutt dogs, for instance, are a mix of several purebreds. This is not merely a pedantic concern. People infer personality traits from a mutt based on what they (usually, wrongly) think her lineage is. "She has floppy ears and a tawny coat. So she must be part Labrador and therefore good with kids." This inference is obviously problematic for practical, not merely scientific, reasons. Perhaps we should replace "mixed breed" with "non-purebred."
38. "11 Facts about Animal Homelessness," DoSomething.org, https://www.dosomething.org/facts/11-facts-about-animal-homelessness.
39. Salman et al., "Human and Animal Factors Related to the Relinquishment of Dogs and Cats in 12 Selected Animal Shelters in the United States," 212–14.
40. Patronek et al., "Risk Factors for Relinquishment of Dogs to an Animal Shelter."

References

Asher, L., G. Diesel, J. F. Summers, P. D. McGreevy, and L. M. Collins. "Inherited Defects in Pedigree Dogs. Part 1: Disorders Related to Breed Standards." *Veterinary Journal* 182, no. 3 (2009): 402–11.

Benatar, David. *Better Never To Have Been: The Harm of Coming into Existence*. Oxford: Oxford University Press, 2006.

Burgess-Jackson, Keith. "Doing Right by Our Animal Companions." *Journal of Ethics* 2, no. 2 (1998): 159–85.

Cohen, Carl. "The Case for the Use of Animals in Biomedical Research." *New England Journal of Medicine* 315, no. 14 (1986): 865–70.

Feinberg, Joel. *Harm to Others: The Moral Limits of the Criminal Law*. Vol. 1. New York: Oxford University Press, 1984.

Friedrich, Daniel. "A Duty to Adopt?" *Journal of Applied Philosophy* 30, no. 1 (2013): 25–39.

Palmer, Clare. "Does Breeding a Bulldog Harm It? Breeding, Ethics and Harm to Animals." *Animal Welfare* 21 (2012): 157–66.

Palmer, Clare. "Killing Animals in Animal Shelters." In *Killing Animals*, edited by Steve Baker, 170–87. Champaign: University of Illinois Press, 2006.

Patronek, G. J., L. T. Glickman, A. M. Beck, G. P. McCabe, and C. Ecker. "Risk Factors for Relinquishment of Dogs to an Animal Shelter." *Journal of the American Veterinary Medical Association* 209, no. 3 (1996): 572–81.

Rachels, Stuart. "The Immorality of Having Children." *Ethical Theory and Moral Practice* 17, no. 3 (2014): 567–82.

Rollin, Bernard. *Animal Rights and Human Morality*. Rev. ed. Buffalo, NY: Prometheus Books, 1992.

Rulli, Tina. "Preferring a Genetically-Related Child." *Journal of Moral Philosophy* (November 2014): 1–30. doi: 10.1163/17455243-4681062.

Salman, M. D., John G. New, Jr., Janet M. Scarlett, and Philip H. Kris. "Human and Animal Factors Related to the Relinquishment of Dogs and Cats in 12 Selected Animal Shelters in the United States." *Journal of Applied Animal Welfare Science* 1, no. 3 (1998): 207–26.

Shiffrin, Seana Valentine. "Wrongful Life, Procreative Responsibility, and the Significance of Harm." *Legal Theory* 5, no. 2 (1999): 117–48.

Singer, Peter. "Famine, Affluence, and Morality." *Philosophy and Public Affairs* 1, no. 3 (Spring 1972): 229–43. Rev. ed.

Young, Thomas. "Overconsumption and Procreation: Are They Morally Equivalent?" *Journal of Applied Philosophy* 18, no. 2 (2001): 183–92.

THE ANIMAL LOVERS' PARADOX?

ON THE ETHICS OF "PET FOOD"

Josh Milburn

The animal lovers' paradox is the fact that animal lovers—people who share their lives with nonhuman companions for whom they feel deep love and affection—typically contribute to more nonhuman animal (NHA) death and suffering than they would if they did not keep companions. This is because dogs and cats (upon whom this chapter will focus) will typically be fed large amounts of NHA flesh, and this flesh is the product of practices that inflict death and suffering as a matter of course. Paradoxically, it could be that the best thing that some people could do to reduce NHA death and suffering would be to stop being animal lovers. This sounds deeply odd, and rightly so. This is not to say that individual animal lovers will *recognize* the oddness of their situation; it is possible that they feel love toward only certain NHAs. When the individual animal lover feels the conflict, she likely faces the *vegetarian's dilemma*: the problem of reconciling "feeding one's [companion] an animal-based diet that may be perceived as best promoting their well-being with concerns over animal welfare [and animal *rights*] and environmental degradation threatened by such diets" (Rothgerber 2013, 77).

There has been some discussion of this issue both inside and outside academia. Despite this, academic animal ethics as a whole has been surprisingly quiet on the animal lovers' paradox and the vegetarian's dilemma. On the one hand, this is surprising, given that it is at the intersection of two key issues in animal ethics: the ethics of NHA-derived foods and the ethics of companionship. On the other, it is unsurprising, as it seems to throw up serious conflicts between our obligations to our companions and toward those NHAs killed for food.

Recent prominent works on animal ethics from a variety of directions have not addressed the issue. For example, Clare Palmer (2010) advocates a contextual animal ethics, in which we have different kinds of obligations to companions than to "wild" NHAs, but does not discuss companion diets, despite considering companions' violence against "wild" animals. Palmer coauthored the recent *Companion Animal Ethics* (Sandøe, Corr, and Palmer 2016) in which companion diet is addressed, but discussions focus upon health, resource use, and environmental impact, rather than the problems with NHA-derived foodstuffs. Alasdair Cochrane (2012) defends an account of justice centered on the interest rights of sentient animals. Though he offers extensive discussions of the injustice of current food practices (2012, ch. 4) and of our obligations toward companions (2012, 129–37; cf. Cochrane 2014), he does not address the conflict between them that arises when we feed companions the flesh of other NHAs.[1] Gary Francione (2007, 2008), who supports the abolition of all use of NHAs, stresses the importance of veganism and, though claiming that we should stop producing more, argues that we must care for existing companions. Despite this, and though he keeps vegan dogs (2007, vi), the issue is not addressed in his major works.

There is, then, a surprising lack of consideration in the animal ethics literature of the ethics of companion diets. One exception to this general trend is the work of Sue Donaldson and Will Kymlicka (2013), who draw a picture of a zoopolis, a mixed human/NHA state. On their picture, different NHAs are awarded different political rights based on their relationship with this state, though all sentient NHAs possess certain fundamental rights, such as the right not to be killed by humans. NHAs who are part of the mixed community, such as companions, are *citizens*, while those who live among but apart from society, such as garden birds, are *denizens*. "Wild" NHAs are *sovereign* over their own communities. Donaldson and Kymlicka are acutely aware of the problem sketched above:

> Amongst our many duties to domesticated animals, we are responsible for ensuring that they have adequate nutrition. And here we encounter another dilemma: do we have an obligation to feed meat to our domesticated animals, particularly if this is part of their (so-called) natural diet? Must we turn some animals into meat in order to fulfil our duties to our domesticated animal co-citizens? (2013, 149)

Ultimately, "dog and cat members of mixed human-animal society do not have a right to food that involves the killing of other animals" (150). Readers may be surprised at the suggestion that companions not be fed flesh and that they instead be fed a vegan diet, but more and more people are now exploring this option. In 2010, research on the ethical credentials of different "pet food" brands was published in *Ethical Consumer* (Brown 2010). Among other things, the report looked at which products contained NHA-derived ingredients and which were the product of animal testing—the latter being a dimension of the paradox I cannot explore here. The report recommended several vegan-friendly brands, including Ami and Benevo—companies that produce vegan foods for both dogs and cats (Brown 2010, 12).

One may think, given their talk of "co-citizens" (2013, 149) and "mixed human-animal society" (150), that Donaldson and Kymlicka's conclusion is a quirk of their framework, and that, if we do not accept their system, we need not accept their conclusion. Here, I could argue that we *should* accept Donaldson and Kymlicka's framework; indeed, it is a very good one. However, it is perhaps more interesting to note that we can construct a very strong argument for vegan companions using premises that, within animal ethics, are not at all controversial. I will now set out this argument, before offering an explanation of the various premises and steps. I will then spend the remainder of the chapter exploring possible objections to this argument and offering some practical suggestions.

Premise 1: It is wrong for us to kill or inflict suffering upon sensitive nonhuman animals unless there is some reason of overriding importance.

Premise 2: The production of nonhuman animal-derived foodstuffs almost always involves inflicting death and suffering upon sensitive nonhuman animals.

Premise 3: Without the consumption of nonhuman animal-derived foodstuffs, there would be no production of nonhuman animal-derived foodstuffs.

Interim conclusion: Given Premises 1–3, the consumption of nonhuman animal-derived foodstuffs is generally wrong, unless there is some reason of overriding importance.

Premise 4: There is generally no reason of overriding importance justifying the consumption of nonhuman animal-derived foodstuffs by our companions.

Conclusion: Given the interim conclusion and Premise 4, feeding nonhuman animal companions nonhuman animal-derived foodstuffs is generally wrong.

Premise 1 is a normative claim uncontroversial within animal ethics. Some profess to hold the view that the death and suffering of NHAs is of no moral significance. Such people will not accept this argument. Importantly, though, it is highly unlikely that an animal lover would hold this view. What, precisely, counts as a reason "of overriding importance" is what I will spend much of the remainder of this chapter examining. Our answers will differ depending upon the ethical framework we adopt. While utilitarians, like Peter Singer

(1995), would allow that the prevention of *greater* suffering is a reason of sufficient magnitude to override a general prescription against inflicting suffering, a more deontological thinker, like Tom Regan (1984), would not allow this. By contrast, in certain cases of self-defense, Regan might allow the infliction of death and suffering, while Singer might not. It is clear that neither greater suffering nor self-defense are in the offing in the current case, but other things might be.

Premise 2 is an empirical claim that would not be denied by anyone familiar with, first, modern farming methods, and, second, animal welfare science. There are enough honest descriptions and images of the kinds of suffering inherent in food production available in various media for me to spare readers the details, but it should be noted that suffering and death are as much a part of egg and milk production as they are of flesh production. And, while past philosophers and scientists have voraciously denied that NHAs experience pain, it is thankfully rare to encounter someone claiming this today. Premise 3, too, is an empirical claim that relies on the realities of the market. If, from tomorrow, there was no demand for NHA-derived foodstuffs, it would not be long before their production ceased. The interim conclusion does not unproblematically follow from premises 1–3. Questions abound about the effects of the behavior of a single individual on the market and the obligation to behave morally when those around us do not. However, let us assume that these can be overcome.[2] Given all of the above, *our continued consumption of NHA-derived products is generally wrong*. We should note that there really are no "overriding" circumstances in most cases. According to both the American Dietetic Association and Dieticians of Canada (Craig and Mangels 2009; Mangels, Messina, and Vesanto 2003), appropriately planned vegan diets are perfectly healthy for people at any stage of their life. Additionally, such diets are easily accessible to almost anyone in the industrialized West. It does not instantly follow that companions must be fed vegan diets, which is why an additional premise is necessary; however, if Premise 4 is correct, then the conclusion naturally follows: feeding companions NHA-derived foodstuffs is generally wrong.

For the remainder of this chapter, I will explore whether there is *generally* a reason of overriding significance that permits the feeding of NHA-derived foodstuffs to our companions. We could certainly construct contrived scenarios where there are reasons of overriding importance: for example, if you and your dog are trapped on an island with edible NHAs but no edible plants, you can surely kill the animals to feed yourself and your dog. However, extreme scenarios do not help us. Instead, I am going to explore four reasons we may think we *generally* have an overriding ethical reason to feed NHA-derived products to our companions. First, I will explore whether making our companions vegan is to force them to live an *undignified* life. Second, I will explore the idea that companion veganism is problematically *unnatural*. Third, I will explore the idea that it is unjustly *freedom-restricting*. Finally, I will consider the most important challenge: whether it is *unhealthy* for the companions to be fed a vegan diet, and what this might mean.

Dignity

Conceptions of NHA dignity may be appealing due to the thought that it is wrong, for instance, to dress a bear in a tutu and have her ride a unicycle *beyond* the fact that it is unpleasant for the bear. Indeed, we may feel that there is something wrong *even if* the bear does not mind and lives a fulfilled, happy life. A dignity-based argument against companion veganism would claim that companions are treated in an undignified way if fed vegan diets. Precisely *why* depends on the particular conception of NHA dignity, of which there are numerous conflicting accounts. For example, Elizabeth Anderson claims that "[t]he dignity of an animal, whether human or nonhuman, is what is required to make it [*sic*] decent for human society, for the particular, species-specific ways in which humans relate to them" (2005, 283). Lori Gruen's account, on the other hand, is almost the polar opposite. She says that "[m]aking other animals 'decent for human society' is precisely what it means to deny them their dignity"; instead, "we dignify the wildness [of NHAs] when we respect their behaviors as meaningful to them and recognize that their lives are theirs to live" (2011, 154–55).

It is not clear how either of these accounts could oppose veganism for companions; in making companions vegan, we precisely make them "decent" for NHA-respecting society, while, as they are not "wild," the extent to which companions could have "wild dignity" is unclear. Tying carnivorous diets to dignity is thus a problem with these "relational" approaches to NHA dignity, but it is even more so with "individualist" accounts of NHA dignity, which tie dignity to some kind of trans-specific capacity.[3] Take Michael Meyer's account (2001), according to which all sentient beings possess "simple dignity." Simple dignity, though, is more about moral standing than about particular kinds of treatment, so it seems that simple dignity and vegan diets have no clear relationship, diminishing its usefulness to the opponent of companion veganism.

Martha Nussbaum's (2006) account is a paradigm example of the "species-based" approach to dignity. She says that a NHA's dignified existence

> would seem at least to include the following: adequate opportunities for nutrition and physical activity; freedom from pain, squalor and cruelty; freedom to act in ways that are characteristic of the species . . . ; freedom

from fear and opportunities for rewarding interactions with other creatures of the same species, and of different species; a chance to enjoy the
light and air in tranquility. (326)

This account is placed within Nussbaum's capabilities approach, according to
which justice is about endorsing various key capabilities. Capabilities are inherently species-dependent (resting upon a controversial Aristotelian notion of
"species"), and so whether a companion has an important capability tied to
flesh-eating, meaning it would be disrespectful to endorse veganism for that
companion, depends on how we understand that companion's species. If a dog
is understood as a member of the species *Canis lupus*, along with wolves, then
perhaps she has an important flesh-eating capability. If dogs are members of the
species *C. familiaris*, then this possibility is less plausible: the species has arisen in
tandem with humans, and so human norms would define that species' norms. The
same is true of cats, whom we may understand as members of *Felis silvestris*, along
with wildcats, or as members of *F. catus*. However, *even if* we consider dogs and
cats to be members of *Canis lupus* and *Felis silvestris* respectively, veganism need
not be undignified. Nussbaum argues that

> [s]ome capabilities are actually bad, and should be inhibited by law. . . .
> No constitution protects capabilities *qua* capabilities. There must be prior
> evaluation, deciding which are good, and, among the good, which are
> most central, most clearly involved in defining the minimum conditions
> for a life with . . . dignity. (2006, 166)[4]

The mere fact some NHA has the *capacity* to x does not mean that she could
not have a dignified life without x. As I have argued, we do have good reason
to believe that companions' eating of flesh is "actually bad," and so it is *not* the
kind of capability we should promote. Nussbaum openly endorses this kind
of picture; she argues that the natural is not always good (400), and indicates
that NHAs' "harm-causing capabilities" are probably "not among those that
should be protected by political and social principles" (369). By way of example,
she points to a zoo that, rather than providing her with prey, provides a tiger
with a ball on a rope (370–71). "Wherever predatory animals are living under
direct human support and control," she suggests, "these solutions seem to be the
most ethically sound" (371). Though vegan companions are not mentioned, it
seems to be the same kind of problem, and so warrants the same kind of solution. Ultimately, Nussbaum's account offers no support for the suggestion that
we feed flesh to our companions, while her own words seemingly oppose the
practice.

I have suggested that key accounts of NHA dignity do not support the claim that we should feed companions flesh, but, in so doing, have taken for granted that accounts of NHA dignity can be useful at all. This idea is controversial (Cochrane 2010; Zuolo 2016). It is possible, first, that dignity does not *add* anything to existing discussions (Macklin 2003) and that accounts of dignity are reducible to other concepts. If so, accounts of NHA dignity fail the requirement that they are non-redundant (Zuolo 2016, 3). Furthermore, accounts like Meyer's, although serving to confer moral worth or standing on individual NHAs, do not offer guidance for action (Zuolo 2016, 3), and so offer little to the present question. Issues of space mean that exploration of problems with dignity is impossible, but it is worth noting a final worry often raised: that appeals to "dignity" are pure rhetoric, and that the term is used merely to justify whatever it is that is being defended. This idea is put eloquently by Singer, who notes that "[p]hilosophers frequently introduce ideas of dignity . . . at the point at which other reasons appear to be lacking, but this is hardly good enough. Fine phrases are the last resource of those who have run out of arguments" (1974, 113; cf. Macklin 2003). So, not only is it unclear how a dignity argument could ground opposition to vegan diets for companions, but there is an open question about the value of dignity arguments (especially in animal ethics) in the first place.

Naturalness

The idea that something is "natural" is found in some accounts of dignity, but it can be separated from them. A naturalness argument against feeding vegan diets to companions would look something like this:

Premise 1: Companions are naturally flesh-eaters.
Interim conclusion: To allow them to be flesh-eaters would promote what is natural.
Premise 2: Promoting what is natural is (prima facie) good.
Conclusion: Allowing companions to be flesh-eaters is (prima facie) good.

There are at least two contentious elements here: the first is the identification of the "natural," and the second is the claim that the "natural" is good. The good of naturalness is sometimes articulated in environmental ethics, but it is controversial. There are many "natural" things that we consider to be very bad, including suffering, starvation, and disease. Further, the claim that something is "natural" is often a smokescreen for oppression. Examples abound: racism and sexual abuse are called "natural"; homosexuality and gender equality are declared "unnatural." However, even if these problems can be overcome, it is difficult to see how the defender of flesh foods for companions can invoke naturalness without throwing the baby out with the bathwater, as it is hard to frame an account of "naturalness" in which companions *themselves* are not unnatural. On the view of the environmental ethicists John Rodman, Holmes Rolston III and (previously) J. Baird Callicott, for example, companions are problematic precisely because they are *unnatural*, or have been *denaturalized*, and so have become "living artifacts" (cited in Cochrane 2014, 158). Even if we have doubts about the claims of these thinkers, it would be oddly selective to defend companion flesh-eating on the grounds of naturalness without also *criticizing* practically every element of the institution of companionship. Consequently, even if we are to promote naturalness, there is no easy way to use this to oppose companion veganism: if arguments about naturalness apply, they likely apply in ways bad for companionship.

Even if we can overcome these problems, the argument is incomplete. The "goodness" of the "natural" diet would have to be compared with the badness of its consequences. Even if some (bizarre) person believed naturalness to be the *only* good, it remains unclear that she should oppose vegan companions; depending on her account of naturalness, it could be that a vegan dog is "less unnatural" than animal agriculture, and, given that animal agriculture results in catastrophic levels of land use, harmful emissions, and chemical pollution, the institution is contributing on an enormous scale to the *destruction* of nature. It is probable that more "naturalness" would be promoted if the world were to convert to vegan diets for companions.

Perhaps a more reasonable challenge grounded in naturalness would take the following form:[5] companions have natural inclinations toward flesh (or, would naturally seek out flesh), and we have an obligation not to interfere with (or, more strongly, to promote) their natural inclinations/actions. I do think this argument is more compelling than the previous one, but that is because it is essentially a freedom-based argument with added naturalness considerations; while "naturalness" does not add much to the argument, it does *detract* from it, insofar as it raises problems. Specifically, the proponent of this argument has the difficult tasks of identifying the "natural" (compounded by the above considerations about the unnaturalness of companions), defending the *value* of the natural, and finally weighing this value with the problems (including problems of unnaturalness and destruction of the natural) associated with feeding companions flesh. In all, I suggest that the proponent of this argument would do better to drop the "naturalness" claim and focus on freedom. Therefore, it is to that argument that I now turn.

Freedom

An argument often heard in defense of *human* consumption of flesh is that people should be free to choose what they consume. We recognize this argument for what it is in some contexts; we do not think that people should be free to choose to consume *human* flesh, for instance. Many animal lovers also oppose the freedom to eat dogs and cats; the outrage at the annual Yulin Dog Meat Festival in China is illustrative. It cannot be the case, then, that the promotion of companion freedom or autonomy necessitates that the companions be permitted to eat whatever they like. Nonetheless, a freedom-based argument could be made to support flesh-based diets for companions. One could appeal either to the freedom of the *companions* to eat what they would prefer, or perhaps to the freedom of the *guardians* to feed to their companions what is convenient. Donaldson and Kymlicka consider but dismiss the former. "We have made a point of enabling animal agency," they write, "[s]o why, in the case of diet, are we advocating that meat should not be among the choices offered to them? Because the liberty of citizens is always constrained by respect for the liberties of others" (2013, 150). They are surely right, and the point stands whether or not we share the authors' conception of citizenship. It is perverse to suggest that companions' interest in having food that they prefer (if they do prefer NHA-derived foods), or guardians' interest in feeding easily accessible food to their companions, should outweigh the interest that sensitive NHAs have in not having suffering inflicted upon them and not being killed. These are some of the most central interests a being can possess.

It is worth remembering that the majority of companions in the West are not given much freedom concerning their choice of diet, and are simply fed the canned food that their guardians have chosen. However, it is perfectly consistent to imagine a companion having considerable choice while remaining vegan. There are multiple vegan "pet food" brands available, as well as plenty of tried-and-tested recipes posted online. And there is no reason to rely wholly on processed or cooked foodstuffs. Donaldson and Kymlicka illustrate the way that companion choice can be promoted while still working within the confines of veganism:

> It's true that humans need to ensure that dogs meet their nutritional needs, and that they don't overeat, or eat foods that will poison them. But this still leaves a large area in which dogs can express their food preferences and make their own choices. Through trial and error (and choice amongst options), it became perfectly clear to us that our dog Codie's favourite foods included fennel, kale stems, and carrots. And peas were so prized he

simply helped himself from the veggie garden. Fruit really wasn't of interest. On the other hand, his buddy Rolly was mad for bananas. Dogs have individual preferences, and (to varying degrees) the competence to make choices based on their preferences. (2013, 109)

Codie, clearly, is given far greater choice when it comes to food than the vast majority of companions. The promotion of companion autonomy should not be understood as in conflict with the demand that companions be fed a vegan diet.

Health

I now move on to the most pressing challenge to companion veganism. It might be said that while we do have an obligation to abstain from inflicting suffering upon and killing sensitive NHAs, this obligation is overridden by the fact that our companions require the flesh of NHAs to be healthy. There is received wisdom in the area (Donaldson and Kymlicka 2013, 143; Rothgerber 2014) that while dogs can thrive on vegan diets, cats may not be able to. Indeed, it is not hard to find authoritative-sounding statements endorsing this claim. For example, on the popular website WebMD, Roxanne Hawn quotes Cailin Heinze (a veterinary nutritionist) as saying that, "[f]or cats", a vegan diet is " really inappropriate. It goes against their physiology and isn't something I would recommend at all. For dogs ... vegan diets can be done, but they need to be done very, very carefully" (Hawn 2011). Hawn also quotes the guardian of cats fed a vegan diet, who explains that her cats are happy and healthy (2011). It is not hard to find anecdotal evidence of vegan cats thriving on the one hand and angry condemnation of guardians of vegan cats on the other.

Here is not the place to solve this particular dispute, especially as the scientific literature seems equivocal. In a review of the evidence, Kathryn Michel concluded that the nutritional adequacy of some commercially available vegan cat foods has been "called into question," but did not claim that vegan diets are necessarily unsuitable (2006, 1275–77). By contrast, a study (Wakefield, Shofer, and Michel 2006) examining individual cats found that vegetarian diets (including vegan diets) did not have the adverse health effects expected. Lorelei Wakefield, the veterinarian who was the lead author of the latter study, runs VegetarianCats.com, a website with information about vegetarian and vegan diets for companions. She is of the view that a plant-based diet for cats is possible, having raised vegan cats, but can be difficult, especially if the cats have pre-existing health problems.

Given the conflicting comments from experts, this fourth challenge seems a serious one for my argument. Were cats unable to survive on a vegan diet, and assuming that they could not be provided flesh in a respectful way, it could be that we would have to explore whether there was some way we could balance our positive duties toward cats with our negative duties toward other NHAs. One solution, unthinkable to some, would be companion cats' extinction. Though we may have good reasons to think cats' extinction would be a bad thing, we also have very good reasons to be opposed to continuing to feed flesh to cats. Another possible solution, though one perhaps equally problematic, is genetically modifying cats away from carnivory. The way forward seems unclear.

But let us take a step back. The issue of companion diet is more complicated than I have previously allowed. First, our obligations concerning dogs and cats may be different, given their different physiologies.[6] Second, our obligations concerning companion diet have both *moral* and *political* dimensions. The moral dimension focuses on the actions of guardians, while the political dimension focuses on the actions of the state and society—for example, decisions about research funding. In the case of dogs, the moral and the political dimensions are close: we should want to see dogs converted to veganism. For individual animal lovers, this means careful research and a change in companion diet. For states, the obligation will, in the medium-term, mean the banning of flesh-based "pet food." More immediately, it might mean information campaigns and subsidies on vegan dog foods, both of which could be funded by a tax on flesh-based dog foods.

With cats, individuals and states appear to have somewhat different obligations. Individual animal lovers should not want to risk their companions' health. For guardians who are confident that they can provide a suitable vegan diet for their cats, this is the right choice, but such individuals may be in a minority. The solution for others is *minimizing* the amount of animal protein fed to companions. Preferable to a wholly flesh-based diet would be feeding cats "half vegetarian biscuits and half organic wet meaty food" (Brown and Welch 2010). A mixed diet could be combined with the seeking out of the most ethically viable NHA-derived products for companions: organic, free-range, "happy" meat still involves the infliction of an early, gruesome death, but at least there is typically *less* suffering. Perhaps there are better possibilities: the eggs of rescued chickens might be viable, but such chickens would not exist in a world in which chickens were not kept for their eggs. Though perhaps unpleasant, "road kill" provides a source of flesh that would be wasted otherwise. "Dumpster-diving" provides another alternative; again, though, dumpster-diving (which is criminalized in some jurisdictions) is a possibility only so long as we live in a society where NHA-derived products remain a "normal" part of the human diet, and so will hopefully become less viable in time.

Political solutions would involve seeking out a just alternative to current cat diets, perhaps through research funding. Most obviously, veterinarians can learn more about cat physiology and diets and so come to understand how they might easily thrive on vegan diets. For example, taurine is a nutrient that cats typically acquire from animal flesh, but vegan taurine supplements are already available—further development in this area is easily conceivable. Animal welfare scientists might be able to discover that certain NHAs are actually unthinking, unfeeling entities, in which case they would not be covered by the typical approaches to animal ethics. If these NHAs could be used to feed our cats, then it seems that the dilemma could be averted.

Research from animal ethicists and other normative theorists, too, could suggest creative solutions to the problem—both temporary and permanent. For example, in a world in which humans and dogs were vegan, there would be much space on which we could develop the most humane possible forms of farming.[7] I defend an alternative elsewhere (Milburn 2015), suggesting that while the discovery of some nonsentient NHA that is suitable as a food source for cats would be ideal, in the meantime, we could be permitted to feed to cats those NHAs for whom sentience is *plausible*, but not *likely*, such as certain shellfish. Importantly, I argue that we may have different obligations concerning our cats' diets than our own; while we could feed certain shellfish to our cats, we would not be permitted to eat them ourselves. (Individual animal lovers, if they are confident that shellfish could provide a suitable food source for their companions but are not confident that a wholly vegan diet could, could follow this route.) The question of companion diets is not solely a scientific one, but something to which normative theorists could offer much.

Concluding Remarks

I began this chapter with the observation that there is an oddity in the fact that in being an animal lover—someone who shares her life with a nonhuman animal companion—one often contributes to more NHA death and suffering than one would otherwise. This "animal lovers' paradox" is closely related to the vegetarian's dilemma, a term that refers to the conflict veg(etari)ans feel when it comes to the possibility of feeding flesh to their companions. I presented an argument in favor of feeding vegan diets to our companions, before exploring four possible challenges. Arguments from NHA *dignity* face the problems of stating precisely what is meant by dignity, and of clarifying why a vegan diet is undignified. In addition, we may have reasons not to endorse dignity arguments at all. Arguments from *naturalness* face problems in explaining why naturalness is good, and encounter problems when it comes to companions in the first place. Further, even if naturalness is good and a vegan diet is unnatural, the badness (including destruction of the natural) of companion carnivory surely outweighs the goodness. The challenge from NHA *freedom* pits two animal ethics ideals against each other, but companions' interest in having a wider variety of food choices cannot override the fundamental interests other NHAs have in not being killed or made to suffer, and, further, a vegan diet is not incompatible with a high degree of dietary freedom for companions anyway.

The final challenge considered was the most important. The fact that it may not be *healthy* for companions (especially cats) to be fed a solely vegan diet leads to important distinctions that need to be made. With dogs, our moral and political obligations seem to fit neatly together; these companions should be converted to vegan diets. With cats, however, our moral and political obligations seem to diverge.[8] While individual animal lovers should seek to limit the death and suffering in their cats' diets, completely eliminating them may not always be possible. However, as a political community, we should be funding research into how the suffering and death currently entailed by cats' diets can be removed entirely. With further research, good will, and wider awareness, we can hope that all members of our community—humans and companions—can come to survive and flourish in ways that are respectful of the fundamental interests of sensitive nonhuman animals.

Acknowledgments

I am thankful for helpful discussions with a variety of people who have engaged with me on this topic. My particular thanks go to my doctoral supervisors—David Archard and Jeremy Watkins—Christine Overall, and the participants (including Matteo Bonotti, Jens Tuider, Anne Barnhill, Jan Deckers, Chris Thompson, and Aaron Crowe) at the Political Theory and the Normative Challenges of Food Governance panel, MANCEPT Workshops 2015, University of Manchester. Thanks are also owed to Katherine Wayne, who originally got me interested in the topic of companion diets and introduced Christine to my work. Finally, I thank the Department of Employment and Learning, Northern Ireland, which provided funding for my research at Queen's University Belfast.

Notes

1. In private correspondence, Cochrane has told me that companion diet is an issue to which he has given considerable thought. Like me, he considers it an important ethico-political issue, and not simply a question of veterinary nutrition.
2. Readers unhappy with this assumption should consider a world in which many products are made with slave labor. (Note that I am not making a claim about the

comparative badness of slavery and animal agriculture.) We may worry about the effect that we as individuals can have on the institution of slave labor, and we might be surrounded by family and friends who happily consume the products of slavery—perhaps they talk about how it is "natural," "normal," "necessary," or "nice" to use slaves (cf. Piazza et al. 2015). Nonetheless, we would surely have an obligation to avoid the products of slavery, especially if it was easy for us to do so, and given that our abstention could convince *others* to refrain.

One might object that this thought experiment would only have an effect upon the current question if we held that the consumption of NHA-derived foods was just as bad as human slavery. However, the fact that we would and should continue to abstain from the products of slavery in the imagined case shows us that the stated concerns are not overridingly significant; the burden of proof would be on the person who objected to veganism to illustrate why these counterarguments were convincing for veganism but not slavery.

3. I have borrowed the tripartite split of NHA dignity accounts into relational, individualist, and species-based from Federico Zuolo (2016). Hybrid positions are possible; Anderson's account is a hybrid species-based/relational account, for example.

4. Nussbaum talks of human dignity, but there is no reason to think that NHA dignity is any different.

5. Thanks to Anne Barnhill for this point.

6. This is not a speciesist claim. Physiological differences are, here, morally relevant.

7. Thanks to Chris Thompson for this observation.

8. This divergence is not unique to the current problem. For example, in the UK, all medicines are tested on NHAs, so vegans face a dilemma when ill. Refusing medication cannot be the answer, but neither can we ignore the ethical demands upon us. As individuals, the best solution may be to accept medication tested on NHAs, but nonetheless demand that it does not contain NHA-derived ingredients—to *minimize* impact. As with companion diets, though, our moral and political obligations diverge in interesting ways; even if we are reliant on the products of vivisection, we retain an obligation to oppose it politically and socially.

References

Anderson, Elizabeth. 2005. "Animal Rights and the Values of Non-Human Life." In *Animal Rights*, edited by Cass Sunstein and Martha Nussbaum, 277–98. Oxford: Oxford University Press.

Brown, Katy. 2010. "A Nation of Animal Lovers?" *Ethical Consumer* (123): 12–16, 34–75.

Brown, Katy, and Dan Welch. 2010. "The Ethics of Veggie Cats and Dogs." *The Guardian*, May 24. http://www.theguardian.com/environment/blog/2010/may/24/vegetarianism-pets-national-vegetarian-week-cats-dogs.

Cochrane, Alasdair. 2010. "Undignified Bioethics." *Bioethics* 24 (5): 234–41.

Cochrane, Alasdair. 2012. *Animal Rights without Liberation*. New York: Columbia University Press.

Cochrane, Alasdair. 2014. "Born in Chains? The Ethics of Animal Domestication." In *The Ethics of Captivity*, edited by Lori Gruen, 156–73. Oxford: Oxford University Press.

Craig, Winston J., and Ann Reed Mangels. 2009. "Position of the American Dietetic Association: Vegetarian Diets." *Journal of the American Dietetic Association* 109 (7): 1266–82.

Donaldson, Sue, and Will Kymlicka. 2013. *Zoopolis*. Oxford: Oxford University Press.

Francione, Gary. 2007. *Introduction to Animal Rights*. Philadelphia: Temple University Press.

Francione, Gary. 2008. *Animals as Persons*. New York: Columbia University Press.

Gruen, Lori. 2011. *Ethics and Animals*. Cambridge: Cambridge University Press.

Hawn, Roxanne. 2011. "Should Your Pet Go on a Vegetarian Diet?" WebMD. http://pets.webmd.com/features/vegetarian-diet-dogs-cats.

Macklin, Ruth. 2003. "Dignity Is a Useless Concept." *British Medical Journal* 327 (7429): 1419–20.

Mangels, Ann Reed, Virginia Messina, and Melina Vesanto. 2003. "Position of the American Dietetic Association and Dietitians of Canada: Vegetarian Diets." *Journal of the American Dietetic Association* 103 (6): 748–65.

Meyer, Michael. 2001. "The Simple Dignity of Sentient Life: Speciesism and Human Dignity." *Journal of Social Philosophy* 32 (2): 115–26.

Michel, Kathryn. 2006. "Unconventional Diets for Dogs and Cats." *Veterinary Clinics of North America: Small Animal Practice* 36 (6): 1269–81.

Milburn, Josh. 2015. "Not Only Humans Eat Meat: Companions, Sentience, and Vegan Politics." *Journal of Social Philosophy* 46 (4): 449–62.

Nussbaum, Martha. 2006. *Frontiers of Justice*. Cambridge, MA: Harvard University Press.

Palmer, Clare. 2010. *Animal Ethics in Context*. New York: Columbia University Press.

Piazza, Jared, Matthew Ruby, Steve Loughnan, Mischel Luong, Juliana Kulik, Hanne Watkins, and Mirra Seigerman. 2015. "Rationalizing Meat Consumption. The 4Ns." *Appetite* 91: 114–28.

Regan, Tom. 1984. *The Case for Animal Rights*. London: Routledge and Kegan Paul.

Rothgerber, Hank. 2013. "A Meaty Matter. Pet Diet and the Vegetarian's Dilemma." *Appetite* 68: 76–82.

Rothgerber, Hank. 2014. "Carnivorous Cats, Vegetarian Dogs, and the Resolution of the Vegetarian's Dilemma." *Anthrozoös* 27 (4): 485–98.

Sandøe, Peter, Sandra Corr, and Clare Palmer. 2016. *Companion Animal Ethics*. Chichester: Wiley.

Singer, Peter. 1974. "All Animals Are Equal." *Philosophical Exchange* 1 (5): 103–16.

Singer, Peter. 1995. *Animal Liberation*. London: Pimlico.

Wakefield, Lorelei, Frances Shofer, and Kathryn Michel. 2006. "Evaluation of Cats Fed Vegetarian Diets and Attitudes of Their Caregivers." *Journal of the American Veterinary Medical Association* 229 (1): 70–73.

Zuolo, Federico. 2016. "Dignity and Animals. Does it Make Sense to Apply the Concept of Dignity to All Sentient Beings?" *Ethical Theory and Moral Practice.* doi: 10.1007/s10677-016-9695-8.

14 THE ETHICS OF ANIMAL TRAINING

Tony Milligan

Adherence to liberal norms concerning the avoidance of cruelty (on all occasions) and domination (where possible) does not require us to buy into the entire package of a "liberal" standpoint by contrast with something else. We can, and arguably ought to, be more piecemeal in our attitude toward the liberal tradition and what it has to offer— particularly so with regard to its resolute individualism. Nonetheless, even a pared-back commitment to liberal norms is enough to generate a reasonable unease about our relations with other creatures. More precisely, we *ought* to be uneasy about the dominance that we exercise over domestic companion animals or, in familiar terms, "pets." (I will switch between these two terms for ease of engagement with the literature, although the former is my preferred terminology.) Paradoxically, this sense of unease may be our saving grace in a difficult situation that we have inherited rather than made and that could not itself be ended (through species extinction) without injustice. The absence of such a sense of unease would indicate not so much that we are at home with our pets but that we are too much at home with our role as the dominant partner in a very unequal relationship. In what follows, I will adopt a broadly genealogical approach toward the ethics of training in order gain a sense of how we have arrived in our current predicament and the vague sense of unease that is part and parcel of a broadly liberal response to it.

An Unsettling Dominance

The dependency of animals goes to the heart of this problem. While we humans are ourselves dependent beings, by virtue of the fact that we are social creatures, the dependence of companion animals upon us seems to be of an entirely different order. And while this may be more the case with dogs than with cats or with a tortoise rather than a rodent, it is dogs that I will focus upon because of their obvious capacity for communication and reciprocation, together with their capacity for adopting at least some of our norms and delights. As a familiar point, the dependence of dogs upon humans is, in some ways, closer to the dependence of human infants upon human adults than it is to our mutual interdependence upon each other. Thanks to generations of breeding for non-threatening traits, companion animals (again dogs in particular) come with built-in neoteny, the presence of infantile characteristics that are simultaneously endearing and disabling, a process of unilateral disarmament that has put at least some of their dangerous ancestral weaponry beyond regular use. Such infantile characteristics make it difficult for domestic dogs to slip free of human control while still enjoying any sort of good life.

And here, as Donna Haraway has pointed out, we need not buy into any manner of flattering creation narrative in which man makes himself and then proceeds to make a special canine companion for himself out of the available raw materials.[1] The timeline for this looks increasingly implausible; dog lineage diverged from the main wolf lines much earlier than previously thought, and the divergent groups may not have been domesticated for several thousand years afterward (Skoglund et al. 2015). But even without the notion of the modern dog as, in all key respects, a man-molded infantile shadow of the wolf, we may still recognize that "we" (in the sense of "we humans," a moral community stretching back in time) have neutralized "them."

Yet no matter how pervasive the analogy of the companion creature and the infant is, it is also notoriously misleading. "They are my children," someone might say of their dogs or cats, even though the animals in question are fully adult and (in the case of rescued animals) may have endured hardships that we would find it difficult to imagine. We understand what is meant by such words and may even sympathize with them as an expression of love. They are words of affection and even of identification, a recognition that "these particular creatures help to make me who I am," or that "I would not fully be myself without them." More ambiguously, we might think of a claim that is not directly about an animal's infantile status, the claim that "they are part of the family," and this may be closer to the truth, although they remain anomalous family members, part of the family group but non-citizens within the larger political community to which our families belong.

In the case of certain kinds of dogs, Staffordshire Bull Terriers being an obvious example, comments of this sort are also the stuff that tragedies are made of. Owners can, and in some cases do, lose sight of the reality of who and what they share their homes with, that is, creatures who remain capable of great harm but who have been inserted into a human-dominated environment where infants are present. When this is done, safety requires an acknowledgment that adult animals are not truly infants, that they are not the stuff nurseries are filled with. They are not our children or anyone else's. Yet while un-childlike, they certainly are still dependent. But even in their dependency, their dissimilarity to a child remains clear because (unlike that of most children) it is entrenched. The companion animals in our midst will mature physically and, in more disturbing ways, sexually, but they will never grow up to become our social equals. We can socialize and train them, but we cannot prepare them for a post-dependent state. And so, when they are trained, exactly what they are being trained *for* and what the justification of such training *is* remain open questions. Yet whatever sorts of narrative we construct on this issue, looking after an animal may at some point turn into looking after a grownup being with more-or-less fixed habits and a stubborn reluctance to change. The obvious thought, then, is to fix matters before this stage is reached, or to be initially strict-to-be-kind when already-adult animals come to stay in our homes.

For those who have been dog owners, these thoughts about showing the creature who is the boss may seem to be thoughts of a common sense sort, but they are thoughts that presuppose a basic level of legitimacy for the institutions of companionship and training. What is troubling is that, upon reflection, the reasons these institutions are legitimate are not entirely obvious. That is to say, we ordinarily feel confident that they are and must be legitimate, that there can be nothing wrong with keeping a dog and training her, unless some sort of physical or psychological abuse is involved. Yet we could well be at a loss to give a plausible explanation of what might license our actions if ever called upon to do so before an audience of those who have never been raised around dogs and have never had a dog of their own.

As a counterfactual point, a point about how the world might have been had things gone differently, it is extremely unlikely that we could provide a satisfactory justification for some initial act of canine domestication unless we were to do so by appeal to the questionable idea that humans matter in an overriding way and more than anything else. Relatedly, accounts of the distant past that appeal to a voluntary decision by wild canids to become camp followers in return for food scraps seem to be optimistic in their reading of events.[2] They may provide an explanation for why dogs might have come into our midst, but without explaining why they would stay without being placed under restraint. Our relation to contemporary dogs may well emerge out of a historical injustice, one that now shapes our inability to be fully just in all respects. More precisely, it probably emerges out of a large number of historical injustices and out of an initial assertion of dominance over creatures whose capacity to resist was no match for our devious human wiles.

Even today, as opponents of pet ownership are quick to point out, there is something servile or at least undignified about the predicament of even the most well-cared-for companion animals. But while notions of dignity sound suspiciously like a reversion to nineteenth-century aristocracy-inspired narratives of animal nobility and virtue, there is nonetheless something to be said for an analysis of human affection for companion animals as a phenomenon that still is thoroughly permeated with a vaguely humiliating dominance, which (as Yi-Fu Tuan notes) is not always separable from affection.[3] Unlike our children, or at least unlike most children in our liberal societies, we train our dogs to fit into special niches within our world and to do so in ways that are convenient, amusing, or (in the case of seeing-eye dogs) functional to us. Their own standpoint and priorities seem to come in a very poor second.

It is difficult not to regard this entire arrangement as something of an imposition. And from this thought a variety of critiques flow: *extinctionist arguments* that, while we must make do with the animal guardian-companion animal relation for the current generation or proximate generations, the ultimate goal should be some form of extinction of the dependents in order to avoid future violations of animal rights (Francione 2007); *ecological attacks* upon the institution of pet ownership as the production of second-rate, faked-up beings who are neither one thing nor another (Callicott 1980);[4] and *political attacks* upon the relation of owner to pet as escapist or bourgeois, a power play by agents who in other aspects of their lives fail to make their proper mark upon the world.[5]

The latter, at least, can have an unsettling ring of truth to it. We tend not to keep chimps as pets, and this is not because our ethical sensibilities will not allow us to coerce our relations. These same sensibilities have, after all, been rather too weak to prevent the ongoing annihilation of all other primates. The absence of chimps from our homes is also not because they lack the mental competence of dogs. Rather, the opposite is true. Chimps seem too smart to be polite, well-behaved, or, more bluntly, submissive to our whims. As a rough generalization, the smarter the creature, the more reluctant she will be to surrender her independence and will. And this is not simply a view that emerges from the ranks of animal rights activists. It also seems to be a part of the experience of animal trainers, at least on the account of Vicki Hearne (Hearne 2007, 27). According to the latter, resistance is often taken as an indication of the potential to excel that may then be channeled through the training process. Dull and submissive dogs do not make champions.

Training of the sort that Hearne writes about so knowledgeably sits toward the sharp end of the practices that critics of the human-pet relation have found objectionable: *we* lord it over *them* in ways that require our dominance to emerge and their autonomy to be brought to heel. And here, the autonomy in question need not meet exacting requirements. Kantian autonomy need not be at stake.[6] It need not require a typical human-like rationality or the capacity to act upon maxims for reasons, yet this autonomy (whether or not we choose to call it "personhood") is nonetheless real and, more awkwardly, difficult to evade or to ignore. There are things *they* want to do and things *they* do not want to do, but some of the former are things *they* want to do only because *they* have been trained to do them and encultured into the desires in question. Dogs are others—willful, desirous, and (when untrained) often recalcitrant in the face of our wishes. If domesticated dogs really were akin to our slaves (which would be odd because they are not, collectively, a labor force), they would be akin to the kind of slaves who have become "preference adapted," trained into adopting their masters' point of view or some extreme and tenacious parody of the latter. This is hardly ideal. In an era of the rejection of even soft and subtle forms of coercion, ours is an unsettling dominance.

Responses to Dominance

Responses to this predicament vary. Understandably, *extinctionism* does not strike those who are outside of animal rights circles as at all plausible. Even inside such circles it represents a minority viewpoint associated mainly with what is known as "abolitionism." The latter, in turn, varies from account to account but usually involves a rejection of the mainstream animal rights movement as morally corrupt or "welfarist" and not truly interested in rights at all. On different accounts, abolitionists advocate the abandonment of all campaigns for reform that fall short of a complete abolition of animal use; or active opposition to such campaigns (rather than merely non-involvement); or a conditional support for some campaigns but only where the immediate goal is the abolition of a particular practice of use rather than its modification. Other campaigns then remain entirely opposed or off-limits. Instead, the priority is the dissemination of veganism, which tends to be understood in a specialized sense that involves ideological commitments in addition to dietary practice. Although a minority view even among activists, the emergence of abolitionism within the animal rights movement during the 1990s has helped to popularize support for an extinctionist approach, although this tends to have little practical significance in a day-to-day manner. Abolitionists are often, in their own right, pet-owners, although the notion of ownership and animal property jars with their outlook.

It is tempting to say that this absence of practical consequences of embracing extinctionism, beyond the minimal restraint of breeding that many non-extinctionists also practice, is symptomatic of the intractable presence of pet ownership. Whatever the rights and wrongs of its historical antecedents, the

30,000-or-so-year-old connection to companion animals seems to run too far into the fiber of our being, too far into our lives to be overridden by any theory-driven considerations. And by this I do not mean to dismiss the role of writing about animals within an explicitly articulated ethical tradition. Rather, my suggestion is that we are probably entitled to be skeptical about viewpoints entailed by some or other ethical theory when they conflict with deep levels of our emotional responsiveness and hence with our sense of what matters in a deep way.

When theories do this by, for example, announcing that it is wrong for humans to bring other humans into being or that the value of a human, a dog, and a fly are one and the same, the thought is that we are entitled to assume that the theories themselves have gone astray, that the devil in the conclusions indicates one or more flaws somewhere in the initial assumptions or else in the argumentative detail. In more formal terms, arrival at such "fearless thoughts" is often taken to provide a *reductio* of the arguments in question. And, in the case of favoring extinction over training, this seems to make at least some sense. Extinctionism requires endorsement of a peculiarly strident form of human authority. What greater indication of human dominance could there be than our even deliberating about ending the lineages of other creatures who are absolutely no threat to our own social group? It presupposes entitlements of an even more wide-reaching sort than those assumed by any common or garden-variety animal guardian or professional animal trainer.

But if our best response to human dominance is not a theory-driven extinction, what then? A continuation of a punitive "I am the master" dominance, of a sort that emerged out of the nineteenth century and continues in narratives of man, the pack-leader? That hardly seems likely. Here, the analogy with children does seem to carry some weight. Victorian ideas about the need for children to be both seen and heard, but only when being soundly disciplined, hardly carry sway. The notion that physical punishment was a basic requirement in childrearing tends to occur only in the more salacious early-morning television programs or in reruns of *Little House on the Prairie*. What it has taken with it is any sense of confidence in our entitlement to physically discipline the companion animals in our lives. And this partial renunciation of physical force is part of a more general trend. As part of a broader reaction to the punitive dimensions of early behaviorism, the second half of the twentieth century witnessed a softening of the power that owners were to wield by means of behaviorist methods of positive reinforcement, with the emphasis upon the positive. With regard to animal training, punishment was *out*, although "correction" might remain, and rewarding with treats was definitely *in*.

The great exemplar of this approach, and one that is still very much in use, is the "click and treat" regime. Desired behaviors are immediately acknowledged by pressing a "clicker," which is associated with a treat. When the animal hears a click, it knows that it has done well and that something good is on its way. The clicker's role is rather like that of the theme tune of a favorite TV show. This helps the dog to identify the desired behavior in question. Thanks to successive modification of such softened exercises of power during the later twentieth century, dogs no longer needed to be put on neck chains and yanked into submission in the manner that was ultimately distilled into *The Koehler Method of Dog Training* (1962). They were to be bribed, albeit bribed under conditions with a loose similarity to drug-dealing, in the sense that dependence upon the good stuff is increased over the course of time. The competition was also eliminated, with alternative sources of comparable satisfactions removed, making the securing of treats (which might have been a biscuit, praise, or anything that pleased) reliant upon conformity to the trainer or owner's wishes.

What helped to rationalize such approaches in the 1970s and after, during times when the issue of animal rights had begun to make its way into the press for the first time since the early years of the century, was, first, the way in which it genuinely did displace forms of physical punishment that seemed out of keeping with the high priority that all good, liberally minded agents place upon the avoidance of cruelty; and secondly, a tendency to reduce animal wellbeing down to pleasures and pains rather than indexing wellbeing to any notion of true autonomy, a reductionist move that we would be reluctant to make in the case of humans. Our wellbeing and enjoyment of a good life turn out to be surprisingly complex accomplishments involving many things.[7] Comparable complexity in the case of dog companions has always tended to be denied. As long as the animals were not suffering anything resembling actual physical pain of less-enlightened days, non-punitive training made a great deal of sense. But what clicker training also encouraged, at least when presented as some sort of comprehensive fix for the inherent inequality of the training situation, was a level of self-deception about the exercise of power.

Susan Garrett's popular training manual, *Ruff Love: A Relationship Building Program for You and Your Dog* (2001), represented something of a reaction, with its reinforcement of the idea of the *reciprocity* of animal and owner (training as, in a sense, *being with*), combined with a startling commitment to total human supervision, 100 percent of the time. When the trainer or owner was not able to be present, crating the animal was recommended (resulting in some unfavorable but not entirely misleading comparisons to abduction) (Garrett 2011). Donna Haraway refers to this approach as "Positive Bondage" with good reason (2003, 43). Essentially, it represented a qualification of positive reinforcement techniques with a particular emphasis placed upon a certain kind of ruthless *honesty* about the process itself. For the trainer, sincerity and integrity were key virtues, but they were essentially human virtues. They were the traits that allowed us to be humane but above all consistent (and this in turn was taken as the key requirement for mutual human-animal understanding). On such an approach, the entire ethical burden of the well-formed reciprocal relation could not be carried by human sympathy or compassion for the animal, and some level of diligence on the part of the latter. In a move reminiscent of eighteenth-century model prison theory, actions and outcomes were to be charted and measured, detailed and recorded, on the assumption that animal trainers were inclined to be fundamentally dishonest about several aspects of the process, not the least of which was their rate of success in getting the animal to do what was actually required without physical force.

While aspects of such an approach (quantification, crating, and continuous presence) have been qualified or dropped, the reciprocity at its heart remains key to contemporary training manuals. Good trainers, on the relevant conception, have not simply mastered techniques for getting things done. Rather, they have learned how to listen to and trust the animal, even (in some contexts) more than they trust fellow humans. This is the familiar, philosophically sophisticated approach that we find in Vicki Hearne's *Adam's Task: Calling Animals by Name* (2007, 13). This picture is, of course, better in many respects than a humanely-informed behaviorism, in which the animal is a sort of black box utterly beyond our comprehension or beyond any need of being understood. And it incorporates a conception of the animal's potential for growth in capacities, moral and other, that may be brought out through the training process, to the animal's own great advantage. We like our skills (in music, sport, and languages) and animals too like theirs, but both must be taught. In this understanding of the training relation, the dog is owed something. In fact, it is owed several things, including, in language that echoes Koehler, the consequences of its mistakes.

Following a line of thought that has become dominant within feminism and widespread in post-1970s ethical theory, rights for Hearne emerge in relational contexts rather than being among the brute gifts of nature. But what this means has always been a matter for some debate. On Hearne's account, it means that animals acquire rights in the training context and during the latter rather than before. It is the training context that sets up relations of obligation, expectation, and trust. Strangers who approach an animal and issue commands as if they were part of this relation when they are not, or who randomly reach out their hand and offer scent without invitation, may rightly be rebuked and disobeyed by the animal without suggesting that the animal's own training process has in any way gone wrong. The training of the human, on the other hand, may well have gone wrong, and this may help to explain their unreasonable expectations and unwelcome familiarity.

A convenient upshot of such an approach is that it precludes any straightforward critique of the training process itself. If rights emerge only once the interactions of trainer and trainee are up and running, then any notion of preexisting rights that might preclude the latter can be rejected. Here, I will take it that there is a good deal to be said for the relational understanding of rights but perhaps less so for Hearne's restrictive understanding of what this means. Her rather strident article in *Harper's Magazine*, "What's Wrong with Animal Rights" (1991), attacking conventional animal rights theory, did little to endear her to an activist movement with an emerging abolitionist wing that was increasingly inclined to regard soft power as, in many ways, the main enemy. (The thought here was that if we stopped hiding behind campaigns for "better," more humane, forms of exploitation, then the nakedness of the process would be exposed.[8]) But even without such reactions, there is a concern that Hearne's loyalty to the broad vision of Koehler may well leave us with an under-constrained account of legitimate, ethically-defensible modes of training.

This remains a plausible suspicion, even though there is a case for saying that Hearne, the feminist movement, and others were perhaps correct about the limitations of traditional rights theory: those aspects that insisted that rights were underpinned by the possession of properties (such as sentience or being the subject of a life) that might belong to a being considered in utter isolation from all other beings.[9] This older, non-relational idea of rights fails to do justice to the point that the securing of a worthwhile conception of animal rights would need to involve altered ways of relating, on the part of both humans and nonhumans, rather than a cessation of relations between the two. Outside of the bounds of the odder versions of neoliberalism, we would not, of course, think of human freedom as a cessation of certain kinds of interaction with others, as a matter of being unleashed and unimpeded. Thinking of animal freedom in such a way (including conceptions required for some plausible form of "liberation" or "abolition") seems similarly reductionist. Autonomy of the best sort, the sort that fits any being for a flourishing existence in any society whatsoever, requires skill, competence, and, in the case of social animals, the cultural enhancement of traits. Learning to read and write is a basic requirement in our own societies; without it, the agent is always missing out. Being left alone is not obviously the ideal, liberated condition.

Socialization Versus Training

The most detailed general account of the possibilities of our being with other creatures in a mutually respectful but taught and trained way is Donaldson and Kymlicka's *Zoopolis: A Political Theory of Animal Rights* (2011), a text best known for its problematic idea that companion animals might become citizens of a better (but still flawed) world. Like Hearne, and (in his own way) Koehler, they regard a failure to socialize animals who have to live among us as a form of abuse. If any members of a community (mixed or otherwise) are to flourish within that community, they need to be equipped with the capabilities required in order to do so. Consequently, "if we also think of cats as members of a mixed human-animal community, then the right of basic socialization encompasses the norms and knowledge needed for cats to flourish in that mixed society, and not just in cat society" (Donaldson and Kymlicka 2011, 124). Additionally, what is required here is socialization in both directions. *They* need to learn how to live with us, and *we* need to learn how to live with them.

An additional wrinkle in this picture is that companion animals such as dogs of course need to learn about far more than just getting along with humans. In the case of a dog, for example, the community in which she will have an opportunity to flourish will include various different humans and non-humans. Given this, "She needs to be housebroken, to learn not to bite or to jump up on people, to be wary of cars, and not to chase the family cat (unless it's a play chase!)" (Donaldson and Kymlicka 2011, 125). And such socialization is learned partly from the humans but also, in part, from the nonhumans. In the case of cats, something may have to be done to mitigate the worst of their devastating harm to birds (although there are limits to what can ever be done about this).

However, unlike Hearne et al., Donaldson and Kymlicka draw a fairly strong distinction between socialization and training in order to try to secure a far stronger constraining of legitimate modes of interaction:

> [B]asic socialization is different from training for particular forms of labor (such as training dogs to be guide dogs for the blind). Socialization involves the basic and general skills/knowledge that individuals need to learn (insofar as possible) in order to be accepted into social community—like establishing control over bodily processes and impulses, learning basic communication, rules of social interaction, and respect for others. Training, on the other hand, is about developing a particular individual's capacities and interests. (2011, 123)

I take it that what they have in mind here is a distinction rather than a rigid dichotomy. Given that both socialization and training involve communication, one-and-the-same act might, from time to time, be classified as both rather than having to count as one at the expense of another. Yet, on the whole, training is viewed as *inessential* to flourishing in a way that socialization is not. Dogs can take it or leave it and still do well, although we may make their completion of the socialization process contingent upon a successful training process, for example, by allowing association with other dogs only in a training context, thereby boosting their enthusiasm for the latter and, at the same time, making training essential to their wellbeing (as a brute, contingent fact).

Socialization, on this approach that treats it as a basic entitlement, is to be guided by a number of general principles, with two standing out: first, it is not a right to mold individuals but a responsibility to recognize them as members of the community who have a need for skills in order to thrive; secondly, socialization is not a lifelong process of control and intervention but a temporary process ideally attended to when the animal is young (Donaldson and Kymlicka 2011, 125). What comes after this stage is a fuller autonomy. The way in which socialization is carried out also matters. Play is ideal, and a key means of socialization among various wild but social animals (including wild canids). Broadly, "Many social animals, like humans, are generally amenable to socialization through methods of positive reinforcement and gentle correction" (Donaldson and Kymlicka 2011, 126). If, instead, humans revert to harsh measures, it is an indication of our lack of patience and respect. A symptom of this lack of respect is the familiar leader-of-the-pack-view that dogs must be dominated by humans by some process in which the latter establish themselves as alpha dogs. The kind of domination that is then modelled, as any good ethologist will affirm, is actually what happens when canid social structure goes wrong. Ordinarily, the latter is based upon more-or-less stable families of related members and not upon packs that are thrown together and held in check by a continuous testing of the dominance of those at the top through intimidation and violence. From a trust standpoint, reliance upon familial ties, rather than naked force, makes a good deal of sense.

Here, of course, we might allow for exceptions to this more consistently liberal approach, especially in cases where something genuinely has gone wrong. One of Hearne's grounds for defending Koehler so vehemently in the face of multiple criticisms of his harsh methods was the reasonable point that for many of the dogs brought to him, it was their last chance.[10] Under such circumstances, for lack of any better way, extraordinary measures might perhaps justifiably be taken in order to save their lives. But this hardly represents the norm, and it supplies a poor model for regular practice. Additionally, none of the above, including the fairly strong socialization/training distinction, implies that training is *never* legitimate, simply that it is something in addition to what a companion animal ordinarily needs in order to live and thrive among us.

This *something in addition* generally involves performing tasks for us, and at least some of these tasks will be questionable or straightforwardly indefensible. Hearne, for example, has a great interest in the animal skills shown in hunting, but the value of their cultivation might well be put in doubt by ethical reservations about hunting itself. But does such concern about the purposes toward which training is likely to be geared carry over into all cases of animal use? If we adopt a position of hostility to any sort of use of animals, as certain specialized instances of animal rights theory do (extinctionism most notably), then it will be automatically ruled out. However, there are good grounds for rejecting such a view.[11] After all, we humans use each other in order to accomplish things all the time, and in many cases our training (including that of students and career academics) is geared toward such use. Employment, generally, is *use* but it is not always or necessarily *abuse*, or at least it is not the kind of abuse that we can readily displace given our prevailing social context.

On a more positive note, Donaldson and Kymlicka insist that the kinds of advantages that animals themselves can derive from training are, just as Hearne claimed, real. They draw an analogy with a human who is given (or rather *gently coerced into*) music lessons as a child because the parents recognize the advantages for the child that may then accrue. Yet their overall verdict on actual training (as opposed to socialization) is not positive:

> Viewed in this light, much training of domesticated animals is exploitative. Most therapy and assistance animals are not trained to develop their own potential and interests, but moulded to serve human ends (the same goes for horse riding, animals in the entertainment industry, and most other kinds of animal work). . . . Even so-called positive reinforcement is usually thinly disguised coercion. If the only way a dog gets treats, play time, or affection from others is by performing tasks to please them, this is blackmail not education. (2011, 141)

The possibilities for exploitation always remain high. "In between the donkeys whose presence in the sheep pasture keeps predators at bay, and the seeing-eye dog who undergoes months of intensive training in order to spend most of his life serving as a tool for others, we cross the line from use to exploitation" (Donaldson and Kymlicka 2011, 142). And here we might think of the predicament of seeing-eye dogs: ignored and virtually subject to a form of social death in public, with other human beings told to avoid interaction and even eye contact. On the tough judgement call about seeing-eye dogs, I find it difficult to disagree. Although some modification of practice might have a more persuasive justification, the existing practice does seem to be exploitative and could only be justified if we humans happen to have a license to exploit in nonviolent ways.

Conclusion

Where does this genealogy of ways of relating leave us? It leaves us where we began, with the sense of liberal unease about domination and control, but without any reasonable way to comprehensively remove either, and with some plausibly justifying narratives in favor of sustaining this sense of unease. We are where we are, in part, because of the injustices of the past and the competing demands that they have helped to place upon us. It seems that, even if we permanently abandon (as we no doubt should) the kinds of physically punitive forms of training that belong in a different era, we will still be left with a great many grey areas and some tough negotiations to protect animal autonomy rather than any blanket and uncritical approval of positive reinforcement or bribery by treats. Even the contentment of the animals themselves, supplied with a steady stream of the latter, will not justify all (any more than it might once have justified the contentment of the palace slave). Yet the standards that we set on human-animal interactions need not obviously be higher than those we set for reasonable, morally defensible interactions between humans. And this means that neither perfect altruism nor absolute license seems to be a particularly good fit. Perhaps it is simplest to say that the use of animals, like the use of our fellow humans, need not be guided *only* by their interests.

Yet animal interests have to come into consideration at some point, and they must surely do so in ways that do not presuppose any standing entitlement to neglect their autonomy or wellbeing or to permanently compromise the former in the name of the latter. The basic questions here will then concern the goals and methods of training and especially the extent to which animals are coaxed (like piano-playing children) rather than coerced (like primates) into following instructions. We may then have to ask about the extent to which we are genuinely enhancing their autonomy rather than compromising its exercise in the name of something else, such as skill, display, entertainment, or aesthetics. But this looks suspiciously like an ordinary moral problem rather than a special sort of puzzle. That is to say, it looks like the kind of difficulty that we face every day, with each other, simply as a consequence of living in the midst of people who are owed a great many things from ourselves and who owe us a great deal in return. When training is determined to be potentially of overall benefit to the animal itself (and is thus a good candidate for justification), it will require a good deal of sensitivity to those points at which an animal's reluctance to engage in the process indicates a merely temporary state of mind, in which case some persuasion to avoid dropping out makes sense. But on other occasions we may have to recognize and respect the fact that even the most sociable of animals simply does not want to play.

Notes

1. Donna Haraway critiques the myth of human self-making and then dog-making in favor of a process of "becoming with" (2008, 3–4).
2. Stephen Budiansky (1997) argues that dogs more or less volunteered themselves into our service in return for campfire scraps and security. But there is a good deal of shifting between individual creature rationality and what makes sense for a species in this account.
3. The entangling of these matters is the persistent theme of Yi-Fu Tuan's classic, *Dominance and Affection: The Making of Pets* (1984).
4. Callicott's ideas have subsequently undergone change, with an acceptance of the legitimacy of rights in the domain of domesticated creatures (see Milligan 2015, 150–52).
5. Gilles Deleuze and Félix Guattari (2013, 265–66) advance an anti-bourgeois critique of pets.
6. Alasdair Cochrane (2012) argues for a robust, more-or-less Kantian, account of autonomy, which rules out nonhumans with some possible exceptions of primates and cetaceans.
7. The animal rights movement is rather older than is sometimes imagined. Henry Salt's seminal *Animals' Rights Considered in Relation to Social Progress* (1892) marks the emergence of a clear intellectual justification for rights attributions, and it influenced generations of radical thinkers, including Gandhi. However, the issue can be traced back into the eighteenth century and was strongly connected to discussions of women's rights.
8. I provide an overview of the abolitionist position in Milligan (2010, 115–35).
9. Regan's account of being a subject of a life as the basis for rights is the most obvious case of an account of rights that focuses upon non-relational considerations (Regan 2004, 243). This focus is strongly linked to a heavy reliance upon the "argument from marginal cases," an argument that is far harder to run once relational considerations are taken into account. For Regan's account of the latter, see Milligan (2015, 49–66).
10. See Hearne (1991, 38, 46, 49, 204, 217) for Koehler's harsh responses to critics of animal discipline as "humaniacs" (repetition of which comes suspiciously close to a tacit sympathy for Koehler's view).
11. Among contemporary advocates of animals rights (in a mainstream sense), Cochrane is probably the most forthright defender of certain kinds of animal use. His *Animal Rights without Liberation* (2012) presents a plausible case for the possibility of defensible use in a range of contexts. But this is not to be confused with advocacy of anything remotely like the status quo and may not be compatible with some of our existing cultural norms and socio-political arrangements.

References

Budiansky, Stephen. 1997. *The Covenant of the Wild*. London: Phoenix.

Callicott, J. Baird. 1980. "Animal Liberation: A Triangular Affair." *Environmental Ethics* 2 (3): 311–38.

Cochrane, Alasdair. 2012. *Animal Rights without Liberation*. New York: Columbia University Press.

Deleuze, Gilles, and Félix Guattari. 2013. *A Thousand Plateaus: Capitalism and Schizophrenia*. Translated by Brian Massumi. London: Continuum.

Donaldson, Sue, and Will Kymlicka. 2011. *Zoopolis: A Political Theory of Animal Rights*. Oxford: Oxford University Press.

Francione, Gary. 2007. "Animal Rights and Domesticated Nonhumans." *Animal Rights: The Abolitionsist Approach* (blog). January 10. http://www.abolitionistapproach.com/animal-rights-and-domesticated-nonhumans/.

Garrett, Susan. 2001. *Ruff Love: A Relationship Building Program for You and Your Dog*. South Hadley, MA: Clear Run Productions.

Garrett, Susan. 2011. "What is 'Ruff Love' Really?" *Say Yes! Dog Training* (blog). April 4. http://susangarrettdogagility.com/2011/04/what-is-ruff-love-really/.

Haraway, Donna. 2003. *The Companion Species Manifesto*. Chicago: Prickly Paradigm Press.

Haraway, Donna. 2008. *When Species Meet*. Minneapolis: University of Minnesota Press.

Hearne, Vicki. 1991. "What's Wrong with Animal Rights." *Harper's Magazine*, September, 59–64.

Hearne, Vicki. 2007. *Adam's Task: Calling Animals by Name*. New York: Skyhorse Publishing.

Koehler, William. 1962. *The Koehler Method of Dog Training*. New Jersey: Prentice-Hall.

Milligan, Tony. 2010. *Beyond Animal Rights*. London and New York: Continuum.

Milligan, Tony. 2015. *Animal Ethics: The Basics*. London and New York: Routledge.

Regan, Tom. 2004. *The Case for Animal Rights*. Berkeley, CA: University of California Press.

Salt, Henry. 1892. *Animals' Rights Considered in Relation to Social Progress*. London: George Bell & Sons.

Skoglund, Pontus, Erik Ersmark, Elftheria Palkopoulou, and Love Dalen. 2015. "Ancient Wolf Genome Reveals an Early Divergence of Domestic Dog Ancestors and Admixture into High-Latitude Breeds." *Current Biology* 25 (11): 1515–19.

Tuan, Yi Fu. 1984. *Dominance and Affection: The Making of Pets*. New Haven: Yale University Press.

15 ANIMAL ASSISTED INTERVENTION AND CITIZENSHIP THEORY

Zipporah Weisberg

Animal Assisted Intervention (AAI) is a fast-growing practice across North America. Animal Assisted Therapy (AAT) and Animal Assisted Activities (AAA), the two main forms of AAI, incorporate animals into a variety of programs designed to promote the healing, recovery, and wellbeing of vulnerable people. AAT is defined as "goal-directed intervention" and typically involves bringing animals into therapeutic contexts to help clients achieve specific emotional, psychological, cognitive, and physical goals. AAA, on the other hand, is "non-goal directed" and often consists of bringing animals into long-term care facilities such as nursing homes, hospices, hospitals, and psychiatric facilities to visit and socialize with residents (Evans and Gray 2012, 601).

Research indicates that the presence of animals in therapeutic contexts is highly beneficial for both the care workers and the clients (Johnson 2011; Fine 2010; Morrison 2007). Animals can help build rapport and trust between people, reduce loneliness, anxiety, and depression, lower blood pressure and cortisol levels, inspire physical activity in the elderly, motivate children to achieve learning goals, and help people with autism spectrum disorders develop social functioning skills (Baun and Johnson 2010; Evans and Gray 2012; Johnson 2011; Grandin, Fine, and Bowers 2010). The participation of animals in therapy is also known to reduce physical pain and speed up recovery times for patients who have undergone surgeries and other invasive medical procedures (Chandler 2011, 211–12, as cited in DeMello 2012).

Unfortunately, the animals involved in AAI are not always treated with the same respect and care they offer their human counterparts. In fact, they are often victims of exploitation. Tzachi Zamir identifies six forms of exploitation animals are at risk for in AAI: "limitations of freedom" (e.g., confinement and a strict, relentless daily work regimen); curtailing of "life determination" (e.g., deciding for animal how their lives will unfold and the activities they will be engaged in); coercive training (e.g., obedience and submission training); "social disconnection" (e.g., breaking up natural social groups among animals to employ the services of one member, resulting in its subsequent isolation); "injury" (e.g., rough handling by care worker or client); and "instrumentalization" (i.e., being treated as tools for human use and benefit) (2006, 181–82).

One of the reasons AAI is often exploitative is that there are no universal standards of practice, no universal selection procedures for animal participants, and no "systematic or empirical evaluation of the potential risks to animals imposed by current practices" (Serpell et al. 2010, 481). In 1996, the Delta Society (now PetPartners.org) published *Animal-Assisted Therapy: Standards of Practice*, but as standards and not regulations, the contents are not binding (and it is not even clear if this self-published handbook is still in use and if so, how widely). Each organization that runs or supports AAI ultimately determines its own standards of practice and defines its own selection processes. If they do follow the Delta Society's standards, the focus is primarily on "broad criteria, such as reliability, predictability, controllability, and suitability" of animals and whether or not they pose a risk of transmitting zoonotic diseases.

Less concern, however, is shown for whether or not the animals themselves wish to participate (Fredrickson-MacNamara and Butler 2010, 113–14). Although in the past decade the focus has shifted from risk prevention and reduction to the relationships among animals, "handlers," and environment, the animals' needs and perspectives are still underrepresented (Fredrickson-MacNamara and Butler 2010, 115–16). To be sure, organizations that support AAI, such as the American Veterinary Medical Association (AVMA) (2016), have produced a set of comprehensive guidelines for implementing Wellness Programs, as they call them, without harming animals. They cover substantial ground and in significant depth and detail. Among other things, they suggest that "animals across the spectrum [of] AAI services [should be] 1) healthy (in part to reduce the bidirectional risk of zoonotics transmission); 2) behaviorally appropriate for the program, and 3) protected from being harmed by the program." They also indicate that "all factors including species, age, breed, temperament, and any risk factors that could jeopardize an animal's health and welfare should be considered." They further insist that dogs and cats under six months of age should not be involved in AAI and that the program should "be flexible and tailored to fit the changing needs of individual animals as they age and as a result of participation in AAI programs." They even suggest, rather progressively, that animals who take part in AAI should be given "vacations." Additionally, AVMA recommends monitoring animals' wellness by making sure that their vaccinations are up to date, and suggests that wellness programs should be flexible enough to accommodate the changing needs of animals as they age or as a result of participation in AAI. These and many of the other guidelines AVMA has proposed are significant, salient, and indeed vital. If upheld, AVMA's guidelines would very likely make a positive difference to the lives of animals enjoined to participate in AAI.

However, despite their relative breadth and depth, these guidelines ultimately fall short of ensuring that animals involved in AAI will not be mistreated, or even that they are appropriate candidates in the first place. This is in large part because, for all their apparent detail, they are still in effect quite vague, given the vast variety of species potentially recruited to AAI and the diversity of practices they may be expected to engage in, not to mention the potential violations to which they are subject, the latter of which get almost no mention in the guidelines. Finally, as guidelines, rather than legally binding entitlements, rights, or regulations, these measures are only optional and therefore potentially ineffectual.

To transform AAI into an ethical practice that mutually benefits its human and nonhuman animal participants, sets of guidelines and piecemeal reforms are insufficient. These measures, though potentially beneficial, do not target the root causes of exploitation, one of which is the instrumentalization of animals for AAI. I suggest here that for AAI to become truly non-exploitative, it must be embedded within a broader protective political framework in which all animals are recognized as active members of interspecies communities. In this chapter, I argue that Sue Donaldson and Will Kymlicka's animal citizenship model (2011) provides just such a framework.

Despite my strong reservations about adopting a specifically *liberal* conception of citizenship, or citizenship theory more generally, for that matter, there are a number of key features of Donaldson and Kymlicka's proposal that are especially pertinent to the development of non-exploitative AAI and are well worth exploring here. To be sure, I am not arguing that to transform AAI into a healthy practice, the adoption of citizenship theory is necessarily required. Structural transformation within and beyond the context of AAI can occur in many ways, and indeed may even preclude the adoption of a citizenship model, liberal or otherwise. However, it is my view that an experimental foray into how AAI might unfold under the rubric of Donaldson and Kymlicka's novel interspecies citizenship theory is useful: 1) as a way of imagining how citizenship theory may manifest itself in practice, and 2) as a way of imagining how AAI might benefit from the seismic shift in human–animal relationality that interspecies citizenship would likely entail.

Citizenship promises animals the fundamental right to express their subjective good and agency in all matters that affect their lives, including whether or not they are comfortable working with humans in therapeutic environments. From this crucial entitlement stems a series of concrete positive rights and "relational duties" that nonhuman animal citizens would be owed under the animal citizenship model, including a personal identity outside their work, non-coercive training methods, duties of protection, medical care, rights of residency and mobility, and institutional, financial, and social support. Citizenship theory also indirectly offers criteria by which to ascertain which animals are and are not appropriate for AAI, with dogs emerging as the most suitable.

I explore here the possibility that if AAI were embedded within the larger political framework of citizenship that Donaldson and Kymlicka propose, animals participating in AAI would, at least in theory, be guaranteed comprehensive protections and entitlements that are not likely to fall under the remit of superficial and precarious reforms. I begin by demonstrating why, both within and outside the context of citizenship theory, dogs are the best candidates for non-exploitative AAI, before moving on to discuss in detail how the key citizenship entitlements and rights outlined above would protect dogs who participate in AAI from exploitation and promote their flourishing.

Dogs: Ideal Candidates for AAI

As a result of loose standards and relaxed selection criteria, a dizzying array of animals with very different species-specific needs, territorial preferences, and degrees of intra- and interspecies sociability are enlisted in AAI programs, including rabbits, guinea pigs, hamsters, mice, capuchin monkeys, dolphins, miniature horses, miniature pigs, llamas, alpacas, African parrots, birds, horses, donkeys, and reptiles. The majority of these animals are fundamentally ill-suited to AAI. Their involvement *necessarily* entails restricting their freedom and undermining their self-determination in potentially catastrophic ways. As Serpell et al. (2010, 486) point out, wild animals as well as many small mammals and birds are at a very high risk of abuse and suffering in the context of AAI. They tend to find close interaction with human beings stressful, they are confined to cages for the majority of their lives, and the techniques used to train them and ensure ongoing compliance and correct performance of tasks are inherently abusive. Programs that use capuchin monkeys to assist severely disabled people, for instance, "found it necessary to neuter and surgically extract the canine teeth from the monkeys before they can be used safely with such vulnerable human partners" and to equip them with remotely controlled electric shock collars and harnesses (487).

Donaldson and Kymlicka's political model militates against involving wild animals in AAI because doing so not only would lead to physical harm and suffering for the animals but also, by making them dependent on human beings for survival, would interfere with their exercise of "competent agency" and violate their fundamental claim to self-determination, self-governance, and sovereignty (2011, 175–76). The only fitting candidates for non-exploitative AAI would be (some) animals that fall within the category of "domesticated animal citizens," most notably dogs.

Dogs are the most obvious candidates for AAI for several reasons. Dogs are naturally sociable, thrive on positive social interaction with humans and other animals, and are adept at cooperation and teamwork. They are also trusting, trustworthy, affectionate, and loyal. It is no coincidence that dogs are already one of the most popular choices for AAI (Canadian Agency for Drugs and Technologies in Health 2014). But restricting AAI to dogs is not sufficient in and of itself to avoid exploitation. A robust political framework, such as animal citizenship, must already be in place in which to ground AAI.

Who qualifies as a domesticated animal citizen and why? Donaldson and Kymlicka (2011) maintain that domesticated animals such as dogs, cows, cats, and pigs, among many others, ought to be considered citizens because they share their lives with us, form intimate relationships with us, and are members of our familial, social, and political communities. Though they may not be able to engage in deliberative reasoning, domesticated animal citizens ought to have a direct "say" in how the communities of which they are a part are organized (99). In other words, animal citizens must be able to express their subjective good and agency (107). They point out that dogs regularly express both of these things "through a vast repertoire of vocalizations, gestures, movements, and signals" (such as tail wagging, barking, and nuzzling), some of which have developed to enable them to communicate with humans (109). While, as we saw above, wild animals are independent agents, dogs and other domesticated animals who have come to depend on humans for survival are better categorized as "dependent agents," but they are agents nonetheless and must be ensured the opportunity to make meaningful choices about their lives (104).

This basic feature of citizenship already has far-reaching implications for AAI. If we keep animals' subjective good in mind, the kinds of AAI dogs might be involved in will depend not just on their species, but also on their personal histories, their personalities, and their preferences. The question would shift from "How can we make this animal do what we want her to do to suit our purposes?" to "What does this individual require to flourish?" and "How could her involvement in AAI promote her flourishing?" (96). To figure out whether or not a dog "consents" to a particular form of AAI, it would be important to ensure that she knew she had other options, or that her participation was optional, not obligatory (140). If she seemed uninterested in AAI or tended toward other activities instead, this should be interpreted as non-consent.

Respecting animals' agency and subjective good also means that dogs and other animals should never be purpose-bred to serve as ideal candidates for AAIs (or for anything else). As AAI is rising in popularity, so are "in-house breeding programs," especially for "service" animals (such as "guide dogs" and "wheelchair dogs") (Serpell et al. 2010). This is incompatible with my application of citizenship theory. Breeding AAI animals is deliberately geared toward predetermining their subjective good and limiting their agency to ensure compliance and optimal performance.

Different Forms of Citizen Canine Cooperation and "Work"

For citizen canines who do express an eagerness to contribute to AAI, there are several kinds of "work" they can participate in without being exploited, provided they are protected by strict regulations designed to promote their subjective good and the meaningful expressions of their agency. "For example," Donaldson and Kymlicka explain, "a gregarious dog might enjoy accompanying her human on social work visits to hospitals or homes for the aged." Other dogs might "use their superior sniffing skills, without excessive training required, to assist humans in detecting tumors or incipient seizures or dangerous substances, or tracking lost individuals" (2011, 140). Some dogs would clearly provide great comfort to the sick and dying in hospitals, and might take pleasure in offering such support, provided they were comfortable in institutional settings, showed an aptitude for being gentle with emotionally and physically fragile people, and preferred calm, quiet interactions with people to noisy, boisterous exchanges. Many dogs would probably also enjoy acting as co-therapists in the context of psychotherapy, particularly, and perhaps only, if the therapist is their primary human companion. One can imagine very affectionate dogs thriving in scenarios where they engage in unstructured, spontaneous interaction with the client, such as petting, cuddling, and playing.

Some dogs might flourish most in walking therapy, where, as the name suggests, a client and therapist go on walks with the dog. As long as the dog is not subjected to irrational assertions of control and is not constrained or restricted with a "halty" or a muzzle, both of which are obviously uncomfortable, obstructive, and relentlessly irritating for dogs, but is given ample space to move around on a lengthy lead (used for the dog's protection against vehicles), walking therapy is clearly a wonderful way for clients to develop an appreciation for and learn from dogs' admirable capacity to immerse themselves entirely in their surroundings, meet and greet people in a friendly manner, and ensure the safety and well-being of their humans.

Other dogs might be well suited to play an active role in some forms of AAI with more specific learning or therapeutic goals. Some dogs might participate as co-therapists in speech and language therapy for people suffering from aphasia by, for example, engaging in "conversations" with the clients. Still others might enjoy participating as co-therapists in physical therapy sessions, in which the client pets or grooms a dog for muscle strengthening and so on. Finally, some citizen canines, particularly those who gravitate toward children, might very much enjoy participating in programs offered by the Therapy Dogs United ACE Program (2014) (also known as Animal Care for Exceptional Children and Adults) for school children. In this program, dogs make weekly visits to schools, where they are undoubtedly the center of most children's attention and can give and receive affection and/or perhaps engage in social play with children, which is a cherished and highly meaningful activity for most dogs (Bekoff 2002, 125–26).

A dog may express her agency in these contexts in any number of ways, including helping to shape the terms of the relationships. She might indicate where and how she would like to be petted or groomed, what kinds of games she would like to play, what kinds of activities she likes and dislikes, and when she would like to take a break, rest, and replenish herself, or go outside to relieve herself. If she is participating in an AAI at a school and some children are interacting with her inappropriately, she might want to withdraw and opt out of the activity. She should not be required to sit through exercises designed to improve interpersonal skills if, for example, the client's efforts are proving unsuccessful and they are harming or annoying her (the dog) as a result. Dogs may not be able to conceptualize the specific cognitive or emotional needs of the clients, but they are often much more attuned to humans' emotional states and capabilities than we give them credit for. For example, dogs are highly skilled at social play and uphold a variety of "rules" and "norms" based on fairness, morality, and reciprocity (Bekoff 2002, 126–28). Kids prone to aggression and lacking a sense of boundaries, for instance, could learn how to play more fairly through the dog's example.

There are undoubtedly many other kinds of AAI in which a variety of dogs would enjoy participating, but it is beyond the scope of this chapter to explore them all. What is important to recognize is that whatever AAI a dog (or any other animal) is involved in, their citizenship status would ensure that they "have the same opportunity human citizens have to control the conditions under which they contribute to society, and to follow their own inclinations in terms of how they live their lives, and with whom they spend their time" (Donaldson and Kymlicka 2011, 140). Crucially, any dogs (or other animals) involved in AAI might express their agency in different ways on different days and in different stages of their life, an issue I address below.

As I will now discuss, Donaldson and Kymlicka's theory of citizenship offers a number of other entitlements and positive rights that would ensure that animals who take part in AAI are guaranteed this kind of autonomy, and are protected from exploitation more generally.

Selves, Not Tools

Under the citizenship model, it would be unacceptable to reduce dogs (and other animals) to their "function" in the therapeutic context, as is often currently the case. One of the entitlements of citizenship is having a personal identity outside any specific activity or form of labor one engages in. Donaldson and Kymlicka's relational theory of justice presupposes that animals "have inviolable rights in virtue of their sentience or selfhood, the fact that they have a subjective experience of the world" (2011, 31). This selfhood and subjective experience of the world extends far beyond the work they engage in. It is cultivated and defined by a wide variety of experiences, activities, and relationships. If it were limited to specific tasks the animal was expected to accomplish, the animal would not have an opportunity to blossom, and would very likely wilt. It is therefore paramount that we choose the terms we use to refer to them carefully. Animals should not be referred to as "tools" or "adjunct tools," as they typically are, because these terms explicitly objectify them as instruments for human use. Many practitioners refer to them as "therapy animals." While this is an improvement, it nevertheless reifies animals as therapy providers, rather than as subjects in their own right. Better terms, which would be more consistent with citizenship theory and the relational justice it advocates, would be "co-therapists," "participants," or perhaps "co-workers."

A change in terminology is also required with respect to the humans involved. At present, therapists and AAI practitioners and volunteers are typically referred to as animal "handlers." But this term only perpetuates the view that animals are objects to be handled, manipulated, and controlled, not unlike machinery. If animals and humans are together seen as co-therapists and so on, the collaborative nature of their work is highlighted, and the equal, if different, contribution they both make is underscored. This is not a semantic exercise, but an important conceptual intervention.

It is also important never to characterize human AAI practitioners as "using" animals, as is so often the case. Non-exploitative relationships between species can never revolve around use, benefit, and welfare considerations, or what Jean Harvey (2008) calls the "utilization with welfare safeguards" model currently in vogue in AAI (161). Even if an argument for non-exploitative use among humans could be made, I think the risks are too high to make the same argument for animals, given how inextricably the use and abuse of animals have been historically intertwined. To properly underscore and support animals' agency, within and beyond the context of AAI, it is best to avoid the language of use altogether. In the words of Fredrickson-MacNamara and Butler, "To ensure quality, respectful programs it is critical that animals are never 'used' in animal-assisted interactions, but treated as partners in a mutually respectful relationship" (2010, 126).

Non-Coercive Training and Socialization

Under the citizenship model, animal co-therapists would never be subjected to coercive or abusive training practices such as long-term restraint and confinement (Donaldson and Kymlicka 2011, 141). By the same token, animals should not be rewarded solely for successfully carrying out a given AAI task, but should be praised for their loveliness in their daily lives (141). Because coercive training and selective positive reinforcement deliberately disable agency and force animals into submission, it cannot be abided in a citizenship model. To avoid undermining dogs' agency, it is necessary to abandon a number of existing AAIs, such as behavioral therapy programs that involve teaching inmates of detention centers to teach "obedience commands to therapy animals" (Fine et al. 2010, 199), and inmates of prisons to train "service dogs," such as the Puppies Behind Bars (PBB) program.

In these programs, there are two concerns: the subjection of the puppies/dogs to coercive and usually intensive training regimes, and the reproduction of unjust relations of power of which the inmates are themselves victims. The PBB website tells us that it is devoted to "training inmates to raise service dogs for wounded war veterans," including sufferers of post-traumatic stress disorder (PTSD) and traumatic brain injury (TBI), and to training explosive-detection canines for law enforcement (Puppies Behind Bars 2016). It explains further that "Labrador retriever puppies are raised and trained in prison from the age of eight weeks until they are ready to be placed with a veteran," usually at about 20–28 months old (2014). By the time they are placed with a veteran, they will have learned "eighty-five commands" required by the industry. While the training regime provides inmates with a focused activity and an opportunity to spend time with animals, the puppies undoubtedly undergo tremendous stress in the process of "learning" eighty-five commands in a short period of time. The training regime is undoubtedly grueling and exhausting and frustrates many of the puppies' basic needs (e.g., for spontaneous, unstructured play, runs and walks outdoors, and comfortable "down time" on someone's lap or in their arms).

Furthermore, the program teaches inmates that their empowerment depends on reproducing and reenacting domination, and subjecting other vulnerable beings to the same punitive and authoritarian measures to which they are subjected in the penal institution.

A much healthier and more constructive approach to personal empowerment for people who are already deeply entangled in abusive power relations can come from learning to empathize and engage cooperatively with dogs, listen to them, and work with them to find mutually beneficial solutions to problems. Learning to communicate with dogs on their own terms, while at the same time teaching them how to perform certain tasks and respond to certain instructions using positive reinforcement techniques such as offering treats and other rewards for successful performance of a task, would enrich the social skills of both parties. Prison training programs should also provide plenty of unstructured interactive time between the dogs and their human counterparts. They should be provided with ample space in which to run, play, and cuddle together at will.

That said, some forms of dog training are not necessarily problematic from a citizenship perspective, depending on the dog's personality and the training techniques employed. Some animals "thrive on learning, testing, and developing their abilities, accomplishing tasks, and engaging in cooperative goal-oriented activity" (Donaldson and Kymlicka 2011, 141). If a dog can learn, for example, to detect the onset of panic attacks in a veteran suffering from PTSD by, for example, spending a few sessions being gently attuned to changes in the veteran's manner, posture, facial expression, tone of voice, and so forth, there is no risk of exploitation, and the AAI practice should go ahead as planned. A dog would be particularly suitable to providing the gentle and protective affection a severely traumatized human being might need to heal, while the human's need could translate into profound love for and devotion to their companion canine.

Importantly, citizenship would ensure that the onus is not entirely on the animal to adjust to human expectations, but that the responsibility is distributed equally between humans and animals. In any political community, "basic socialization" is also "presupposed" (Donaldson and Kymlicka 2011, 123). In general, basic socialization entails helping new members of a community to "channel" their "readiness" to "learn," "explore," "figure out the rules," and "find their place" (123). "Socialization involves the basic and general skills/knowledge that individuals need to learn (insofar as possible) in order to be accepted into social community—like establishing control over bodily processes and impulses, learning basic communication, rules of social interaction, and respect for others" (123). Socialization, Donaldson and Kymlicka point out, is distinct from (non-coercive) training. In any political community, all citizens must know how to engage with each other in socially appropriate ways, ways that enable each other's agency and wellbeing and facilitate constructive interactions, while reducing interpersonal conflict. The point is not to flatten the possibility for lively public discourse, debate, or activity, not to mention critical thinking, dissent, protest, and socio-political transformation. The point is, rather, to ensure that all members of the community feel comfortable and safe enough to express themselves and be themselves without risking physical or emotional harm and without encroaching upon or violating the liberty of others.

Of course, not everyone agrees on what "appropriate socialization" consists of (Donaldson and Kymlicka 2011, 124). In many cases, different rules apply to humans and animals. One obvious difference concerns permissions and restrictions regarding physical contact. In general, cultural differences notwithstanding, humans tend to allow and enjoy immediate physical intimacy with dogs. The latter might pounce on our laps or lick our faces at the first meeting, and we might respond with tender caresses and kisses. A similar degree of physical contact might be appropriate with some children (e.g., the child of a close friend, where trust is already established), but is generally not appropriate between adults meeting for the first time in all formal and most informal settings (at least in North America). On the other hand, while physical contact is usually mutually reinforcing between humans and dogs, dogs can sometimes frighten people by jumping up on them, so it is important to gently train them not to do so. Yelling at and hitting dogs is not an appropriate way to assert limits, but coaxing them out of the behavior using treats or other measures is. The point is that under the aegis of citizenship, the different needs of the different members of society are balanced and an environment of mutual respect prevails.

In the context of AAI, mutual socialization is particularly important. Dogs visiting patients in an intensive care unit, for example, must be socialized to know how to remain quiet, not bark, not run around wildly, and not jump on the patients. But the humans involved must also know how to interact with dogs in a way that respects their boundaries and needs as well. They must know how to touch a dog appropriately and how to elicit certain responses from the dog without resorting to violence or aggression. As Fredrickson-MacNamara and Butler (2010, 117) point out, all too often therapists, clients, and volunteers do not know how to interrelate with animals appropriately. Dogs should not have to pay the price for humans' ignorance. The onus should be on humans involved in AAI to spend the time to learn about dogs by receiving direct instruction and training from specialists in animal behavior, reading books, and watching educational films as a supplement. This will ensure that the humans involved in AAI understand and comply with dogs' "rules of the game," rather than expecting them to understand and comply with ours.

Duties of Protection and Medical Care

As citizens, domesticated animals are also owed "duties of protection." This means that humans must protect them from "harm from human beings, harm from other animals, and more generally harm from accidents or natural disasters" (Donaldson and Kymlicka 2011, 132). Crucially, in a citizenship framework, these duties are not merely ethical ones, but political ones with legal weight. Harms to animals should be deemed criminal acts, while positive duties should be upheld (132). In the context of AAI, these duties of protection from harm must be met in several ways. Animal participants of AAI should be protected by labor laws that stipulate that they must be provided with opportunities for rest, food, water, and play (140). Jason Hribal puts it especially delicately: "[T]he next time you cross paths with a service dog, your perspective should be turned upside-down. Don't glance from above: 'Wow, look at that beautiful, well-trained dog!' But instead, question [from] below: 'Hey! does that dog ever get a fuckin' day off?'" (2006). We should not only ask this question of service dogs, but of all dogs (or other animals) providing AAI services.

All animal co-therapists should also be protected from harm from both clients and therapists, who are both often ill-equipped to attend to the animal's needs. Alison Hatch (2007) recounts one story of a client in a residential center hitting a shelter dog in the face. The volunteer recounts, "I had a dog in my arms, and I brought it closer to this one person who I thought seemed to want to see the dog, and that person just swatted the dog in the nose!" (43). In this case, there appears to have been malicious intent on the part of the client who invited the dog into her/his personal space only to cause harm to the dog. Any client who behaved in this way would have to be removed from the program and/or provided with empathy training or other forms of guidance on how to engage with animals respectfully. As noted above, many volunteers and practitioners are ill-equipped to work with animals and must also be provided with proper education and socialization to prevent them from mistreating animals. Finally, citizenship also entitles animals to medical care and other forms of institutional, social, and financial support accorded (at least in theory) to human citizens (142).

We can imagine how these citizenship rights could be upheld in the context of a program like PAWS (Pets Are Wonderful Support) (2016) in San Francisco, which is devoted to providing this kind of support for a variety of vulnerable human beings, including "people with disabling HIV/AIDS, other disabling illnesses, and seniors 60 and older." PAWS makes it possible for vulnerable people to share their lives with companion animals without having to compromise the animals' wellbeing as a result of financial difficulties, mobility and health issues, and so on. The services PAWS provides include offering a pet food bank, providing and funding veterinary care, and providing in-home care such as cat care, dog walking, transportation, emergency foster care (for example, if someone passes away or feels they can no longer live with an animal), and grooming (PAWS 2016). Under a citizenship model, though, it would be important that organizations like PAWS monitor more than just the basic physical health of the animals. They would have to make sure that the animals' subjective good was being promoted and that their agency was being enabled. If, for example, a dog or cat was well fed and healthy, but otherwise depressed, a care worker would have to figure out why this was occurring and take measures to alleviate it. If the dog or cat was expressing a desire to live elsewhere, have more space, have more toys, and so forth, the care worker would have to meet these demands.

Rights to Residency and Mobility

Animal citizens are guaranteed rights to permanent and stable residency in a safe and comfortable environment and rights to "mobility and sharing of public spaces" (Donaldson and Kymlicka 2011, 123). This means that in no cases should an animal of any species be confined in a kennel, crate, or cage outside of short, temporary periods—during transport, for example. Residency and mobility rights are based on "a very strong presumption against any form of restraint or confinement, except in cases where individuals pose a demonstrable threat to themselves or the basic liberties of others" (129). At present, service dogs are typically confined in kennels for the first eight weeks of their lives, ostensibly to "protect" them from exposure to environmental dangers and diseases (Serpell et al. 2010). This is cruel and unjust treatment and is incompatible with the citizenship model.

The restriction on confinement also translates into "a positive right to sufficient mobility providing access to an adequate range of options needed for a flourishing life" (129). Not only should animals not be confined, but they should also be given ample opportunity to move around freely in ways that are appropriate to them. For example, whether involved in AAI or not, all dogs should be able to go on long off-leash runs and walks on a regular basis. There should be sufficient parks and off-leash zones within urban centers to facilitate access, particularly for people who do not have vehicles. Overall, as members of the social and political community, animals engaged in AAI should not be hidden from the community. They have a right equal to that of human citizens to visibility, to the sharing of public space, and to determining how the public space is designed. At present, most public spaces are designed with human and commercial interests in mind. Cars on city streets and highways plow through animal habitat, causing scores of violent deaths on a daily basis. For dogs, cats, and other domesticated animal citizens, not to mention liminal and wild animals, living in proximity to humans carries enormous risks. Constitutive of enabling animals' agency and promoting their subjective good is providing safe public spaces for animals to "do their thing" without risk of injury and death.

Finally, under the citizenship model, animals involved in AAI must be guaranteed residency and mobility rights, as well as duties of protection, medical care, and so on, after they are no longer willing or able to participate. Humans owe to them a lifelong commitment to providing a safe, comfortable, and peaceful environment for them to live and grow as individuals before, during, and after their participation in AAI. This means animals cannot be abandoned, neglected, or killed when their work tenure is up and that their special needs must be attended to when they reach old age or develop illnesses. Like humans, they must be guaranteed a secure place in the community and the institutional, financial, medical, and social support a flourishing life at any stage requires. While a dog may have shown an interest in engaging in AAI at one stage in her life, for example, she may lose interest at another stage and should not only be able to discontinue her work in AAI but also be provided full canine retirement benefits.

Conclusion

Animal Assisted Intervention is a rapidly expanding practice, and for good reasons. In its best form it can be mutually reinforcing for both the humans and nonhumans, most notably dogs, involved. It can encourage meaningful, reciprocal, and long-lasting relationships between human clients and canine co-therapists. It can help humans heal from trauma, and offer dogs an opportunity to flourish in ways that build upon the natural inclinations many of them have to engage with humans as their companions, guides, helpers, playmates, and protectors. But AAI also carries with it grave risks to dogs' (and other animals') wellbeing and flourishing. Among other things, it can involve abuse, neglect, violence, and the frustration of natural behaviors. It also risks reinforcing the oppressive view that other animals are instruments for human use to be consumed and disposed of at will. Over the years, there have been well-intentioned efforts at reform and standardization of AAI. But so far, it seems that the animals involved are not universally provided with the robust and comprehensive protections and entitlements they deserve. Although this might not be the only approach, one possible way to ensure that AAI develops into a practice that enables the flourishing of all the parties involved is to embed it in a wider protective political framework such as citizenship. Whether or not we accept Donaldson and Kymlicka's theory of citizenship, we can certainly see the advantages of according animals' political status within an interspecies community. With regard to AAI in particular, our foray into Donaldson and Kymlicka's "zoopolis" demonstrates that fundamental changes in animals' status, entitlements, and rights are required if they are to thrive and avoid being harmed as participants in this practice.

References

American Veterinary Medical Association. 2016. "Animal-Assisted Interventions: Guidelines." https://www.avma.org/KB/Policies/Pages/Animal-Assisted-Interventions-Guidelines.aspx.

Baun, Mara, and Rebecca Johnson. 2010. "Human/Animal Interaction and Successful Aging." In *Handbook on Animal-Assisted Therapy: Theoretical Foundations and Guidelines for Practice*, 3rd ed., edited by Aubrey H. Fine, 283–99. Boston: Academic Press.

Bekoff, Marc. 2002. *Minding Animals: Awareness, Emotions, and Heart.* New York: Oxford University Press.

Canadian Agency for Drugs and Technologies in Health. 2014. "Therapy Dogs and Horses for Mental Health: A Review of the Clinical Effectiveness." http://www.cadth.ca/media/pdf/htis/aug2012/RC0381%20Therapy%20Animals%20final.pdf.

Delta Society. 1996. *Animal-Assisted Therapy: Standards of Practice.* Bellevue, WA: Delta Society.

DeMello, Margo. 2012. *Animals and Society: An Introduction to Human-Animal Studies.* New York: Columbia University Press.

Donaldson, Sue, and Will Kymlicka. 2011. *Zoopolis: A Political Theory of Animal Rights.* Oxford: Oxford University Press.

Evans, Nikki, and Claire Gray. 2012. "The Practice and Ethics of Animal-Assisted Therapy with Children and Young People: Is It Enough That We Don't Eat Our Co-Workers?" *British Journal of Social Work* 42: 600–617.

Fine, Aubrey H. 2010. "Incorporating Animal-Assisted Therapy into Psychotherapy: Guidelines and Suggestions for Therapists." In *Handbook on Animal-Assisted Therapy: Theoretical Foundations and Guidelines for Practice*, 3rd ed., edited by Aubrey H. Fine, 169–91. Boston: Academic Press.

Fine, Aubrey H., Dana O'Callaghan, Cynthia Chandler, Karen Schaffer, Teri Pichot, and Julia Gimeno. 2010. "Application of Animal-Assisted Interventions in Counseling Settings: An Overview of Alternatives." In *Handbook on Animal-Assisted Therapy: Theoretical Foundations and Guidelines for Practice*, 3rd ed., edited by Aubrey H. Fine, 193–222. Boston: Academic Press.

Fredrickson-MacNamara, Maureen, and Kris Butler. 2010. "Animal Selection Procedures in Animal-Assisted Interaction Programs." In *Handbook on*

Animal-Assisted Therapy: Theoretical Foundations and Guidelines for Practice, 3rd ed., edited by Aubrey H. Fine, 111–34. Boston: Academic Press.

Grandin, Temple, Aubrey H. Fine, and Christine M. Bowers. 2010. "The Use of Therapy Animals with Individuals with Autism Spectrum Disorders." In *Handbook on Animal-Assisted Therapy: Theoretical Foundations and Guidelines for Practice*, 3rd ed., edited by Aubrey H. Fine, 247–64. Boston: Academic Press.

Harvey, Jean. 2008. "Companion and Assistance Animals: Benefits, Welfare Safeguards, and Relationships." *International Journal of Applied Philosophy* 22 (2): 161–76.

Hatch, Alison. 2007. "The View from All Fours: A Look at an Animal-Assisted Activity Program from the Animals' Perspective." *Anthrozoös* 2 (1): 37–50.

Hribal, Jason. 2006. "Jesse, a Working Dog." *Counterpunch*, November 11. http://www.counterpunch.org/2006/11/11/jesse-a-working-dog/.

Johnson, Rebecca A. 2011. "Animal-Assisted Intervention in Health Care Contexts." In *How Animals Affect Us: Examining the Influences of Human–Animal Interaction on Child Development and Human Health*, edited by Peggy McCardle, Sandra McCune, James A. Griffin, and Valerie Maholmes, 183–92. Washington: American Psychological Association.

Morrison, Michele L. 2007. "Health Benefits of Animal-Assisted Interventions." *Complementary Health Practice Review* 12 (1): 51–62. doi: 10.1177/1533210107302397.

PAWS. 2016. http://www.shanti.org/pages/paws_about_us.html.

Puppies Behind Bars. 2016. "About Us." http://www.puppiesbehindbars.com/mission.

Serpell, J. A., R. Coppinger, A. H. Fine, and J. M. Peralta. 2010. "Welfare Considerations in Therapy Animals." In *Handbook on Animal-Assisted Therapy: Theoretical Foundations and Guidelines for Practice*, 3rd ed., edited by Aubrey H. Fine, 481–501. Boston: Academic Press.

Therapy Dogs United. 2014. "Home." http://www.therapydogsunited.org.

Zamir, Tzachi. 2006. "The Moral Basis of Animal-Assisted Therapy." *Society and Animals* 14 (2): 179–98.

16 "SEX WITHOUT ALL THE POLITICS"?

SEXUAL ETHICS AND HUMAN-CANINE RELATIONS

Chloë Taylor

In "Rethinking Bestiality: Towards a Concept of Interspecies Sexual Assault" (1997), Piers Beirne describes watching a work of pornography titled *Barnyard Love*, which depicts humans having sexual relations with a variety of species of animals. As Beirne observes, the ways that the different species of animals responded to sexual interactions with humans varied drastically. At one extreme, small animals such as eels and hens clearly suffered greatly, and in at least one case died, due to the sexual uses to which humans put their bodies. In the middle of the spectrum, large quadrupeds such as cows and horses appeared to Beirne to be bored by their sexual interactions with humans, continuing to eat, defecate, and urinate even while humans manipulated their genitals. Beirne is cautious in assuming that he can interpret these animals' body language, however, and suggests that the apparent indifference of these animals "might actually have been calculated detachment on their part, a coping strategy for numbing the pain inflicted on them by yet another of the myriad ways in which their lives are routinely invaded, inspected, and disposed of by humans" (1997, 318). At the other extreme, however, were dogs, who were "engaged in sexual activities with women" in the film and "seemed energetically to enjoy such human attention" (318). Beirne writes, "To me, at least, it did not seem possible that such canine enthusiasm could be trained by off-camera training designed to suppress more genuine emotions of grief and pain" (318).

Beirne's account indicates that anyone considering the welfare of animals will recognize the immorality of sexual relations between humans and small animals such as eels and hens. Dogs, however, appear to be the "hard case" from an ethical perspective. As Peter Singer's infamous review, "Heavy Petting" (2001), makes clear, a utilitarian approach will not allow us to categorically condemn sexual relations between humans and dogs. Singer writes,

[S]ex with animals does not always involve cruelty. Who has not been at a social occasion disrupted by the household dog gripping the legs of a visitor and vigorously rubbing its [sic] penis against them? The host usually discourages such activities, but in private not everyone objects to being used by her or his dog in this way, and occasionally mutually satisfying activities may develop. (2001, n.p.).

Contra Beirne's and Singer's assumption, at least one account of human-canine sex suggests that dogs who engage in sex with humans must be rigorously trained to do so. A 2013 interview with a sex-trafficked woman who trains puppies to have sex with women includes the following account:

There are special dog farms in many countries that train dogs to [have sex with humans]. I personally work as a trainer in such farms in Germany, Belgium, and Sweden. They employ me to help the dogs get used to the human female. After about half a year of concentrated effort, the dogs fuck like devils. . . . I also have two dogs living in my cottage and they have never fucked with other dogs, only with humans. Often the clients will bring dogs of their own, these are of course trained dogs, too. (Zalupin 2013)

Although the woman interviewed observes that she "loves" the sex with dogs, it is unclear how the dogs feel. The fact that it takes "a year of concentrated effort" to get the dogs to "fuck like devils" suggests that bestiality does not come naturally to them. Nevertheless, the dogs can be trained to engage in bestial acts with a vigor that even a critical viewer such as Beirne reads as enthusiasm, while chickens, eels, and cats cannot.

It is perhaps because of this performance of enthusiasm that dogs are today the most common species choice of zoophiles. Moreover, the characteristics that zoophiles claim make them prefer nonhuman animals to humans—playfulness, affectionateness, non-judgmentalness, loyalty, and unconditional love—are particularly characteristic of dogs. Sexual relations with the more aloof cat are relatively rare; this is likely because zoophiles (who distinguish themselves from "bestialists," or people who have sadistic sex with animals) want at least the appearance of consent and enthusiasm from the animals with whom they have sex. Zoophiles consider themselves animal lovers, and want to believe they are in relations of reciprocal love. Dogs accommodate these desires of zoophiles more than any other species. Within a broader consideration of the ethics of human-animal sexual relations, human-canine sexual relations are thus worth dwelling on, both because these are the cases in which the immorality of the relations is least obvious, and because they are one of the most common forms that bestiality takes today.

I will argue in this chapter that the medicalized and identity-based categories of "zoophile" or "zoosexual" mask the particularities and politics of which humans are having sex with which animals. It is significant that the people having sex with animals are overwhelmingly white and male, that the animals they are having sex with are domesticated, and that the most popular sexual partners are canines. Any adequate account of the phenomenon of zoophilia, I argue, must interrogate the power relationships entailed in domestication, and in human-canine relationships in particular, as well as the kinds of privilege involved in white masculinity that result in the gendering and racialization of zoophilia. Contra Singer and the discourses of zoophiles, I contend that the apparent performance of pleasure and thus consent on the part of dogs is insufficient for understanding whether sex between humans and dogs is exploitative, and masks structures of privilege and domination. What is necessary is to analyze the structure of domestication as a power relation that produces the (apparent) sexual consent of (some) domesticated animals, as well as the kinds of privilege that enable (some) humans to experience such consent as reciprocal love. This privilege is first and foremost human privilege within relations of domestication, but it also intersects to a considerable degree with male privilege and white privilege.

Ecofeminist scholars have criticized masculinist approaches to animal ethics, such as Singer's utilitarianism and Tom Regan's theory of animal rights, in a number of ways that apply to Singer's analysis of bestiality. Ecofeminists have argued that these approaches are extensionist, with the rationalist, white, male, able-bodied and -minded human remaining at the center (the obvious bearer of rights and moral consideration), even as the circle of moral consideration expands outward to include other beings in virtue of their bearing similarities to the man at the center (Cuomo 1998). Ecofeminists have also argued that the clear desire of male animal ethicists such as Singer to distance themselves from charges of emotion and sentiment indicates that they remain embedded in a masculinist rationalism that has historically justified the domination of animals, as well as the domination of women and people of color, and so is unlikely to be the means to animals' salvation (Donovan 1990). Moreover, while Singer and Regan compare speciesism to racism and sexism, or see these as analogous forms of discrimination, they do not see these oppressions as interlocking. In contrast, ecofeminists have argued that the logics that result in the domination of women, the cognitively and physically disabled, people of color, and animals are not analogous but interconnected. Building on these insights, in this chapter I argue that the exploitation of animals by zoophiles is part and parcel of a male sex right that has resulted in the exploitation of women and, as feminists have argued, has done so along axes of ability, race, and class. In this chapter, I will thus turn an intersectionalist feminist lens on the phenomenon of zoophilia, to show why a utilitarian analysis of the phenomenon is inadequate.

Why White Men?

Historical studies of court records indicate that, in both the "old" and "new" worlds, bestiality was an overwhelmingly male crime and was, moreover, policed by women (Liliequist 1991; Murrin 1998). Bestiality was frequently associated with adolescence and sexual deprivation, and was particularly prevalent in agricultural contexts. Although in some cases bestiality became a "habit" that men continued into married life, it was associated with "a boy's culture" (Liliequist 1991, 414) and with unmarried men in an era that condemned extramarital sex. Boys and men were understood to turn to nonhuman animals because of sexual deprivation rather than as an expression of an orientation. Zoosex was problematic because it undermined species boundaries, and not because it violated the nonhuman animals. Indeed, there seems to have been no inclination to see nonhuman animals as victims in these cases, and these animals were executed and considered defiled and thus inedible.

Today, in contrast, bestiality ranges from online "zoo" communities and bestiality porn to Furry Fandom, and has been medicalized as a paraphilia. As has occurred with other psychiatrized "sexualities," "zoophilia" has been taken up by the individuals so labeled as a sexual identity or orientation, and an unsuccessful liberation movement has been launched. Despite the efforts of zoophiles to gain acceptance through comparisons of their cause to the gay liberation movement, the public is more likely to compare "zoos" to pedophiles than to homosexuals, and zoosex is widely viewed as a form of cruelty to animals (Cassidy 2009).

Despite the differences between the historical and contemporary phenomena of bestiality, sex between humans and nonhuman animals remains a typically male activity. Sex therapist Hani Miletski's (2001) study draws on interviews with 82 men and 11 women who have sexual relations with nonhuman animals, and all the cases that she discusses in a sustained manner involve men and canines. Miletski also cites Hunt's study (1974), for which "reported incidence of bestiality was 4.9% for men and 1.9% for women" (Miletski 2001, 85). Psychologist Andrea Beetz draws on a sample of 113 men and 3 women in her study (2005). Colin Williams and Martin Weinberg's study (2003, 525) involved 114 zoophile men and no women. At the meeting of zoophiles that Williams and Weinberg attended, "The 28 attendees were mainly young men but did include a woman, the zoophile wife of a male zoophile" (525). Christopher Earls and Martin Lalumière write that "zoophilia seems to be an overwhelmingly male phenomenon (there are few cases of female zoophiles and these are often partners of male zoophiles)" (2009, 608). Without considering any social or political explanations for why more men than women might identify as zoophile, they conclude that "the male sexual preference system is more vulnerable than the female preference system with respect to developmental perturbations" (608).

Significantly, Williams and Weinberg also note that all 114 men in their study were white (2003, 525). As they observe, the zoophiles in Miletski's study were also "preponderantly White" (532). Earls and Lalumière's case study also involves a white male (2009, 606). None of these authors attempts to explain the racialization of the zoophile phenomenon. Such demographics lead Alok Vaid-Menon to ask, "Why is the Zoo full of White people?" (2013, 10). Vaid-Menon observes that in the documentary *Zoo*, one member of a zoophile community states, "Most of the people who were part of our group were white, but we did have a few who were black, there was a Hispanic who came once" (10). Vaid-Menon notes that, in this way, "[t]he white zoophile implicitly acknowledges the (problematic) racial makeup of the community and uses a distinctly neoliberal logic of tokenization to deflect any racial critique" (10). Vaid-Menon contends that "experiencing this closer affinity to non-human animals [that zoophiles express] is the extension of a white subjectivity in our colonial modernity—that the ability to choose to identify with a non-human animal, rather than be interpellated as one, reflects white privilege" (11). In other words, given the dehumanizing strategies of white colonists and slave-owners, it is more fraught for a person of color to identify as a zoophile than it is for a white person.

Further connecting zoophilia with colonial subjectivity, Vaid-Menon cites zoophiles who praise zoosex because when taking a nonhuman lover, you need not "discuss the difference between Monet and Picasso, it just doesn't exist for their world. It's a simpler and more plain world and in those moments you can get disconnected. It's a very intense, wonderful kind of feeling" (2013, 14). Such a description of zoosex as an "escape from the shackles of Western modernity has a history that is rooted in the sexual white body," Vaid-Menon observes, and resonates with the language of "Queer-desiring European men, such as Edward Carpenter and E. M. Forester, [who] journeyed to the East in search of the liberatory 'Other,' 'freed from Western sexual taboos'" (14). As Vaid-Menon writes, "Oriental men served as 'traditional, primitive, sexually uninhibited repositories of the escapist sexual fantasies' of these white men" (14), much as nonhuman animals serve for zoophiles today.

Vaid-Menon argues that zoophilia entails the domination of nonhuman animals in addition to being premised on human superiority, and is thus caught up with the human-animal binary as well as other interlocking oppressions, such as racism and colonization. Expanding on the concept of "homonationalism" developed by queer theorists to describe the ways in which homosexuality has been incorporated into the ethics of neoliberal democratic citizenship, Vaid-Menon furthermore describes the discourse of zoophiles as "zoonationalism": white male zoophiles, like white gay men, demand recognition as having the same rights and privileges as straight white men. Rather than situating themselves in allegiance with the deviant or queer, zoophiles want to be recognized as normal, and to maintain all the privileges of their first-world male whiteness as well as an anthropocentric privilege to use nonhuman animals as they will.

Although Vaid-Menon is astute in questioning why the "zoo" is full of white people, and in showing the interconnections between anthropocentrism and colonial, racist, and homonationalist attitudes, like the sociological and clinical authors discussed above, he does not ask the equally pressing question: Why is the zoo full of *men*? I argue that zoophilia is a male phenomenon because of what feminist political theorist Carole Pateman calls male "sex-right" (1988, 1). Sheila Jeffreys describes this perceived right as "the privileged expectation in male dominant societies that men should have sexual access to the bodies of women as of right" (2008, 328). Pateman's examples of male sex-right include compulsory heterosexuality, marriage, and prostitution. Interestingly, zoophiles often "marry" their animals, and the discourses of zoophiles resonate not only with the discourses of colonial men but also with the discourses of clients of sex workers. While I do not wish to compare the companion animals of zoophiles to sex workers (because, contra Pateman, I do not believe that sex workers are necessarily victims in the way that nonhuman animals owned by zoophiles are), I do want to compare zoophiles to the *clients* of sex workers.

Sex work clients, like zoophiles, are a group that is also vastly overrepresented by men. Male clients of sex workers, despite paying for sex, tend to believe that the sex workers they hire have a special fondness for them, are amazed by the sex, and would like to date them (Sanders 2008). Clients nearly uniformly believe that they are special to the sex worker and not like her other clients. At the same time, clients stress that what they like about sex with sex workers is the lack of politics (feminism), judgmentalness, and responsibility for an interpersonal relationship that goes beyond the sexual-monetary transaction. Similarly, one zoophile in Williams and Weinberg's study notes that nonhuman animals "are just friendly and non-judgmental" (2003, 528). Another states that "[l]ove with an animal is how love should be—a lot less complicated with no strings attached" (531). Another study participant praises zoosex because "[a]nimals do not judge you[:] they just love and enjoy the pleasures of sex without all the politics" (527). In Earls and Lalumière's case study, the zoophile notes of his "mare-wives" that "I can . . . be with them at any time I want. Life's good" (2009, 606). Although the zoophiles in Williams and Weinberg's study are having sex with domesticated animals whom they have purchased and who have nowhere else to go—and are thus in relationships of extreme power imbalance—and although they refer to their sexual partners as "its," they insist that the sex is consensual (Williams and Weinberg, 2003, 526). Indeed, the majority of the zoophiles in Williams and Weinberg's study state that their nonhuman animal sexual partners are "in love" with them (2003, 529) and praise their love as "unconditional" (527).

As in accounts of sex work on the part of clients, the advantage of zoosex that is repeatedly noted by zoophiles is that by having sex with their domesticated animals, they can have precisely what they want when they want it with no complications and without having to concern themselves with the other individuals' judgments. Moreover, zoosex allows zoophiles, like clients, to project their fantasies of reciprocated desire onto their sexual partners without the inconvenience of a rebuttal. I would thus expand on Pateman's argument by saying that when women are *not* providing the kind of sexual services that some men think they require—e.g., when clients complain that prostitutes are "cold," while other women are "judgmental" and "political" (feminist)—these same men feel entitled to use another species of animal to satisfy their sexual and emotional desires. Conveniently, a dog will neither be "cold" like a prostitute nor "judgmental" like a non-sex-worker human, nor will a dog introduce politics into the relationship. On the contrary, one's companion canine is the paradigm of warmth, enthusiasm, and uncritical acceptance.

The discourses of zoophiles are also similar to those of men who buy "real dolls" (life-sized sex dolls) and fantasize about "sexbots," as represented in Allison de Fren's documentary, *The Mechanical Bride* (2012). Once again, the vast majority of consumers of "real dolls" are men. Like zoophiles, doll-lovers claim to have an emotional relationship with their dolls. Resonating with the zoophile who praises sex with animals because you need not compare Monet to Picasso with them, one appeal of "real dolls" put forward in this documentary is that you need not take them to *The English Patient*; dolls, like dogs, will not judge your intelligence or level of culture. As a man who manufactures "real dolls" explains,

Men I think love . . . something they can control. . . . And finally a trigger word is *"you own her."* Why is that? A couple theories I have. One, maybe men have been beaten down and berated so much by this feminism stuff, that we used to be able to drag a woman by the hair, this is instinct for us [points to the head], to drag the woman by the hair into your cave and to have your way with her, this is instinct, now we have to be so politically correct [grimace]. . . . I agree with that, don't get me wrong, that's the proper way, but there is an instinct there that you *own, own, own* this woman.

While sex workers are at most rented, sex dolls, like companion animals, may be purchased. Another man interviewed describes the appeal of a "sexbot" in the following way: "You can tell her to do anything and she'll do it." While "real dolls" are unaffordable for most consumers,[1] and sexbots remain a fantasy of the future, men can easily purchase a dog to have a compliant, enthusiastic, and non-judgmental sexual partner whom they quite literally *"own, own, own."*

Why Dogs?

The species most often involved in bestiality trials in historical records are agricultural animals, although cases involving dogs are also common. In a post-agricultural age, it appears that sex with dogs has become the most common form of bestiality. Beirne explains,

> [I]n most Western societies—where pet ownership has dramatically increased and where, with the rise of "factory farming," there has been a steady decline in the percentage of the human population living in agricultural areas or residing with farm animals inside their houses—it cannot be certain that it is farm animals who are nowadays the most common objects of interspecies sexual assault by humans. (1997, 330)

Beirne's point should be qualified. Setting aside the many contemporary cases in which farm workers have been recorded raping animals (cases that the agriculture industry itself characterizes as abuse), the agricultural industry's term for devices used to inseminate female animals is "rape rack" (Gillespie 2014, 1331). This indicates an acceptance on the part of farmers that what is happening in agribusiness is a routine sexual assault of female animals. Both male and female agricultural animals are involuntarily sterilized, and male animals are forced by humans to ejaculate through manual and electrical stimulation. Sexual assault of both female and male animals thus continues to be a standard practice in animal agriculture, and animal agriculture could not function without it. Given the scale of animal agriculture today, it is thus plausible that agricultural animals remain the most common victims of sexual assault by humans.

Farmers do not identify as zoophiles, however, and are not psychiatrized as having a paraphilia; among people who identify as "zoos," and who are subjected to psychiatrization on these grounds, dogs are the most common sexual object choice. Miletski's study of 82 men and 11 women "revealed that the most popular animal sex partner for men (74 = 90%) and women (11 = 100%) was a male canine. Second most popular for men (59 = 72%) and women (8 = 73%) was a female canine" (2001, 86). Sociologists Williams and Weinberg have also undertaken a study of zoophiles, and observe the following:

> A variety of species were involved [in the first sexual encounters of zoophiles with other animals], mainly equines (29%) . . . or dogs (63%), but also reported were cats (2 cases), cattle (2 cases), a goat (1 case), a sheep (1 case), a chicken (1 case), and a dolphin (1 case). Among those who reported currently having sex with an animal, 51% had a dog as a partner and 37% had an equine (while the remaining animals included goats, pigs, cats, and sheep). . . . Whether currently having sex with a dog or an equine, almost all said they had been in love with an animal partner and perceived an animal partner to have been in love with them. (2003, 529)

The popularity of dogs among zoophiles is partly a matter of cost and convenience (equines being relatively expensive and difficult to house), but the preference clearly goes beyond this, since cats are also cheap and easy to house, but are not popular among zoophiles. I suggest that the popularity of dogs among zoophiles is due to their unmatched malleability to human ends.

Studies of pet culture indicate that dogs, more than any other companion animal, serve a wide range of roles for humans, including those of child, grandchild, spouse, or parent (Shell 1986). To this list, Heidi Nast adds that dogs are highly amenable to being our best friends and lovers. As she writes, "[P]ets (especially dogs) today supersede children as ideal love objects; they are more easily mobilized, require less investment, and to some degree can be shaped into whatever you want them to be—a best friend, a lover, an occasional companion" (2006, 302). Dogs, more than any other companion species, provide a remarkable "anthropomorphic malleability" (302). Nast documents the ways that this malleability has resulted in dogs' becoming the objects of an extraordinary pet culture, including canine camping gear, pet Olympics, Dog Scouts of America, canine massage, pet cloning, dog yoga (doga), formal dancing with dogs, dozens of dog-love magazines, the Bowlingual radiomicrophone dog collar that translates a dog's bark into human language, a plethora of books on dogs ranging from biographies to training guides, and genetic, psychological, and linguistic studies of dogs, including the multi-million-dollar Dog Genome Project (funded by private breed clubs) and dog psychology centers such as Cesar Millan's Dog Psychology Center in Los Angeles and the Canine Behaviour Centre in Northern England. As Nast makes clear, there is no comparable cat culture, most likely because cats simply would not put up with such activities as Cat Scouts of America or formal dancing classes.

For some, the malleability of dogs compared to humans and non-canine companion animals means that dogs not only supersede humans in the role of family member or friend, but also are an ideal object of sexual and romantic love. Dogs provide the kind of love that can easily blur the lines between pet-ownership and zoophilia, between companionship and a passionate affair. Dogs, unlike humans and other companion animals—such as the famously "independent" cat (Jabr 2015)—offer the possibility of passionate adoration *without any risk of rejection*.

While several authors have recently argued that zoophilia has the potential to be liberatory for animals (Brown and Rasmussen 2010; Rudy 2012; Nast 2006; Cassidy 2009), I contend that a feminist analysis of zoophilia indicates that it is, rather, another example of speciesist domination. While Nast and Rudy suggest that zoophilia subverts human supremacy because it implies that animals, as sexual partners, are our equals, feminist analyses of institutionalized hetero-sexuality and marriage make clear that men having sex with (and even loving) a particular kind of being does not indicate that they see or treat those beings as their equals. On the contrary, sexual and love relations such as marriage can be means to reinforce subjection and domination; moreover, these relations, as in the zoophilia and "real doll" cases, may be closely bound up with ownership and property relations.

Why Feminism?

Singer's (2001) argument is that not all sex with animals causes pain and thus not all sex with animals is immoral; some bestial acts, because they bring pleasure to both nonhuman animals and humans, could even be seen as morally good. One of Singer's primary examples is the dog who rubs his penis against a human's leg at a party. Singer's implication is that because the dog has apparently expressed sexual desire for a human in this way, it would be morally acceptable to have sex with the dog. Other utilitarians have expanded on Singer's point by arguing that because most sexual consent between humans occurs nonverbally, it is sufficient to accept nonverbal cues on the part of nonhuman animals as indicative of sexual consent.[2] It is possible that Singer is projecting his own (privileged, adult, male, white, human) subjectivity onto the dog in interpreting the party scenario: if Singer rubbed *his* penis against someone's leg at a party, this would mean that he was up for sex when the guests leave, and so he assumes this is also true for the canine. Should we necessarily assume that what is true of Singer is true of a domesticated dog, however? Should we make a similar assumption about a child who behaved (in a way that adults interpret as) sexually at a party?

As Beirne (1997) does in his description of bestiality pornography, we should exercise caution when judging our ability to interpret animal behavior, especially when we have a vested interest in interpreting it in a particular way. As Beirne notes, passivity that looks to us like indifference (and hence consent) may mask suffering and be a coping strategy. Similarly, what looks like desire for sex to us may in fact be desire for attention or agitation on the part of a dog (or child). If we were to agree that humans can interpret when their companion animals (or children) are nonverbally consenting to sex based on their body language, we would be authorizing humans who have a strong investment in seeing consent to decide when consent has been expressed. Feminist scholarship on sexual harassment, sexual assault, and child abuse, however, has shown that men have a strong tendency to see sexual flirtation in the actions of women and children that the women and children never intend, and fail to register negative cues. Barbara Gutek's (1992) study of sexual harassment, for instance, shows that men are prone to interpret virtually *everything* their female coworkers do as sexual and directed at them, much as child molesters arrogantly misinterpret the affection and intimacy of children as purposeful attempts to arouse (Alcoff 2000). Similarly, zoophiles are likely to misinterpret affectionate or restless behavior on the part of pets as sexual "come-ons," and to interpret bred and trained docility as consent. Given the power dynamics between humans and the animals they *own*, and between adults and the children they *raise*, domesticated animals and children are particularly ill-equipped to extricate themselves from sexual relations with their owners and adults.

In her chapter, "In and Out of Harm's Way: Arrogance and Love" (1983), Marilyn Frye develops understandings of coercion, oppression, and arrogance that serve well to analyze the discourses of zoophiles. Frye argues that we have too simplistic a notion of sexual coercion when we think that an act "will not count ... as coerced unless the ... victim ... is literally physically overcome to the point where the rapist (or rapists) literally physically controls the movements of the victim's limbs and the location and position of her body" (54). In fact, a being is coerced not only in situations where she cannot make any choices, but also in situations where the manipulations of another mean that she will almost certainly do as that person wants, since the only available alternatives are even less appealing. In most situations of coercion, one makes choices, yet ultimately acts in a way that one would not have in the absence of manipulation (56–57). While some forms of coercion involve violence, in situations where an oppressor wants to have an ongoing relationship with a victim, he will often manipulate her psychologically or transform her into the kind of individual he wishes her to be.

Importantly, Frye's primary example of coercion in which the victim's world and psyche are transformed is the domestication of animals. Frye describes numerous ways in which humans alter animals into means to their ends, including breeding them to have particular "tempers and capacities," training animals "from a very young age to tolerate various bindings and harnesses," "suppressing certain tendencies to twitch, shy, buck, stamp or flee," and the use of conditioning "to habituate the animals to certain responses to certain human actions and noises" (1983, 58). As Frye writes, "In the end, by its [sic] 'second' nature, acquired through processes appropriately called 'breaking' and 'training' and by physical restraints placed on it [sic], such a beast can do very little which does not serve some human purpose" (59). Perhaps most crucial of the transformations that Frye describes are centuries of selective breeding. Dogs have been bred for traits that humans find desirable, including neotenization (the retention of juvenile characteristics in adults) and docility. These are the kinds of animals with whom zoophiles are having sex, and who (zoophiles say) consent to this sex and are in love with them. In fact, dogs have been so transformed to suit the purposes of humans that it is highly complex to speak of them consenting to anything their owners do.

For Frye, the domestication of animals is a striking instance of oppression, and, much like Gayle Rubin's use of the term "domestication" to describe the sex/gender system (1975, 158), it serves as a simple case through which we can consider analogous, intra-human forms of oppression such as the physical and psychological "breaking" of sex slaves by pimps. Of such slaves, Frye writes, "Like any animal, the other is not in the nature of things ready-made to suit anyone's interests but its own" (1983, 59). Thus, as occurs in the domestication of animals, those humans must be transformed, and this transformation "must extend beneath the victim's skin": "In particular, the manipulations which adapt the exploited to a niche in another's economy must accomplish a great reduction of the victim's intolerance of coercion" (60). We see this kind of coercion in the case of zoophiles' relationships with animals; these animals have been transformed not only into docile bodies, but also into beings who are emotionally and psychologically bound to the humans who manipulate them.

In "Animal Friendship as a Way of Life" (2016), Dinesh Wadiwel takes up feminist analyses of sexual consent to discuss the case of zoophilia, acknowledging, as Singer does not, that zoophilia takes place within relations that are always already saturated by power. Particularly relevant is Wadiwel's discussion of how dog training practices complicate the possibility of meaningful consent on the part of canines. Wadiwel cites puppy training guides to demonstrate that puppies standardly undergo disciplining that renders them desensitized and docile to human touch; they learn to submit to touching that displeases them, such as manipulation of their teeth and feet. Since such training may be necessary for a domesticated dog's health (to trim nails, clean teeth, and make vet visits manageable), it is not objectionable in itself; it *is*, however, objectionable to take advantage of such an animal's docility to have sexual relations with him. Given the complexities of imagining what sexual consent could look like within contexts of domestication, and in the context of human-canine relations in particular, Wadiwel is critical of Singer's use of dogs as an example of a case in which humans and nonhuman animals can have mutually pleasurable and consensual sexual relations. As Wadiwel notes, "Beyond an awareness of threshold practices that might be identified as 'cruel,' there is little in Singer's essay to illustrate an awareness of how the social and political context of our relationships with animals might frame how we understand the possibility of human/animal sexuality" (292).

According to Beirne (1997), we should reject the view that zoophilia is a paraphilia because—much like many other activities that psychiatrists have tended to pathologize, such as intrahuman rape and purchasing sex—the sexual assault of nonhuman animals is a widespread or, in the Durkheimian sense, "normal" male activity. Indeed, in their account of observing a meeting of zoophiles, sociologists Williams and Weinberg describe being struck by how normal the men were (2003, 525). The zoophiles demonstrated to the male sociologists how they have sex with the animals present and "laughingly related" the animals' sexual "reputations," and yet Williams and Weinberg write that "at no time did we see any ill treatment of an animal" (525). Far from the men fitting the "cultural conception that zoophiles were sick or dangerous," Williams and Weinberg note that "the gathering was strikingly reminiscent of a fraternity get-together" (525)—fraternities being very "normal" spaces of masculinity that are also, of course, notorious for sexual violence. Following feminist critical animal theorist Carol Adams (1995), Beirne argues that "sexism and speciesism operate not in opposition to each other but in tandem. Animal sexual assault is the product of a masculinity that sees women, animals, and nature as objects that can be controlled, manipulated, and exploited" (1997, 117). In conclusion, we might thus say that zoophilia—and human-canine sexual relations in particular—is not so much a sexual orientation (as "zoos" claim) or a symptom of a mental disorder (as psychiatrists claim), as it is part of what feminists have called a rape culture.

Notes

1. The Classic Real Doll starts at $5,699, while the Wicked Real Doll starts at $6,749. See https://www.realdoll.com/.
2. This point was argued by a utilitarian philosopher on a panel on bestiality at the Good Sex/Bad Sex: Sex Law, Crime and Ethics conference held in Prague in May 2010.

References

Adams, Carol. 1995. "Bestiality: The Unmentioned Abuse." *The Animals' Agenda* 15 (6): 29–31.

Alcoff, Linda. 2000. "Phenomenology, Post-Structuralism, and Feminist Theory on the Concept of Experience." In *Feminist Phenomenology*, edited by Linda Fisher and Lester Embree, 39–56. Dordrecht: Kluwer Academic Publishers.

Beetz, Andrea. 2005. *Bestiality and Zoophilia: Sexual Relations with Animals*. West Lafayette, IN: Purdue University Press.

Beirne, Piers. 1997. "Rethinking Bestiality: Towards a Concept of Interspecies Sexual Assault." *Theoretical Criminology* 1 (3): 317–40.

Brown, Michael, and Claire Rasmussen. 2010. "Bestiality and the Queering of the Human Animal." *Environment and Planning D: Society and Space* 28 (1): 158–77.

Cassidy, Rebecca. 2009. "Zoosex and Other Relationships with Animals." In *Transgressive Sex: Subversion and Control in Erotic Encounters*, edited by Hastings Donnan and Fiona Magowan, 91–112. Oxford and Brooklyn: Berghahn Books.

Cuomo, Chris. 1998. *Feminism and Ecological Communities: An Ethics of Flourishing*. New York: Routledge.

de Fren, Allison, producer, director, editor. 2012. *The Mechanical Bride*. Los Angeles: Stream America Inc. http://www.mechanicalbridemovie.com/index.html.

Devor, Robinson, director. 2007. *Zoo*. New York: THINKfilm, DVD.

Donovan, Josephine. 1990. "Animal Rights and Feminist Theory." *Signs* 15 (2): 350–75.

Earls, Christopher M., and Martin L. Lalumière. 2009. "A Case Study of Preferential Bestiality." *Archives of Sexual Behavior* 38 (4): 605–9.

Frye, Marilyn. 1983. "In and Out of Harm's Way: Arrogance and Love." In *The Politics of Reality*, 52–83. Freedom, CA: The Crossing Press.

Gillespie, Kathryn. 2014. "Sexualized Violence and the Gendered Commodification of the Animal Body in Pacific Northwest U.S. Dairy Production." *Gender, Space, and Culture: A Journal of Feminist Geography* 21 (10): 1321–37.

Gutek, Barbara. 1992. "Understanding Sexual Harassment at Work." *Notre Dame Journal of Law, Ethics, and Public Policy* 6 (2): 335–58.

Hunt, M. 1974. *Sexual Behaviour in the 1970s*. Chicago, IL: Playboy Press.

Jabr, Ferris. 2015. "Are Cats Domesticated?" *The New Yorker*, October 23, http://www.newyorker.com/tech/elements/are-cats-domesticated.

Jeffreys, Sheila. 2008. "Disability and the Male Sex Right." *Women's Studies International Forum* 31 (5): 327–35.

Liliequist, Jonas. 1991. "Peasants against Nature: Crossing the Boundaries between Man and Animals in Seventeenth- and Eighteenth-Century Sweden." *Journal of the History of Sexuality* 1 (3): 393–423.

Miletski, Hani. 2001. "Zoophilia—Implications for Therapy." *Journal of Sex Education and Therapy* 26 (2): 85–89.

Murrin, John M. 1998. "'Things Fearful to Name': Bestiality in Colonial America." *Explorations in Early American Culture* 65 (Special supplemental issue): 8–43.

Nast, Heidi. 2006. "Loving . . . Whatever: Alienation, Neoliberalism and Pet-Love in the Twenty-First Century." *ACME: An International E-Journal for Critical Geographies* 5 (2): 300–327.

Pateman, Carole. 1988. *The Sexual Contract*. Stanford, CA: Stanford University Press.

Rubin, Gayle. 1975. "'The Traffic in Women': Notes on the Political Economy of Sex." In *Toward an Anthropology of Women*, edited by Rayna R. Reiter, 157–210. New York: Monthly Review Press.

Rudy, Kathy. 2012. "LGBTQ . . . Z?" *Hypatia* 27 (3): 601–15.

Sanders, Teela. 2008. *Paying for Pleasure: Men Who Buy Sex*. Devon: Willan Publishing.

Shell, Marc. 1986. "The Family Pet." *Representations* 15 (Summer): 121–53.

Singer, Peter. 2001. "Heavy Petting." *Nerve*. http://www.utilitarian.net/singer/by/2001----.htm.

Vaid-Menon, Alok. 2013. "My Little (Homo)Nationalist Pony: A Critique of Zoophilia." Undergraduate Thesis, Program in Feminist, Gender, and Sexuality Studies, Stanford University. https://searchworks.stanford.edu/view/fs953jp5133.

Wadiwel, Dinesh. 2016. "Animal Friendship as a Way of Life: Sexuality, Petting and Interspecies Companionship." In *Foucault and Animals*, edited by Matthew Chrulew and Dinesh Wadiwel, 286–316. Leiden: Brill.

Williams, Colin J., and Martin S. Weinberg. 2003. "Zoophilia in Men: A Study of Sexual Interest in Animals." *Archives of Sexual Behavior* 32 (6): 523–35.

Zalupin, Andrei. 2013. "The Woman Who Trains Dogs to Have Sex with Humans." *Vice Magazine*, December. https://www.vice.com/en_ca/read/training-a-dog-to-have-sex-with-humans.

17 THROW OUT THE DOG?

DEATH, LONGEVITY, AND COMPANION ANIMALS

Christine Overall

Philosophers have devoted much thought to whether or not death is bad for human beings, whether death should be postponed, whether or not a longer life is a better life, and whether or not our human lives should be extended. These important questions can also be asked about nonhuman animals. In this chapter I investigate whether, in regard to our animal companions, especially cats and dogs, a longer life is a better life.

I first make some general remarks on the idea of death that is relevant to this question, an idea that is necessarily tied to the concept of longevity. Then I evaluate and reply to three arguments purporting to show that, for animals in general, a longer life is not a better life: first, that death is not bad for animals; second, that death is bad for animals but not as bad as it is for human beings; and third, that merely having *some* life is good enough for animals, so that premature death is not bad for them. I argue that all of these arguments are unsuccessful, and hence that we have good reasons for believing that, for companion animals as for human beings, a longer life is a better life. I conclude with some brief remarks about the practical implications of this argument for our responsibilities toward companion animals.

The Concept of Death

The word "death" is, of course, ambiguous. It is customary to distinguish death, an event by which a life ends, from dying, which is a process, and from being dead, which is a state (e.g, Luper 2009, 41–44; Rosenbaum 2010, 176–77).

By characterizing death as an event, philosophers such as Stephen Rosenbaum have become tangled in the question of whether or not death, as an event, takes time. On the one hand, Rosenbaum writes that "death is roughly the time at which a person becomes dead. . . . [D]eath is the portal between the land of the living and the land of the dead; the bridge over the Styx" (2010, 176–77). Yet on the other hand he says that it is not clear whether death is "a part of a person's lifetime, although it may be a (very) small part. Also, it is not clear that it takes time or, if so, how much time it takes" (177).

Treating death as an event also generates some unnecessary metaphysical quandaries about the badness of death. For example, in treating death as an event, some philosophers have been moved to ask *when* death is bad. Thus, Geoffrey Scarre thinks that one's death is bad *before* it occurs:

> The view that death harms the ante-mortem person involves no metaphys-
> ically objectionable notion of backwards causation. The claim is not that
> what happens in the future can causally affect what has happened in the
> past, but that a person who was going to die young was harmed all along
> by his impending demise, unapparent though this may have been at the
> time. (2007, 94)

But this view has a surprising implication: if one is harmed all along by one's impending early demise, then it is better to die at twenty than at thirty. The longer a person lives, the worse her death must be, because there is that much greater time in which her impending death is harming her. Yet it is hard not to see the deaths of the twenty-year-old and the thirty-year-old as about equally bad (in the absence of other circumstances, such as irremediable suffering).

Moreover, if the harm of one's future death occurs throughout one's life, then it would seem that the death of a ninety-year-old is worse than the death of a fifty-year-old. This implication contradicts our usual, and sensible, assumption that, provided one's life has afforded a reasonable range of opportunities and experiences, death in old age is not as bad as death in middle age.

These errors result from asking axiological questions about death as an event. Instead, what is philosophically interesting is not so much death as an event but death as *the end of the life of a being*. In this respect, death is not an event but a terminus, not something that takes time but rather something that divides two times. This, I contend, is the sense of "death" we are using when we philosophize about the inevitability of death or about dealing with death. We are not speaking of a discrete event, *but rather of the fact that life has an end*.

Thus, questions about the value of death are questions about the axiology of the fact that life ends; they cannot be answered separately from questions about the value of various lengths of life. Because death in this sense is the end of life, the value of death is relational: its value is determined by its relationship to the quality and length of the life it terminates. What makes death bad, when it is bad, is the fact that it terminates something of value, the life that it ended. Therefore, in order to know whether or not death is bad for an animal, we must investigate what, if anything, makes an animal's continuing existence valuable.

Death Is Not Bad for Animals

David Velleman argues that death is not bad at all or in any way for nonhuman animals. According to Velleman, an animal—he uses the example of a cow—cannot conceive of himself as an enduring individual; what he cannot conceive, he cannot care about; so the cow cannot care about "which sequences of momentary goods it [sic] enjoys" (1993, 354). Although good and bad things can happen to a cow, they are good or bad only at specific times. "There is no timeless dimension of value along which the cow progresses by undergoing successive benefits and harms. Hence the various benefits accruing to a cow at different moments must not add up to anything at all, not even to zero" (356). Given that "a cow cannot care about extended periods in [his] life . . . [t]he totality of this subject's life simply has no value for him, because he cannot care about it as such, and because its constituent moments, which he can care about, have values that do not accumulate." Thus, death does not take anything from the cow, since he cannot accumulate momentary wellbeing, and it does not "detract from the value of the cow's life as a whole, since a cow has no interest in [his] life as a whole, being unable to care about what sort of life [he] lives." Velleman concludes, "[T]here is no moment at which a cow can be badly off because of death" (357).

Reply to Velleman

It is not true that companion animals, at any rate, cannot conceive of themselves as persisting individuals in any way. Companion animals certainly act as if they understand themselves as persisting individuals. For example, my cat Nekko's constant meowing at me starting at 2:00 p.m., following me from room to room, and trying to lead me into the kitchen, all suggest that she has an anticipation at least of a near future in which I feed her. Self-oriented behaviors such as Nekko's, which are directed at eliciting actions from human beings or from other animals, indicate an ability to anticipate and even plan for events (involving the animal herself) that have not yet occurred.

These behaviors are evidence that companion animals understand themselves to persist. An animal's sense of herself as a persisting being may be shorter in duration than that of adult human beings. But in that sense, it may not be too different from the sense of herself as a persisting being that my three-year-old grandson has. Nekko's sense of the future may extend, perhaps, to an anticipation of the next few hours. But once there, her sense then extends for another few hours. And so on. She has a series of overlapping senses of herself as a persisting being. Thus, Nekko is connected to her own future, probably not so differently from how a human toddler is connected to his future, and to that extent, Nekko is able to accumulate good moments.[1]

But even if (contrary to what interactions with companion animals seem to suggest) nonhuman animals do not and cannot conceive of themselves as persisting individuals even in this limited way, it is not clear how that putative fact is supposed to mean that depriving an animal of a longer succession of good moments is not harmful to the animal. What matters is not whether companion animals have a far-reaching sense of their future or an ongoing sense of self-continuity, but rather, whether they have a future at all, and what sort of future it is. As Steven Luper puts it, "It seems entirely reasonable to say a life that contains years of pleasure which an animal cannot recall is better for that animal than a life that contains only a few minutes of pleasure which the animal can recall, just as your life and mine are better for the pleasures we have forgotten" (2009, 164). Moreover, as Krister Bykvist points out, Velleman's view implies, most implausibly, that we cannot say that a future full of terrible suffering is worse for an animal than a future of great pleasure (2014, 320).

It is hard to see why an animal's "caring about" extended life must be the criterion for the badness of death. Velleman seems to be saying that, in order for any being to be harmed by her own death, that being must be capable of a kind of *meta*-judgment about her own life. She must not only be capable of enjoying life; she must also care about enjoying life. If "caring about" is an extra evaluation of one's life, in addition to simply enjoying a succession of momentary goods, the question is why this extra evaluation is necessary in order to make the succession of moments good for the animal.

Alistair Norcross shows that having a preference for future existence does not necessarily add much even to human beings' global wellbeing. For example, a person who never considers the future is almost as much benefited by having preventive dental treatment as a person who does anticipate her future. Each will enjoy increased wellbeing by taking steps to avoid future pain from dental problems (Norcross 2013, 468–69). Norcross also asks that we imagine two animals, each of whom has many desires. One of them, Charles, but not the other,

Harold, also desires to continue to exist. Charles's desire for continued existence does not necessarily make his death qualitatively worse than Harold's death; it would really depend on the extent and strength of Harold's desires (Norcross 2013, 469–70). As Frederike Kaldewaij asks, "[I]s someone who just enjoys life as it comes harmed much less by death than someone who has his life completely planned out already?" (2008, 60). Surely the answer is no.

Indeed, companion animals may often enjoy their temporary pleasures—extended or not—even more than many human beings do. Companion animals greet each day anew (Overall 2003, 146–47). By this I mean that provided they are reasonably healthy and able-bodied, they take pleasure, often exuberant pleasure, in the activities of their ordinary lives, appreciating simple activities and pleasures over and over again, as if experienced fresh each time. Unlike adult human beings (but like infant and toddler human beings), companion animals do not seem to have a sense of the middle or distant future, which can be feared or dreaded, or of the past, which can be regretted or longed for. They live very fully in the present and close future, and are able to enjoy the same or similar activities—eating, playing, cuddling, or running—over and over again. For this reason it could be said that, compared to adult human beings' enjoyment, the pleasures of the moment are, for companion animals, unalloyed and pure, and arguably for that reason even more valuable than (many) humans' present moments, which are often contaminated with worries and fears about the future, or regrets and nostalgia for the past.[2]

When companion animals enjoy such activities and have prospects for a future in which they will have additional enjoyments, their lives are worthwhile, and death—the termination of their lives—is bad for them.

Death Is Not as Bad for Animals as for Human Beings

David DeGrazia (2007) rejects the view held by Velleman that nonhuman animals cannot accumulate enjoyments. He cites the pleasures that dogs can get from their extraordinary olfactory and auditory capacities. DeGrazia states clearly that, if we compare the pleasures afforded to human beings and to dogs—as well as to "many other mammals with rich sensory worlds"—it is by no means clear that the human being's total *quantity* is greater (61). Nonetheless, according to DeGrazia, we can make the "considered judgment" that death is not *as* bad for nonhuman animals, such as dogs, as it is for adult human beings (57).

DeGrazia appeals to Tom Regan's well-known lifeboat case (1983, 324). "If a lifeboat is sinking with several normal human beings and a dog aboard," says DeGrazia, "where it is clear that all will drown unless someone is thrown overboard, nearly everyone agrees that it is morally right to sacrifice the dog" (2007, 57). DeGrazia's explanation for what he takes to be this near-unanimity is what he calls the "Unequal Harm of Death Judgment" (UHDJ). The UHDJ is not justified merely on the basis of the length of life of different beings (DeGrazia 2007, 60);[3] nor can it be accounted for by reference to varying amounts of happiness different beings experience (61), or by reference to the varying quality of different beings' objective prudential values (such as autonomy, accomplishment, and personal relationships) (62).

Instead, he says, our differential judgments about the harms of death, and our willingness to throw the dog overboard, can be justified by Jeff McMahan's Time Relative Interest Account (TRIA), which highlights the ways in which different beings are "psychologically 'invested' in, or connected with" their future possible life (DeGrazia 2007, 65). So the importance of death to a victim is *discounted* based on any "weakness in the psychological unity that would have connected the victim at that time with himself in the future" (65). Psychological unity is a function of the richness of a subject's mental life, "the proportion of the mental life that is sustained over the stretch of time in question," and the "degree of internal reference between earlier and later mental states" (65–66).

Thus, according to DeGrazia, an animal such as a snake has very little self-awareness over time, and "[i]f one snake were to die before reaching his natural life span and another with equal prospects for a decent snake life came into existence, that state of affairs would not seem significantly worse than for the first snake to have survived without another coming into existence. . . . With a snake, it is almost as if the future he loses due to death might as well have belonged to another snake" (65).

Hence, writes DeGrazia, "all are likely to agree . . . that death itself harms a normal human in ordinary circumstances more than it harms a dog or, for that matter any (or nearly any) nonhuman animal" (60). He also says that infants are not as harmed by death as an older person is. He writes, "Other things equal, death seems to harm a 10- or 25-year-old more than it harms an infant" (63). The death of the ten- or twenty-five-year-old is tragic in a way that "infantile death cannot be for its victim" (64).

Reply to DeGrazia

Do we now have a good reason for thinking that, although (contrary to Velleman) animals can accumulate a large quantity of pleasures in their lives, nonetheless, death is not as bad for them as it is for adult human beings? There are three reasons for rejecting psychological investment or unity as a criterion for evaluating the degree of badness of death.

DeGrazia himself provides the first reason for rejecting it. In the course of evaluating and discarding putative reasons for believing that death is less bad for the dog than for an adult human being, he rejects an objective-list approach—the view that autonomy, accomplishment, and deep personal relationships enhance one's wellbeing (whether one desires or enjoys them or not), and that nonhuman animals lack the capacity for these objective goods (DeGrazia 2007, 62). DeGrazia's reason for rejecting the objective-list approach is relevance. He suggests that the features that may well be objectively good for human beings just may not be relevant to nonhuman animals, and therefore "this approach owes us some plausible account of what capacities or conditions have special weight across species and why they have special weight" (62). He also points out that founding claims of qualitative superiority on an objective-list approach is so "convenient" as to "invite[] reasonable concerns about dogmatism" (62).

Insisting on psychological investment and unity as the criteria for the evaluation of the degree of badness of death in sentient beings such as companion animals is similarly "convenient" and invites concerns about "dogmatism." For the badness of death for dogs and other companion animals then turns out to be lower than for human beings mainly because they are not (like) "normal" human beings. But it is inappropriate for the degree of value of death for nonhuman animals to be assessed solely by reference to criteria that, like worldly accomplishments, have little or no connection to their lives. If animals are inherently incapable of x—despite being inherently capable of y and z, which contribute importantly to a good life—it is unfair to suppose that only the possession of x makes death bad, but not the possession of y and z. While dogs may have a low degree—if any—of psychological investment in and unity with their own futures, they do have capacities for enjoyment of life and repeated indulgence in pleasures, however simple, and the forging of connections with human beings or other animals. It is the termination of these capacities that makes death bad for them.

A second objection to DeGrazia's reason for regarding death as less bad for animals than for human beings is that in lifeboat cases, it would justify us in first throwing out the dogs and cats, then throwing out the infants, and then, in order, the one-year-olds, two-year-olds, and three-year-olds.[4] Even a six-year-old, compared to an adult, may have a smaller proportion of mental life sustained over her lifetime, and may have fewer memories, less developed anticipation of future experiences, and fewer intentions with regard to the future, all of which are part of what DeGrazia means by "internal reference between earlier and later mental states" (2007, 66). If the criteria that justify throwing out the dog also justify throwing out the infant, followed by any toddlers on board, then there is some problem with the criteria that purport to justify throwing out the dog. The prospect of tossing a three-year-old human being out of a lifeboat in order to save the "normal" older humans is surely a reductio ad absurdum of the claim that death is less bad for sentient beings with lower degrees of psychological investment and unity. Hence, we should have further doubts as to whether psychological investment and unity are the sole appropriate and adequate criteria for evaluating the badness of death for all sentient beings.

The third reason for rejecting DeGrazia's criteria is related to the locus of evaluation. What validates the TRIA, according to DeGrazia, is simply the fact that it explains "our considered judgments about the harm of death" (66). To whose judgments is he referring? Who exactly are the people who are giving "our considered judgments"? Presumably only adult human beings, not young children or nonhuman animals.[5] It is suspiciously convenient that those who are claimed to be less harmed by death are precisely those who have no input into the lifeboat decision about whom to sacrifice.

Moreover, although I am, presumably, a member of the category of "normal human being," I do not accept DeGrazia's "considered judgment." I regard all the potential deaths in the lifeboat case with horror, and would be unwilling to throw any of the passengers overboard. I only hope if I were ever in those circumstances that I could find the personal strength to volunteer to jump overboard myself. The question is whether I am the only person who would reject the judgment that the dog (followed by any available babies and toddlers) should be tossed from the boat.

I doubt it. The reality is that even "normal" persons in the lifeboat would have different reactions to the deaths of an infant, a two-year-old, a ten-year-old, a twenty-five-year-old, and a dog, and this fact is significant. Must we discount their opinions? Are we to say, because they do not share DeGrazia's considered judgment, that they are irrational or simply mistaken, or that their lives are emotionally and morally impoverished?

People's judgments about whom to sacrifice would not necessarily be based on the extent of psychological investment and unity of each individual. Unlike DeGrazia, some might not dismiss the importance of the length of life, along with the opportunity for positive life experiences that is usually but not always associated with the length of life, as a possible criterion for the badness of death. Others might decide whom to throw overboard based on their concern for or relationship to the individuals. Just as some people might have a closer concern for or relationship with an infant or a two-year-old than to anyone who is older, some people would feel—and have—a stronger concern for or relationship to the dog than to any of the people in the boat.[6]

DeGrazia claims that an extraterrestrial would share his judgment about the expendability of the dog (2007, 58), thus suggesting that there is a god's-eye or objective view of what is right in the situation. I am not convinced. Given that people's "considered judgments" about whom to toss from the lifeboat are not likely to be unanimous, and that people do not necessarily use psychological investment or unity to ground their judgments about the harm of death, DeGrazia may be *assuming* what he ought to be trying to prove: that the dog and the infant are harmed less by death than is the twenty-five-year-old. He calls it a "considered judgment," but his treatment of it makes clear that it is foundational for him, and that if it is contradicted by other criteria—such as the desire-satisfaction account of the harm of death, or the theory that the harm of death is a function of lost opportunities for valuable future experiences, both of which are relevant to companion animals—he is not willing to abandon his foundational belief about who is less harmed by death. It is always those beings with lower psychological unity (DeGrazia 2007, 67).

Perhaps, then, what underlie the views of people like Velleman and DeGrazia about the value of death for human and nonhuman animals are their fundamental feelings about human beings of various ages and about nonhuman animals of various kinds. According to DeGrazia, "[i]f one snake were to die before reaching his natural life span and another with equal prospects for a decent snake life came into existence, that state of affairs would not seem significantly worse than for the first snake to have survived without another coming into existence" (2007, 65). It may seem to DeGrazia that all snakes are alike and interchangeable, but—even though he lacks self-awareness—for the snake, his life is not substitutable with others. Death happens to *unique* individuals.

Premature Death Is Not Bad for Animals

As Jeff McMahan pointed out in a recent lecture (2013), many people are committed to the view that provided animals are raised humanely and killed painlessly, it does not matter *when* they are slaughtered for human consumption, use, or expedience; nor does it matter that they do not live out their natural life spans. This view permits animals used for food to be killed at only a fraction of their life span potential,[7] and animals abandoned at shelters to be routinely killed, whatever their age, if there are no potential adopters. In other words, the thought is that premature death—prematurity being defined by reference to what is species-typical—is not bad for animals. Those who support this point of view believe that, provided their lives are at least worth living, the mere opportunity to exist—even briefly—is enough for these animals, and animals' potential life span has no moral relevance. Thus, self-described animal lover Kathy Rudy writes,

> Buying meat, eggs, and dairy from local farms where animals have long, happy, and natural lives on pasture is animal centered, I believe, even if we kill them for their meat eventually. . . . They get to spend days walking in sunshine, eating good food, mating, loving their young, enjoying the beautiful earth. We give them the chance to have this life, we pay for the land and the grass and the water, and eventually we get to eat their eggs, milk, cheese, and meat. It's not a bad deal for either side. . . . If I were a Redcap chicken, say, I would rather have a farmer raise me and let me proliferate, even if she is going to kill me to eat in the end. That way, my kind get to stay on this planet; in many ways, that could mean more to me than my own life. (Rudy 2011)

Reply to Rudy

Of course, we can only wish that most domesticated animals could have, before they are slaughtered, the long pleasant existence so idyllically depicted by Rudy. The evidence is all too overwhelming that most of them live in misery (Francione 2000). But I doubt that Rudy's arguments apply even to those who do have good lives. Animals do not possess the cognitive ability to understand the idea of species continuity, and they surely do not have opinions about its value. It makes no empirical sense whatsoever to imagine individual animals choosing their *own* slaughter as the price for "proliferation" of their *species*. More important, however, we can legitimately ask whether beings who *are* able to process such complex ideas would choose, as Rudy believes, a life of reasonable comfort, followed by slaughter in the prime of life, in order to be eaten by members of another species. I certainly would not, and I suspect most other human beings would not.

It is not at all implausible to suppose that premature death is bad for animals. Much of our behavior is based on this supposition. In natural disasters, for example, efforts are often made to save nonhuman animals, even (or especially) when their "owners" may be missing or even dead. And if we come upon a lost cat who is not able to fend for himself, we take him to a veterinarian or the Humane Society, or home to be cared for, even (or especially) if he appears to have no particular relationship to other human beings. We recognize, that is, that we have reason to protect an animal from death, not only for the sake of her human companion, if and when there is one, but for her own sake. These behaviors indicate that we value animal lives and consider them to be worth saving. Indeed, as Tristram McPherson points out (2014, 683), although causing pain to an animal for, let us say, the sake of art would be morally wrong, we regard it as morally permissible, even laudable, to cause pain to an animal (via surgery, for example) if doing so will save and thus prolong the animal's life.

This observation suggests that it is not just the avoidance of inflicting pain on nonhuman animals that is morally important; it is also the preservation of their lives. And it is not just having *some* life that matters for them, but having a reasonably full life span. Given that animals are capable of the kinds of enjoyments Rudy describes, it makes sense to suppose that the continuation of their lives is good for them. It is a mistake to assume that human beings are so different from nonhuman beings that premature death harms us but not them.

Some Implications

My arguments so far indicate, first, that death *is* bad for companion animals; second, that the claim that their death is *necessarily* less bad than death is for human beings lacks justification; and third, that *premature* death is bad for companion animals. Our default moral assumption should therefore be non-maleficence: we should not kill companion or other nonhuman animals, should not routinely allow them to die, and should where possible save them from premature death. If someone is going to kill an animal or refuse to save it, the burden of justification rests on that person.

Provided that the animal's life is good, then for that animal, a longer life is a better life. A companion animal's life is good when she is flourishing, a state that requires the optimization of her wellbeing—including the experiences of pleasures of eating, play, companionship, and rest—and the satisfaction of many of her desires.

Animals do not have a psychological investment in their own future in the way that (many) human beings do. Thus, if categorical desires involve long-term projects toward whose fulfilment one is working, then companion animals do not have categorical desires. But if categorical desires are defined as desires for something that provides a good reason to go on living, something that makes life worth living (even if those things are not long-range goals), then companion animals very often do have categorical desires: a desire to eat again, to play some more, to explore further, to enjoy affection, companionship, or sex, or to sleep again.

Animals do not simply eat to live; they also live to eat. Kaldewaij writes, "Animals do not only have desires like eating when they are hungry, desires to alleviate frustration. They actually like eating, grooming, rolling in the mud, play-ing, etc. Such desires give their life instrumental value, just like whatever we find valuable makes our lives worth living" (2008, 61).[8] But in my view the actual enjoyment of pleasures is more fundamental than are the desires for them. It is because animals are capable of these enjoyments that their desires for them are morally significant. Indeed, the capacity for enjoyment of x may persist even when a desire for x is not consciously present. For example, an animal can be accurately described as a being who loves to play, even when she is temporarily asleep or ill and not feeling any conscious desire to play. Thus, Aaron Simmons describes animals' desires as "enduring [and] dispositional" (2009, 387); that is, they can continue to exist even when they are not phenomenologically present.

But even if a longer life is a better life for companion animals, one might won-der nonetheless whether deliberate efforts should always be made to extend their lives. For when an animal has little or no prospect of any future enjoyments, then the animal's worthwhile life is over and her death is not bad. And Bernard Rollin asks whether the opportunity for a longer life is worth the cost to the animal of significant and severe suffering. Animals cannot weigh future benefits against current suffering and cannot make their own considered choices about medical treatments:

> An animal *is* its pain, for it is incapable of anticipating or even hoping for cessation of that pain. Thus, when we are confronted with life-threatening illnesses that afflict our animals, it is not axiomatic that they be treated at whatever qualitative, experiential cost that may entail. The owner may consider the suffering a treatment modality that entails a small price for extra life, but the animal neither values nor comprehends extra life, let alone the trade-off this entails. (Rollin 2011, 431, his emphasis)

Obviously, I would not argue for extending the lives of animals who are suf-fering without relief or prospect for improvement. I agree with Rollin that an animal's serious, unremitting, pointless, and irremediable pain is a reason not to prolong her life. But arguably some cases of painful procedures to extend life might be justified, and others not. The extraction of teeth or removal of a tumor may involve present pain that is more than offset by additional years of wellbeing for the animal. Although the animal cannot know that her future after medi-cal treatment will be good, human companions are at least sometimes justified in making the judgment that the prolongation of the animal's life is defensible based on the likelihood of future wellbeing. As McMahan has argued, "[T]hird parties have a present reason to ensure that a *future* interest is satisfied rather than frustrated that is equal in strength to their present reason to ensure that an equivalent *present* interest is satisfied rather than frustrated" (2013, his emphasis). For these reasons, I assume that not only is it prima facie wrong to kill or fail to save companion animals; it is also *not* wrong to devote resources to keeping a companion animal alive, although the limit of such efforts will be set by such factors as the effectiveness of treatment, the animal's quality of life, and the availability of scientific, medical, and healthcare resources for both human and nonhuman beings.

Just like her human companions, the dog in the lifeboat has only one life to live.

Acknowledgments

I am grateful to the late Jean Harvey for motivating and inspiring me to think and write about this topic. I also thank Josh Milburn and Tina Rulli for their insightful and careful feedback on an earlier draft of this chapter. Any remaining problems are, of course, my own responsibility.

Notes

1. As Krister Bykvist puts it, "[S]ince cows and many animals can care about the parts that make up their future lives, we need not deny that their futures are overall good for them" (2014, 320).
2. This is not to say that companion animals' experiences are "disconnected," as Christopher Belshaw believes (2009, 117). I do not see why a companion animal's experiences would not be a smooth continuum—interrupted, of course, by sleep, but nonetheless still appearing (and how else can our experiences exist for us?) to be continuous.
3. For this criterion would imply that infants are more harmed by death than older human beings are, a view that is "highly implausible," according to DeGrazia (2007, 67).
4. Along with those of any age who are severely cognitively disabled.
5. The judgments of those who are not "normal human beings" would likely not accept DeGrazia's "considered judgment." I imagine if a puppy were to be thrown overboard, and her canine mother witnessed the act, she would oppose it. Also, I am not sure that children would favor discarding the dog, or a younger child.
6. In an article tellingly titled, "The Love That Dare Not Bark Its Name," Mikita Brottman describes her dog Grisby as one of the most important beings in her life: "Since I disliked being apart from him, I stopped taking plane trips and attending conferences.... If I couldn't bring him with me to a social function, I'd leave early or skip it altogether.... People like to make fun of those who love their dogs

'excessively,' but who decides how much love is too much? Why can't we let ourselves take dog love too seriously?" (Brottman 2014, B20).

7. Bruijnis, Meijboom, and Stassen refer to the "normally intended productive life" of cows, and argue for increasing it to 8 years—this, despite the fact that "a dairy cow can reach the age of 20 or more" (2013, 193).

8. Thus, either animals do have categorical desires (if defined as desires for activities that give them a reason to go on living), or having categorical desires (if defined as desires to realize long-term projects and goals) is not necessary to making an animal's death bad, because such desires are simply irrelevant to their lives (even though an absence of categorical desires might make some human beings' deaths not bad).

References

Belshaw, Christopher. 2009. *Annihilation: The Sense and Significance of Death*. Stocksfield, UK: Acumen.

Brottman, Mikita. 2014. "The Love That Dare Not Bark Its Name." *The Chronicle Review* 61 (2), September 8: B20.

Bruijnis, M. R. N., F. L. B. Meijboom, and E. N. Stassen. 2013. "Longevity as an Animal Welfare Issue Applied to the Case of Foot Disorders in Dairy Cattle." *Journal of Agricultural and Environmental Ethics* 26 (1): 191–205.

Bykvist, Krister. 2014. "Killing and Extinction." In *The Cambridge Companion to Life and Death*, edited by Steven Luper, 316–29. Cambridge: Cambridge University Press.

DeGrazia, David. 2007. "The Harm of Death, Time-Relative Interests, and Abortion." *Philosophical Forum* 38 (1): 57–80.

Francione, Gary L. 2000. *Introduction to Animal Rights: Your Child or the Dog?* Philadelphia: Temple University Press.

Kaldewaij, Frederike. 2008. "Animals and the Harm of Death." In *The Animal Ethics Reader*, 2nd ed., edited by Susan J. Armstrong and Richard George Botzler, 59–62. London: Routledge.

Luper, Steven. 2009. *The Philosophy of Death*. Cambridge: Cambridge University Press.

McMahan, Jeff. 2013. "Killing Animals and Causing Them to Suffer." Lecture presented at Queen's University Department of Philosophy Colloquium series, October 21.

McPherson, Tristram. 2014. "A Case for Ethical Veganism: Intuitive and Methodological Considerations." *Journal of Moral Philosophy* II: 677–703. doi: 0.1163/17455243-4681041.

Norcross, Alistair. 2013. "The Significance of Death for Animals." In *The Oxford Handbook of Philosophy of Death*, edited by Ben Bradley, Fred Feldman, and Jens Johansson, 465–74. Oxford: Oxford University Press.

Overall, Christine. 2003. *Aging, Death, and Human Longevity: A Philosophical Inquiry*. Berkeley, CA: University of California Press.

Regan, Tom. 1983. *The Case for Animal Rights*. Berkeley, CA: University of California Press.

Rollin, Bernard E. 2011. "Animal Pain: What It Is and Why It Matters." *Journal of Ethics: An International Philosophical Review* 15 (4): 425–37.

Rosenbaum, Stephen E. 2010. "How to Be Dead and Not Care: A Defense of Epicurus." In *Life, Death, and Meaning: Key Philosophical Questions on the Big Questions*, 2nd ed., edited by David Benatar, 175–89. Lanham, MD: Rowman & Littlefield.

Rudy, Kathy. 2011. "With Veganism and Animal-Rights Causes, a Middle Ground Is Always Best." *University of Minnesota Press Blog: Books, Media and More*. August 31. http://www.uminnpressblog.com/2011/08/with-veganism-and-animal-rights-causes.html.

Scarre, Geoffrey. 2007. *Death*. Montreal: McGill-Queen's University Press.

Simmons, Aaron. 2009. "Do Animals Have an Interest in Continued Life? In Defense of a Desire-Based Approach." *Environmental Ethics* 31 (4): 375–92.

Velleman, J. David. 1993. "Well-Being and Time." In *The Metaphysics of Death*, edited by John Martin Fischer, 329–55. Stanford: Stanford University Press.

18 THE EUTHANASIA OF COMPANION ANIMALS

Michael Cholbi

Intense debates regarding the ethical justifiability and legal wisdom of human euthanasia (and its close cousin, assisted suicide) have occurred in many societies over the past half century, despite the fact the numbers involved are vanishingly small. In those jurisdictions that permit assisted dying, only 3 percent of all deaths result from such procedures (Statistics Netherlands 2012; Warnes 2014). In contrast, euthanasia of companion animals is almost commonplace. Exact numbers regarding how many companion animals are euthanized each year by their owners are hard to come by. But given that the Humane Society of the United States (2014) estimates that 2.7 million animals from companion species are euthanized each year in shelters, and Americans own about 164 million pets, one can only assume that the number of euthanasias of companion animals performed at guardians' requests must number in the millions per year. In any case, it seems clear that euthanasia of pets is far more the norm than human euthanasia will ever be. Still, that euthanizing companion animals is not ethically controversial does not mean that it raises no complex ethical questions. My aim here is not to upend the popular conviction that this practice is morally permissible. Rather, my primary task is to clarify the underlying ethical issues and, to the extent possible, render more precise the conditions under which euthanizing companion animals is morally justified.

The euthanasia of companion animals and the assisted killing of humans share a superficial similarity: both involve the use of medical means to bring about the end of a creature's life for beneficent reasons. But I first argue that modeling the ethics of euthanizing companion animals on the ethics of euthanizing human beings is implausible. The bromide that companion animal euthanasia should be "humane" or done "humanely" in fact obscures the very different ethical terrain of human and animal euthanasia. For very few of the ethical considerations that count in favor of (or against) euthanizing humans apply straightforwardly to nonhuman animals. Indeed, euthanizing companion animals might more accurately be seen as a species of (potentially) justifiable homicide, the justification of which turns almost entirely on our duties to protect or promote animal wellbeing. I then argue that the familiar *comparative* account of the value of death provides the best account of when prematurely ending a companion animal's life through medical means is morally justified. Very roughly, this account implies that there is an approximate right time for an animal to die, namely, at that point at which additional life would be neither a benefit nor a harm to it. I augment this approach by proposing that knowingly failing to euthanize a companion animal at the optimal time fails to respect such an animal and can treat it merely as a means (though not in the usual Kantian sense of that phrase). I conclude by reflecting on why guardians of companion animals, as opposed to others, are both morally permitted and morally obligated to euthanize companion animals (with the assistance of veterinary professionals). These moral entitlements, I propose, rest on the guardians' distinctive knowledge of an animal's history and wellbeing.

Let us start with two caveats regarding nomenclature: First, I will use the term "companion animals" here, despite the allegation that doing so is "politically correct" (Varner 2002, 460). I intend the term in a literal sense, as designating any animals with whom human beings can be companionate. This will include most pets, but may also include service animals or domesticated animals from whom labor is sought. Companionship, in other words, is compatible with animals playing other roles in human affairs. This usage leaves open precisely which species of animals can serve as human companions (whether, for example, fish or insects might be human companions). Second, for reasons that become clear later on, I will refer to those human beings with whom animals are companionate and who bear special moral obligations toward those animals as those animals' *guardians* rather than as their owners.

Animals and the Human-Assisted Dying Debate

Unsurprisingly, recent debates about human euthanasia have been dominated by discussions of *voluntary* euthanasia, euthanasia that takes place with the consent of the person killed. *Involuntary* euthanasia is ruled out by the widespread belief that the willful killing of another human being against her will (except in cases of self-defense) is among the most serious of moral wrongs. Furthermore, since voluntary euthanasia counts as suicide, that is, as intentional self-killing undertaken in this case with the assistance of others, the moral debate about human euthanasia has been couched in terms of whether human beings may permissibly end their own lives, and if so, whether others (particularly physicians) are permitted to facilitate such self-termination.

However, this framework simply cannot be repurposed to address the euthanasia of nonhuman creatures. Admittedly, humans euthanizing animals may be "helping" those animals to die (more on this shortly). But this does not make the euthanasia of companion animals "voluntary" in the sense deployed in debates about human euthanasia. Although the right to autonomy—that is, the right to make one's own decisions, particularly regarding key life matters such as life and death—has played a central role in advocacy for human euthanasia, it has essentially no role to play in the morality of euthanizing animals. Animals do not consent to their own deaths, nor would it make sense to ask them to do so. Animal euthanasia thus does not count as suicide in the ordinary sense. Rather, it is better classified as *non-voluntary* euthanasia, the beneficent killing of a being neither in concert with, nor contrary to, its consent.

Nor are many other considerations commonly brought to bear on the human euthanasia debate applicable to the euthanasia of nonhumans. For example, most religious arguments intended to show the impermissibility of suicide appeal to premises that, within the relevant religious traditions at least, exclude nonhuman animals. That life is a gift from God; that humans are made in God's image; that God entrusts our bodies to us but that they not belong to us; that life is sacred; that suicide amounts to our abandoning our assigned post in life: it is not clear how such premises could apply to the killing of nonhuman animals (Cholbi 2011, 39–53). Indeed, the dominant strain of thought within Western monotheism has sharply differentiated between human beings, who have rational souls, and animals, who do not. This difference is in turn alleged to be the putative moral basis for humans' right to use animals for their own purposes. In any event, we cannot take our cues regarding the euthanasia of nonhuman animals from religious arguments concerning human euthanasia.

Likewise, other arguments aimed at establishing the moral impermissibility of suicide do not readily extrapolate to nonhuman euthanasia either. Kant's argument, that suicide violates a duty to oneself resting on the moral demand to treat rational agency as having dignity rather than price, applies only to creatures with "humanity," that is, with the capacity to rationally determine their ends and the best means to those ends. And while we cannot rule out nonhuman animals' having such a capacity, Kant's argument nevertheless sets a high bar for which creatures are morally forbidden to end their lives (Cholbi 2000). I am similarly skeptical that libertarian arguments for the moral permissibility of suicide (appealing to the notion of self-ownership) or communitarian arguments for suicide's moral impermissibility apply to animals either.

Finally, many of the psychological facts that shape human attitudes toward death are probably not present in animals. All animals die, but human beings, it has been claimed, are the only animals with the conceptual sophistication and reflective capacity to grasp their own inherent mortality (Becker 1997, 27). This claim strikes me as plausible but not indisputable. Animals no doubt have a strong survival instinct, and many species of animals grieve (King 2013). Still, the moral significance of death for human beings is shaped by attitudes that presuppose some incipient awareness of death, attitudes that we likely do not share with animals. Other animals probably cannot conceptualize the finitude of their lives (Regan 1983, 111), and to the extent that animals are self-conscious, their self-consciousness is more episodic than narrative, a more punctate awareness of themselves in time than an awareness of having a life span organized into temporal or developmental stages (childhood, adulthood, etc.) (Strawson 2004). Animals' fear of death is therefore far less mediated by their beliefs and attitudes than our fear of death is. Animals also lack the existential fear of death, the fear of nothingness or of the obliteration of one's subjectivity (Behrendt 2010). To the degree, then, that the morality of euthanizing companion animals depends on whether death harms such animals, the harms in question are more direct than in the human case, rooted primarily in intrinsic facts about animals' welfare rather than in facts constituted by whatever attitudes animals may have toward death.

My proposal is, therefore, that we will not learn much about the morality of euthanizing animals, companion or otherwise, by looking to the debate about euthanasia or suicide in humans. If euthanizing companion animals is to be morally justified, it will instead be on the basis of its being a form of justifiable *zooicide*.

Animal Wellbeing and the Comparative Account

Let us suppose, then, that the central consideration that should shape deliberation about euthanizing companion animals is the welfare of these animals. How can this consideration be used to develop an account of the conditions under which companion animals ought to be euthanized?

Here we may appeal to the *comparative account* of the value of death (Rollin 1992, 112–13; DeGrazia 2002, 61). Assume that a person's death is the cessation of his or her existence—that there is no afterlife, as it is standardly understood. It may seem to follow, as Epicurus thought, that death is of no consequence to us, that is, inasmuch as death is the cessation of a person's existence, death ought to be a matter of indifference to the person who dies. If death is not a condition *we* ever occupy—if one's own death marks the beginning of the state of the world after one exists—then it might appear that death can neither benefit nor harm us. But such a claim is counterintuitive. Death, many believe, can be bad for us, or at least can be bad for us at a certain time. A person can die too early. Conversely, a person's current or future quality of life may be so dire that death may be a blessing to her. Such conclusions are difficult to sustain if judgments about the value (or disvalue) of death rest on comparisons between being alive and being dead, where the latter is arguably not a state of a person at all.

Advocates of the comparative account argue that this is the wrong basis on which to ground judgments of death's value. The value of death, according to this account, is measured by comparing the actual life of a person who dies at a given time to the life that person would have had by continuing to live. Suppose that Agatha in fact dies at time t. Let us call the life she actually lived her *t-life*. Suppose further that had Agatha not died at t, she would have died at a later time n. (Imagine that Agatha receives a treatment for her cancer that extends her life for one year.) Let us call this alternative life, the life she would have had if she had died at n rather than at t, her *n-life*. To ascertain whether Agatha's dying at t was good, bad, or indifferent for her, we compare how good her t-life was to how her n-life would have been.

1. If her t-life was better than her n-life would have been, then Agatha would have been worse off if she had survived until n. Agatha thus benefitted from dying at t.
2. If her n-life would have been better than her t-life, then Agatha would have been better off if she had survived until n. Agatha was thus harmed by dying at t.
3. If Agatha's t-life and her n-life would have been equally good for her, then her dying at t was neither a benefit nor a harm to her. Her living to n would not have been better than her living to t, nor was her living to t better than her surviving to n.

Note that on the comparative account, the value of death is measured by comparing two lives: a person's actual life, the life she had by dying at a particular time, and the counterfactual life she would have had if she had lived longer. The comparative account therefore avoids the arguably impossible comparison of being alive with being dead. Rather, it indexes the value of a person's life to the time at which death occurs and to the time that it would have occurred otherwise.

The comparative account of death's value can be extended quite readily to the deaths of animals. Suppose a twelve-year-old pet dog, Ridge, has developed cancer and that Ridge's guardian is considering whether to euthanize him. Assuming that animals do not survive death and are not immortal, the central ethical consideration here is whether euthanasia would be a benefit or a harm to Ridge at this point in time. According to the comparative account, Ridge's guardian should euthanize Ridge at a given point in time if doing so satisfies the condition described in circumstance (3) above regarding Agatha. That is, euthanizing Ridge is warranted to the extent that at the time of the act of euthanasia, Ridge does not stand to gain by living longer, but also loses nothing by dying at that point. Ridge would thus die at the right time: Were Ridge's guardian to euthanize him at that point, Ridge would have lived his *optimum life span*. He would have gotten the most out of his life, given its particular circumstances and contingencies. But Ridge also cannot get any more out of life. Further life would therefore be neither a benefit nor a harm to him.

In the case of human beings, it may appear that the comparative account leaves out considerations relevant to the morality of euthanasia. As noted earlier, religious claims, autonomy, the human psychological conceptualization of death, and so forth are all thought to bear on the morality of euthanasia, but they evidently do not bear on the euthanasia of companion animals. Moreover, the comparative account of death's value invokes an account of harm that may be controversial when applied to human beings. Some argue that for a person to be harmed is not for that person to be made worse off than she would otherwise have been. Rather, harm occurs when a gap or clash is created between a person's will and the state in which a person finds herself (Shiffrin 2012).

This does not seem to be a legitimate criticism of a comparative account of death's value for companion animals, however. While animals can certainly have their desires thwarted, a good deal more psychological machinery is necessary for such thwarting to constitute what Shiffrin understands as a gap between a creature's will and her circumstances. Harms, as Shiffrin understands them, result from a mismatch between a creature's lived experience and her circumstances such that the creature is unable to endorse or identify with the main components of its life (Shiffrin 1999, 123). It would be surprising, I think, for even highly sophisticated nonhuman animals to have the self-conceptions and deliberative insight needed to endorse the circumstances of their lives. Thus, whatever shortcomings the comparative account may have with respect to harming humans, these shortcomings do not mar it as an account of harming nonhuman animals (Rabenberg 2015, 3). The morality of companion animal euthanasia can largely be reduced to the kinds of considerations adduced by the comparative account, namely, whether euthanizing a companion animal would be a harm or a benefit to it. If so, then death's value for nonhuman animals rests on how their lives are made better or worse overall by dying at various points in time. Hence, death is not always the worst fate an animal can undergo; it may be worse to live too long. But nor is death never a harm to an animal either, for death may arrive too soon.

Nonetheless, that the morality of euthanizing companion animals can be largely reduced to a question of animal wellbeing does not imply that wellbeing itself can be reduced to a single factor. Our dualistic philosophical heritage may encourage us to think of animals in overly mechanical terms, crudely physiological systems for whom pleasure and pain are the sole measure of wellbeing. Such hedonism contains a grain of truth: that an animal's future portends little pleasure and a great deal of pain can be a powerful, sometimes even decisive, consideration in opting to euthanize it. However, at least two other factors are relevant in thinking about the overall quality or value of a companion animal's life. The first is *species-typical functioning* (Rollin 1992, 132). Species of companion animals have patterns of behavior that are characteristic of those species. So whereas cats are generally more solitary creatures, dogs are highly social creatures dependent on life in a pack. Hence, for a dog to have an illness or condition that precludes it from pack activities (play, etc.) detracts more from its overall wellbeing than would the same fact for a cat. The second is *personality*. Companion animals of the same species nevertheless vary significantly in their idiosyncratic preferences and tastes. A condition that would undermine the wellbeing of a curious, independent-minded outdoor cat may not undermine the wellbeing of a more docile "lap cat." Thus, both how a companion animal's life feels, as well as the animal's capabilities, shape its current and prospective quality of life. Those seeking to determine whether an animal has reached its optimum life span need an understanding of how all of these factors undergird animal wellbeing.

One worry about using the comparative account is that it seems to require more precision in our judgments regarding animal wellbeing than is possible for us. Will one's sick pet reach its optimum life span today, tomorrow, or next week? Here I believe we can only ask of animal guardians to seek out the best evidence possible and to make the best judgments they can in light of that evidence. No doubt most companion animal euthanasias do not occur *precisely* at the point of the animal's optimum life span. But the most we can demand of guardians in this regard is conscientiousness and awareness of the possible sources of distortion in their decision-making. Some sources of distortion (for example, financial considerations) can lead guardians to euthanize too soon. Others (for example, guardians' strong emotional attachment to their animals) can lead guardians to euthanize too late. In any case, those guardians who opt for euthanasia *near* the point of optimum life span need not be blamed for doing so.

One surprising implication of my account of the conditions under which euthanizing a companion animal is morally justified is that it implies that such acts of euthanasia are never *merely* permissible. That is to say, it is never the case that euthanizing a companion animal is morally optional, that is, neither morally forbidden nor morally required. For if a companion animal is euthanized prior to the point of optimum life span, then this wrongs the animal. However, if the euthanasia of a companion animal occurs at, near, or after the point in time at which the animal enjoys an optimum life span, then euthanizing the animal was obligatory, not simply morally permissible. Thus, it may sometimes be wrong to *forego* euthanizing a companion animal. This may happen when the guardians of companion animals are too blithe regarding the animals' condition and wait beyond the point of the animals' optimum life span to euthanize. In such cases, guardians do not show adequate respect for their animal companions.

The notion of "respect" is closely associated with Kantian ethics, which maintains that we are to respect persons or rational agents. Yet, as Harry Frankfurt suggests, there is a more general sense of "respect" in which it denotes treating an individual on the basis of those properties of that individual that make it significant or valuable as the sort of thing it is:

> Treating a person with respect means dealing with him exclusively on the basis of those aspects of his particular character or circumstances that are actually relevant to the issue at hand. . . . [A] lack of respect consists in the circumstance that some important fact about the person is not properly attended to or is not taken appropriately into account. In other words, the person is dealt with as though he is not what he actually is. The implications of significant features of his life are overlooked or denied. Pertinent aspects of how things are with him are treated as though they had no reality. (1999, 150)

Failing to respect an individual overlooks the crucial aspects of that individual's reality, particularly "how things are" for that individual. An animal companion that is euthanized at a point in time when its overall quality of life declines with each passing moment has not been adequately respected. For what is "relevant to the issue at hand," what should be "properly attended to" or "taken appropriately into account" in this instance, is precisely the steady decline in overall wellbeing the animal faces by continuing to live. This "reality" should be determinative in deciding to euthanize a companion animal.

In a similar Kantian vein, if the animal's guardian is so strongly attached to the animal that she keeps the animal alive beyond its optimum life span, then this fails to respect the animal and in fact treats the animal merely as a means (Cholbi 2014). Again, this is not to say that the animal is thereby treated merely as a means in a standard Kantian way. Animals (I am assuming) lack the features of practical rational agency necessary to make them ends in themselves in

Kant's robust sense. Nevertheless, to keep an animal alive beyond its optimum life span for one's own material or psychological purposes is to conceptualize the animal as a tool utilized in the service of one's own ends. The companion animal is thus seen as lacking a moral standing of its own, rooted in the sort of creature it is. Not to euthanize an animal at the point of its optimum life span, based on the best evidence available to us, is therefore wrong because of its cruel effects on the animal—as it amounts to willfully deciding that an animal will live less than the best life available to it—but it also betokens a lack of respect for the animal as a being separate from oneself, with interests and a point of view of its own, worthy of consideration in its own right.

A Guardian's Right to Euthanize?

The previous section offered an account of *when* and *why* companion animals ought to be euthanized. This section addresses the question of *who* may determine if and when an animal companion is to be euthanized. Note that this is not the question of who may perform the euthanasia procedure. For reasons of safety, efficacy, and wellbeing, only veterinarians or those with comparable medical training should perform the procedure (though the extent to which repeatedly performing animal euthanasia is traumatic for animal care professionals is easy to overlook [Rollin 2011, 56–59]). Rather, the question at hand is to whom the decision to euthanize is delegated. It may seem natural to suppose that only a companion animal's guardian may make such a decision. Yet the fact that guardians and veterinarians may reasonably disagree about when a companion animal should be euthanized underscores that some argument is necessary to defend the supposition that the choice to euthanize belongs to an animal's guardian.

A guardian's right to determine when a companion animal is to be euthanized rests on the guardian's having a certain *authority* with respect to the animal. The relevant sense of "authority" is not rooted in the fact that guardians of companion animals are typically "in charge of" them or that many companion animals are trained to respond to their guardian's commands. The authority in question is instead moral. To say that guardians may decide when a companion animal shall be euthanized because they have authority with respect to such animals is to posit an asymmetrical entitlement wherein guardians exercise discretion. In what might such authority be rooted? One possibility is to root it in a property relation wherein guardians own their companion animals (Rollin 1992, 308). This proposal is promising because property ownership confers exclusive authority on a property owner with regard to her property. It entitles her to determine its location, how it is to be treated, and so on. Thinking of companion animals as property also helps explain why guardians may be responsible for harms caused by such animals. If a pet dog bites its neighbor, attributing responsibility to its guardian can be justified by seeing the dog as property with respect to which the owner failed to exercise due care (as when a property owner permits a backyard fire to get out of control). Conversely, understanding companion animals as property can help to justify the thesis that others have obligations to respect a guardian's animal qua property (Cooke 2011).

Nevertheless, that guardians have the right to decide on euthanasia for their companion animals because they own these animals should be rejected. For one, it would seem to prove too much: typically, property owners have no duties to their property. Rather, property ownership serves only to impose duties on other people (duties to refrain from interfering with, destroying, stealing, etc., property belonging to others). Hence, if our companion animals were our property, we would have no duties to them at all. Indeed, it would not be impermissible to torture them, destroy them at any time for any reason, and so forth. For these reasons, companion animal ownership cannot plausibly be modeled on "full liberal ownership" (Cooke 2011, 267).

In response, some have argued that animals are self-owners to whom their guardians have a form of legal title or authority, or that other nonstandard forms of ownership could allow for animals having moral standing that precludes various forms of mistreatment (Cooke 2011, 265–66). Perhaps so. But I doubt that most animal guardians conceptualize their moral responsibilities as flowing from their ownership of their animals. Rather, I imagine that while conscientious companion animal guardians think they have moral responsibilities concerning those animals *akin to* those of property ownership, they do not see ownership as the most *fundamental* moral relationship they have with those animals. Indeed, to call an animal one's companion is to imply that whatever asymmetry of authority may exist between companion animals and their guardians, it coexists with a certain moral symmetry. The relationship is a partnership, wherein each partner has a distinct role to play. The guardian's role is that of caretaker to the animal, imposing on the guardian various duties of care. To think of our authority with regard to companion animals as rooted in ownership is at odds with the understanding of the animal-guardian relationship as one in which each partner has something at stake. Whatever guardians' authority consists in, it must be compatible with our sense that our relations with companion animals morally compel us to act on their behalf, that they are not objects to be manipulated for our interests.

We should therefore not be misled by our normal patterns of speech—wherein we refer to "my pet" and the like—into concluding that our authority with regard to companion animals is proprietary in nature. But a challenge remains: how is it that a companion animal guardian, a person who stands in a unique relationship to the animal, has the specific authority to decide on euthanasia, given that (as I argued earlier) the facts relevant to making this decision correctly are not themselves relational facts? If all that matters morally to deciding whether to euthanize a companion animal is that doing so makes possible an optimum life span (or something close to it) for that animal, then it does not seem to follow, without additional argument at least, that the animal's guardian is especially or uniquely entitled to make such a determination. The challenge is to show how companion animals' own moral status (the moral relevance of which is independent of animals' relationship to their guardians) can nevertheless be reconciled with the special entitlement of guardians (who do stand in a distinctive relationship to their animals) to determine the conditions of companion animals' deaths.

A better route to justifying a guardian's right to determine when a companion animal is to be euthanized is *epistemic*. On this model, guardians have a right to euthanize because of their intimate knowledge of their animal companions. Tony Milligan observes that it is tempting to suppose that the relationships guardians have with their companion animals are likely to introduce sentiments of attachment, sentiments that may serve as an obstacle to guardians acting in the best interests of their companion animals. The sentiments associated with guardianship, we might think, can only distort, rather than clarify, whether a companion animal ought to be euthanized. Milligan instead argues that having a companion animal is an educative process because of the "depth and continuity" of the relationship guardians establish with companion animals (2009, 404).

As I argued earlier, there are other factors beyond hedonic considerations that guardians must take into account in deciding when to euthanize. One I have already gestured at: an animal's individual personality. Due to personality differences, one and the same physical debility can be devastating to one specimen of a given species but far less consequential for another member of that species. The "depth and continuity" of a guardian's relationship with an animal provides her knowledge of the animal's personality, which can in turn make her uniquely situated to judge the significance of a particular physical debility for that animal's wellbeing.

Milligan further proposes that guardians are uniquely situated to understand what ethical significance to assign to an animal's affective states, including pain. He argues that guardians have unique access to the unique narrative of a companion animal's life, and only via knowledge of this narrative can pain (and other states) of an animal be assigned their proper significance. Milligan provides an example of two dogs with identical medical prognoses, levels of suffering, and so forth. It matters to whether the dogs should be euthanized that one of the dogs underwent years of cruelty and mistreatment prior to rescue by its guardian. It would be cruel to subject this dog to a reintroduction of pain, but less cruel to permit the other dog to be subject to such pain. Animal stories matter, Milligan argues, and inasmuch as decisions to euthanize are end-of-life decisions, they are also end-of-narrative choices requiring intimate understanding of the animal's particularity. Guardians' authority to euthanize companion animals is therefore epistemic in nature: "Animal guardians can (and often will) be epistemically privileged participants in end-of-life deliberations because they can (and often will) be the people who are best placed to bring the relevant narrative of a pet's life into view" (Milligan 2009, 411).

Grounding guardians' authority over their companion animal's being euthanized answers the challenge I identified earlier. For on Milligan's picture, guardians' authority is rooted in a relational epistemic attitude (their knowledge of the animal's life narrative) whose object is a non-relational ethical fact (the narrative itself). The duty to euthanize at the point of optimum life span thus rests on the nature of the animal itself. The guardians have authority with respect to such decisions but not because (as in the ownership account) they have authority *over* their companion animals.

In my estimation, Milligan's proposal is best seen as an analogue of a familiar picture regarding end-of-life choices for human beings. When a human patient is no longer able to make such choices competently, an individual presumed to be knowledgeable about the patient's life history and values steps in to serve as the patient's proxy. So too for companion animals, except that they never were able to make such choices. The crucial difference is that in cases of human proxy judgment, a human proxy is supposed to make the judgment the human patient would have made were she able, whereas in cases of guardians choosing an end-of-life path for a companion animal, the guardian is not a proxy for what the animal patient would have wanted. Milligan does not make the claim that animals themselves fashion narratives regarding their conditions and, given the aforementioned episodic nature of much of animal consciousness, he is wise not to attribute such narrative self-awareness to animals. Moreover, it is unlikely that animals can make the kinds of judgments the comparative account of death's value requires, that is, judgments comparing their lives up to a given moment in time with lives they might have by continuing to live. In this respect, guardians are not proxies but custodians, bringing to bear on decisions regarding euthanasia knowledge regarding their companion animals that the animals themselves lack.

Conclusion

To reiterate: superficial similarities notwithstanding, the euthanasia of companion animals cannot rest on ethical foundations similar to those that ground assisted dying in humans. The former instead rests largely on animal wellbeing, and the comparative account of the value of death should guide guardians' thinking about when the proper moment to euthanize a companion animal is. The authority guardians have to make decisions regarding companion animal euthanasia rests on their special knowledge of the animal's life history and personality. And though perhaps it should go without saying, companion animal euthanasia should be performed painlessly and swiftly.

As Bernard Rollin observes, companion animals are sometimes euthanized for trivial or appalling reasons: because guardians have planned a vacation and forgot to plan for their companion animal's care, because guardians failed to provide adequate training for the animal, because a grown animal is less cute than a young animal (Rollin 1992, 220–21; see also Yeates and Main 2011). The view proposed here rejects these sorts of egocentric rationales, but I do not intend thereby that the interests of guardians are utterly irrelevant to whether a companion animal should be euthanized. Medical care for diseased animals can be astonishingly costly, and guardians at least have the right to take that into account when determining when animals should be euthanized.

I have largely abstained from grounding my arguments regarding companion animal euthanasia in any greater theoretical account of the nature or source of our duties to such animals. However, my arguments accord well with the widely shared view that the nature or source of these duties is that human guardians voluntarily undertake a relationship with a companion animal, thereby rendering that creature dependent upon a specific human companion for its wellbeing (Burgess-Jackson 1998; Cooke 2011, 267–70). But if such relationships are the source of our special obligations toward companion animals, then the duties ensuing from these relationships may be circumscribed by the interests of the other party to the relationship. Even though special relationships (friendship, familial relationships, etc.) generate duties that are more morally demanding than our generic relationships to others, even these duties have their limits. We are certainly not required, for instance, to do everything possible to keep companion animals alive. The nexus between guardians' interests and their obligations to their companion animals is obviously thorny, and I make no pretense of offering precise prescriptions as to how to balance guardian interests with the wellbeing of companion animals when it comes to decisions regarding euthanasia. Still, in identifying the conditions under which the euthanasia of companion animals is justified in light of their interests, I hope to have brought clarity to one half of this moral ledger.

Throughout this discussion, I have assumed that the animals whose euthanasia we are imagining are animals that are already someone's companion. My discussion might therefore appear irrelevant to the pressing ethical question of the euthanasia of *potential* companion animals, that is, the euthanizing of members of pet species housed in animal shelters. Sadly, millions of shelter animals are euthanized annually for want of a guardian. Granted, certain elements of my account cannot be extrapolated to shelter animals. They lack guardians with the sort of species- and organism-specific knowledge that comes from a longstanding relationship. However, their caretakers must still euthanize responsibly, and my own account of the conditions under which the euthanasia of companion animals is justified at least suggests the contours of an account of the ethics of euthanizing shelter animals.

In particular, there will be a point at which the continued life of a shelter animal is not a benefit to it, at which time euthanasia would be morally required on the grounds that the animal's optimum life span has been reached. The distressing fact is that the point of optimum life span for shelter animals is likely to be much earlier in its life than for companion animals who have morally decent human guardians. Shelter animals may live in crowded, unsanitary conditions inimical to their social needs; may lack adequate food, shelter, or medical care; and so forth. And regrettably, there are fewer spaces in shelters than there are unwanted animals. Therefore, to try to keep all prospective companion animals living in shelters alive in conditions of want would be worse for each of these animals. As a form of shelter population control, euthanasia has a role in ensuring that a larger portion of shelter animals do not live long enough that they would have been better off dead. This is not to deny the moral urgency of improving shelter conditions, or better yet, taking measures to reduce the population of unwanted members of companion animal species. Even so, euthanasia of shelter animals can serve as the best response to a far-from-ideal reality.

References

Becker, Ernest. 1997. *Denial of Death*. New York: Free Press.

Behrendt, Kathy. 2010. "A Special Way of Being Afraid." *Philosophical Psychology* 23 (5): 669–82.

Burgess-Jackson, Keith. 1998. "Doing Right by Our Companion Animals." *Journal of Ethics* 2 (2): 159–85.

Cholbi, Michael. 2000. "Kant and the Irrationality of Suicide." *History of Philosophy Quarterly* 17 (2): 159–76.

Cholbi, Michael. 2011. *Suicide: The Philosophical Dimensions*. Peterborough, ON: Broadview Press.

Cholbi, Michael. 2014. "A Direct Kantian Duty to Animals." *Southern Journal of Philosophy* 52 (3): 338–58.

Cooke, Steve. 2011. "Duties to Companion Animals." *Res Publica* 17 (3): 261–74.

DeGrazia, David. 2002. *Animal Rights: A Very Short Introduction*. Oxford: Oxford University Press.

Frankfurt, Harry. 1999. "Equality and Respect." In *Necessity, Volition, and Love*, 146–54. Cambridge: Cambridge University Press.

Humane Society of the United States. 2014. "Pets by the Numbers." http://www.humanesociety.org/issues/pet_overpopulation/facts/pet_ownership_statistics.html.

King, Barbara. 2013. *How Animals Grieve*. Chicago: University of Chicago Press.

Rabenberg, Michael. 2015. "Harm." *Journal of Ethics and Social Philosophy* 8 (3): 1–32. http://www.jesp.org/PDF/harm.pdf.

Milligan, Tony. 2009. "Dependent Companions." *Journal of Applied Philosophy* 26 (4): 402–13.

Regan, Tom. 1983. *The Case for Animal Rights*. Berkeley: University of California Press.

Rollin, Bernard. 1992. *Animal Rights and Human Morality*. New York: Prometheus.

Rollin, Bernard. 2011. *Putting the Horse before Descartes*. Philadelphia: Temple University Press.

Shiffrin, Seana. 1999. "Wrongful Life, Procreative Responsibility, and the Significance of Harm." *Legal Theory* 5 (2): 117–48.

Shiffrin, Seana. 2012. "Harm and Its Moral Significance." *Legal Theory* 18 (3): 357–98.

Statistics Netherlands. 2012. "Deaths by Medical End-of-Life Decision; Age, Cause of Death." Last modified July 11. http://statline.cbs.nl/StatWeb/publication/?VW=T&DM=SLen&PA=81655ENG&LA=en.

Strawson, Galen. 2004. "Against Narrativity." *Ratio* 17: 428–52.

Varner, Gary. 2002. "Pets, Companion Animals, and Domesticated Partners." In *Ethics for Everyday*, edited by David Benatar, 45–75. New York: McGraw-Hill.

Warnes, Sophie. 2014 "How Many Choose Assisted Suicide Where It Is Legal?" *The Guardian*, July18. http://www.theguardian.com/news/datablog/2014/jul/18/how-many-people-choose-assisted-suicide-where-it-is-legal.

Yeates, James, and D. C. J. Main. 2011. "Veterinary Opinions on Refusing Euthanasia: Justifications and Philosophical Frameworks." *Veterinary Record* 168 (10): 263.

INDEX